HANNA

Country Fair

Country Fair

The Month-by-Month Countryside Companion

Edited by Macdonald Hastings
with A.G. Street

Introduction by Sir Max Hastings

This edition first published in 2007 by

Prion
an imprint of the
Carlton Publishing Group,
20 Mortimer Street,
London W1T 3JW

A catalogue record for this book is available from the British Library

ISBN 978-1-85375-627-6
Typeset by e-type, Liverpool

Printed in Spain

CONTENTS

INTRODUCTION

There was a time, little more than half a century ago, when the British countryside was still a place of whirling corn binders and stooks in the fields, of grazing livestock and thatched cottages overwhelmingly inhabited by farm-workers. Fishermen cast lines of dressed silk, garden produce was bottled rather than frozen, and wild birds flourished in a pre-pesticide landscape. Agriculture was the largest single industry in Britain, its wartime achievements celebrated. Farmers were important people, whom politicians provoked at their peril. Some rural homes were still lit by oil lamps. Rabbits and pigeons formed a significant part of many countrymen's diet, as well as prized sporting quarry. The well-known Wiltshire farmer and writer A.G.Street responded contemptuously to an urban critic's denunciation of the cruelties of chasing foxes: 'I would no more seek to defend foxhunting than I would ploughing, sowing, reaping, or any other event in the country calendar.'

This was a world my father, Macdonald Hastings, loved passionately. He was a hybrid, a weekend countryman, who became famous in his day as a journalist and broadcaster, first making his reputation as war correspondent of the great magazine *Picture Post*, then becoming the idol of a generation of children as 'Special Investigator' for the legendary boys' weekly *Eagle*.

He was the last editor of the *Strand Magazine*. When the *Strand* closed, Father turned his mind to starting something of his own. He joined forces with Arthur Street, a close friend, raised some money from friends, and created *Country Fair*. 'The most that any editor can do,' he wrote in its first issue of July 1951, 'is to create the sort of magazine that he likes himself and hope that his tastes will be shared by other people. This is the magazine I have always felt that I would like to do…I've always believed that the worst thing that happened to Adam and Eve…was when they went to live in city streets.'

For six years thereafter, every month, he produced a publication that became a niche classic. He recruited some of the great writers of the day, to become his regular contributors on rural topics: Constance Spry on flowers, 'B.B.' on shooting, Roy Beddington on fishing, Arthur Street on farming, James Fisher on birds, James Robertson Justice on falconry, Maxwell Knight (who was head of MI5) on wildlife. My mother, Anne Scott-James, wrote a 'Weekender' column. He persuaded famous local inhabitants to pen essays on their own counties: Anthony Armstrong on Sussex, H.E.Bates on Kent, John Betjeman on Middlesex. The animal caricatures on each cover, drawn by Hanna, were memorable works of art, which I still use as table mats.

Country Fair was a celebration of the countryside, reflecting my father's romantic vision of rural England and its history, as well as providing a wealth of practical information about game cookery, fly-tying, pest control, ferreting, pressing flowers, decoying pigeons. It never made money, indeed it nearly ruined father and his friends. Always a dreamer, he never attempted to match the magazine he wanted to publish with the cash available to fund it: he merely marched happily onward until the day came when the bank called time. *Country Fair* was sold, and eventually merged into another title. Father's fantasy was over, but gosh, how he loved it while it lasted. Today, its volumes comprise a wonderful tribute to a vanished world. We should not over-idealise those days, because there was a lot wrong with them. Britain was broke. Many rural people lived in poverty. Cottages without indoor sanitation were not much fun for their occupants. Today, most country-dwellers enjoy vastly better lives than did their forebears of the 1950s. But things have been lost, big and important things: an innocence; an intimacy between the soil and the animals and those who gain their livings from them; a sense of community; a delight in belonging. All these elements are captured, I think, in this selection of writings and illustrations from the old *Country Fair*, which would delight my father as much as it delights me, his son. He died in 1982, his joy in the glories of the countryside undimmed by age. Those of us who have inherited his passion are grateful that he preserved in print so much that deserves to be remembered, for a new generation to savour today.

MAX HASTINGS
March 2007

JANUARY

IN PRAISE OF WINTER

Far from being a fair weather countryman, I confess that, secretly, I even prefer these icy-fingered days of mid-winter. The trees, I think, are almost lovelier in their nakedness than they are when they are decked in leaf. The hedgerows are for me infinitely more mysterious and fascinating at this time of year than they are when you can't look at a bird's nest without a stinging nettle licking your hand.

Admittedly I am prejudiced because I share some of the tastes of the terrier. Nothing makes me feel happier, or better inside, than a good hunt or a good day's shooting. Further, I am a lazy gardener; and at this time of year I feel a glow of satisfaction as I peer through my frosty bedroom window when I am shaving in the morning to think that absolutely nothing is growing, that the ground is as gooey as a hard-centred chocolate and that I can pretend to be an enthusiastic gardener without the slightest sense of guilt that I ought to be up and out and doing some work.

Having just returned from a journey to South Africa, of all places, I realise more than ever that I am a cold weather creature.

I like the nip of the frost. I can derive an aesthetic pleasure from the sheer absence of things that bite. And it is an undeniable fact that, although it is well-nigh impossible to remain cool in a hot climate, there are always ways of keeping warm in a cold one.

No day can be really beautiful without a fire for companionship at the end of it. Nothing inculcates such a sense of wellbeing than the warmth that comes out of exercise on a cold day.

But if I say a word about this in my own house, my wife goes off into a tantrum. Her idea of heaven is to swelter on some tideless Mediterranean shore, where the only field sport is swatting mosquitoes and the weeds grow in nearly every month of the year.

M.H.

WILD LIFE

Under the snow, snowdrops, violets and primroses are safely sleeping. Above move shivering rooks, thrushes and starving lapwing and golden plover, easy morsels for wandering fox and stoat and crow. These are the weaklings which have failed to move agilely enough to the frost-free climate of the Lusitanian seaboard (Southern Ireland, West Wales, Cornwall, Brittany to

Spain). But finches, tits, jays, nuthatches, magpies and other hard-bills find sufficient food in seed and hibernating insect to survive a month of snow and frost, although they may draw nearer to the warmth of human homes to seek scraps.

Tracks in the snow are fascinating study: a whole episode of the day or night employ of a wild animal is writ there for our unravelling. The faster the pace the fewer the tracks, as hind feet leap precisely, economically, into the spoor left by fore feet (fox, hare, rabbit, squirrel). Many a tale of tragedy or escape is told by tracks of predator and prey coming together, and predator's track alone moving away – the stalking spoor from bush to bush, the sudden leap, the smudged area of capture, are plainly marked in the snow.

Suddenly, overnight the bitter anticyclonic east wind is gone. The morning air by contrast is almost hot; snow seeps away in a flood. Under the rain in the leafless woods, elder and honeysuckle are delicately budding; in the tree-tops, catching the fitful wind and sun, stormcocks (mistle-thrushes) begin fluting so finely that many have thought the blackbird was in song a month early. But the whistle of the stormcock is wild and sweet and monotonous, lacking both the rich subtle variation and the squeaky end notes of the blackbird's song.

The male robin's tender notes grow more full and prolonged, as the female ceases to sing or to defend her territory, and moves to partner him in an early nest in the old kettle in the hedge. The dunnock (hedge-sparrow) shuffles his wings and with mincing steps and high-pitched ditty defies his rivals and courts his little brown hen. The oxeye (great tit) repeats his saw-whet double note. The twink (chaffinch) tentatively announces "Pretty,

pretty," trying over the prelude to full February song while still flock-minded. In the pine branches the yellow, busy crossbill hen is already gathering twigs for her early nest, while the crimson, idle cock whistles his loud monotonous note of happiness and challenge.

In filtered shade dog's-mercury flowers while trees are bare. In the sun the first yellow of lesser celandine glitters with promise of spring.

R.M.L.

B y the time January is fairly launched we shall be very lucky if some proper hard weather has not come our way: frost certainly; snow probably; while, in between, bright but cold days may compensate us. If a really severe frosty spell arrives, this is when those wildfowl I wrote of before will seek sanctuaries well inland.

In winter one ought to think of the birds first of all; for when the countryside is held in winter's icy grasp many birds feel the effects of cold before any other living creatures. Not for them the protected hibernacula of toads and snakes or dormice. Birds must keep up their body heat if they are to survive, and for this they must obtain stores of potential energy – otherwise food. So far as we are able to, let us help them by adapting our bird-table menus to their needs. Sunflower and hemp seed (the latter is better if crushed) will be relished by all the true seed-eaters, and a few others as well; fat, of course, and pieces of boiled potato, too, will help. Mealworms for robins will be particularly sought after, and very valuable they are. See that the birds' water does not remain frozen, and melt the ice in the bird bath frequently.

Hard-weather problems certainly exist for birds, but extreme cold spells sometimes bring south the lovely waxwing – the berry-eater in chief. This magnificent bird with its pastel plumage – black, white, yellow and red wing feathers, and longish crest-like head feathers, whose black bib and diagonal eye stripe give it a rather angry-looking expression – will often descend on any berry-bearing shrubs.

Bird song? Well, the mistle-thrush will tell you quite early in the morning – probably before you are up and about – if the day is to be a milder one; robins, hedge sparrows and wrens will strike up, and so will the pretty little marsh tit. If you have a rookery near you there will soon be signs of activity; for it is some time in January that these gregarious members of the crow tribe start to prospect the trees in which they will subsequently nest.

So far as mammals go there will be the chance, when the ground is snow covered, or white with heavy frost, to see the tracks which beasts of varying size will leave. Describing tracks in words is a hard task, but take it by easy stages. Try to satisfy yourself by your own endeavours that the rabbit, for instance, really does put its hind legs down on the ground in front of its forelegs; or that the tracks of a hunting cat will *register* exactly – that is to say, the print of the hind foot will be placed precisely in that of the fore foot. The same applies to the fox, but these will show traces of the claws, while cats will not.

M.K.

THE VEGETABLE GARDEN

January weather is often a nightmare to the gardener who is behindhand with digging, but he who is well on can do many odd jobs with smug satisfaction in the warmth of the potting shed. Every opportunity must be taken to get all ground turned over provided no frost or snow is dug in. Hydrated lime can still be applied.

Jerusalem artichokes may be planted towards the end of the month in rows 2 feet apart and 1 foot between the tubers. It is vital to use a good strain, otherwise a cluster of objects the size of walnuts will result. This vegetable can be utilised to form a windbreak for small spring-sown seeds.

Give yourself time to study the seed catalogues and plan the cropping programme with care. Bear in mind that long-standing crops such as sprouts, broccoli, kales, savoys, etc., should be grouped together. Brassicas should never occupy the same ground two years running. Avoid freshly manured ground for carrots and beetroot, otherwise coarse and mis-shapen roots will develop. Reserve the manure for sprouts, cauliflowers, broccoli, celery, lettuces, etc.

Beware of ordering quantities of different varieties because they sound exciting. Stick to the type that suits the locality but pay great attention to the strains that follow on well. For example, select a stump-rooted carrot for earlier and an intermediate for main crop. With intelligent ordering, a supply of cabbage can be maintained the whole year round.

Reserve a small part of the garden for experimenting with lesser-known varieties, but play for safety with the bigger plots, otherwise there will be disappointments and the pot will suffer. Consider the possibilities of intercropping such as lettuces or dwarf beans between the celery trenches. Space is so often wasted.

Overhaul equipment when the weather is had. Cutting tools should be sharpened and handles looked to. Clean the mowing machine and have the knives reground. Fruit-nets should be inspected. Buy a book on "Netting" and repair them. This is a fascinating and simple occupation.

E.B.

T here are many times when it is infinitely wiser to keep one's feet off the soil than on it. Even digging is best avoided when the earth turns up in sodden wet lumps. Restrain the urge to get on with the job unless conditions are suitable. If all is well, dig hard, for remember that the longer the time for the frost to do its work, the better. The onion bed, in particular, should be prepared, manure dug well in and absolutely clean. Leave the surface rough to facilitate breaking down in spring. Onions must have firm ground, so hasty preparation in the early spring should be avoided.

Continue to review last year's efforts and plan for the future. Plan a space for two little-grown vegetables. The delicious Mangetout pea and the climbing purple-podded French bean. Carter's sugar pea is a well-tried variety of the former and the same firm has an excellent purple-podded bean. The Mangetout pea has large fleshy pods which are cooked whole when young. A delicious vegetable, popular on the Continent. Although purple when picked, the bean turns green when cooked. Besides being most attractive to look at, growth is prolific and flavour excellent. Every garden should also produce a small quantity of the haricot bean for drying. The well-known Comtesse de Chambord is probably the best and is much used for canning. Also consider the globe artichoke – best grown from offsets, seed being a long job. Even if not eaten they are quite lovely for decoration both from the leaf and flower point of view.

Arrange seed of early potatoes – such as Home Guard or Epicure – in shallow boxes "eye end" up and place in a light, frost-proof shed. This method helps the production of an early crop.

If the weather is dry, Jerusalem artichokes may be planted this month. It is absolutely essential to get a good strain, otherwise hours will be spent trying to dig up things the size of walnuts. Plant in rows thirty inches apart, twelve inches between tubers and about six inches deep. If planted with thought, Jerusalem artichokes can be an excellent windbreak.

It will be quite easy to appreciate the value of hoof and horn meal during this month. The brassicas which have received a dressing will show a deeper green colour and the sprouts, especially, will have benefited. The buttons are larger and firmer and the stem is longer. This is obviously one of the most valuable organic fertilisers. Easy to apply and adds necessary humus. The finer ground variety should be used for the quick-growing crops such as lettuce.

E.F.

THE FLOWER GARDEN

January need not be a dull month in the garden and with careful selection and planting can easily give us a foretaste of things to come. The first choice for a January flowering shrub must be the Chinese witch hazel – *Hamamelis mollis*. Its rich, bright yellow, frost-resistant flowers scent the whole garden and are especially beautiful when seen against a dark background. A good companion is the almost white *Viburnum fragrans* or the newer hybrid *V. bodnantense*, both of which are scented and a most attractive rose-pink when in bud. Even the smallest garden can find room for *Daphne Mezereum* in either the crimson or white form, but it needs to be planted in its permanent position for, like all daphnes, it resents being moved.

If there is space for a small tree *Prunus subhirtella autumnale* cannot fail to please, flowering as it does from November until March. A most pleasing effect can be obtained by planting around the base of any of these shrubs some of the varieties of *Erica carnea* of which King George is the best.

It is a little early for the majority of the bulbs but the early snowdrops will soon be with us. Beneath any deciduous tree, hardy cyclamens thrive and deserve to be widely planted, for a succession of flower can be arranged – *Cyclamen Coum* is the January flowering species. The Algerian *iris unguicularis* is one of the most beautiful of the genus and at the base of a sunny wall in poor soil will soon belie its reputation of being a poor flowerer. The Christmas rose must not be forgotten despite the ease in which its flowers are damaged by the weather. The green *Helleborus corsicus* is an ideal plant for the shady corner or under trees, and its flowers last from November until June. There are many more January flowering plants, but these will provide a start towards brighter winter days.

The preparation of the site for sweet peas should be as thorough as possible and deep cultivation and a liberal supply of manure will be amply repaid. An additional benefit is a dressing of bonemeal worked into the topsoil so that this slow-acting manure is immediately available when planting or sowing takes place in early spring.

The tops of herbaceous plants can be cut down and any alterations made to the border. Overcrowded clumps should be lifted, retaining only the outer healthy portions of each root. All herbaceous plants appreciate feeding and a dressing of well-rotted compost should be forked between the clumps when other work has been completed.

C.P.

A wet autumn will greatly delay work, and one of the first tasks of the New Year must be to catch up with arrears. Whenever the weather is suitable the opportunity should be taken to complete the planting of shrubs and roses which may have had to be heeled in because of bad weather at planting time. Vacant plots should be dug over, leaving the surface rough so as to gain the full benefit of frost action which is usually severe next month. Of special importance is the preparation of the site for Sweet Peas, which need deep cultivation and an ample supply of manure or well-rotted compost. Slow-acting manures such as bonemeal are most valuable but should be applied during cultivation if the plant foods are to be readily available to the young plants when they are put out in early spring. Herbaceous plants also need attention, their dying tops being removed, any crowded clumps divided or adjustments made, and then the whole border forked over, working in manure or compost.

A really bright display in January can be provided by groups of the many varieties of *Erica carnea*. This is one of the few members of the Erica family which are tolerant to lime and being completely hardy it is suitable for almost all gardens. Like all Heathers it shows to the best effect when planted in groups, and can be used in the rock garden or as an under-planting for winter-flowering shrubs. They quickly cover the ground and are admirable labour-saving plants, but are essentially a plant for the natural parts of the garden and do not look well in formal beds. *Erica carnea* itself is rosy red, but two early-flowering varieties gracilis (bright pink) and King George (deep crimson) make an excellent contrast. The flowering season goes on until April and other kinds are Prince of Wales (soft pink) Vivelli (dark red), Springwood (white) and its form Springwood Pink.

The majority of winter-flowering shrubs are very sweet scented and providing the weather is reasonable the garden in January can be really delightful. Two of the most popular shrubs are *Hamamelis mollis* and *Viburnum fragrans*, the former being one of the finest shrubs throughout the year. The charming Winter Sweet (*Chimonanthus praecox*) needs a sunny position if it is to flower well, and whilst its yellow form luteus has larger flowers it is not quite so fragrant. Mahonias, with their lovely terminal heads of lemon-yellow flowers and most attractive foliage, must be planted in their permanent positions when small, for they resent root disturbance.

C.P.

THE FRUIT GARDEN

In many gardens the raspberry is not grown as well as it might be. As with strawberries, it is becoming increasingly affected by virus disease, which results in thin, weak canes and poor fruit. This disease, known as Raspberry Mosaic, is thought to be carried by insects such as aphids, which can quickly spread the trouble from infected to clean canes. Thus the folly of planting new stock near infected rows is obvious. Certified, virus-free stock of some varieties is available and, if possible, these are the plants to buy.

The most vigorous raspberry today, and probably the most desirable, is "Mailing Promise." This early variety gives an abundance of strong canes and a heavy crop. As a second choice we can recommend "Mailing Exploit," and for a late one "Norfolk Giant." The best yellow-fruited variety is "Antwerp," a free cropper and of good flavour. No newly planted canes should be allowed to crop the following summer. They should be cut back to about nine inches above ground level at the end of February and then finally removed when the new growth has developed from ground level.

When restocking the fruit garden advantage should be taken of the wide range of gooseberries available. Planted in well-prepared ground bushes will crop for many years given the correct treatment. The variety renowned for dessert purposes is the famous yellow-fruited ' Leveller,' which like all yellow varieties should not be sprayed with lime-sulphur. Other dessert varieties are the red-fruited "Whinham's Industry" and "Lancashire Lad." Such varieties are seldom seen nowadays but are still well worth their place. Probably the best all-round gooseberry is the green 'Lancer.' This variety has a good upright habit and fruits heavily and regularly. An excellent variety which can be picked green as early as May is "May Duke," the berries turning red later in the season. Often recommended is "Whitesmith," a good all-round white gooseberry of particularly fine flavour and a heavy cropper.

SEASONAL NOTES: At this time of year fruit is particularly

acceptable and a well-managed fruit store gives a good return. Frequent inspections should be made—an ideal job for when one is kept indoors by the weather. Any decaying fruits should be burnt and slightly marked specimens put aside for immediate use.

Out of doors newly planted trees should be firmed thoroughly by heavy stamping after frost. It is as well to stress once again the importance of firming when actually planting.

G.R.W.

———•———

PLANTING AND STAKING: Any planting still not completed should be pressed ahead this month wherever the ground and weather conditions permit. After setting each tree the soil around the roots should be well firmed. In connection with this, staking and tying are two salient points, especially with young trees in exposed positions. When tying it is important to see that the main stem does not rub against the support. This may easily be prevented by wrapping the trunk with a small piece of old bicycle tyre at the tying point. Alternatively, one of the new plastic ties can be used.

NOVELTIES: Apart from everyday fruits, many people like to grow one or two novelties. Such a practice is to be admired and suggestions would include such interesting things as "White Grape" – a white currant – filberts, cobnuts and grafted varieties of walnuts. Various hybrid berries can also be planted, and amongst these there is the Veitchberry, a cross between the blackberry and raspberry, the Worcester Berry, the result of a gooseberry and blackcurrant cross, and the Phenomenal Berry, which might be described in general terms as a large-fruited loganberry.

PRUNING: At the present time, pruning is one of the main tasks on hand and it is as well to consider a few of the principles governing these operations. Where trees are growing vigorously and, possibly, making excessive growth at the expense of fruit bud formation, any pruning should be reduced to a minimum. It must be remembered that in pruning the root system is not touched, and where vigour is excessive hard pruning will induce even more growth. Conversely, where growth is weak and the occurrence of fruit buds excessive, the surface area to be nourished by the roots should be considerably reduced by hard pruning. This should include the removal of a percentage of fruit buds, thinning of established spurs and reducing any new growth to one or two buds. The interesting theory of a balanced root/branch ratio is utilised where trees are grown as cordons and dwarf pyramids.

One of the major difficulties in pruning is the treatment for overgrown trees. As already noted, excessive vigour calls for light pruning, but where neglect is apparent a certain amount of thinning will be necessary. Badly placed growths causing overcrowding are best removed completely, and if needs be whole branches taken out. In most cases it is advisable to spread such operations over a period of at least two years, as wholesale thinning in one season is liable to upset the balance of the tree.

G.R.W.

Pruning the Apple Trees

The over-pruned apple tree must be one of the most common problems in a new garden. Sometimes they are bush trees which have had every lateral shoot spur pruned hard for years, making ugly, gnarled spurs with a forest of young shoots, like a shapeless porcupine. Often the trees themselves are too close together as well. We are lucky if there is not woolly aphis living in the gnarled spurs and scab fungus on the young shoots as a result of this overcrowding.

This state of affairs often occurs on old espalier trees, particularly along the top branches, where the zealous pruner has been determined that the tree shall *not* shoot above the top of the wall, and has pruned hard down to the buds level with the top. This overcrowded, fruitless condition cannot be remedied in one year. All the shoots grew out last summer and will take another summer in the light and sun before their buds can turn into fruit buds, which could fruit the year after that. So it is no good expecting fruit of any quality the next year, however wisely they are pruned.

The treatment to bring these unfruitful trees round to bearing is to thin out these long shoots, cutting them out completely so that there is no bud, however small and dormant, left; even cutting out a lump of old spur with it where possible. It is vital to let light and sun reach the remaining shoots, which should be left entirely alone to form fruit buds. But don't get too excited as the tree begins to look better and cut out everything the first year, as this would be too much of a shock and promote more growth, which is what you are trying to avoid. It is well to cut out half only the first year, and quarter the next, and quarter the one after, taking three years over the renovation.

If the trees are too close together, shading each other and by leaving shoots alone they are interlacing, it would be foolish to try to keep them all and we should dig some out with a bold heart.

The espalier that has all "gone to the top" can be renovated in a similar way, thinning out shoots and chunks of spur entirely and leaving the rest alone. We will have to be content with shoots above the wall for a year or two until the tree is cropping again, and then we will be able to cut down to fruit spurs. It is amazing how the lower branches become young and active again when more balanced pruning is carried out, and the tree does not have to spend all its energies on sending out armies of shoots along the top of the wall.

R.D.

SHOOTING

ONE can never reckon either snipe or woodcock anything of a certainty in this country, though in Ireland you can depend on them, provided no one else has got there first. But where in any normal year we get both woodcock and snipe moving in from the Continent in early November, these migrants seldom stay long and the first really hard frosts are usually enough to make them continue their trip to Ireland.

Dependent on Continental weather, successive small migrations occur and suitable water meadows near the coast often hold an unexpected number of birds. All too often a heavy migration comes in toward the end of January, but these birds are as a rule in such poor condition that they are not worth shooting.

There seems to be no real rule which indicates a likely day for snipe, and it is worth keeping an eye open for reports of "Ice in the Baltic" and other remote weather items. One snipe addict I know used to place great faith in the number and condition of worm casts on his lawn, and he certainly bagged birds on most unlikely days.

Unfortunately changes in agriculture have played havoc with some meadows sacred in the past to grazing and to snipe in their season. I do not know if snipe are selective in a taste for worms but a good deal of the old "rough" has been snuffed up and replaced possibly by more nutritious grass. This may mean not only inadequate cover but possibly some chemical fertiliser was applied which was also a worm killer.

All I can say is that many of us are agreed that corners which used to be worth looking into for the occasional cock and meadows usually good for a leash of snipe have seemed more than usually barren in these last two seasons. Let us hope that it is simply a seasonal variation and not due to someone letting off atom bombs in the great breeding areas.

Woodcock are, because of their low flight, dangerous birds at a covert shoot.

H.B.C.P.

FISHING

This is the month for looking over the salmon tackle in readiness for a chance invitation or a well-laid plan for early spinning. The Loch Tay opening ceremony in January heralds another season and next month there will be more opportunities. Test the spinning lines. Don't give angular pulls at the line but straight, strong tugs. Soak them and try again. I have tested a line dry, only to lose a big fish through a break when it was wet. Wooden minnows can be painted at home; celluloid or Perspex fins renewed and swivels oiled and freed from rust.

Spoons (very useful in coloured water) can be polished and leads looked over and sorted into their respective weight categories. The gaff can be sharpened hopefully and the splice revarnished, though many rivers demand the use of a tailer or a net until May, when the kelts have gone. Remember to take down reels, oil them and put back the drum without pinching the line. If you want a little practice, have a go at the pike. They like the cold, and spinning for them to me is preferable, if less lucrative, than sitting on a camp-stool and watching a live bait. Seldom, however, does the spinner catch bigger fish than the user of snap-tackle.

Until the middle of March the stool fraternity can continue to sit and fish fine for roach or less fine for the other fellows called coarse. Well protected against the cold with hands in pockets and rod propped on a V stick, the angler can watch his float and occasionally warm his inside by not too frequent gulps from an attendant bottle. Such a method is not conducive to the best sport; for to be successful (certainly for roach) the fisherman must have his hand ever ready to strike. But we are not all so hardy and not all find it easy to contemplate as fishermen should when the warmth is not within us.

Trout fishermen can spend time usefully by trimming branches and cutting away the brambles that in spring and summer will deplete his fly box. But do not make the casting too easy. The bunkers add interest, give the fish a more sporting chance and will, if left in sufficient quantity, provide words new and ancient to regale other casters within hearing. January, if wet (should February later fail to fill the dyke), will give the trout streams a good flush out, clearing away the mud and providing more congenial surroundings for the food-harbouring weed.

If you have a day with the bream don't forget to see your bait is on the bottom, because the fish stands on his head to take it. They prefer it to be stationary or slowly dragging along the bottom.

R.B.

Is it my imagination, or is there an element of truth in a theory I have that the best treatment for seasonal colds, and a lot of other minor ailments, isn't bed and a hot-water bottle but fresh air and hard exercise? Remedial exercise, in fact?

I know that nothing is more calculated to shoot up the temperatures of professional medical men than the private speculations of laymen on matters of this kind. But, as I'm told that old wives and witches were aware of the curative qualities of a penicillin-like fungus several hundred years before the scientists got on to it, it may be that I'm ahead of the medical practice of my times, too.

I started thinking about it when I was re-reading the diaries of the great nineteenth-century sportsman Colonel Peter Hawker. Hawker, who was a bit of a hypochondriac, was always dosing himself up with various poisonous mixtures. Poor chap, he was ill, on and off, most of his life. But, when all else failed, when he was "trembling with ague" and "sick as a dog," he'd put his gun under his arm and do a hard day's work in the shooting field. Again and again, he recorded that by the end of the day he had cheated his doctor of five golden guineas!

Personally, when I have a heavy cold nothing gives me such relief as a hard walk. In the open air I can forget I've got a cold. It's inside, in an armchair, in front of a warm fire, that it swarms out of the nose and makes my head sing like a comb full of bees.

When I've had a gastric chill, which has doubled me up in the office in London, I've got rid of it in one glorious day's march over the Downs.

It seems to me that it must be a good thing to make the body work like that. Yet the traditional cure is just the opposite.

M.H.

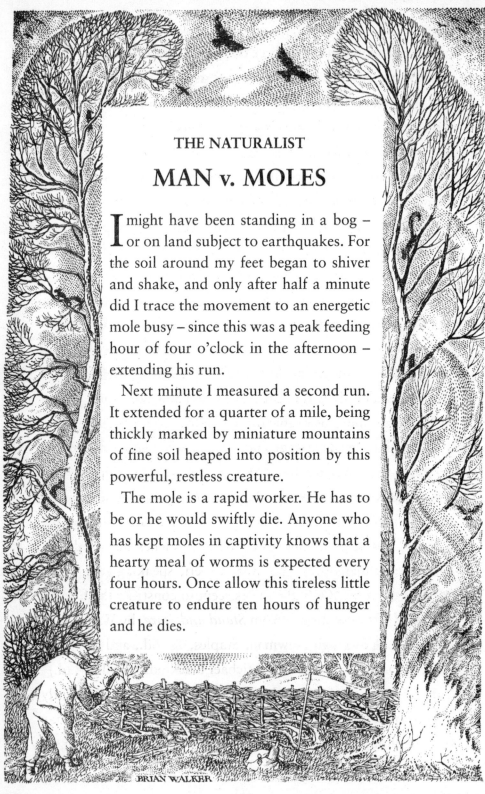

THE NATURALIST

MAN v. MOLES

I might have been standing in a bog – or on land subject to earthquakes. For the soil around my feet began to shiver and shake, and only after half a minute did I trace the movement to an energetic mole busy – since this was a peak feeding hour of four o'clock in the afternoon – extending his run.

Next minute I measured a second run. It extended for a quarter of a mile, being thickly marked by miniature mountains of fine soil heaped into position by this powerful, restless creature.

The mole is a rapid worker. He has to be or he would swiftly die. Anyone who has kept moles in captivity knows that a hearty meal of worms is expected every four hours. Once allow this tireless little creature to endure ten hours of hunger and he dies.

BRIAN WALKER

It was only recently when I grasped just what this must mean to the mole. A voice on the telephone asked me if I would please rear a young cuckoo; reluctantly I accepted the bird, only to find it was a mistle-thrush who soon demanded forty, fifty and even seventy worms a day.

It was never easy to secure these worms. It became immensely difficult by the time the bird had consumed his 500th worm from my garden. Only the kindness of neighbours, who sent me pints of worms gathered in their own gardens and dropped into tins, enabled me to rear this young bird to maturity.

After that I began to look with more kindly eyes upon the maddening mole, who ruins many a fine lawn and blunts all too numerous ploughs with his hundreds of little molehills. When to this mischief is added the fact that his beautiful velvet fur is for ever in demand, it is not hard to understand how some expert mole-catchers have been able to earn £40 a month at their trade.

Yet though men have waged war on the mole for many centuries, few have ever paused to study his behaviour. Hence our strange ignorance about his ways. Recently two eminent authorities have written about moles. One said: "The females construct the fortress ... a large mound often eighteen inches high and nine feet in circumference." The other expert, speaking with equal authority, wrote: "Only the males seem to construct the fortress ..." (The first quotation is from *Stand and Stare*, by Walter J. C. Murray and L. Hugh Newman, Staples, 7s. 6d., and the other from *Mammals in Britain*, by Michael Blackmore, Collins Ltd.)

The mysteries of the mole do not end there. It is frequently asserted that the creature seldom comes to the surface. This may be true, though I suspect that the mole comes out into the open more often than we suppose. I have found five moles run over along a single mile of main road in the course of one summer. Their nesting "fortresses" are lined with grass, leaves and even moss, which could only be gathered above ground. Again, it is surprising how often the village boy prowling around after birds' nests or looking for lost cricket balls returns with a frightened mole in the hand.

Again, does the mole mate for life? Or do most of them become polygamous as many naturalists suspect? And is the mole really blind?

This is a question frequently asked. As long ago as 1768, Robert Smith, Rat-Catcher to Her Royal Highness the Princess Amelia, wrote: "Moles are supposed by some people to be entirely blind, it being in many places proverbial to say 'as blind as a mole.' But this is a mistake, for they have eyes as well as other vermin, but very small, appearing scarcely larger than the head of a common pin, but sufficient to serve their purpose, their residence being generally under the earth."

The moles I have handled seemed hopelessly bewildered by strong sunlight. It is certain that their sharp sense of smell, possibly assisted by acute hearing, is the means by which they find their prey.

For proof of their sharp hearing, one has only to stand beside a mole-run when its owner is near. A single cough, a grunt or even loud breathing seems to frighten the creature away.

It is what the Royal Rat-Catcher, Robert Smith, called "the residences" of the moles which make them so unpopular. A single mole, extending its run by as much as fifty yards in a day, may swiftly spoil years of work. The mole digs with his powerful forefeet, which possess something of the shape and appearance of the human hand. At first the creature pushes all the loose soil against the sides of his underground passage. But soon too much soil may collect around him, and this he shoves upwards with his sturdy shoulders – despite the sanctity of the lawn above.

In some areas of England – Devon and the West Country, for instance – buzzards have sometimes come to the gardeners' rescue and captured a mole or two: occasionally a tawny owl may seize one. The badger, too, sometimes finds the mole a useful substitute for its stable diet of worms, young rabbits, honey, roots and insects.

Young moles – born in the nesting fortress – are blind at birth, but their eyes open after three weeks and they leave their home about a fortnight later. What happens next? Gardeners finding moles ruining their lawns might curb their annoyance and devote a little time to observing the habits of this mysterious creature.

Have they increased in number, one wonders, since the professional mole-catcher became as scarce as the bittern? Except in Ireland – fortunately (from the gardener's point of view) free of them – they are abundant wherever the moist soil attracts earthworms.

G.C.

THE NATURALIST

THE STORY OF THE RED DEER

O n the roof of the Cairngorm Mountains is a vast shallow plateau among the 4,000-feet hills. It is a wild windswept place of brown peat-hags and yellowish-green sweeps of mountain pasture, with grey granite cairns, acres of tumbled boulders and little pits of ice-cold water. From January to May it is completely covered by frozen snow.

All through the winter and spring, herds of red deer have been feeding in the glens at the foot of the mountains; but in June, when the grass begins to grow on the tops, the various herds come up to that high plateau – the Great Moss, as it is called – from miles around, assembling there in greater numbers than anywhere else in Britain. I have counted 600 deer at one time on the Moss, with a hundred or two more in the high corries of the surrounding hills.

The big stags, about one hundred in number, usually graze together in a single herd on the higher rim of the Moss, where their great antlers are clearly silhouetted against the horizon three miles distant. In April their antlers had dropped off and they had become very bad tempered, rearing up on their hind legs and boxing each other with their fore-feet, for the "velvet" knobs of the newly growing antlers are too tender for them to spar in the normal way with their heads. By the end of June, however, some of the big fellows are fully antlered again, though still in "velvet," their antlers covered by a protective skin, which will not finally wither and peel off in long strips until the horn of the antlers has hardened in August.

The young staggies, with only a tine or two projecting from each antler, run with the big fellows, others with the hinds. Many hinds are also accompanied by last year's calf, though by this time they are almost as big as their mothers. The first of the new year's calves are born early in June. Sometimes I have surprised a hind by herself. Instead of trotting or cantering away on those long springy legs of hers, after a preliminary stare at me, she advances towards my collies, stamping the ground with one fore-foot. If I sit down to watch her, she takes up her position on a nearby knoll, keeping me under close observation. And there she stands, giving a warning yelp from time to time. She has a newly born calf lying up not very far away.

The calf, however, is not hidden, like the young of most wild animals, but lies curled up on the grass. Its smooth head, with its large bluish-brown eyes, is turned back over its fore-legs, which are stretched out to their full length, though the yellow hooves are doubled under; its crinkled nose, soft and still unformed, pulses in and out with its breathing; little tufts of white hair sprinkle its brown coat. It neither moves nor blinks when the dogs sniff at it, as I sit beside it smoothing its coat. Its head seems too heavy to lift.

Opportunities for handling the calves are, however, limited, for within five days of its birth – during which period its mother returns to feed it twice a day – it is already sufficiently strong and agile to accompany her and run with the herd. And even before this time, if one comes suddenly upon one of these ruddy-coated, dappled-white babies, it will get up from its couch and trot away swiftly, while its mother canters off in the *opposite* direction.

If the wind is blowing from or across the deer, it may be some minutes before they become aware of me walking quite openly down the hill. When I am at any distance from half a mile to one hundred yards of them, however, one or two of the hinds begin to grow uneasy, pricking up their long diamond-shaped ears in my direction. And then some old mother-hind, with a dirty-yellow "moth-eaten" coat, utters a lion-like cough. Her warning cry touches off pandemonium, with the old hinds coughing and yelping, the yearlings blaring, staggies grunting, and calves bleating squeakily. The various herds and small groups begin to run together, stopping and starting, from all quarters of the Moss, and the whole concourse of three hundred or five hundred – the herd of big stags among them – canter across the Moss and climb reluctantly up from these pastures to the high corries.

By the end of July all the calves have been born, but the deer continue to inhabit the Moss for another six or eight weeks. Then the hinds begin to make their way down to the lower hills immediately above the glens. At the same time the herd of big stags breaks up and a curious thing occurs. All through the spring and summer these big fellows have been mute or have uttered only low grunts, but now a new sound is heard on the tops – the wailing and snarling of stags, roaring at one another from hill to hill across the glens and lochs.

October is the mating season, or rut, of the deer, and the stags follow the hinds down to the glen hills. Then a wide-antlered stag may appear out of the grey mists on the crest of one hill and, advancing to its extreme end, raise his head, round his mouth and roar defiance across the 1,000-foot chasm to another stag on the next hill. There may be fifteen or twenty stags roaring on the hillsides around a single glen at one time. It is a most impressive sound – a deep menacing lowing, ending in a lion-like cough.

But it is more sound than fury, for the stags behave like collies with sheep. Each stag tries to round up as many hinds as he can for his own harem and, at the same time, to prevent other stags from running away with the hinds he has collected. Stags do fight with those massive antlers during the rut, of course – sometimes to the death, by some accidents of antlers interlocking or a chance blow – but, for the most part, they are content to vent their fury in roaring at a distance or chasing one another. Meanwhile, the hinds continue to graze quietly – during those intervals, that is, when they are not being herded and chivvied by their lord.

By the beginning of November most of the stags are worn out with their tremendous exertions and have either gone back to the high tops, if the weather is open, or to their favourite winter corries, and only an occasional roar is heard in the glens.

As the snow creeps down the hills, the deer venture farther afield in search of food over the moors and glens and down to the pine forests. Then, winter sets in at its hardest. But the big stags still go up to the tops from time to time, and I can watch them through my binoculars marching along the dazzling white crest of the hills five or six miles from my house.

R.P.

THE NATURALIST

One winter afternoon, I encountered a badger wandering leisurely beneath the tall firs of a Cornish coppice. What followed was the most exciting experience in thirty years as a naturalist.

I hid in a dense clump of willows and focused my field-glasses just in time to see the badger pause and sniff at the base of a beech tree. It had found a wasps' nest. Then it started digging. Its short strong legs, equipped with efficient claws, threw the earth in all directions, and within a few minutes hundreds of drowsy wasps were buzzing around it; but the badger took no notice of them, its thick jacket of coarse wiry fur protecting its body from their stings.

It fed lavishly. Wasps as well as honey must surely have gone down its throat, and it was not until it was sated that it showed any concern for the battalion of buzzing wasps. One of them had apparently found a tender spot, causing the badger to rub its nose violently in the herbage and finally to roll over and over on the ground to dislodge the wasps entangled in its furry coat.

I was able to follow it back to its underground fortress. Fortress is the right word. There were eight large entrances, all connected with corridors running back into the sandy hillside to a depth of more than a hundred feet, each of these big enough to allow the inhabitants to move about freely. As the average badger is about fourteen or fifteen inches in height, and weighs up to thirty pounds, we can get some idea of the digging needed over years before such a stronghold was established.

Near one of the entrances was a quantity of fern, leaves and other vegetation which had obviously been recently collected. Strewn lightly over the ground, it led me to believe, from my previous knowledge of badgers, that this was fresh bedding which one of the inhabitants had gathered, for the badger is an ideal housekeeper. I also noticed near the sett two rabbit skins neatly turned inside out, a sure indication that a badger had dealt with them.

It looked as if a small colony of badgers might be in the sett. I decided to watch, and that evening by six o'clock I was in position a few yards from the old sandy burrow, where I had an uninterrupted view of at least five entrances.

Suddenly I became conscious of a white-striped face peering from the main entrance to the sett. After listening a few minutes it cautiously emerged, to squat on its doorstep and sniff the evening air in all directions. The moonlight by then was almost as clear as day, and no sooner had the first badger moved away into the shadows of the coppice than another appeared – but it came out backwards. I had never seen this happen before and doubt if I will ever see it again, for normally every badger (and I have watched scores) is cautious enough to test the conditions on the outside before showing itself; but this one had no misgivings, and as it reversed out of the corridor it pulled a bundle of soiled bedding behind its front paws.

This it dragged some distance away from the entrances and then piled together the fresh bedding, to which I have already referred, and using its nose bundled it through the doorway. During the next six hours I saw five different badgers leave that sett, three of them being noticeably smaller than the other two.

Exactly when the badger first came to this country nobody seems to know, but it is Britain's oldest mammal. Its life history is far from complete.

According to some, it is an unmitigated nuisance and should be destroyed because of its fondness for poultry, but I am convinced that many of the depredations with which badgers are charged have been the work of foxes. It would be stupid to deny that cases of badgers raiding poultry-runs have been proved; such robberies are not, I am convinced, a characteristic of badgers. Their main food is rabbits, rats, mice and other small mammals, many of which are dug up from their underground nurseries before they are old enough to leave home. Adult rabbits are also pulled from the trapper's gins, for a badger could not chase a rabbit down; but although mainly of a carnivorous appetite its dietary also includes certain vegetable matter and many insects.

Badgers are not hibernators in the true sense of the word, but during a spell of particularly cold weather I have known them to lie up for several days. Yet, on the other hand, I have often traced their footprints when the ground has been covered with snow. Indeed, winter affords many opportunities for tracking wild creatures, for even if no snow has fallen, the damp paths and muddy lanes tell the story of where they have wandered.

B.M.N.

THE DOG MAN

ON BUYING A GUN DOG

A reader has asked for a few hints on choosing a good gun dog. This is rather like being asked for a few hints on choosing a good wife – only more difficult, for he does not specify the type of dog, whether a spaniel or a retriever or what not. Obviously, the choice of a gun dog must be largely a matter of personal preference, but there are, I think, a few broad lines of approach worth bearing in mind.

Presumably you will choose a puppy. It is surely much more satisfactory than buying the ready-made article, even if you haven't the time to train it yourself. The point is *when* to choose your puppy. If you're wanting a pet above everything else, there is no doubt about it: it is best to buy your puppy between eight and ten weeks old. But if you're wanting a gun dog for work as well as companionship, get it as late as possible. This isn't as easy as it sounds, for the breeder will want to get rid of his puppies as soon after they're weaned as he can. Still, if you can buy your pup at six months old, so much the better.

And don't let yourself be mesmerised by pedigree. It happens all too often. Of course, you will want a good pup, a well-*bred* pup; but do remember that that does not of necessity mean a well-*born* one. Indeed, if someone offers you a pup by a field-trial champion out of a bitch who was a champion on the show bench (and even more so the other way round), my advice is – change the subject.

Remember that a colt sired by a Derby winner out of an Oaks winner has never yet won the Derby, nor I believe finished in the first three. Mind you, I have absolutely no objection to a champion as a sire or to a champion as a dam, provided that they can *work*. It is much more important in selecting a gun dog to know the working qualifications of the sire and the dam than it is to have champions close up in the pedigree. And in this connection you might think how many times you have seen a field-trial champion out at an ordinary shoot.

And then you must make up your mind about sex. If you have only one dog (and most people in these days are limited to one), it must be a dog, because it is not liable to be out of action just when required. But if you have two, then do have one bitch. Of the two, I much prefer the bitch (in the same way, I believe, most huntsmen prefer the bitch pack), for they are the most delightful of shooting companions.

Those three points decided, what are you to look for in choosing your puppy? This is the most difficult thing. If you're to make a good choice, you should know something about conformation, and there are some fairly definite rules about this – about what sort of shape a gun dog ought to be for the job it has to do – which you can learn. And, having learnt them, you're just as likely to make mistakes as the chap who doesn't know a thing about conformation.

Obviously you won't pick a puppy that is overshot or undershot: obviously you won't pick one with too small a mouth. You will go for a good deep chest and a short back, for well-sprung and nicely arched ribs. These are the obvious points, and you will pick them. In addition, I always like to see a gun dog with his hocks well under him. I forget who said that he liked to see a gun dog stand like a polo pony, but that man knew his stuff. It's advice I have never forgotten.

But when you remember all these points, and a hundred other little ones, and when you find them all in one animal, it still doesn't mean that you will have picked a good gun dog. There are things about a good gun dog that defy nice classification: you either know them or you don't. You are, as it is also with horses, a good judge of a dog or you are not. But I do believe that you can become a good judge of a working dog (as opposed to a bench dog) with practice. With practice you can even pick them out as pups without making too many mistakes – once you have learned to look at their heads, that is.

You see, all the things that go to the making of a good working gun dog – pace and nose, and so on – are valueless if the dog hasn't got the brains to make the best use of them. Pick the pup that looks sensible, even if he isn't as handsome as some of the others. The eyes will give you a pretty good indication if he has got any sense or not. Don't worry about their colour.

There seems to be a strong prejudice against light-coloured eyes in a dog: a sign of treacherous temper, people will tell you. That is absolute nonsense. There are just as many treacherous tempers in dark eyes as light. It's the expression that matters.

Then you want to look at the shape of the head as well. A big head does not necessarily mean brains. What you want to look for is, when seen in profile, a small but distinct step in the outline of the head. What you do not want is a "wedge-shaped" head. The scientists may laugh at this – I don't know if they do or do not, and care less – but ninety-nine times out of a hundred a wedge-faced dog is an obstinate dog and will be sour-tempered and a shirker by the time he is four.

Be fussy over the choosing of your puppy. Don't get flustered if the breeder looks at his watch in a pointed manner. After all, he is only selling a puppy: you are buying the companion of years.

B.V.F.

Dogs in Armchairs

With the approach of the colder weather I start waging a battle against Vicky (our Lakeland terrier), who decides that at the first sign of a snap in the air the armchair in the now disused drawing-room is just the place for napping. True, this habit was winked at at one time, but the chairs have just been expensively covered and I've vetoed it. With of course the usual absence of co-operation any man gets from his wife and daughters where animals are concerned. "Oh, it doesn't matter just once in a while" (once in a while being, of course, every time the dog wants to) and "Daddy, how would you like to have to lie on a hard carpet?" (the true and logical answer to this being completely unacceptable to any child and most women.

Vicky knew it was forbidden but, sensing support from other females, always took a chance when I was upstairs in the study and everyone else out. I used to come down, catch her ensconced and mildly chastise her on the scene of the crime, as for other misdemeanours. No use. She'd be back again in half an hour, till after a while the punishment motif sank into her small mind to the extent that I'd hear a quick pattering across the hall as I descended and find her all innocent in her basket in the kitchen. Again I would chastise her, carrying her back to the drawing-room, my idea still being that next time she was tempted she would associate the beating with the chair and desist.

Once again no use. Though in a short while Vicky had learned to nip off the chair the moment she heard me leave the study and more or less tiptoe across the hall, I would feel the cushion, find it warm and again haul her off to punishment, extremely puzzled as to how the hell I had found out this time.

By now we were just approaching the stage when I should come down very suddenly to catch Vicky blowing on the seat of the chair to cool it down, but before this happened I had a brilliant idea.

Vicky has always been rather nervous of small but sudden noises: a spoon dropping off the table or a gun-shot in the distance will invariably send her straight to the dark corner under the refrigerator, where alone she feels safe from the malevolence of the world. So I merely borrowed a couple of the kitchen mousetraps and laid them ready set on the chair seat. For the next few days I used to find them sprung and Vicky cowering in her refuge – known to us as "High Dudgeon" by the way – and thereafter she was cured. Just another triumph of *homo sapiens* over the lower forms of life.

A.A.

THE BOTANIST

DAFFODILS & ALL THAT

Save in spots which are unusually favoured by the climate, there are few wild plants in flower this month, and such plants as are in flower are, for the most part, too well known to form the subject of a special article. But it occurs to me that, since one of our winter-flowering plants is the snowdrop, the occasion is opportune for discussing the whole race of which the snowdrop is a type: the so-called Monocotyledons.

The monocotyledons form one of the two races into which all flowering plants are divided. The great majority belong to the other race: the Dicotyledons. In dicotyledonous plants every seed contains, in addition to the embryo of the stem and root, two primary leaves: these are the cotyledons. If a characteristic seed, e.g. a hazel nut, is examined, it can readily be split into two halves. The monocotyledons, on the other hand, contain only the one primary leaf.

Monocotyledons – I apologise for this clumsy name, but I didn't invent it – have many other characteristics in common. A high proportion of them have tuberous roots, corms or bulbs: nearly all the flowers raised from bulbs, which make so brave a display in the spring, are monocotyledonous. Again, the parts of the flower – the sepals, petals, stamens, stigmas and so on – are in threes, or multiples of three, whereas, in dicotyledonous plants, they are normally in multiples of two or five. And again, the leaves are, more often than not, unserrated and with parallel veins: typical are the sword-like leaves of such plants as iris and gladiolus. One does not have to be deeply versed in botany to be able to recognise at a glance the more characteristic "monocots." Consider, for example, four very lovely flowers, all of them favourites with poets and descriptive writers: the snowdrop, the daffodil, the yellow iris (or "flag") and the wild hyacinth, known south of the border as the bluebell. All these are typical. They are probably the best known of our native monocotyledons, though many others are familiar to everyone who knows the countryside.

The yellow iris, found all over the country in marshy soil and by the banks of rivers, is the prototype of many beautiful plants known to gardeners. It is also historically interesting as the original fleur-de-lis. We have another iris, less well known: this is *Iris Foetidissima*, the stinking iris, or gladdon. It has small purple flowers and, as its name implies, a most offensive smell.

To the same family belong the true crocuses, which, in their wild state, are very rare; the much commoner autumn crocus (or colchicum) is, however, not a true crocus but a lily. Yet another relative of the iris is our wild gladiolus. I have never seen this flower, but it is said to grow in the New Forest.

A second family of monocotyledons includes two of the flowers already mentioned, the snowdrop and the daffodil. The snowdrop in its native state is not common, but, where it does grow wild, tends to grow in profusion. It will be in bloom towards the end of this month. Soon after – "before the swallow dares" – comes the daffodil; and, to my mind, no display of cultivated daffodils, of which there are now so many varieties, presents a more enchanting spectacle than do wild daffodils in their native habitat. The jonquil and the white-petalled narcissus (pheasant's eye) are, of course, closely related to the daffodil. We have some wild narcissi, but they are believed not to be native to this country.

The largest class of native monocotyledons is the lily family, which includes a number of flowers that, at first blush, seem to have little in common. In addition to the bluebell and its close relative, the squill, we have a wild asparagus (a cliff plant); Solomon's Seal; lily of the valley; several species of garlic; the Star of Bethlehem; the snake's head or fritillary; a somewhat uncommon wild tulip; the bog asphodel; and herb Paris. This does not exhaust the catalogue of "lilies" but those I have not mentioned are of little interest save to specialists.

Of the flowers just referred to many are very beautiful – particularly in their native setting – and I have never ceased to delight in them. Bluebells, for example, grow in such profusion in meadows and copses that, when in flower, they can transfigure the countryside. As a boy I lived near Lady Bath's home, Longleat:

the bluebells there literally covered acres, and my father, who was an artist, spent many happy days painting them. Another great delight is the fritillary, once fairly common in Oxfordshire, though I am told it is tending to die out. And another is the bog asphodel (*Narthecium*). Its flowers are little yellow stars, and we used to travel many miles to look for them.

The oddest member of the lily family is the plant known as butcher's broom. The flowers, which are very small, appear to be stuck on to the middle of the leaves. These, however, are not true leaves, but modified stems, serving a somewhat similar purpose.

There is one other family of monocotyledons which I have not so far mentioned: I propose to deal with it later in a separate article. This is the orchid family, to which quite a number of our most interesting wild flowers belong. Most of them come into flower in the summer, and maybe I shall write about them then.

H.P.

WHAT EVERY COOK
SHOULD KNOW ABOUT

HARES

THE hare is at its best when in its first season, and it is not always easy to decide on the age of full-grown specimens. In general the belly hair is lighter and less tawny than in older hares, but I think on the whole the ears are the best test, as in a young hare these are tender and flexible rather than gristly, and can be easily split from top to bottom by a sharp tug. Some keepers go by the skin on the inside of the thigh, which in young animals is easily tearable.

Now hares are by their nature athletic animals and in order to get them really tender they need treatment. First long hanging and then proper "marinading." If these are not done there is a tendency for the dish to be dry, deficient in flavour and stringy in texture.

The purpose of a "marinade" is double. It makes the meat tender and enhances the flavour, and in the case of an essentially lean animal such as the hare the oil in the marinade is a substitute for non-existent fat. Joint your hare and lay the pieces compactly in a deep covered dish or casserole. To the hare add a marinade made in the following proportions:

Olive oil: 6 dessertspoonfuls.

Wine vinegar: 2 dessertspoonfuls (if malt vinegar alone is available it must be weakened in the proportion of half malt vinegar, half water).

6 bay leaves.

A liberal *bouquet garni* of sprigs of thyme and rosemary, chopped parsley is added, then two good-sized strong onions cut in thin rings.

The amount of marinade is dependent on the pot, but there should be enough to almost cover the joints. In this mixture they are steeped with occasional turning for at least twenty-four hours before the hare is cooked or jugged. If the latter process is in view, a glass or two of port is added to the marinade.

Jugged hare is the classic dish, and when all is said and done it is the best way to cook hare, but you should have this decision in view as soon as the hare is in the larder, for it is as well to save the blood and liver. The blood can be added to the marinade, but the liver is better very lightly poached and set aside while the joints are in the marinade.

The real secret of perfect jugged hare is long, *low* simmering, and it is a dish which takes time. Remove the joints from the marinade, dry them and dust with flour. Fry them lightly in butter or bacon fat till nicely brown. Then fry a handful of bacon cut in dice and with continuous stirring a cupful of diced onions. These should go to straw colour, not deeper.

Put the hare, the onions, bacon and most of the marinade into a casserole, and if necessary add stock. Stick the cover down with flour and water paste and set it in a very low oven to simmer for two or three hours. About half an hour before serving, cut up the poached liver and rub it through a sieve. Take the lid off the hare and taste the juice. It can now be seasoned with salt, pepper and possibly a little more herbs. Make a flour and butter *roux* and add some of the hare gravy to produce a moderately thick sauce. To this add the sieved liver, another glass of port and a little redcurrant or rowan jelly, possibly a squeeze of lemon if these are not sharp enough. Return this to the casserole, this will blend with the remainder of the gravy, and allow to cook very lightly till ready to serve.

Serve with redcurrant jelly and forcemeat balls. These should be made separately and with a good deal of rosemary. They can be added to the remains of the jugged hare later, but for first appearance are better cooked apart.

There are variations on jugged hare. It can be expanded by the addition of cubes of steak or it can be contracted for the smaller family by only "jugging" portions of the hare and treating part as a plainer roast. The best section for individual treatment is the *râble* or saddle, the portion from the back of the ribs to the hindlegs. Try this with a cream (or in these days "top milk"!) sauce. Chop the saddle straight through into convenient joints and simply cook it very slowly for an hour in enough cream to cover it to half depth in which you have put half a tea-cupful of finely minced shallots. A glass of wine is stirred in just before serving, and it is as well to serve snippets of toast in order to lose no drop of this delectable sauce!

When hare is plentiful, as it often is in a shooting household, one craves for variety, and in point of fact one can accommodate hare in a variety of ways. The basis is invariably hare joints fried in butter, but you can make a "stew" sauce with chestnuts and prunes which is excellent. Another has a basis of chopped olives, which as they are salty requires some care. The balance has to be carefully judged by taste and lemon juice or wine added till it is satisfactory.

H.B.C.P.

VICTOR MacCLURE'S
SCOTTISH KITCHEN

A bleak month, but all the more reason for keeping bleakness off the table. If the finer game-birds are past their best, there are wildfowl, woodcock and hares, and there is venison to supplement the ordinary butcher-meat, still good. Among fish – skate, eels, prawns and shrimps, haddock and cod – you may see the "poor man's turbot," brill, on the slab. Don't despise it. It responds to generous treatment with gelatinous court-bouillon better than cod or haddock. And that's the trick of it, to give it the jellied sappiness which belongs to its richer cousin.

Make a bouillon, then, with any odds-and-ends of veal, an onion spiked with two cloves, a carrot, a bouquet of parsley, thyme, and a bayleaf. Add a generous glass of white wine (not sherry), or a couple of tablespoonfuls of wine vinegar. Take the black skin off the brill. Butter an earthenware dish, strew it with sliced mild onion, or onion blanched. Lay your fish on this. Pour the strained bouillon over it. Put the lid on, or cover it with buttered paper. Let it poach in a moderate oven for fifteen to twenty minutes. Pour the liquid off the fish, and keep the fish warm and moist under paper. Make a *roux* of equal amounts of butter and flour, stir in your liquid. Quietly incorporate the yolk of an egg, cream if you have any, and a handful of peeled shrimps. Pour this sauce over the brill. Return to the oven for seven minutes. Brown off gently under the grill.

There may be that old cock-pheasant which uselessly occupies the attention of the hens. The gamekeeper thinks he would be better dead. Good. You can't roast him. Well, cook him in a casserole old Gloucester fashion – with chestnuts.

If you cook the old bird whole, you will need more stock to cover him. I would say, then, discard thought of appearances and have the better dish. Cut the bird up. If you want the drumsticks, draw those bony tendons from them with a pair of pliers. If not, put the drumsticks with the rest of the carcase, which you break up, the neck and so on, into a pot for addition to the necessary stock. Brown the pieces in a stout pan with butter and diced onion, and with some diced mushrooms if handy. Take the pieces out when browned, and keep warm.

Put your stock into the browning-pan, spoon it round to collect the caramel, add a good glass of red wine or a smaller one of port or madeira, reduce the stock to such quantity as will cover the pieces well. Butter a serving casserole, lay in it a couple of cross-sliced carrots and the white of one stick of celery cut into two-inch lengths. Get ready a bouquet of herbs, but add to it one clove of garlic crushed (optional) and the green tops of the celery. Tie the bouquet in a bag of washed muslin for handy removal. Put it in the casserole. Now lay the pheasant pieces on top, pepper and salt judiciously, and pour the reduced stock over. Let the bird's liver cook in the pot for five minutes. Put the casserole in an oven at about 325 deg. Fahr.

Prepare your chestnuts by slitting nine to a dozen slightly. Put them in a pan, pour boiling water over them, and boil for five minutes. Cool, shell and skin them. Put them under the grill to dry a little, then sprinkle them with salt, and roast them by shaking them in melted butter. Add them to the contents of the pot. The old bird will need cooking for nearly two hours. When ready to serve, chop the liver up finely. A Frenchman would flame the sauce with port and brandy before adding the liver. You needn't. Simply add the liver to the liquid in the casserole. Remove the bouquet bag, cook for a few minutes longer; Brussels sprouts are the traditional accompaniment to this dish.

Probably the best winter vegetable is the leek. We Scots have a way of treating it which makes a dish worth serving alone. You trim, say, two dozen moderate-sized leeks to the white only. Wash in lukewarm water and in several changes of cold. Drain and dry them. Butter a lidded dish and lay the leeks out on it. Chop up two tablespoonfuls apiece of carrot, onions, parsley, green celery top. It isn't Scots to add green peppers, but one may. Season cautiously with salt, pepper, nutmeg, powdered thyme, and add two bay leaves. Pour over enough meat-stock to cover. Cover with buttered paper, put on the lid, bake at about 350 deg. Fahr. for thirty-five to forty minutes.

By this time the liquor should be well absorbed and the leeks tender. Take out the bay leaves. Pour over the leeks a good half-pint of Béchamel sauce with the beaten yolks of two eggs added. Return the dish to the oven for a quarter of an hour to twenty minutes. Shake half a cup of breadcrumbs in butter under the grill, not letting them get too crisp. Sprinkle them over the dish, and brown under the grill.

Country folks don't need, possibly, to economise on leeks. But I wouldn't, myself, throw the green tops away. I would save the tender blades of the centre, blanch them for five minutes, then drain them. I'd wash the coarser parts thoroughly, and boil them in slightly salted water until I had a good leek infusion from them. Then, depending on what I had handy, I would either add clear brown stock to the infusion or with white stock and the leek infusion concoct a cream soup on a *roux* of flour and butter, probably adding a small cup of single cream. In either case, I would cross-cut the tender leek centres into thin strips, sprinkle them on the soup, cook a little, and serve. With the thick soup, I'd very likely fry some diced bread in butter until crisp, and sprinkle them on the soup at table. And I should have, if a not very nourishing soup, one that would start a meal very nicely and not be wanting in vitamins.

V.M.

WHAT EVERY COOK
SHOULD KNOW ABOUT

WILD FOWL

A seasonable hard spell may involve one in what is called wild fowling but is really shore shooting on ice-cold, wind-swept mud barrens. Not the least of the penalty for this activity is the work one has to do attempting to make something passably edible out of the odd things in the bag. Curlews, gaudy oyster-catchers, knots, redshanks, turnstones and godwits, they are all tougher than fowl, fishier than fish and oilier than red herrings! Even respectable birds like the common wild duck or mallard can be disappointing if shot at the seaside.

There *are* some birds which are worth cooking and of those the golden plover is undoubtedly the best. Of the ducks, pochard, teal and wigeon are not too bad, but in the winter you can be almost certain that they will be all fairly fishy. As to the geese, they are if hung for weeks still so tough that their resemblance to fisherman's old boots is pronounced in flavour, scent and consistency. Nevertheless, hardy people do eat them, but since the supply of new free dentures by the State has stopped they are possibly declining in popularity.

In general, all these beachcombing birds taste of fish oil, and the shore and tide-water birds taste of fish and mud, an unfortunate combination. Thus all methods of preparation and cooking are devoted to reducing or marking their shortcomings. In all cases they are better skinned than plucked, and though some people advocate cutting out the backbone from top to tail it makes little difference. The best thing is to concentrate on really pungent sauces which smother the bird's flavour.

Colonel Peter Hawker used to travel with a bottle of olive oil, a pot of anchovies, a bottle of lemon acid and one of the strongest and darkest cayenne pepper. With this nearly anything could be dressed or smothered.

His celebrated sauce to wildfowl was: Port wine, one glass; sauce á la Russe, the stronger the better, one tablespoonful; ketchup, one tablespoonful; lemon juice, ditto; lemon peel, one slice. Shallot, one large sliced; cayenne pepper (the darkest, not that like brick dust), four grains. This to be scalded, strained and added to the gravy from the roast bird. Sauce Russe is unknown today but Harveys is a possible descendant. It must also be remembered that in 1825 glasses and tablespoons were far larger than today.

Another way of using some of the amphibious birds to the best advantage is to make them into the well-known soup "Bitok á la Russe." It is a soup founded on raw beetroot, cabbage, any other handy vegetables and whatever is available in the way of meat for "stock" purposes. Remove the breasts and any other meat which can be easily removed with a sharp knife from the bird, duck, coot, goose or curlew. Chop up the chassis and add it to the Bitok stock of raw beetroot, cabbage, etc. The beautiful beetroot colour will change to orange as cooking proceeds. Now a real Bitok contains a little meat and, above all, fried cabbage; so you cut your bird meat to dice and fry it up with sliced cabbage, which should be fried enough to begin to brown a little. Drain off as much of the fat as you can (Russian cooks omit this) and add the cabbage and meat fry to the Bitok after removing the original bits of bird chassis from the stock pot. It is as well to remove some of the surplus stock of boiled cabbage and rather exhausted beetroot, though some of the latter can be retained if you want a Bitok with a good deal to eat in it.

Let your bird meat and fried cabbage simmer for at least an hour in the stock. For the sake of colour, grate up a raw beetroot and simmer out a bright magenta solution in milk. Now thicken your Bitok with a little "roux" or Robinson's Barley, which is nearer the Russian buckwheat flour they use.

Now taste the stock, which will be cabbagey, beetrooty and seabirdy; add your colouring of bright red beetroot essence, salt and pepper and add red wine vinegar in dessertspoonfuls till the soup has a taste not vinegary but on the sharp side – it should be slightly sour. It will alter surprisingly and, despite the odd ingredients, becomes a first-class soup. It is served very hot (but not boiling, as this would spoil the colour) and you can reinforce it with fried bread squares but, above all, add at the table sour cream or soured top milk, about a tablespoonful to each person.

Actually a good white stock is the preferable basis, but water and a little meat extract, etc., will do at a pinch. It is essentially a soup one flavours with beetroot and vinegar, etc., during the last ten minutes, and it can be served either cleared or as a sort of soup stew.

H.B.C.P.

WHAT EVERY COOK
SHOULD KNOW IN

JANUARY

There are some kinds of food which are particularly appropriate to really cold weather. The simplest of all is pea soup, made with milk which has been highly flavoured with bacon rinds or the skin off a piece of ham, or best of all, a knuckle of ham itself. Pea flour is rather a variable commodity but the best kinds are now nearly back to prewar standards. Pea soup for people returning with a good appetite from outdoor sports needs to be made rather thicker than it would be if it were simply to begin a meal, and calls, above all, for quantities of fried bread *croûtons* and dried mint to be sprinkled on it. The best way to deal with the *croûtons* if the family demand is large is to "deep-fry" a lot in oil, drain them on old newspaper and any surplus can be kept in a closed jar or tin. They warm up fairly well. On the other hand the *croûtons* ought to be done in bacon fat and are far nicer if they are – but it is not easy to find enough bacon fat for a quantity.

Associated with pea soup is lentil soup. It has rather a more pronounced flavour of its own and some varieties of lentils seem to taste stronger than others. I prefer the red variety. The lentils are steeped overnight in water with a lump of washing soda as big as a hazel nut in it. This is said to be a charm against the flatulence associated with these and other dried pulses. As with pea soup, a ham flavour is essential but a good deal of mace and a few cloves or allspice help. Rub through a wire sieve, as you never get a really smooth lentil soup unless you filter out all traces of lentil and simply thicken the water or milk they have boiled in. As a rule lentil soup needs a little thickening with arrowroot or cornflour otherwise it tends to "settle" too quickly.

Lentils make rather a good dish to serve with − not in − a stew with a good gravy. They should be cooked in good stock and then baked in the oven when they burst like miniature chestnuts. The ideal way is long slow cooking in a slow oven adding from time to time as much stock as they will take as they expand during the cooking. They stand up very well to the traditional "garlic and tomato" of Italian cookery, and will take up a certain amount of olive oil while cooking.

H.B.C.P.

HOME HINTS

With the New Year begins the season of Children's Parties. Here are a few ideas: I have always thought it a good idea to begin with tea. Food, and plenty of it, seems to put young guests at their ease, and to encourage the party spirit. A large cake made and decorated like a little house, with a roof of almond paste and sugar roses round the door. Gingerbread men. Biscuits iced like dominoes. Little pastry cases made like small boats, with a rice-paper sail, set on a green jelly sea. A more elaborate cake made like a merry-go-round, with a striped awning and posts made of sugar-sticks.

Children are all individualists, and this last idea may appeal more than all the rest: a small pink cake for each child, with his or her name written on it in chocolate water icing.

Here are the recipes:

GINGERBREAD MEN:

Special cutters for these may be had at some large stores. If none is at hand, cut out a stencil in stiff cardboard, and cut round it with a small sharp knife.

3 tablespoons golden syrup
1 tablespoon brown sugar
¾ oz. margarine
¾ oz. lard
1 dessertspoon milk
½ lb. flour, sifted with a pinch of salt
½ teaspoon bicarbonate of soda
1 teaspoon ground ginger
½ teaspoon mixed spice
Some glacé icing

Heat the syrup, milk, sugar, margarine and lard to boiling-point and cool. Pour on to the flour mixture and mix well. Set aside for an hour. Roll out on a lightly floured board to about ¼ inch in thickness and cut out the men. Lay carefully on a greased baking sheet and bake at 375 deg. F. (Regulo 5) for just under 10 minutes. Cool, and with glacé icing make buttons, eyes, mouth, etc.

DOMINO BISCUITS:

  5 oz. self-raising flour
  2 oz. sugar, castor or granulated
  White and chocolate glacé icing
  4 oz. margarine

Cream margarine and sugar together until well blended, and work in the flour. Spread the mixture on a greased baking sheet to the depth of about ½ in. Bake at 375 deg. F. (Regulo 5) for 10 minutes; turn out on a cake tray, and cut when cold into neat oblongs. Ice with white glacé icing like a set of dominoes, making dots and lines with chocolate icing, piped through a paper cornet.

M.B.R.

ODD-JOB MAN

It's funny how a sudden old-fashioned emergency can throw people into a complete panic; a chimney on fire, for instance.

One Sunday evening a little while ago I was disturbed from a somewhat tepid interest in "What's My Line?" to answer an agitated knocking at the door. And there was a neighbour in near hysterics. The chimney was on fire, she was alone in the house, and please would I do something. They haven't a telephone or I'm sure she would have used that.

The first thing to do if you find that soot in the flue has caught alight is to shut windows and doors in order to cut down the supply of air. Then spread a generous layer of salt on the fire. That will damp it down, and you will be able to take a lot of the coals away with a shovel and bucket. Roll back the carpet and hearth rug to prevent damage from falling soot, and on no account throw water on the fire.

If there is still no sign of the fire diminishing, then call in the fire brigade.

In any event, prevention being better than cure, have the chimney swept at regular intervals.

W.P.M.

THE FOX HUNTER

CLOTHES & THE HUNTING MAN

Excepting a few state occasions, the hunting field is the only remaining place where an Englishman may dress gaily without being accused of eccentricity.

There is something of the peacock hidden away in the make-up of nearly every healthy man and, after clothing himself soberly for the rest of the week, he finds an indescribable, if partly hidden, joy in dressing up on a hunting morning. Then, turned out in scarlet coat, yellow waistcoat, white breeches and shining topper and boots, no wonder he oozes bonhommie and goes around distributing shillings to lads who open gates for him or catch his horse when he falls off it. On such a morning his good feelings even extend to his enemies, and he finds himself calling out a cheery "Good morning!" to old Hardnut who got the better of him in the City last month. After all, this is a fine hunting day, and so on. Even if he comes off in the first twenty minutes and leaves one of his scarlet tails on a strand of barbed wire, or steeps his white breeches in muddy water and yellow clay, it will have been worth dressing up for.

Or he may be a farmer who has spent his past three days in driving a tractor up and down an unending field and worrying about a sick cow and the price of pig meal, and his evenings in filling in stacks of pointless forms. He has not even had the satisfaction of doing these things in the rather "natty" costume of the farmers of bygone years. Tractor oil and the need to save time have put him in overalls and gumboots while on the farm, and an ordinary tweed suit for market days. But on this, a hunting morning, having made a hurried round of the farm, he kicks off the gumboots, and with them his worries, and becomes the jovial yeoman of tradition as he puts on hunting clothes. Perhaps the black melton coat is straining a little at the buttons and the velvet hunting cap which, as a farmer, he is privileged to wear, shows a trace of green. What does it matter? The coat is beautifully cut by the same family of tailors who made his father's clothes and *his* father's before that, and he can hear the mare whinneying because she, too, knows this for a hunting morning.

The custom observed by many hunts of asking farmers who come out with them to wear black coats and hunting caps came into being for a very good reason. It is done so that others may easily recognise the men over whose land they may be riding and who, therefore, should be treated with courtesy.

All forms of hunting headwear, whether caps, toppers or bowlers, are something more than marks of distinction or of decoration. They are also designed to act as crash helmets, and you have only to rattle your knuckles on the crown of one to realise its strength.

A hundred years or more ago there was more variety in hunting dress. Costumes were even gayer than they are at the present time, but then so were all men's clothes. Perhaps the wearers were less shy of being labelled as individualists. Colours were not confined to scarlet and black. As for that nondescript form of dress known as "ratcatcher," well, it was unknown except on the backs of members of the fraternity from which it took its name. Hunting fields of those days often included coats of blue, green, brown, buff and yellow, while legs were encased in garments which varied from cavalry pattern overalls to very tight breeches and tasselled hessian boots.

Unusual colours have not vanished entirely from the modern hunting field, but they have come to be associated with certain hunts. For instance, the hunt servants of the Berkeley wear yellow coats with black collars, the livery of the noble family after which the hunt is named. At one time this hunt claimed as its country all the district between Berkeley Castle in Gloucestershire and Charing Cross, and maintained kennels at both places.

When the Berkeley country was split up, another hunt, the

Old Berkeley, came into being, and this also adopted yellow as the colour of the hunt servants' livery. When this hunt was further divided into East and West packs, the O.B.H. (East) retained the yellow coat, while the O.B.H. (West) adopted red coats with yellow collars. This is the explanation why some hunt staffs turn out in yellow coats. It has nothing to do with any political aversion to the more customary foxhunting colour as was imputed by one newspaper!

The oldest hunting colour is, as might be expected, green, and coats of this colour are still worn by the hunt staff of the Duke of Beaufort's hounds, and by the Duke himself in his capacity of master and huntsman. Members of the hunt wear the Beaufort family colours, blue coats with buff facings. The Heythrop was originally an offshoot of "the Duke's" and here again the hunt staff sport green. A few other packs, among them the Gellygaer and the Nant Fawr in Wales and the Royal Artillery on Salisbury Plain, favour green for their hunt staffs, as, also, do the Romney Marsh Foxhounds, which were originally harriers.

There are at least two Welsh packs which clothe their staffs in brown coats, and, farther north, several other hunts, among them the North Tyne and the Border, choose steel grey as their colour.

There is no space here for going into the question of whether the correct term for the most favoured hunting colour should be scarlet, red or pink, although it is one which crops up annually in the sporting press. Personally, I prefer "scarlet," which is what most professional huntsmen call it.

Although hunt staffs and a number of followers continue to turn out in bright colours, there are now more black and grey coats to be seen in the hunting field than was the case in our grandfathers' time. This is not the only change. Coats have become shorter. The old-time riding coat had skirts that came well below the knees and which were a good protection against weather. The swallow-tailed coat gives little protection, but looks superb on a tall, slim-waisted man. Anyhow, perhaps protection matters less in these days of motor transport. The long hack home has become a thing of the past except for those who refuse to be parted from their horses.

Yet, while actually riding "with one eye for hounds and the other for the country," whether taking the fences as they come or looking for lanes and a handy line of gates, the hunting man – and woman – needs to guard against our English climate. So hunting costume is not merely a form of fancy dress. Breeches are cut (we always hope) so that, besides *looking* right, they do not wrinkle behind the knee and so that the top knee button fits exactly into the little hollow place which God designed for that purpose. Coats, too, must be as nearly as possible weatherproof. The hunting stock is worn for the same reason that sailors wrap a towel round their necks inside their oilskin collars. It is an excellent way of stopping rain from running down between the shirt and the body.

As for the famous John Peel, he was a hill huntsman and turned himself out in a very long-skirted coat of hodden grey and a rather rough top hat. The words of the song, of course, are correctly "coat so *grey*," not "gay," as it is so often sung.

J.I.L.

FEBRUARY

WILD LIFE

In February spring approaches the door and may well knock on it. On all sides the eye of the naturalist can perceive signs – some obvious, some more subtle – which show that before long the full glories of what is surely the best of all seasons will be with us. Everything seems to be astir, though we cannot actually *hear* all that goes on. Nevertheless, we certainly do hear many samples of bird song – fair tastes of concerts to come. Finches are tending to split up their flocks and spread out prior to pairing. These birds sing fitfully at such times, but some of our other regulars – blackbirds, for instance – will be singing quite strongly.

Perhaps one of the most definite signs of awakening life is the reappearance of those butterflies which spend the winter months in hibernation. In the house the tortoiseshells which have been lurking in dark corners and behind pictures on the wall may be disturbed by energetic and early spring-cleaners;

and if the days are sunny these butterflies will, if allowed, fly outside and provide a pleasing spot of colour in the garden. Before the month is out the bright yellow brimstones may also be seen on the wing.

In some of our warmer regions, notably in the extreme south-west, frogs will be spawning, though the bulk of them will not do so until late in the month or in early March. Newts, too, can often be seen in ponds; but they will not court and then deposit their eggs (each carefully wrapped in a leaf of pondweed) for some weeks yet.

The reptile world is no exception to this early activity, for both grass snakes and adders may be observed in sheltered spots when the sun comes out. So will slow-worms – those legless lizards which so often get mistaken for snakes and suffer in consequence.

Badgers have their cubs in February, though this fact was not definitely established until quite recently when Ernest Neal's researches proved this beyond doubt. A badger sett will be worth visiting from now onwards; for although at the moment the sow will be occupied underground, there will he many evidences of work afoot. There will be signs of fresh diggings, and the bringing out of stale bedding and its replacement with new. Many observers used to think that at the time when the cubs are born the sow would not tolerate the boar anywhere near her, but I have satisfied myself that this is not the case. Not unnaturally he spends more time hunting and rooting than she does, but he is there in the sett just the same, though possibly occupying a separate apartment.

M.K.

Early nesters this month ravens, sometimes long-eared owls, sometimes herons, sometimes mallard. Eggs of tawny and barn-owl have been recorded though not until the second half of the month. Bitterns start booming in the fens of East Anglia.

Several animals come out of hibernation towards the end of the month, especially if fairly warm – notably frogs and bats. "Skylarks mount and essay to sing" wrote White, and he, as might be expected, has many other records of returning bird song this month – jackdaws, chattering on churches, missel-thrushes and yellowhammers, black-birds whistling, great-tits "attempting their spring note," and robins, chaffinches, marsh-tits. Brown owls hoot, and partridges pair.

February my usual month for visit to bird-place of boyhood – duck-decoy in plantation at corner of River Nene, in ancient water meadow. But the waterfowl are not what they used to be, for ten years ago the river was deepened, and the meadows drained. Of the hundreds of white-fronts of a decade back there is now not one, and the packs of ducks are small.

Rooks make much business and noise at their old rookeries on sunny afternoons, and may start rebuilding in earnest. Short of food this month, they'll raid the potato clamps if they're not frozen solid, and just this month they'll be spending much time on the ploughland, especially in Scotland.

Snowdrops, crocuses, green hellebore and pilewort. The male bloom on the hazels. The field-crickets open their holes, and the first brimstones stirred from hibernation by the low February sun flit about the empty woods like wandering leaves.

J.F.

THE FLOWER GARDEN

In the early months of the year much of the charm and beauty of our gardens is provided by bulbous plants. From the first glistening white snowdrop to the late-flowering tulips, the majority need very little attention and a selection can be made which is suitable for the rock garden, for naturalising in grass, for planting at the base of deciduous trees or for more formal bedding schemes. Almost every garden has its snowdrops, crocuses, narcissi or tulips but there are many other bulbous plants worthy of consideration.

One of the earliest to flower is the hybrid winter aconite *Eranthis Tubergenii,* with its large yellow buttercup-like flowers. A little later *Scilla siberica* and *Chionodoxa Lucilie,* planted together in masses, will form a lovely carpet of blue, however uncertain the weather may be. The more popular grape hyacinths increase rapidly and combine well with groups of the dwarf *Narcissus triandrus* or *N. Bulbocodium. Erythronium Dens-canis,* the dog's-toothed violet, with its pink flowers and marbled foliage, is most valuable for planting beneath trees, but the taller and more variable American species, *E. californicum* and *E. revolutum,* succeed best in the rock garden. In a damper situation, *Fritillaria meleagris* always arouses interest despite the fact that it can be seen wild in some parts of the country. One must not forget the hardy cyclamen, the lovely blue *Anemone apennina*, the snowflake *Leucojum vernum*, or the many rarer varieties of our common bulbs which combine to give an ample choice for even the most discriminating gardener.

The pruning of wall shrubs and climbers leads to many queries, but in most cases little attention is needed except for the removal of overcrowded or dead growths. Wisteria, however, needs hard pruning to produce its long racemes of flower, and following the shortening of the long growths in August to five leaves, the spurs should now be shortened to two dormant buds. Similar treatment should be afforded to the deciduous ceanothus, buddleias and ornamental vines. Winter shrubs are best attended to immediately after flowering, growths of *Jasminum nudiflorum* being thinned and those of shrubs such as the winter sweet shortened back. Clematis fall into several sections, but with the exception of the Jackmanii group, which need severe pruning to produce large flowers, the majority are best thinned and a certain number of growths cut back to the base each year. Hydrangeas benefit from the removal of the dead flower heads but otherwise do not need pruning.

C.P.

———·•·———

U NDER GLASS: If possible sow in gentle heat (about 50 deg. F.) half-hardy annuals like ageratum, antirrhinum, nemesia, petunia and stocks. In an unheated greenhouse or cold frame, hardy perennials such as delphiniums may be sown. Soil for seed boxes should be sterilised with chestnut compound to prevent "damping-off."

Remove Dahlia tubers from their winter store and place in sterilized boxes of soil to start into growth for taking cuttings next month – this can only be undertaken in a heated greenhouse.

Take cuttings of decorative chrysanthemums, including both mid-season and late varieties, as early as possible. Ideal type of cutting is about 3 in. long, sturdy, not soft, and growing direct from the soil, as distinct from the old stem. Make the cut immediately below soil level to include a blanched portion. With some varieties, notably Friendly Rival, stem cuttings are unavoidable, as no basal shoots are produced. Stem cuttings are more successful if not taken too high up the stem.

IN THE OPEN: Keep sharp look-out for slugs, always liable to attack shoots of perennials like delphiniums as they push through the soil. Use a proprietary preparation such as "Abol" slug bait if necessary.

Rose trees may still he planted unless the ground is frost-bound, sodden or sticky. Try and complete soil preparation not less than three weeks previously, to allow the ground to settle. Perfect drainage is always essential, therefore break up the subsoil by thorough digging, adding humus-forming material such as compost and hop manure – don't add farmyard manure unless the land is in poor heart. Bonemeal and peat should be incorporated in the top spit. Plant firmly and make sure that the trees are not allowed to dry out beforehand – cover the roots with sacking or cloth until ready to plant, or dip the trees in a pail of water for half an hour unless the weather is very cold.

If roses are planted in late February they should be pruned

before planting, and cut back to four or five eyes from the base in the case of bush trees; standards to, say, six or seven eyes. Climbers and ramblers planted at this time are reduced to about half their length, but leave climbing hybrid teas alone or they may revert to the bush form.

Late – flowering shrubs such as buddleias, Hydrangea paniculata and Ceanothus Gloire de Versailles are pruned this month. Cut back last year's growth to within two or three buds of the main stems.

N.P.H.

THE VEGETABLE GARDEN

Work for this month can almost be summed up in two words: make lists. The more thorough your lists, the better crops you will get; providing, of course, that you follow up your decisions. This is about the only time of year when pencil and paper are more practical than fork and spade; in fact, if there is frost or snow on the ground it should not be so much as stepped upon. And if it has been dug and left rough – as it should be by now – there is the great satisfaction of knowing that the weather is working on it much more effectively than tools could just now.

First, make a list of all the kinds of vegetables you have ever grown, putting them under two headings: those that were successful, and the failures or generally poor crops. The ones that are consistently good are the ones to grow again; obviously your ground suits them, or you have studied their needs and have a flair for growing them well; these, too, are the ones to concentrate on if you have in mind prize exhibits this year. The failures need careful thought if you mean to master them. Try to find the reason for their poor performance, and if it is something that can be remedied, give them another chance. But it is both disheartening and a waste of ground to continue sowing, for example, carrots, if your soil simply will not grow good carrots.

Your next list, the selection of future crops, will also be divided into at least two sections: one for the really essential vegetables; another for untried, unusual, or "experimental" ones. This is where you will need some seed catalogues, and if you haven't already got them, send to the best seed merchants, including those specialising in unusual varieties. The first list you made will help you to decide what you want to grow this year, and if your completed list is bigger than your available ground, some of the "non-essentials" will have to be struck off – or put on a waiting list.

Another, more detailed, list should be made by looking up the kind of treatment (preparation of soil and so on) for each kind of vegetable you intend growing. This may seem a lot of bother, but there just isn't time to hunt for information once the season really gets going; if you get together, now, all the necessary details for cultivation, these can be pinned up somewhere inside the tool-shed, where a quick glance will tell you all you want to know.

C.M.

———•••———

It is difficult to make definite statements of work to be done in February, owing to the fact that the last fortnight can be very busy, or, on the other hand, one can equally well be forced to spend it sheltering from pelting rain or hard frosts.

If it is dry on top, fork over ground which has lain rough during the winter, in preparation for early seed beds. Prepare celery trenches. Dig out two spits deep, place well-rotted manure in the bottom of the trench and replace one spit. Quick-growing crops such as radish and planted-out lettuce can occupy the trench before being required for the main crop and the ridges formed by the unwanted spit can be levelled out and utilised for dwarf beans, early cauliflower, lettuce, etc., at a later date. Deep soil is essential for this operation.

Make a small sowing of a long-pod broad bean. Plant two inches deep, 8 inches between the beans and 18 inches between the rows. Peas may be sown in a sheltered position towards the end of the month. Use an early dwarf variety such as Meteor, Little Marvel, etc. Spinach can also be put in.

Plant shallots and garlic on ground which is loose. Allow 12 inches between rows and 6 inches between plants. Shallots should be pushed lightly in with the tops showing, and garlic cloves must be covered by about an inch of soil.

Choose a favourable moment to lightly fork, or, better still, hoe the autumn-planted spring cabbage bed, but do not apply any fertilisers until later.

If a new rhubarb bed is required, now is the time to plant. It is essential for the ground to be well manured and absolutely clean. Divide old crowns and replant pieces which have at least two eyes. This bed will not be fit for pulling until the following year.

If parsnips show signs of sprouting, they should be lifted and stored in a cool shed or under a wall.

E.B.

THE FRUIT GARDEN

Root-pruning. On the better types of soils one is often faced with the problem of a fruit tree which, although growing away very strongly, fails to produce any fruit. The tree may flower adequately and yet set no crop, in which case the lack of a suitable variety nearby for cross pollination can be suspected, or even frost damage if the garden is in a known frost pocket. There is often the case, however, of the tree which produces little or no flower at all because of the excessive amount of wood growth that is being produced annually. The natural reaction is to prune away the unwanted wood and open up the tree generally, but when the following summer arrives one realises that such treatment has not had the desired effect but rather the reverse of it, for the tree is a mass of new growth.

The reason for such a disappointing result is that the over-vigorous root system – which the tree must have had to produce wood so freely – has remained untouched and therefore unchecked. Such vigour invariably points to the probable existence of several large "tap" roots which, if allowed to remain, will be the indirect cause of the tree's unfruitfulness for many years ahead.

The best remedy for such a state of affairs is "root-pruning." This can be done anytime during the late autumn or winter providing the soil is not too wet. With a young tree it is comparatively simple to lift it, prune back any tap roots and then replant it. This is done by first taking out a trench around the tree and about three feet from it; then by the use of a fork the tree is carefully undermined and lifted. The large tap roots are best cut with a sharp knife or pair of secateurs, making a long slanting cut on the underside and a much shorter one on top. Such a cut ensures rapid healing of the wound and probably more important encourages the formation of fibrous roots – the type which go hand-in-hand with the production of fruit buds. The tree is then replanted in exactly the same way as for any new fruit tree, replacing the soil *very firmly* and evenly around the well-spread roots.

With larger trees which cannot be lifted the answer is to root-prune one side and then the other a year or so later rather than all in one operation. On trees so treated pruning should be very *light* until cropping commences, and adequate staking to avoid "wind-rock" is an obvious essential. After treatment, a surface mulch of old manure or compost is advisable to avoid drying out and to encourage formation of fibrous roots.

G.R.W.

This is the season for apple pruning, and by now the job should be well under way. Some trees are spoiled by wrong pruning but more often by the lack of it. In the initial four or five years the aim is to form a well-balanced framework of branches rather than encourage fruiting. To obtain this, hard pruning is necessary and as a general rule about one-third of the current season's growth should be removed. With upright-growing varieties prune leaders to outward pointing buds and spreading varieties to an upward pointing bud. The leaders which will form the main branches in time should be well-placed vigorous growths; any other very strong shoots are best removed completely, moderately vigorous shoots shortened to three or four buds and weak ones to one or two buds. Occasionally a short shoot can be left unpruned as such growths are the first to fruit. If *all* the shoots are left unpruned then the majority will be quick to form fruit buds. While this would appear to be the shortest way to heavy crops it is not so in the long run. At this stage fruit is produced at the expense of growth, without which a shapely tree can never be formed.

Once the framework has been built up a different type of pruning is employed. This is in no case as hard as that of earlier years as the aim now is to encourage the formation of fruit bud. It is probably at this stage that pruning appears to follow no logical sequence to the average gardener. Although pruning does vary from variety to variety, depending on the type of growth produced, such types can be divided into definite groups. The first is those varieties which readily produce short spurs such as "Cox's Orange Pippin" and, incidentally, many varieties of pear. With these, new growths are pruned back to three or four buds as vigour is seldom really excessive.

The second group can be conveniently called long-spurred varieties with examples like "Laxton's Superb." In this case growth is more vigorous and to ensure formation of fruit bud must not be pruned so drastically. Stronger growths should be cut to six or seven buds whilst a proportion of shorter ones may again be left unpruned.

In the third group are the tip-bearers – that is those varieties which habitually form fruit bud on the tips of young shoots. A typical example is "Worcester Pearmain." Here up to a half of shorter growths are left unpruned providing the tree is vigorous enough to carry them. The remainder are cut back to five to six buds to encourage new growth.

G.R.W.

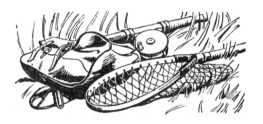

FISHING

From now until the start of the trouting, my mind will be set on big pike. This is the time to catch them. The real monsters

– and they are most of them females – may be four or five pounds above their autumn weight by now, the balance being made up by ripening spawn. A daily newspaper is at this moment offering £100 for the first English or Welsh pike of forty pounds to be captured. Their money is, I think, fairly safe, at least for a long time to come, but many anglers will be busy working out the best way to relieve them of it.

The first thing to be considered is what match-anglers and speedway fans call the "venue." The obvious waters to hold such a fish are: the Wye, which has turned up more pike over thirty pounds than most other rivers put together; the Hampshire Avon, which holds the present record of 37 lb. 8 oz.; the Broads, with especial reference to Barton Broad; lastly, the Midland and London reservoirs.

I think that a fish of this tremendous weight is likely to be king of a beat in a river or lake. For this reason all stories – provided they can be reasonably checked first – of monster pike that haunt such-and-such a bend or eddy should be followed up.

The next question concerns bait – should it be alive, dead, or just spinning? The list of better than thirty-pounders taken on spinners is impressive; it even includes Mr. John Garvin's 53 lb. Lough Conn record. All the same, where the presence of a big fish is known or suspected I would settle for live bait. After all, a big pike has more to lose than a small one by dashing about after its prey.

I believe, too, in the big-pike-big-live-bait theory. In this instance I wouldn't call five- or six-inch roach large. For a possible forty-pounder I would much rather tackle up with a two-pound roach (if I could catch one first) or even with a young jack of anything up to four pounds. This size of bait plainly demands some new thinking about hooking devices. I'm certain I should settle for fewer than the thirteen hooks with which Tom Morgan caught his Loch Lomond fish of 47 lb. 11 oz. Three big triangles would probably be enough, for a forty-pound pike isn't going to nibble at its food.

The odds against any weekend anglers getting that forty-pounder accordingly to plan are astronomic, especially when one takes into consideration that such a fish is probably only really on the feed once in a fortnight. But there will be a lot of fun in trying and the methods used should catch a lot of big pike, if not a record-breaker.

C.W.

SHOOTING

February sees the close of the real shooting season, but the days are beginning to draw out a little, and there are usually appointed days when a sort of mass onslaught is made on the pigeons. It is certainly an inspiring noise to hear the steady crackle of musketry, and it is pleasing to hope that the disturbed birds will fly to your own "hide," as you are probably half perished with cold! In point of fact all you probably see are rather annoyed pigeons, extremely alert and flying far too high to warrant the expensive discharge of a cartridge. In counties which are not too heavily wooded, these pigeon shoots are, however, tolerably effective.

On the other hand there is always the possibility that there may be snipe in appropriate or even inappropriate places. Snipe are very mobile and astonishingly good at forecasting weather, so if you hear on the wireless that hard weather is spreading from somewhere else and coming towards you, it is worth while pottering round some of the marshes to see if a few visiting snipe have come in. You will probably find that you have shot off all the number eight cartridges at marauding jays, and will have to use ordinary number six. I think it does make a difference – but the small shot never give you the chance of that incredibly long shot at snipe, which you pace out with pride, and then conclude you need fresh glasses!

Actually I think that February is the only time to review the faults of the last year. Birds you know were properly "tapped in" leaked out along hedgerows and were seen impertinently running away. Yes, running, probably laughing too much to fly! So you need to prowl your own coverts and get a pheasant's-eye view of things. Probably the undergrowth has gone leggy, and is bare underneath, while a breast-high jungle of old bramble and rose has led you to believe there was ample cover, and the birds would lie like stones. Well, you can do a bit with a slasher and improve things a little. You may find that the age-old wire netting, which used to ensure a good rise and no leakage, is flat, worn out, or has been lifted a foot or so off the ground by exuberant brambles.

It is really a case of "Do look now!" for if you put it off till you can get the woodman or someone to come round with you, everything will have started growing and you will again be deceived. Incidentally, you will again want some number eight, as you will find the place swarming with jays and possibly some grey squirrels, and if you do see one of those damnable old cocks, well, any Bench will let you off if you produce a psychiatrist's evidence that from early childhood you had been unable to distinguish a pheasant from a squirrel.

H.B.C.P.

THE BIRD-WATCHER

POOR COCK ROBIN

WHAT happens to dead birds? This is a question every ornithologist is asked and none has been able to answer without some reservation. Dr. David Lack, Director of the Edward Grey Institute for Field Ornithology at Oxford, has shown in an interesting way just how great is our ignorance of the causes of most birds' death. He examined the "returns" of blackbirds that had been marked by British bird-watchers under the National Bird-marking Scheme. He found that no fewer than seven in every ten had been simply recorded by the observers as "found dead."

From an analysis of the individual history of large numbers of nests, ornithologists now know the average losses of eggs and fledgelings in the nests of several of our commonest birds. And from an analysis of the ringing records we also know a great deal about the expectation of life of such birds after they have left the nest. There is a short period (often in July) just after the fledgelings have flown from the nest when we know less than we would like about their mortality; but it is also true that an insurance actuary with slide rule and tables could work out a more accurate life policy rate for a blackbird, song-thrush, robin or chaffinch than for a Chinese soldier or a member of a Balkan government.

We are, however, still pretty ignorant about the *causes* of their deaths. Unquestionably, a large percentage of birds in an area at any time is doomed to be eaten by other animals, and quite a surprisingly large percentage is doomed to die by accident. Thus, the domestic cat is perhaps the commonest predator of the nestlings of such common garden birds as do not nest in holes. And very many birds suffer accidental death in man-made things like fruit-netting and the apparatus of his communication (road, railway and air traffic, telegraph, telephone, power and radio wires). Many birds are shot and trapped. It has been calculated, for instance, that of every three wild mallard fledged, one is shot.

There is here an interesting paradox. While a large proportion of common wild birds fall victims to predators, especially when they are young and inexperienced, it is not likely that their population, their density over a given area, is controlled by these predators to any important extent. Rather is it the other way round. It is the abundance of the prey that controls the population of the predator. Indeed, the only predator that can be relied upon to affect the numbers of its prey is Man! This is because he is too efficient. Indeed, he can only enter into a balanced relationship with his prey when he accepts the task of keeper as well as that of killer, cherishes the animals that he kills and limits voluntarily the crop that he takes.

There are, of course, other exceptions to this general rule. Thus, certain of the wild animals which Man has wittingly or unwittingly introduced, such as rats, may destroy the populations of their own prey. But in the long run, in natural conditions, the predatory animals arrive at a balanced, though often fluctuating, relationship with their prey, which it takes a cataclysm of Nature or the interference of Man to upset. The numbers of common birds are probably controlled mainly by the abundance of the food which they are adapted to eat and not by the abundance of the creatures which are adapted to eat them.

It seems to be true that blackbirds and thrushes can (and do) lose about half their output of eggs and young to predators during the breeding season, without their fundamental population being materially affected. Yet one exceptionally icy February, by closing down the food supply, can kill a smaller total number of birds, yet cause a setback to the population from which it may need more than one breeding season to recover.

Before the war, Dr. Julian Huxley and I devised a method of recording the adventures and fate of the contents of birds' nests on cards. With subsequent improvements, the card has become the nest record card for the British Trust for Ornithology, and a thousand or more are now filled in every year by observers all over the country. Some of these observations have been analysed, and we now know a good deal about the fate of eggs and young in the nest. Thanks to the records of the ringing scheme we now know a little about the fate of fledgelings between leaving the nest and the first of August (though not as much as we would like) and a lot about their subsequent fate. Dr. Lack found that from every hundred robins' eggs, seventy-three are likely to hatch and fifty-seven young ones to leave the nest. By the first of August following, fifteen more of these young robins will be eaten or die, leaving forty-two. A year later, only twelve of these will survive, a year later only four, a year later two, a year later one, a year later probably none.

The fate of blackbirds gives a slightly different version of the same pattern. From a hundred eggs, sixty-four hatch, fifty fledge, thirty survive on the first of August, and of these there survive in subsequent years, on an average, fourteen, eight, four, three, two, one and nought. It is probable that the better survival of robins in the nest is due to the fact that animals of prey, including schoolchildren, find blackbirds' nests far more easily than they do those of robins.

The death of small birds thus normally takes place very early in their potential life. And their expectation of life, once they are adult, is actually a constant, and independent of their age. This is a very interesting situation and has been otherwise found in the animal kingdom only among young male humans of warlike savage races, or of Western races in time of war, and among some fish and some other animals such as oysters. Our knowledge of the possible length of life of birds comes partly from the ringing scheme, but mainly from the records of birds in captivity, of which large numbers have been published by the late Stanley S. Flower. From these records we know that small birds *can* live a very long time – greenfinch nineteen years, chaffinch twenty-two, house-sparrow twenty-three, garden warbler twenty-four, redpoll and siskin twenty-five, goldfinch twenty-seven. Yet, in the wild, the actual expectation of life of an adult of any of these species is not much over a year.

J.F.

THE ENGLISH HEDGE

Undoubtedly the dominant feature of the English landscape is the hedge. Any panorama of the patchwork of fields is laced with hedges and fences, differing widely in form and appearance. These differences are determined by locality, wherein custom, soil and available materials have influenced the style and construction of the hedge.

Historically, they came into prominence at the time of the Enclosure Acts, most of which were passed during the late eighteenth century and early in the nineteenth century. Enclosure had started earlier, in the sixteenth century, but was not generally practised until 160 years ago.

It is often possible, therefore, to determine the age of a hedge by the type of plants used and by its line. Pre-Enclosure hedges were most likely built of mixed plantings of sloe, elder, holly, thorn, privet and hazel and followed the line of the plough thus presenting a curving and winding boundary. The post-Enclosure hedge is straight in line and is far more likely to consist only of thorn.

Farming, in the days before the Enclosure Acts, was communal. Strip cultivation was followed, and hedges were therefore not generally recognised as necessary for anything more than confining the stock. Boundaries were primitive and simply constructed or marked only by boulders or large holes dug in the ground. The first consideration was that a hedge while indicating the boundary and forming a barrier, should produce timber for fuel and fencing posts and at the same time be non-poisonous to stock. Ash (*Fraxinus excelsior*) was extensively planted for this reason, and the bushes were allowed to grow to a considerable height before being cut. The ash trees that still stand as shade trees in our hedgerows today are a legacy of this early hedge planting.

Thorn, either quickthorn alias hawthorn (*Crataegus Oxycantha*) or sloe alias blackthorn (*Prunus spinosa*) seems to have been a favourite plant for farm hedges in post-Enclosure plantings because it is quick-growing, adaptable to all situations, hardy, stands clipping, forms an impenetrable barrier for stock, is cheap, long-lasting and not generally attacked by disease.

With the growing use of coal, timber was less urgently required as fuel and this led to hedges being kept lower and tidier. Before then, brushwood and hedgerows bordering bridle paths had been the only ones to be kept low, in order to foil highwaymen.

Early in the present century the sign of a good farmer was his well-cared-for hedges, but during periods of shortage of labour and urgent food and stock production, fences, hedges and gates seem to be the first to suffer neglect. Now, the present trend for mechanised farming and the consequent need for larger fields is leading to the grubbing up and destruction of many farmland hedges. In some cases, wire fences have been erected as substitutes on purely hygienic grounds, as a fence does not harbour weeds and allows the farmer more space.

In contemplating the English landscape, hedges and fences must be considered to be the same thing, for hedges are fences of living material and serve all the purposes of a good fence and, in addition, afford timber and protection to bird, animal and plant life and add grace and beauty to the landscape. In some counties, notably in the Cotswolds, hedges are planted on the straight and have for many years been constructed this way, either because the soil is shallow or because the land slopes and a drainage ditch is not necessary. In other localities, they are built on a bank parallel to an open ditch, or raised between two parallel ditches. Here, turf taken from the top of the ditches in construction is placed grass side innermost to form a wall along the bank on which the hedge is planted; in some districts, local stone is used to face this bank, giving the appearance of hedge plants growing on top of a wall. When railway property was enclosed, for speed and economy hedges were frequently straight planted, and proved to be as successful as the more elaborately-planted kinds. The method was then more widely adopted, especially on land where the natural drainage was reasonably good.

These various patterns of planting are not just farmers' whims, but change according to local conditions. In Cornwall, granite blocks forming a rough wall and surmounted by gorse provide an excellent example of the stone and plant type of hedge, while on the slopes of the Pennines loose walls of millstone grit are surmounted by hawthorn. Devonshire is famous for its tantalisingly high hedgerows, but these tall screens provide excellent protection from the strong south-west winds that sweep across the Atlantic. Tall hedges are sometimes grown in Kent also to afford protection for the crops, in this case hops. The Leicestershire bullfinch hedge is so called because its original purpose was to keep in the bullocks of the Midland stock-breeding areas, and here a hedge of thorn is planted on a bank parallel to a ditch and the hedge plants allowed to grow to some 15 feet before cutting. In the Midlands, notably Bedfordshire and Warwickshire, many examples of straight planting are to be found because enclosure was practised later than in eastern or western counties.

A hedge that is carefully tended, trimmed or "brushed" regularly with sharp tools and kept free of weeds in the hedge bottom will serve its purpose for years, but will eventually get thin at the base and need attention, so that it does not become too straggly and useless. The art of laying a hedge is a craft, and varies slightly from one locality to another. The operation is also known as "pleaching" (though this is more strictly pollarding) and "plashing" and consists of clearing all weeds, dead wood and rubbish from the hedge bottom and cutting out any stems that are not in line or are unwanted. The remaining stems are slashed near the base and are then bent over to an angle of about 45 degrees and interlaced with upright stakes. Thus the hedge plants are strengthened and the barrier made impenetrable once more. Generally if a hedge is neglected and overhangs a footpath or road, obscuring the view, the owner of the hedge may be required to cut (or even remove) the plants.

Thus comes the question of ownership of a hedge. Legally,

this is determined by the position of the ditch, if there is one, the hedge belonging to the land-owner on whose side of the hedge there is no ditch. Where straight planting has been used the hedge either belongs to both parties (each being responsible for the maintenance of his own side) or to the party who by evidence of fact can claim ownership. Fact can be established according to the deeds of the land or because the "owner" has kept in repair the hedge or fence for a period of twenty consecutive years.

K.N.

THE WAY OF A TRAMP

IT was on a wet and cold evening that I slowed up to him, standing on the grass verge of the road between Newmarket and Bury St. Edmunds. He was not actually thumbing a lift, just standing in the rain like a sodden scarecrow hoping someone would stop for him.

As he got into my little car I at first doubted my wisdom in having done so. Bearded as he was to his eyes he looked villainous. Also he brought with him a powerful aroma of wet humanity, and bacon, fried bacon. Luckily the smell of the bacon, incongruous as it was in such surroundings of dampness, with squelches where there ought to have been sizzlings, overpowered his body odour.

His "thanks" to me for picking him up was in a North Country accent. "You don't come from these parts?" I queried.

"No, Cheshire," was the somewhat sullen reply.

I asked where he had walked from that day. "Royston," he said. That was over 30 miles and not the sort of walk I should have liked in such a downpour. We drove on in silence.

Then, my mind on the weekend that lay ahead of me, I volunteered the information that it was to be something of an occasion as my daughter was having her 17th birthday on the Saturday and my father his 87th birthday on the Monday. This brought the response in a much less surly tone. "My old dad is 76. My mother is 68. They live in Cheshire – Macclesfield."

"What are you going to Bury for – the chance of a harvest job?"

"No, just because I've got to be on t'move somewhere. I can never spend more than a day or two in one place. Always got to be on t'move."

Then I realised that I was entertaining a born wanderer. After that, he spoke willingly and indeed with a sort of enthusiasm.

"Ay," he said "I've got to be on t'move. I bought some pieces of bacon at bacon shop i' Royston and fried 'em back there on t'roadside." "What!" I interrupted. "How do you light a fire in this weather?"

"I look for an old rubber tyre. I mostly carry a bit with me anyroad. That burns with a good flame." (I imagine how bacon would taste when fried over burning rubber.) "Lots of chaps don't cook anything when they are walking. They wait till they get into t'institution at night. All they get there is two slices of bread and marge and a mug of tea. They don't get properly nourished. I always buy my pieces of bacon, fry 'em and make myself a can of tea, so I've got something in me before I get to t'institution.

"Sleeping out's often a cold and wet job. You want to know

how to make yourself comfortable? You always want to fetch up near a barn or farm buildings so that if it's wet you can get inside. You must always take off your boots at night and see your feet are warm. If your feet are warm, your body will be warm. Another thing, if you don't take your boots off your feet will swell and you won't be long on t'road next morning before they'll ache too much for you to walk. I put my feet into a sack" (which he showed me he carried slung on a string round his shoulders) "and my coat over them. Then I put everything under me. It's what you have under you that keeps you warm, not what's on top. Lots of chaps put sacks or straw or what they can find on top, then they turn over in t'night and off it all goes."

As he talked I observed his face. For all its unwashed and unshaven condition it was a decent face. Moreover a young face and it did not surprise me when he told me he was only 29. I offered him a cigarette: he did not smoke – nor, he said, did he drink – except tea.

"Do you know" he went on "I never slept in a bed at all last winter. I got a job in a coalyard, filling sacks, right in Macclesfield. I found myself a loft above pigsties and a stall with fattening beasts. T'chap knew I was there. His pigman used to shout me in t'morning. About six o'clock that was. I'd got a primus stove then and I'd cook my bacon and tea in an empty sty. I stuck that for four months, longest time I've ever been in one place since I was a lad. I made good money too."

"What did you spend it on?"

"I bought tea and bacon" – mention of these two comestibles recurred every few sentences – "and boots. You've got to have good boots when you are, on t'move and a pair only lasts about a month on these hard roads."

"What did your parents in Macclesfield say about your sleeping out?"

"They take no notice of me. Have nowt to do with me, anyway."

Then he told me how lucky he had been during the war, when he served in the Army Catering Corps, and frequent postings from one unit to another satisfied in part his ache "to be on t'move." He appeared to have enjoyed Army life, "all except t'parade ground side. And I'm sorry I never got overseas," he added. No, he was sure his restlessness was not caused by his Army experiences, "because I used to be on t'move before the war, after I had left school. I've always been like it, far as I can remember."

By this time we were running into Bury St. Edmunds. He was explaining why he was not interested in farm jobs, not in such weather. "You take on for a day. You do an hour or hour and a half. Then down comes t'rain and you're off for t'day and only paid for the hour or so. I like piece-work where I can make good money, buy me tea and bacon – and boots – and be off t'next day."

"Then why have you chosen to come to Bury, where the work is preponderantly farm-work?" I asked.

"Oh, I came here two years ago and I thought I'd like to see t'place again."

As I dropped him close to the "institution" – the sort of place which in his opinion was not so good nowadays as "before t'war" – I gave him 2s. 6d. for some bacon. With a "thank you" he got out, and trudged off into the night with his sack, his frying pan and his aura of fried bacon.

S.R.

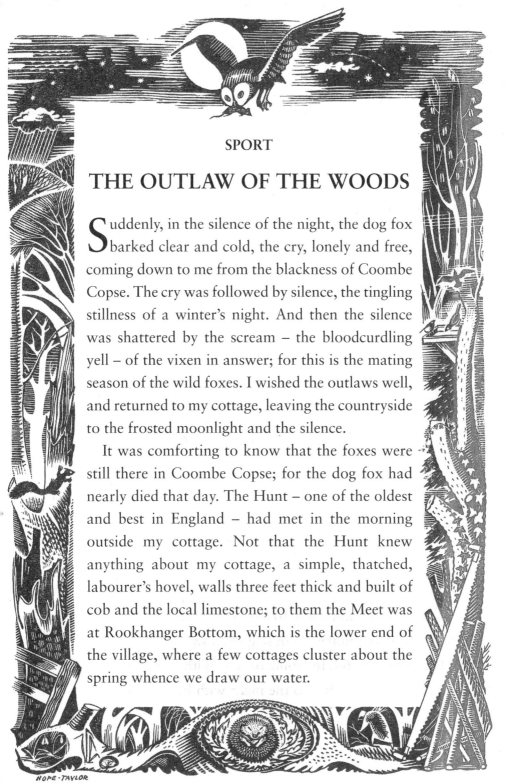

SPORT

THE OUTLAW OF THE WOODS

Suddenly, in the silence of the night, the dog fox barked clear and cold, the cry, lonely and free, coming down to me from the blackness of Coombe Copse. The cry was followed by silence, the tingling stillness of a winter's night. And then the silence was shattered by the scream – the bloodcurdling yell – of the vixen in answer; for this is the mating season of the wild foxes. I wished the outlaws well, and returned to my cottage, leaving the countryside to the frosted moonlight and the silence.

It was comforting to know that the foxes were still there in Coombe Copse; for the dog fox had nearly died that day. The Hunt – one of the oldest and best in England – had met in the morning outside my cottage. Not that the Hunt knew anything about my cottage, a simple, thatched, labourer's hovel, walls three feet thick and built of cob and the local limestone; to them the Meet was at Rookhanger Bottom, which is the lower end of the village, where a few cottages cluster about the spring whence we draw our water.

HOPE-TAYLOR

I was very excited. In the cold mist of the morning they had come, hooves clattering on the frost-bound road, a tide of black, white and tan hounds, sterns afeather, flowing about the Huntsman. High on their lovely hunters sat gallants in pink or ratcatcher, and remote, impersonal Dianas who spoke of the day's prospects in clear voices high above the burring background of conversation from admiring villagers standing outside the throng.

Hounds moved off to draw Coombe Copse, and I followed. Half an hour later I stood on a low hill and watched a fox break away from the trees and run across the water-meadow below the copse.

"Gone away!" came a long shout on the wind. I saw the Huntsman, his coat a vivid splash of colour against the leafless trees, appear at the corner of the wood. "Leu-leu-leu-leu-leu!" came his stentorian shout, and the twang of his horn was almost drowned in the sudden clamour of hounds giving tongue as they streamed out of the wood, full-throated in their joyous rage. Behind cantered several riders.

The fox turned at the withies and headed up over the sticky ploughland to the top of the downs. I watched his small brown body draw a line up over the hill, while far in the rear hounds, combed out now, threw tongue and came relentlessly after him. Behind came the riders, well strung out, the bolder spirits taking the low hedges in their stride, others queuing at the gates and gaps, blaspheming impatiently as they awaited their turn.

The fox topped the far skyline, and was etched, blackly, for a moment before disappearing beyond my ken. And that was the last I saw of him. I stood in a reverie on my lonely hilltop, thinking of the glorious, bucketing fun of riding up hill and down dale on a thoroughbred behind hounds, and all the pageantry of the Hunt spread out across the green and brown countryside; and I thought also of the ineffable sadness of the kill, when the poor bedraggled fox was all-in, and the pursuing humans were pink and perspiring; and even the glorious hounds were somehow tawdy when it was all over. Yet piercingly I wished as I stood there that I was astride a horse again, and part of the pageantry.

I became aware that Tom, the earth-stopper, was beside me. He grinned shyly.

"Li'l old dog varx from Coombe Copse gone away," he remarked.

"Did you stop all the earths?" I asked.

"Ais, I stopped'n all up. Rammed in empty petrol cans to make sure. If thic varx do come back yurrabouts, er wun't find no hidey-holes. Naw!"

"Poor old fox," I said. Tom looked at me beneath shaggy brows. Face, hair, clothes, teeth, all were the colour of earth.

"Yurr," he said mysteriously, after some cogitation, "shall I tell 'ee summat? You won't goo tellin' no one else what I be going to tell 'ee?"

I promised.

"Well, lookat yurr," he said, coming closer. "I allus do leave one earth open in Coombe Copse! 'Tis in a place under the brambles where no one can find'n save the varx. If they dogs don't chup'n, I reckon he'll come back awver to Coombe and down his hole out o' harm's way. That is," he added, "if Master don't put terriers in after 'n."

"You're a sportsman, Tom," I told him. He looked puzzled.

"Naw, I bain't," he said. "The sportsmen be over t'other side o' valley, hunting foxes. If they do catch 'n it wun't worry I – zee, I just like to give the varx a better chance. Tidden no odds to I if he do get away or no."

It is said that hounds lost the scent somewhere on Cheney Down; that they stumbled on it again an hour later; that the dog fox of Coombe Copse came round in a great sweep, was diverted from Look Wood by a 'keeper, and ran in a straight line back to Rookhanger. Presumably he crossed through the Manor grounds to get back to Coombe Copse, for shortly afterwards a small boy, delirious with excitement, came running, shouting, "Yurr come the dogs, yurr they come! They'm all coming, horses and dogs and all – coming droo the village!"

And suddenly in the narrow street there was the belling thunder of hounds' voices, the galloping of hooves. "Gone up towards Coombe, sir," came a voice. A whip cracked. "Leu-leu-leu...! And then the street was empty, save for the people at their doors, and a solitary tired rider, mud-bespattered, clopping slowly past the Providence Inn.

Nov, in the tingling silence of the night I returned to my cottage, feeling very happy because "the li'l old dog varx o' Coombe" was still alive. Once again came the vixen's scream; and I knew that soon there would be whelps up there in the fastness of the earth dug deep beneath the bramble thicket.

J.E.

HOW TO START A VINEYARD

There is absolutely no reason why grapes should not be grown outdoors and good crops harvested in this country, provided suitable varieties and favourable positions are chosen, and proper methods of pruning adhered to.

The choice of vines is important, as only those grown in the cooler regions of Europe stand a chance of ripening well in our climate. Brock reports well on the white Madeleine Royal and the red Gamay Hatif des Vosges. The latter is grown by the French because of its productivity, but only for *vin ordinaire*, not for quality wines. Varieties grown in Germany and Western Switzerland are more suitable for our climate than those in the eastern parts of Switzerland and in the warmer parts of France.

Of the hardy white varieties the Sylvaner Riesling (also called Mueller Thurgau) does well in our climate and so does the ordinary Sylvaner. Riesling is rather late and even on the Continent the grapes are sometimes not gathered till all the leaves have fallen, and frequently the ground is covered by its first snow.

Other white vines suitable for cool climates are Fendant, also called Chasselas or Muscadine, Triumph of Alsace and Chemin Blanc, while very good results have been reported by growing the Hybrid Vines Seyve Villard 5247 and 1276. These vines bear well but may contain a little less sugar than Madeleine Royal.

This is, to my way of thinking, not a serious matter as sugar can always be added to increase the alcohol content of wine. After all, it is a quite common practice in Germany to add sugar or syrup to the must, that is to the juice expressed from grapes, to give a wine of better flavour and keeping qualities.

Of red grapes the one which, beside Gamay, does well in this country is Blue Portuguese. This grape is grown quite extensively in Germany and does well in poor stony soils both there and in Gloucestershire on typical Cotswold soil. It is a vigorous-growing vine and requires more space than normal and also longer extensions. Another red grape which is suited to cooler climates and gives a quality wine is the *Pinot noir fin*, called also Late Burgundy vine. In Germany and in Switzerland this vine is grown for red wine while in the Champagne district of France its juice is used also for champagne as the juice is colourless. A red grape which ripens early in this country, is of good sugar content and gives a deeply coloured juice is Seibel 13053. Red wine made from this grape is of excellent colour.

To produce good crops of grapes requires a knowledge of the habits of a particular vine and of the best methods to obtain fruitful wood. Allowing a vine to grow rampant is all right in hot climates where the harvest is early and where the wood ripens during dry, warm, autumn weather, but in our climate it is necessary severely to restrict growth so as to get ripe and consequently fruitful wood.

PLANTING STOCK, OUTDOOR VINES AND CUTTINGS.
Outdoor vines can now be purchased in this country. As the demand for vines is steadily increasing one may have to buy vines from Germany, France or Switzerland. Such growers are:

Paul Mueller, Gartenbau und Reben, Eltvillea Rhein, Western Germany; Ville Morin Andrieux, 4 Quai de la Megisserie, Paris, France; Jacob Kaltbrunner, Erlenbach, Zurich, Switzerland. To do this one has to apply to the Board of Trade for an import licence stating also the total value of vines plus transport in order to secure the necessary currency for payment. It is highly desirable to arrange for air transport and if the import licence is sent to the grower for inclusion in the parcel of plants then delays at the Customs can be avoided. The plants must be accompanied by a health certificate issued by the appropriate authorities of the country of origin.

PROPAGATION OF VINES. It is, of course, possible to strike cuttings from the ripened wood of vines but the wood must be hard and brittle and crack on bending. Soft or pliable wood is unsuitable. When the vines are pruned in February any hard wood should be cut into lengths containing four or five buds and these cuttings bedded down in moist sand till the spring, when they should be planted into trenches of light soil with about three to four inches of stem protruding, and carrying a bud. The protruding stem should be covered with a heap of soil to prevent the exposed bud from drying out. The shoot which will emerge in the spring should be tied to a stake and allowed to extend to its full length. In the following spring the vine is planted out into position and the ripened cane, which should have been pruned to the desired length in February and on which two top buds should have been retained, is tied to a stake. This forms the stem of the vine and from these two buds shoots will be produced to form a fruiting cane and a replacement cane for the following year. Frequently cuttings only produce a very short growth in the first year or a shoot which is very thin. In that case it should be cut back to the first bud in February and after replanting be covered again with soil. That year's growth will then be cut back to a stem of desired length at pruning time.

LAYING OUT A VINEYARD. The vine is not a demanding plant and grows well in any kind of soil provided it is not water-logged. If it is possible to find a slope facing south or south-east so much the better. If not, choose a somewhat protected site where a hedge or coniferous trees act as a wind shield against the north or west. In dry soil it is as well to plant the vine, which should be a one-year-old plant, by mixing the soil with some peat as vines soon suffer from drought. Clayey soil should be lightened. The soil should be well dug and if not previously used for crops no manure will be required. On the whole no manure should be given till the vines have cropped, then bonemeal and potassium fertiliser can be employed in alternate years and liquid manure prepared from stable manure in the intervening years.

Having chosen a site the vines are planted either for growing on individual stakes or for training on wires. Distances should be about three or four feet apart with a space between rows of four to five feet. The direction of rows or the siting of vines grown on stakes should be arrived at as follows:

Find out the direction in which a planted stake will throw a shadow at midday and, if at all possible, this line should be used as a planting line. This will ensure maximum exposure to the sun.

Vines are planted in autumn or in spring. If vines are purchased in the autumn they should not be top pruned till the spring but only the main and fibrous roots cut back by one-third. Good planting will carry its own reward. The soil should be well dug over and lightened if necessary by peat and sand and some compost incorporated at the bottom of a hole dug out to accommodate the whole plant. If grafted vines are purchased, and those obtained abroad may be grafted, care must be taken that the graft is above soil level. Having set the vine into position the hole should be filled up with light soil, made firm, and soil heaped over the top bud. The cane should be tied to a stake. Unwanted buds are rubbed out in the spring, or if the cane is very thin it must be pruned back to one bud.

PLANTING TIME. In general planting in spring is preferable as root growth is more vigorous in warm soil. Plants for spring planting, if one year old, will probably have been cut back in February to one or two buds. If the plant is vigorous then two buds can be allowed to develop. If not, rub out the unwanted bud, retaining only one, and prevent this from drying out by heaping soil over the stump. In the first year one shoot only is allowed to grow and should be tied to a stake. The second year this is cut at the desired height, which is nowadays much higher than formerly and should be from 20 to 30 inches off the ground. This pruning should be carried out in February or March. The two topmost buds are allowed to develop into shoots which will harden to canes during the same year, while the other buds are rubbed off. These shoots are not allowed to fruit the first year but one of them will act as a fruiting cane in the following year. It should be cut back to six or eight buds and trained out sideways along a wire. To prevent too much sap going into the extremities of the shoot, it is advisable to bend the cane right down to the ground until it starts shooting.

The other cane, which will probably be six feet long, is cut back to two buds which in the same season will produce replacement shoots. These shoots will, in the following year, be treated in the above manner *if*, and this is an important if, the fruiting cane has fruited well. If not then it must remain a second year as a fruiting cane and be spur pruned.

The above method of pruning is called the Guyot method. Spur pruning consists of cutting back each fruiting shoot to a good bud or even to an axil bud. It must always be remembered that fruit is borne on the new shoots arising out of the previous year's growth on any canes older than that. If the wood has ripened well due to a dry autumn, and this is shown by brittleness of the cane, then it will bear well. If the cane bends easily then it is not likely to produce fruit.

There are other methods of pruning used in Germany and it is said that by using more canes and longer extensions the vine is more fruitful. In this method the vine is allowed to carry four or even six canes and similarly four or six shoots are grown for replacement of canes in the following year. The canes are allowed to retain about eight to twelve buds and are bent in a circle and tied back on to the stake. The greater length of cane discourages too much axil growth, which has to be pinched out and thus necessitates less attention during the season.

LEAF WORK. When the cane has flowered it is generally advocated to stop growth at the third or fifth leaf beyond the bunch. Recent research in Germany has indicated that more sugar is produced in the grape if this practice is abandoned and only the tip of the shoot nipped out. Additional pruning consists in topping the replacement shoot at six feet or so.

SPRAYING. One of the most important items towards success in grape growing is the prevention of mildew. Two types are particularly troublesome. One is called Peronospora and the other Oidium. To prevent these, spraying two or three times at three-week intervals with colloidal copper during the early part of the season and following several weeks later by dusting with sulphur has appeared adequate so far. The weather has a great bearing on this and more protection is needed where plants are in a warm, stagnant and humid atmosphere than where the air is bracing and dry. Plants which have been exposed to mildew show scorching of leaves. Such leaves should be picked off and burnt.

CROPPING. Whether the plants are obtained from abroad or from English nurseries it must be emphasised that it takes up to five years to get a good crop from a vine, although it is possible to take a bunch of grapes in the second year, but it is desirable to restrain one's self and not allow the cane to fruit until the third year. Several pounds can be cropped in the third year and increasing quantities in the following years, but over-fruiting will inevitably lead to early exhaustion of the vine and it may take some years for it to become vigorous again. It needs quite a few plants to get grapes for wine making and a 24 ft. row of plants established at 4 ft. intervals will produce in the first year of cropping from 20 to 24 lb. of grapes, sufficient for

1½ to 2 gallons of juice. On the other hand, although patience will be needed to take a crop from a vineyard, the vine is a very much less demanding plant than other fruits grown in this country and will grow in positions quite unsuitable for other cultivation, to give a crop which is definitely favourable to the consumer and which can be of commercial value in this country. Unfortunately it must be emphasised that home-made wines cannot be sold unless they are produced under Excise control and for this a sweets makers licence is required costing £5 5s. per annum. In addition, duty of 10s. 6d. per gallon will be levied on wines produced for sale. One may hope that with the very great interest which is shown in outdoor grape growing and wine making the situation may arise in which the levy of duty on home-produced wine is considered undesirable and uneconomic to collect and will be abandoned, therefore. This was the case some many years ago with a duty on cider when the cost of collection from so many home producers of cider made the collection of duty uneconomic.

If the foregoing information will encourage lovers of wine to establish their own vineyards and try out their hands at wine making it can only react favourably on the consumption of imported wines as every home producer will promptly wish to buy "real" wines to compare with his own production. Furthermore, if home-produced wines should be liberated from the payment of duty then imported wines may also receive some consideration in this respect and increase wine consumption in this country.

S.M.T.

THE APIARIST

THE WINTERING BEES

At the end of my garden, sheltered from the north wind by a thicket, stand four hives. Stripped of the piled-up wooden tiers that caught the sun and held the honey of summer, the factory dismantled, the harvest done, the four hives conserve their inner warmth, offer the least resistance to the weather, and house as snugly as possible the close-packed bees clustered in each.

The winter clustering of bees, this concentration of their life to an inner core, is as gradual as the withdrawal of a tree's sap from branches to root. Wintering bees do not enter into a state of true hibernation, neither do they cling inert after the manner of their wild relative, the queen wasp. Honey bees retain throughout the winter a certain activity and body warmth, which they conserve by feeding on the stored honey. Warm they must be to survive. Whatever the cold outside the hive, a warm temperature must be maintained by the cluster of bees within it.

They keep warm by a constant radiation of hot air; their own system of central heating. To this end they form themselves into a ball, or winter cluster. The bees of this cluster are in constant movement, feeding and changing position. As the outer temperature drops, the ball tightens, the bees rearrange themselves. Those on the outer surface of the mass stand in close formation, heads inward, forming a pattern which is densest at the bottom of the cluster, near the entrance of the hive. The bees of this outer phalanx fan with their wings incessantly, rhythmically, with a peculiar movement, thus expelling outward a current of hot air which comes in contact with the cold air at the hive's entrance. This fanning is so regulated that the outgoing hot air has the same pressure as the incoming cold air which is arrested. The two currents meet, but do not mingle, and the balance of temperature is thus maintained inside the hive. The bees in effect surround themselves with a warm blanket, an invisible aerial envelope, which, though only a few millimetres in thickness, protects them and keeps them warm.

During the raw December, there is, outwardly, no sign of life. But the weather may change, often in a night, from frost to rain, or from bleak east wind to still warmth. The wettest December has days of wonderful clarity – "Bad weather-breeders," say the country people – and on these days, under the pale blue sky, the four bee populations fly out, soon after midday, to void their excrement. But this cleansing flight is precipitate and silent, without the hum of summer. They withdraw immediately into the hive.

In the cold of January there is already a sweetness in the air. Snowdrops and crocus push up; the missel-thrush sings. Could our vision now pierce the hive walls and penetrate through the clustering bees into the centre of the combs, we should see, in a few of the centre cells, a small, curved, white object: the egg of the queen bee. She, too, has felt the turn of the year. She has begun to form her family.

As the days pass, inner activity is made apparent by movement at the hive's entrance. Going out one mild morning at the end of

January, I see the bees scuttling about on the alighting board. They are bringing out their dead. A row of corpses lie there; pitiful, shrunken objects, as light as seed-husks. One worker grasps a corpse in her jaws and her front pair of legs. She staggers with it to the edge and launches herself and it overboard, half-falling, half-flying, to the ground. Shaking out her wings, she flies back to the hive. The other bees are busy. One pulls in front, the other pushes behind. The body is soon thrust out, to be borne away with the wind, or eaten by ants or other insect scavengers.

On the last day of January, the sun gives out warmth as well as light. Joyously, the four populations surge out; black bees, golden bees, whirling, aspiring in their first joy-flight, exorcising the spectre of the winter, proclaiming the advent of spring.

Hereafter there may be grey days, cold days, snow and frost even; but the spell is broken, the sun is ascendant, and all life expands.

V.T.

WHAT EVERY COOK
SHOULD KNOW ABOUT

HARE & GAME PÂTÉS

The end of the shooting season usually coincides with the arrival in the larder of hares well past their tender, care-free youth, and veteran cock-pheasants with cavalry spurs. The obvious solution is game pie or, more precisely, game Pâté.

In more spacious days one bought a pound of lean beef and a pound of pork or veal to furnish a suitable background. The basis of a good Pâté is really half as much meat as there is game, not to mention bacon or ham in moderation. As things are, quantities will have to be left to the fortune of the individual cook.

The simplest form of Hare Pâté is joints of young hare cut to suitable proportions and to some extent boned, lightly fried and then bedded in a bacon-lined pie dish with alternating layers of veal or pork forcemeat. This should go through a mincer twice. The whole is moistened with good stock and it is as well to sieve the hare-liver into this stock, which should be well flavoured with herbs and seasoning. The whole is completed with a paste crust or it can simply be served in an ornamental game pie dish whose cover is a replica of the decorative crust and equally inedible.

The more ambitious Pâtés are all the better if the contents are not only hare but pheasant or any game as well. The fillets from the breasts of the birds and the saddle and best portions of the hare are cut to suitable size. These form the central, more substantial portion of the dish. The remaining meat is cut off the bones and to it is added half its weight of pork or veal and the whole put twice through the mincing machine. This is the forcemeat. For real perfection it should be pounded in a mortar until perfectly smooth, then rubbed through a hair sieve.

The sauce or gravy which is to fill the Pâté needs care in preparation. Make a good strong stock out of the game bones and flavour it rather strongly with thyme and a bay leaf. Fry three finely minced shallots to a light gold colour and make a brown *roux*. Add the shallots to the *roux* and stir in the stock.

Add a little redcurrant jelly and a glass of either Port or Madeira. The latter is preferable. This sauce should be smooth and velvety but not thicker than very thin cream. Cook and stir for about five minutes and taste it. It may require a little tarragon vinegar or lemon juice to sharpen it. Nov add half an ounce of gelatine and stir till dissolved.

Brown the fillets and portions of game in a frying pan and mix the forcemeat in a basin with some of the sauce so that it is about the consistency of porridge. Arrange the game more or less centrally in the tureen and bed the whole down in forcemeat. If it is desired to turn out the Pâté and glaze it with aspic later, a *soufflé* dish covered with buttered paper is handier than the usual tureen. It requires long, slow cooking – three hours at least. When it is cold some of the fat will have risen to the top and will be set. This should be removed from the underlying jelly.

Many things can go into a game Pâté. Hard-boiled eggs, whole, cooked chestnuts and tinned, white, button mushrooms.

Many of the delicious French "Pâté Maisons" use a lighter forcemeat than is usual in England. They incorporate "Panade" which is simply the white crust of bread, soaked in milk for an hour, then squeezed dry in a cloth and put into a saucepan with adequate butter. It is strained and amalgamated over low heat till smooth. It should leave the side and bottom of the pan easily when done. This is mixed with the forcemeat and makes it considerably lighter as well as effecting economy in meat.

There are also available tins of Pork Loaf and Liver Pâtés which are quite suitable as replacing the forcemeat in a game Pâté. If these are used it would probably be better to cook the game separately as it is difficult to combine raw and pre-cooked foods, for they need different timing. It should be borne in mind that a cold Pâté needs a stronger-flavoured sauce than one to accompany a hot dish, so the sauce when hot should taste rather too strong.

One of the best forms of game Pâté is a Boned Pheasant. This involves the delicate operation of getting out the *undrawn* carcase of the bird through the neck and crop aperture. It is not difficult – but it is difficult not to tear the skin during the operation. The bird skin and flesh are then stuffed with a forcemeat stuffing or chopped ham and breadcrumbs with a little suet if the traditional stuffing is preferred. In any case, whatever is used requires good seasoning with plenty of chopped parsley and a very little lemon thyme. Boil in a cloth, after carefully sewing up the holes in the skin with thread. When cooked, the bird is allowed to cool under slight pressure so as to retain some of its natural shape but still to be easier to carve as the back is flattened. Slices cut through should be perfect cross-sections of the bird. The party version should contain a forcemeat with truffles and here again the Pâté de Foie Truffle, which is not Pâté de Foie Gras but veal in place of goose-liver, is suitable. For the remainder of the forcemeat I suggest rabbit. It is handy and either minced in galantines or pounded in Pâtés is usually believed to be chicken. Anyway, a good thick glaze of aspic, put on when the bird is cold, will cover a multitude of blemishes.

H.B.C.P.

THE SKILFUL SCAVENGERS

An old woodman who was cutting a ten-year stand of Spanish chestnuts for fencing and bean-sticks, confessed to having the day before killed two snakes without knowing whether they were adders or grass snakes. He pointed out one victim; the other we could not find. There were, he explained, a few hours between the kills and he could not recall exactly where the second snake had landed when he flicked the body away with a stick.

The one we found was a three-foot-long grass snake. Probably they had been a pair, and it was surprising that a man whose work had long given him close contact with the wild life of the woods should have unknowledgeably slaughtered two such harmless and useful creatures.

The following evening I visited the spot again. This time the absentee showed up, cradled in some tall bramble brush about thirty yards away. She was a female grass snake. I then had another look at her mate, and was astonished to find that his head had been drawn into what might have been his own snake hole. If the female had been still alive, I would have suspected her of a futile attempt to drag her helpless mate under cover. The likely retrievers were therefore sextons, though this was not the usual *modus operandi* of burying beetles. However, it might well be that, a large and long enough hole being handy, the buriers had decided to save time and toil by using it.

At two subsequent visits the three-foot corpse was observed to be progressively disappearing into the cavity, until finally it vanished. Throughout this inspection only the slightest movement of the carcass was noticeable, and not once did an insect expose itself. This was a position wide open to the light of day, and doubtless the beetles, being normally nocturnal labourers, worked only as tractors in the darkness of the hole by day, emerging at night to ease and push the body from outside.

I decided to set a stage for full observation by day. A favourable site seemed to be a spreading birch tree about a hundred yards away, with, beneath it, a space almost completely encircled by bramble, thorn, and five-foot sprouts from old chestnut-tree stumps. The light was subdued, no sunlight penetrated, so I placed here the body of a young rabbit which had been dead about twenty-four hours.

The following evening the corpse was still undisturbed, so was the earth about it. The next day I deferred my call until the late evening, approached the spot quietly, and took up a position whence watch could be conveniently kept for an hour, if necessary. The carcass was now smelling evilly, and it was quite evident that a pair of sextons were at work. I pictured their arrival on the wing, their acute sense of smell piloting them to the corpse, on which they had now started operations.

The sexton belongs to the Coleoptera, beetles whose wings are sheath-protected for, among other things, the business of boring. It is up to an inch in length. One sex is black, in the other the wing cases are crossed with two orange bands. Sextons' aim in life is to entomb carrion, feeding on it as they work, but ultimately to lay their eggs in the carcass, which thereafter ensures a supply of moist food for their larva. Sometimes two pairs of sextons, or even three, are attracted to the same object.

The beetles seemed now to be at work undermining the soil beneath the corpse. But their courage must return with the approach of darkness for, as the light faded, the sextons emerged and, posting themselves about three inches from the body, they began to scoop the earth upwards and outwards, working with head as well as legs. Soon each moved to the adjoining position and repeated the action.

It has been said that a pair of sexton beetles can inter a grown rabbit in a single night, leaving behind no trace either of the animal or of their excavations. But either this is an exaggeration, or the rapidity of burial depends on the number of beetles engaged. I turned up the next evening quite prepared to find that the interment was over, but the body was still there, though it had settled appreciably. Soil loosening beneath the carcass was still proceeding, and I noticed that work at the surface during the night had moved the beetles' earlier earthworks far enough away to permit shovelling from close to the body.

By the next evening operations had so far advanced that the top of the recumbent rabbit was now level with the ground around it. And the following evening I watched the even more remarkable activity of covering up the carcass with loose soil, leaf mould and small sticks and stones. To effect this the beetle alternatively pushes and pulls, bulldozer-like, with two of its six powerful legs, occasionally resting its limbs and using its muscular head and neck.

At my next call I found the rabbit completely covered, and doubtless the female beetle was now laying her eggs in the invisible corpse before flying on with her spouse to wherever her maternal instinct plus the stench of carrion impelled her. The thought set me wondering if sextons were ever lured away from the task in hand should another, more tempting, scent be borne on the breeze. I have twice since put this possibility to the test, but on neither occasion were the beetles deflected from one job to the other, though in each instance the decoy was decidedly more niffy, had been placed down-wind and was within a few feet of the workers.

There are some 150,000 species of Coleoptera, but for sheer foot-slogging industry among beetles the sexton's sole peer must be the scarab, or dung beetle. In appearance it resembles our dor beetle, and probably the best example of the species is the Egyptian scarab, of which the female forms a ball of dung, after laying its eggs in the middle. Having chosen a promising spot, it sinks a deep, perpendicular shaft, returns to its ball, and rolls it about in the sunlight to speed up the hatching of the eggs. The ball has now vastly increased in size. Then, pulling while her mate pushes, between them the beetles work the ball to the hole, tip it in, and fill up the cavity.

J.F.R.

AT HOME

Plants for the herb garden must be renewed, not because they have been neglected, but because we have picked them too hard; slaughtered them, the gardener says.

The fact of the matter is that for anyone with culinary aspirations the herb garden is of vital importance, and since it is natural for each one of us at Winkfield to think that the dish that we personally have in hand is of foremost importance, we are inclined to treat our herbs a little too severely.

I have to admit that one still meets people who do not share this view of the culinary value of herbs, but I believe that this generally denotes that they have at some time or another been victims of excessive enthusiasm. Herbs have their classic and, I would say, indisputable uses in cooking and, in addition to this, they are of course suitable subjects for experiment, but experiments to be made by those possessing a discerning palate.

Flavouring should never be overdone and if, for example, one eats in France a delicate turtle soup, one is not overconscious of the basil used to flavour it.

Here are some of the herbs I am sowing or planting soon and a few of the dishes that they will be needed for; among the most delicious are sweet basil and French tarragon.

Basil has a delicate, perfumed flavour; being a half-hardy annual it will not be sown until the danger of frosts is over, early in May, and then we shall choose a soft evening and water the sun-warmed soil before sowing the seed; if this is done germination is fairly quick. When the herb is ready it will be used for tomato dishes, for soups, for flavouring cream cheeses; sprigs of it will be put into fruit drinks and certainly when we have a dish of mixed herb fritters the tender tips of basil will be in great demand. For salads, for omelettes and for flavouring scrambled eggs and other egg dishes it will be wanted throughout its season.

Tarragon is a perennial herb and each year we try to put in

a few extra plants, partly because of the depredations we make on it and partly because it is not a very long-lasting perennial anyhow, and even at the best of times may have to be renewed every two or three years. Certainly it does not always stand up to its first winter if this should prove to be a severe one. It is most important to get the true French variety, for there is another plant, I think Russian, or possibly German in origin, very free-growing but not bearing the same piquante flavour. I get the true French variety from the Herb Farm at Seal in Kent.

This, of course, is a perfect herb for flavouring chicken, Poulet à l'estragon being a famous dish needs no praise from me, but even a sprig or two put into a chicken roasted in the Continental way (with a little water in the baking pan) gives the whole bird and accompanying gravy a delicious flavour.

Now that cold tables are coming back into the restaurants we see the little blanched leaves of the tarragon decorating dishes of salmon trout, and of course this is an admirable herb for any sauces to accompany fish. If you put tarragon in a salad, it should be used sparingly, for in spite of its delicious spicy flavour it is over-pungent for eating raw; everybody knows that it makes an admirable vinegar, but not everybody realises that it can be bottled in brine for winter use; small bottles should be used because one only needs a small quantity of this at a time and once the bottle has been opened it has to be re-sterilised.

As we use our herbs so heavily we have only room for a limited number of varieties, but three at least of the umbrella-shaped family must be grown. First of all dill, which is an annual. Of this both seed and leaf have a delicate and distinctive flavour and we use it in beaten cream cheeses, for potato salad, and sprigs of the soft green leaves are picked and dipped in batter for fritters; it is also sometimes used to flavour vinegar and I think it is in "Paradise in Sole" that Parkinson mentions the suitable use of dill in connection with cucumber, so forecasting the popular American dill pickle. The seeds are called for in a dressing for a Danish beetroot salad and, indeed, dill is greatly used in Scandinavian dressings and mayonnaises.

I must confess that we grow the ordinary fennel chiefly for its decorative value; it is charming in leaf and in flower. The tender side shoots are sometimes picked, peeled and used in salads, the tender tips are used for fritters and of course the leaves are used for flavouring fish stocks and sauces. The sweet or Florence fennel, a plant with a swollen root-base blanched like celery, is delicious raw, either as a dressed salad or plain like celery with cheese.

I don't find it easy to get the blanched roots to perfection in the garden for so often a drought intervenes and they run up to flower, but still the stems and the side shoots are useful in salads. Fortunately, a taste for this root is beginning to prevail and it is imported in great quantities into this country now.

Coriander, a delicate and graceful plant, has heavy heads of round seeds which weigh down the stems; when ripe they have a faint taste of orange, or rather of orange peel; they are admirable in curries and though they are used when dry for cakes and biscuits and so forth, they really are of greatest value in savoury dishes. A few crushed ripe seeds added to a curry make a great difference to the flavour.

I am being pressed to grow lovage again because of its good celery flavour, so clearly a space will have to be made for this. Chervil, chives, marjoram, savory, rosemary, thyme, bay and horseradish all have their appointed place in the garden and all come in for a good deal of attention.

Rosemary is of particular value in the preparation of marinades for roast meat and fish, and if used carefully, a sprig of it in the pan, when frying potatoes or making bubble and squeak, adds an excellent flavour.

Horseradish is not used exclusively with roast beef but a sauce of it is often made to accompany fish and everybody knows how good a cream horseradish sauce is with smoked trout. We have a rather special soup of spinach and peas in which it is used as a flavouring, and nobody can quite guess where the unusual taste of the soup comes from.

Bay, of course, is used for various soups and stews and marinades and when we are making kebabs of stuffed prunes, dates, bacon and slices of apple, we put a leaf of bay on the skewer between each layer and these impart a delicate and aromatic flavour to the whole.

There is sweet geranium in the greenhouse for the lining of our sponge cake tins and scented mint in the garden for tisanes and for crystallising, and the more I write about it and the more I think about it, I realise how dull cooking would be without these delicious and fragrant herbs.

Finally, I have this year put down two small thyme lawns. Some squares of soil in a yard between blocks of concrete have been planted all over with thyme; after a while we shall be able to walk over these, filling the air with sweet scent and adding a note of interest to a not particularly inspiring spot.

C.S.

THE STUFF OF
ENGLAND'S HOUSES

Old houses reflect unerringly these three things: the kind of country rock nearest them or on which they stand, the period in which they were built and the standard of wealth of their first owners. There are other lesser variations, such as the local tradition of design and craftsmanship.

To get a general idea of how the rocks reflect themselves in the older houses built upon them, it is helpful to have an outline in one's mind of the sequence of the geological systems as they appear when we cross England and Wales from west to east. The oldest rocks are to the west and, successively, newer rocks emerge, in general, on a north-east to south-west line as we move eastward.

In Wales, we have the ancient sedimentary rocks, with some granite intrusions, these being repeated in Devon and Cornwall and in Cumbria. Then come the coal-bearing measures held in the lap of the Carboniferous limestone. These rocks are repeated in the Pennine ridge, with coal measures flanking this upland on east and west.

Then follow the Jurassic limestones, from Dorsetshire through the Midlands to Lincolnshire, reappearing in Yorkshire, especially in the North Riding. From these rocks the well-known Portland, Bath and Cotswold Stone is quarried, the first two "freestones," because of their beauty and ease of working, having travelled far and been used in the larger buildings in the south of England from very early times. Many of London's oldest churches and public buildings are built of Portland Stone. Jurassic limestone also appears in the Vale of Glamorgan, especially at its northern and southern edges.

A wide band of clays and sandstones of later Permian Age with much valley alluvium then follows until we come to the chalk. This stretches, roughly, from Salisbury Plain by way of the Berkshire Downs and the Chilterns into North Norfolk, with the two prongs of the North and South Downs embracing the Weald. Large areas of chalk also extend into eastern Lincolnshire and Yorkshire. Young alluvial rocks of later age make up the rest of England, except for the older gravels, clays and sandstones exposed in places like the Weald. Roughly north of a line joining the Thames and the Severn there may be later boulder clay, left by the glaciers of the Ice Ages and now hiding the basic country rock.

It is from these rocks, glacial moraines and sometimes from ancient castles that the material to build the English house before the 1850s was quarried, and upon these rocks, conditioned by the rainfall, drainage and wind, the trees have grown which supplied the timbers.

Where does this take us in the understanding of the old house? First, there are those built of the very old, hard rocks of Wales and the north of England. From these rocks come slates, sometimes of great beauty.

Rubble walls of flat Pennant and other sandstones appear in houses in South Wales and in the north of England where, in Yorkshire and Lancashire especially, the stone can often be easily worked into squarish blocks. The Carboniferous limestone has characteristic houses, but Jurassic limestones supply square, easily worked blocks from which clean-looking villages have been built in South Glamorgan. The red Devonian sandstone of Breconshire and Devonshire has been used in characteristic houses in those counties.

The sheltered alluvial valleys produced large timber, and there you will find timbered houses following on the stone-built types as, for example, in the Severn Valley or as you coast down the gentle eastern dip of the Cotswolds into the valley of the Thames. From Shrewsbury, "black and white" half-timbered houses penetrate the Severn Valley into the heart of Wales while, on the hills around, stand stone-built farmhouses.

The chalk measures give rise to houses of flint (with brick coigns and arches around windows and doors), or where the rock is hard, as in parts of Wiltshire, built actually of blocks of chalk called "clunch." Ely Cathedral has some "clunch" in its decoration. Sometimes chalk is used, puddled with flints, to make a kind of concrete wall. Such walls in Wiltshire, surrounding gardens, are often thatched to keep the rain from breaking them down. Beeches of the chalk and oaks of the hollows of the chalk Downs and the river valleys of South-East England appear in timbered houses once again.

Beds of alluvial gravels and clays gave rise to brick and tile works. Most of London was built out of bricks made of "London Clay." As you approach Beaconsfield, for example, brick-built and tiled houses begin to appear in large numbers – and there is even a "Gravel Digger's Arms" not far away. As transport improved, bricks to replace rotted timbered walls, and tiles for tile hanging to protect these timbers from the weather, made their way into regions where framed, timbered houses had hitherto been the rule. The golden age of brick came with late Tudor and Stuart times.

Few old houses now exist which were built before Tudor times, although some earlier "cruck houses" have been repaired and modified, while many of the large single "halls" of medieval times have later been provided with chimneys and additional floors, so that they assumed a modern character. Projecting beams carrying upper storeys tell a tale of construction, since the walls at the ends of the projecting beams are used to balance the weight of the upper floors which the old square-shaped, adzed or hand-sawn, beams could not otherwise support with rigidity.

For those who are interested in "collecting houses" here are a few specimens:

1. Houses of Cotswold Stone (e.g. at Chipping Campden).
2. Houses of Pennant Rock (Yorkshire, Lancashire, Glamorganshire).
3. Houses of Devonian – or old Red Sandstone (Brecon, North Devon, Herefordshire).
4. Purbeck (Jurassic) Limestone houses (e.g. at Corfe Castle and in the Purbeck Hills).
5. Black and white timbered houses in regions previously heavily forested (e.g. the Weald and the great river basins of South and Mid-England).
6. Timber-framed and weatherboarded houses of the Thames and other river valleys and of the Weald.
7. Flint-built houses on chalk ridges.
8. Chalk block built houses of Wiltshire.

9. Bath Stone houses. Ashlar walls and sometimes panels of Bath Stone – alternating with flints (e.g. North Wiltshire).

10. Houses of Portland Stone (found over much of South England).

11. Projecting beams in houses.

12. Tile-hung and mixed brick and stone houses of Sussex and Kent.

13. "Kentish rag houses," Tudor, Stuart and Queen Anne houses of brick and stone.

14. Thatched houses and thatched walls in the corn-growing areas (e.g. Wiltshire and Eastern Counties)

15. Brick and tile built houses of London basin and the gravel heaths around.

16. Square stone houses of Pennine regions of Yorkshire and Lancashire.

17. Houses built of stone pirated from ruined castles, abbeys, etc.

F.E.

THE BOTANIST

THE FIRST WILD FLOWERS

When I was a boy, my father – in the true Victorian tradition – did everything he could to encourage "educational" pursuits. Cash prizes were awarded for the first, and second, specimens of any wild flower brought home: a penny for the first and a ha'penny for the second. One could easily clock up five bob in the course of a summer afternoon. This is how I became acquainted with about half of our native wild flowers: my own herbarium contained some 1,200 species.

Reflecting on these happy and carefree days, I have been trying to recall what dozen or so flowers were the first to be found in bloom each year. And here is my list, arranged in their botanical order (the order, that is, in which they appear in any systematic flora): Green Hellebore; Violet; Blackthorn; Moschatel; Coltsfoot; Primrose; Lesser Periwinkle; Speedwell; Ground Ivy; Dead Nettle; Daffodil; Snowdrop. I wonder how many readers will find all these in bloom this month! If you live (as I did when a boy) in Somerset – or, for that matter, in Dorset or in Devon – you may well find these and many more.

The Green Hellebore is, of course, our English Christmas Rose. The white Christmas rose which we grow in our gardens is very closely related. In both cases what appear to be the petals are, in fact, the sepals, and that is why the flowers last so long. Our Hellebore produces, as a rule, some three or four flowers, each borne on a single stem. It grows in meadows and thickets and is comparatively rare.

The Violet everyone knows: none of our flowers is more beautiful in itself or has a lovelier scent. We have many violets besides *Viola odorata*: among them the Dog Violet, very common everywhere somewhat later in the year; and the small Wild Pansy, which grows in cornfields.

Everyone knows the Blackthorn too: the first harbinger of the great rose family to which our flora owes so much. The

Blackthorn, or Sloe, is one of our wild plums, and the flowers, which appear before the leaves, make many a hedge conspicuous at this season of the year. In the Oxfordshire village where I lived for so long, practically every household made its own sloe gin. The catch about this is that, to make good sloe gin, one wants gin as well as sloes!

Just as the Blackthorn heralds the rose family, so does the Coltsfoot usher in the still greater family of composites. Here again, the flower heads, each solitary on its stem, appear before the radical leaves. The Coltsfoot is common everywhere: it grows on waste land, and the more unpromising the soil, the more it seems to flourish. Leave a cinder heap alone for a few months and the yellow stars of Coltsfoot will duly appear.

The Moschatel is common enough in Great Britain, but its pale green flowers are so inconspicuous that it may well never be noticed. Its Latin (or rather, Greek) name is Adoxa, which means "without glory." Strange to say, this little plant – only about five inches high – is a relative of the Guelder Rose and the Honeysuckle. Each stem bears a cluster or four or five flowers, more or less symmetrically arranged. In Somerset its local name was the '"town clock."

The Primrose hardly needs description, even for the non-botanist. Not everyone knows, however, that it has flowers of two kinds: the pistil may be longer than the stamens, so that the latter are not visible; or the stamens may be longer than the pistil. Country children call them "pin-eyed" and "thrum-eyed" primroses. The Primrose hybridises freely with its close relative the Cowslip.

The Lesser Periwinkle is another flower no one can miss. It has shining evergreen leaves, and the colour of its flowers is characteristic: one often reads that a frock or fabric is "periwinkle blue." We used to find it in bloom quite early in January, and it may go on flowering throughout the spring.

The Speedwell, one of our commonest "weeds," is a beautiful little flower, and – were it not so common – would probably be cherished by gardeners. Nearly twenty species of its genus (*Veronica*) grow wild in this country, and a great many more of non-British origin are cultivated. Botanically, the most interesting thing about Veronica is that it is one of the few genera where the flower has only two stamens.

My next two flowers Ground Ivy and Dead Nettle – are labiates. Ground Ivy can be found wherever there are shady banks and hedges. It has pretty little blue flowers and its name indicates the shape of its leaves. It is closely related to that standby of all cottage gardens, Catmint. As for Dead Nettle, it is even commoner than Ground Ivy. There are two species – the white Dead Nettle and the purple Dead Nettle – and both can be found practically everywhere, and in flower all the year round.

Finally, I listed Daffodil and Snowdrop, which both belong to the Amaryllis family, closely related to the lilies. I said something of these flowers in my last article; both have an infinitude of associations, legendary and poetic. Housman, in *The Shropshire Lad*, refers to one legend about the Daffodil:

> And there's the windflower chilly,
> With all the winds at play;
> And there's the Lenten lily,
> That has not long to stay
> And dies on Easter Day.

H.P.

READER'S LETTER

A good pipe: in his kindly review of my book, *The Gentle Art of Smoking*, Mr. Ralph Wightman (Books, December) gently reproaches me for not explaining in "words of one syllable" why a very good pipe tastes so much better than a cheap one.

If by this he wants a brief explanation, I wish it were possible, for it is what every pipe-smoker wants to know and to be convinced about. But "care," "skill," "time" and other monosyllables cannot briefly explain the point any more than they can explain briefly how a sheep-hurdle is made. And like many country crafts, the manufacture of a first-class pipe cannot be hurried; many processes and a great deal of work are necessary. It is this that my book is at pains to explain.

ALFRED H. DUNHILL, 30 DUKE STREET, S.W.I.

MARCH

NOTES FROM THE EDITOR

Someone says to me that every editor should have his own hobby-horses. So what are mine?

The trouble is that I have so many hobby-horses of my own that I'm nervous of being too noisy about them for fear of becoming a bore. Anyhow, I should have thought that most readers of COUNTRY FAIR had guessed most of my prejudices already.

But, for the record, I have no objection to supplying a list. If you don't like any of the items, you've at least got to admit that I've given you fair warning.

1. I think that town life has become so utterly dreary that I'm not surprised that everybody is trying to get themselves run over on the zebra crossings.

2. I like everything about country life except the inability of country people to mind their own damned business.

3. I hate February, and I think we're all suffering from a surfeit of politics.

4. I believe that everyone who knows his onions, these days, chooses a small house to live in, in preference to a large one; a short-barrelled gun in favour of a long one; and a fishing rod not longer than 8 feet for trout or 12 feet for salmon.

5. I assume that all fishermen, jobbing gardeners and shepherds are thoroughly disagreeable until I've got enduring evidence to the opposite. I know that's quite contrary to the romantic conception of "gentle Isaac," "Old Herbaceous," and the loving flockmaster, but my own opinion is based on what Mr. James Fisher refers to as practical field-work. Maybe I've been unlucky, but I doubt it.

6. I hate going for walks for the sake of walking and I loathe driving in cars for the mere sake of "going for a drive."

7. To my taste, a picnic (the wasps and women sort) is the foulest of all social disasters.

8. Seriously, and without reference to my colleague A. G. Street, who may disagree with me, I'm quite sure that, even now, we're not growing nearly as much food as this country is capable of.

9. It is monstrous that, at a time when we're so short of houses, rural cottages, which any competent architect could save, are being condemned and levelled to the ground.

10. The British climate is unquestionably the best climate in the world.

M.H.

WILD LIFE

If we are blessed with normal weather in March it may be said that this month sets the seal on the preliminary of activity which commences in February.

March is the traditional month for the exhibitions of so-called madness among hares; though these delightful animals often go through their comic dancing and boxing acts even earlier than this. It is more than interesting that there seem to be few months in the year when hares have not been reported as holding gatherings and performing weird evolutions of some kind or another. As spring is the breeding season for hares, it would appear that these antics are not necessarily associated with courtship.

Early badger cubs may leave their setts later this month, and the careful and quiet observer may get much enjoyment from watching these attractive little things as they grow in boldness night after night.

Hedgehogs, too, now emerge from their winter quarters and start to feed up on the insects which themselves are becoming more active and plentiful.

The hibernating butterflies referred to last month will be seen more frequently – not only the common tortoiseshell, but brimstones and peacocks as well; and any sunny day will find them seeking out early blossoms from which to restore their depleted tissues.

In the bird world there is plenty to see. Among our resident birds, nest-building gets under way at a brisk pace. Rooks, magpies, jackdaws, water-hens and several more will have started on this operation. Towards the end of the month genuine early arrivals of migrants may be reported – wheatears, chiff chaffs and willow warblers. With them we get a spate of stories of precocious cuckoos which turn out to be small boys!

Toads will be spawning about the third week of the month (unless conditions are unusually cold) and this serves to remind us that the breeding activities of these humble creatures provide one of Nature's unsolved mysteries. It is not yet known how toads find their way to their spawning ponds; but whatever sense or senses may guide them must be very powerful indeed, for toads will surmount considerable obstacles – even climbing over low walls – in order to reach their cherished goal. Up to date no definite answer has been found to this puzzle, though in recent years naturalists have been devoting more and more attention to the problem.

Coarse fishing ends in March, and this heralds the spawning time for most of these fish, though it is perhaps true that many of them might with benefit be left in peace some time before the official close season.

M.K.

There is scarcely a mammal, reptile, amphibian or bird in the British Isles that does not change its habits in some marked way in March; and this applies to residents just as much as to migrants. But of course the migratory changes are the most spectacular, and Britain's army of "ringers" and bird observatory workers will be out in strength manning the coastal and island stations, anxiously scanning the barometer and meteorological chart for the likelihood of "arrival" weather.

In homes all over the country naturalists will be opening their phenological notebooks, and entering the first blowing of flowers, the first emergence of many an insect, the first songs of the finches and buntings, the larks and pipits, the first arrivals of the little spring birds – chiffchaff undoubtedly, yellow wagtail probably, cuckoo most improbably.

Among the most romantic movements in March is the reorganisation of the water fowl. Some, like the whooper swans, have gone, and others, like the Bewicks, are going. Our native Scottish greylags, which usually winter not far from their secret West Highland and Island breeding places, are in full dispersal, turning up on their old breeding grounds in little parties, patrolling restlessly the favoured lochs. The whitefront and bean-geese may take off on their journeys to Arctic and sub-Arctic Russia, and if the spring opens quickly the pinkfeet may begin to leave Scotland and the yellow-billed whitefronts leave Ireland for their remote nesting grounds in Iceland and Greenland; but like the barnacles these usually wait till April.

Setting aside the mallard, which may even have ducklings by March, most of our duck are in the throes of departure or assembly. This certainly goes for shelduck, teal, gadwall, widgeon, pintail, shoveler, and most of the diving ducks; and the big spring arrival of the garganeys is usually in the second half of the month. Rather oddly, scoter remain pretty faithful to their coastal wintering grounds; these sea-ducks seldom begin to change their habits until well into April.

Great crested grebes moulting into summer plumage always assemble in March on their nesting lakes and engage in the fantastic and beautiful courtship activities so felicitously described by Dr. Julian Huxley.

In the garden, the bird-lover checks his bird boxes. These should have been up since October, but, put up as late as March, have safely covered broods of tits the same season; and certainly it is not too late to put up open-type boxes among the creeper on house walls to receive the spotted fly-catchers in May.

J.F.

THE VEGETABLE GARDEN

The germination of seeds must be a continuous process. Once they are roused from dormancy growth must go on, and any serious check will have fatal results. That is why occasional sunshine now – or even several mild days – is not enough to justify sowing long rows of all the main crops. Even if the earth is dry enough to rake smooth, and moist enough to receive seeds, it is better to sow only short rows at present. Be reluctant to empty the seed packets until temperature and soil are in harmony; when they are, all the summer vegetables and salads, with the exception of a few less hardy ones, can be sown. Remember the winter greens also; these need a long period of growth, and sowings of kale, cauliflowers, Brussels sprouts and sprouting broccoli, are a necessary provision for next winter. They will not take up much extra ground if they are sown between broad beans, or other crops which will be over when the greenstuff gets bigger.

As with germinating seeds, so with potatoes which have been sprouted. These are also in an active state of growth, and to put them into cold, wet ground will give them a bad set-back. Far better to leave them in their trays indoors until the ground is ready; but keep them near the light so that the sprouting tips do not become drawn.

Another planting that can be made when the ground is ready is that of globe artichokes. Opinions differ as to whether they are worth growing as a vegetable; some say that they take too much chewing, others regard them as an epicure's dish. Most people agree, however, on the beauty of the flowers (which are also the edible part), and globe artichokes are probably grown more often for decoration than for eating. They like rich soil and should be planted with the tip of the crown just showing, and at least two feet between each plant.

Mint should be moved to a fresh bed every three years to keep it free of rust, and this is the best time to transplant it, or to start a new bed. Unfortunately, mint has earned a bad reputation with its habit of taking over the rest of the garden, and must be curbed from the beginning if it is to stay within bounds. One way of doing this is to sink an iron tub or something similar into the ground, fill it with soil and plant the mint within its rim. This method also disposes of old iron of this nature, but if there is nothing of the kind available, the same end can be achieved by sinking some corrugated iron to make a root enclosure. Mint does not need a rich soil, something moist and light will suit it very well,

C.M.

———•••———

Successional sowings of Broad Windsor broad beans and dwarf peas should be made as early as possible. Carter's Eight Weeks pea is a valuable variety for producing an early pea in a minimum space. Meteor is always reliable. Do not plant too deep. Quick germination is essential. When one batch shows clear drill, put in another. Cauliflowers Brussels and summer cabbage are the first of the brassicas to receive attention. Sutton's Fillbasket is a sprout that stands well and Harbinger for early and Majestic for autumn cutting are the most valuable cauliflowers. Consult your seed merchant about the new preparations for dressing brassica seed against the dreaded flea beetle. Select a strain of stump-rooted carrot for early pulling. These may be sprayed with ordinary T.V.O. between the true leaf stage and before the root is pencil thick – a wonderful control for weeds and a great labour-saver. Parsnips may be treated in the same way.

It is well worth risking a planting of dwarf beans, such as The Prince, during the last week. The safest method of growing onions is to plant out sets which have been raised in boxes. The ground should be raked to a very fine tilth and well firmed. Draw a shallow drill and place the sets, which resemble blades of grass, about four to six inches apart and cover very lightly with soil. By this method, attack by the carrot fly is eliminated and weed control is infinitely easier. A small sowing, of salad onion, White Lisbon, should be made and not thinned out. These are pulled as Spring onions. Leeks should be put in at the same time for transplanting later.

Give the spring cabbage bed a dressing of sulphate of ammonia on a dry day and keep the hoe going to work it into the soil. Take care that the leaves are absolutely dry otherwise scorching will occur. Sprouted potatoes may be planted during the last fortnight. Home Guard and Epicure mature early and have excellent flavour. A late frost may destroy the first shoots but others will develop.

E.B.

———

Growing Asparagus

Only within recent years has the importance of breeding been fully recognised and suitable methods adopted to produce asparagus crowns yielding large heads of high quality and flavour.

Botanists are not agreed that the cultivated asparagus is a dioecious plant, and some think it might be polygamous in flowering habit. It is a fact, however, that breeding from seed from best selected stock of separate male and female plants has produced extra-ordinarily good results.

Those about to raise new plants should use carefully selected seed as most of that commonly offered is merely a by-product of commercial plantings. There are several ways of selecting plants for the production of an improved strain. Male and female blossoms are produced on separate plants and the practice of isolating five or six female plants and one male in the midst of them will improve the strain. All plants used for this purpose must be top-grade in both sexes. Plants to be so used are staked during the growing season, lifted in the autumn and replanted on an isolated plot. The seed produced is then grown on in successive years until a stock is obtained. Breeding plants must be well isolated from other asparagus otherwise bees will cross-fertilise the blossom with disastrous results.

Successful growers, including Mr. A. W. Kidner, maintain there are no varieties: no Conover's Colossal, Early Argenteuil, Giant Argenteuil, Mary Washington or Martha Washington, only strains some of which, in certain respects, are better than others. It is true that only a few so-called varieties or types are given even a pretence of recognition in cultivation and generally speaking any varietal differences are not very clearly defined. The maintenance of good strains is not easy and it is found in practice that unless plants are carefully handled and grown in isolation the stock soon becomes mixed, resulting in immediate deterioration. Improvement in cultivated stocks can be carried out by means of both seeds and crowns. The result to aim at is a strain exhibiting the desirable features. To maintain a strain with the desirable features aimed at, whatever these may be, requires constant selection.

Each stock should produce shoots for a uniform period and for this early and late strains are needed in contrast to the present position of entire dependence on a single mixed strain; vigorous and productive crowns should be pronounced in a selected strain; all sprue and crowns with small buds should be eliminated; a uniformly green colour of spear free from purplish or reddish colour is desirable as green "grass" is better flavoured; plants that branch some distance from the surface of the ground give a greater length of spear.

H.M.

The first rule in gardening is to work the soil and plant seeds only when conditions are suitable. *How*, not *when*, is the most important factor. These notes are given as a guide only; do not forget that weather in March can often upset the best laid plans. The soil must always be dry and friable before any seeding is attempted.

Sowings of maincrop brussels, leeks; summer cabbage and cauliflowers can be made about the second week, also cabbage lettuce and stump-rooted carrots. Tread the ground firmly and use shallow drills. Deeply set seeds in hollow ground will never do well. Practise thin and even sowing on a piece of paper before you begin. It is an art only acquired by experience. Successional sowings of broad Windsor beans, short peas such as Little Marvel, should be made in the middle of the month, also parsley as soon as possible. When one sowing is clearly through, put in another. Avoid having too much at one time. Vegetables must be picked young otherwise they are horrid. Drill a pinch of radish or turnip seed with the lettuce, carrot, etc. These come through quickly and will clearly mark the row and make easy hoeing possible. Herbs may be divided and new beds made. Only plant what can be kept clean.

Thyme, mint, chervil and tarragon are essential. A light dressing of sulphate of ammonia should be given to the spring cabbage bed but only when perfectly dry, scorching results if leaves are wet. Sulphate stimulates growth. Hoeing helps for quick action.

During the last week of the month, plant sprouted early potatoes in well-manured ground. Handle seed carefully and do not break shoots. There is a risk of being caught by late frosts, but a light covering of straw directly they show through will give adequate protection. Do not worry if first shoots are frosted, others will come, merely causing a slight delay.

E.B.

THE FLOWER GARDEN

Magnolias are the most spectacular of the early-flowering trees and shrubs. Although they succeed best in the milder districts, there are some varieties suitable for most areas providing there is shelter from the east and frost pockets are avoided. A well-drained soil is essential and the addition of a little peat or leafsoil is most beneficial. The best time to plant is early spring so that the thick fleshy roots can become immediately active. Magnolias resent being moved once they are established and for this reason should be placed in their permanent positions when small.

For small gardens, M. *stellata* is the best of the early group, with flowers composed of strap-like petals. It forms a low bush and is covered with masses of white or pink flowers. M. *Kobus* and M. *salicifolia* have somewhat similar flowers but are trees, although the latter only reaches about twenty feet and is usually a most handsome shape. M. *denudata* in its best form is undoubtedly the most beautiful of all magnolias, its lovely cup-like flowers of pure white appearing before the young leaves. Its hybrid M. *Soulangeana* is more easily obtained and perhaps a little more robust, but its colour varies from white to purple and the flowers are apt to appear at the same time as the leaves begin to unfold. M. *sinensis, Wilsonii* and *Sieboldii* are all later flowering and ideal for the small garden. They have open pendulous flowers with a mass of crimson anthers in the centre. It is unfortunate that the wonderful large-flowered pink species, M. *Campbellii, mollicomata, Sprengeri Diva* and *Sargentiana*, can only be recommended for the warmer gardens, for despite the fact that they take several years to flower patience is rewarded.

At the end of March or early April newly planted roses of the hybrid tea and floribunda sections should be cut back to about four eyes. Dead and diseased wood together with crowded weak growths should be removed.

The pruning of hybrid teas varies with the variety, but generally the remaining well-ripened lateral growths are reduced to about the fifth bud. Hybrid polyanthas or floribundas respond to light pruning, last season's flowering growths being cut just below the flowering head and any other older wood to about two buds from the base. The young shoots of climbing hybrid teas are tipped to encourage the development of flowering laterals. When this work has been completed the beds may be forked over, incorporating some well-rotted compost, and later given a dressing with a good balanced fertiliser.

C.P.

Lawns

Attention to established lawns this month pays good dividends in summer. In open weather give a good raking and remove any stones brought up by the raking. *Light* rolling is especially valuable now during a dry spell – heavy rolling is usually detrimental. If the grass has started to grow give the first mowing at the end of March, setting the knives fairly high.

N.P.H.

Pruning the Roses

Towards the end of March is the traditional time for rose pruning, though there is a school which favours December or January. I have always been very successful with the orthodox timing and have yet to give winter pruning a fair test. Nevertheless, I must mention the arguments. Briefly, they are that the trees never bleed as sometimes happens with early spring pruning, growth and consequently flowering are earlier, and late May frosts give no trouble, growth being sufficiently far advanced to suffer no real check at this time.

Though forcing the trees to break into premature growth may have no permanent ill effects, it seems to me of doubtful value as these shoots would probably often succumb to very cold weather. So make a few experiments yourself; preferably with established plants, as trees just planted ought to be allowed to establish a proper root system as soon as possible.

Whether you use a knife or secateurs depends on manual dexterity. I've yet to meet a nurseryman who doesn't look at secateurs with the same condescension as the genuine architect regards fake Tudor or sham Gothic. Maybe you can't get quite as clean a cut with secateurs, but provided the rivet is oiled periodically they will make a very satisfactory job of all save really tough wood, for which a small pruning saw comes in useful.

Let us begin with the pruning of newly planted roses. Trees received from the nursery in March are frequently already pruned, and in any case roses purchased during this month should be pruned before planting. Otherwise defer the operation until the third week of March unless you are in the south-west, when a week or so earlier is advisable. In the north and in Scotland wait until beginning of April.

Newly planted bush roses, whether hybrid teas or polyanthas, should be cut back severely to about four eyes from base.

Standards are best pruned to about six eyes. Text books invariably advise pruning to an outward eye to avoid the development of inward growing shoots, but don't worry too much on this score as it seldom makes any noticeable difference to the trees in the long run.

All pruning cuts must be made to a *dormant* eye, since an eye which has already started to "shoot" will almost certainly have been nipped by frost and will eventually produce blind or flowerless growths. It is equally important to ensure that the cut – which should be slanting and not horizontal – is made just above the eye, otherwise the bit of wood that remains may develop die back.

Climbers and ramblers are generally pruned to about half their length before planting, or alternatively in early March before starting on the bushes and standards. Climbing hybrid teas like Etoile de Hollande, Lady Sylvia and Shot Silk are treated quite differently. Severe cutting back would result in reversion to the bush variety, from which they are simply sports. Shorten the tips of the shoots in late March, nothing more.

Arguments persist over the pruning of established trees. Nowadays rather lighter pruning is widely practised, but there is no general answer to the problem. Hard pruning of bushes or standards, especially if delayed until mid-April, may seriously weaken their constitution, besides rendering them highly susceptible to late May frosts. Nor is it true that hard pruning necessarily gives you finer blooms.

On the other hand, where space is limited and you wish, as I do, to grow a large number of different varieties, little or no pruning is inadvisable as it produces lop-sided, lanky plants which occupy considerable room. Light pruning does, however, ensure that the trees start to flower at least a fortnight before hard-pruned plants.

Does light pruning confer increased resistance to pests and diseases? With me Crimson Glory and The Doctor usually suffer badly from mildew, though they make excellent growth and bloom freely. I merely tip the tallest growths, yet very light pruning has apparently had no effect on disease incidence, which is surely largely a matter of varietal susceptibility, combined with other factors such as draughty situations, weather and atmospheric conditions and so on.

All weak, worn out, diseased and dead wood should be cut completely away before you tackle pruning proper. Some gardeners undertake this in autumn, but the precise time is of little importance.

If you aim at very large specimens, remove the useless wood as already described, also any growths which failed to produce satisfactory flowering shoots last summer, and reduce branched stems to single shoots. But remember that you may have to stake your plants and in any case this treatment may not work unless the soil is really fertile, as the trees will be unable to carry the extra top growth.

For my own bush trees I adopt a typical English compromise. After removing the useless wood, I cut back last summer's laterals to four or five eyes. In theory the result is a balanced tree with equidistant shoots, but as each variety and each plant are individuals, perfect regimentation is seldom achieved, nor is it desirable. About three weeks later superfluous eyes are rubbed out, leaving one shoot only to each eye. This treatment produces plants from two to four or more feet in height, depending on the variety. Standards are pruned to about six eyes.

Polyantha pompons such as Cameo and Paul Crampel are pruned fairly drastically to encourage fresh basal growths, which come very readily. Hybrid polyanthas like the Poulsens are treated less severely, last year's basal growths being reduced to the second eye below the flowering head and older wood pruned to about four eyes from the base.

Wichuraiana ramblers like Sanders' White and François Juranville are usually dealt with in early autumn, when new growths are trained in and old wood removed. Varieties such as Albéric Barbier and Paul's Scarlet only require the occasional removal of one or more older growths. Climbing hybrid teas bloom on laterals and sub-laterals, which are tipped back in early March. Rose species seldom require pruning beyond cutting away any very old wood.

N.P.H.

It is only in recent years that the value of Camellias as garden plants has been fully recognised, and this has led to a great increase in their popularity both here and in America. Their shiny dark green leaves can hardly be surpassed by any evergreen, and in addition throughout the spring they are laden with a wealth of blossom of many shades.

When first introduced they were considered to be tender, but the majority are really quite hardy, although in the colder areas it is advisable to give some shelter so as to avoid undue weather damage to the flowers. To be seen at their best they need a lime-free soil to which a little peat or leaf soil has been added, shade from the hottest sun, and an adequate supply of moisture during the summer months. Once established, however, it is surprising what adverse conditions they will withstand and a little care after planting will be amply repaid in future years.

Camellia japonica in its many forms is the most widely planted and there is a vast choice of size, form and colour of blossom. Adolphe Audusson (red), *Chandleri elegans* (pale pink), Lady Clare (pink), *alba grandiflora* (white), *magnoliaeflora* (shell-pink) and *Mathotiana rubra* (deep red) are among the most popular. The development of the hybrid group known collectively as *C. Williamsii* has already led to the beautiful J. C. Williams and Mary Christian both of which are most floriferous and easily grown. The forms of *C. reticulata* can, however, only be recommended for the milder gardens, although they are well worth a trial against a sheltered wall.

C.P.

THE FRUIT GARDEN

Although damage from wind is always a problem near the sea, similar trouble may be experienced in any exposed garden inland. Wind is particularly troublesome to freshly planted trees as constant movement of the trunk prevents the establishment of newly formed roots. In addition, the swaying of the trunk tends to make a hole in the soil around the base of the tree. This can be dangerous particularly on heavy soils as water collecting in these holes often leads to fatal results.

When planting in an exposed position, it is as well to make full use of the tree's own root system by so planting that the majority of the roots point into the direction of the wind. At the same time the tree should be staked. Whether the upright or oblique stake is best is a matter of opinion and, if the former method is adopted, the stake should be inserted before planting if only to avoid damaging any roots. It is also as well to have the stake leaning a little towards the wind so that any subsequent movement merely pulls it upright.

Afterwards, when tying, care must be taken to see that no chafing between the trunk and stake occurs. This can be done by wrapping a piece of bicycle tyre around the trunk and securing it to the stake with cord.

A characteristic feature of the windswept garden is the misshapen tree. Time after time in such cases the value of vigorous growth in young trees is lost when it is carried over by the wind to completely ruin the shapeliness of a tree. The only remedy is to prune hard to the base of those shoots in an endeavour to maintain the original direction of each branch. A system the writer advocates is to prune to one bud above that actually required. A crescent-shaped piece of bark (down to the wood) is then removed immediately below the top bud with a sharp knife. This will reduce growth from that bud without actually killing it, whereas the selected bud just below will grow out at a wider angle than would otherwise have been the case.

A further difficulty in exposed situations is that wind tends to reduce the activities of pollinating insects. As a result many flowers remain unfertilized with a consequent loss in crop. The only practical answer to this problem is the provision of some form of wind-break. Where space is limited this may be provided by a hedge of *Chamaecyparis lawsoniana* setting the plants at 2 ft. apart. An even better plant for the purpose is *Cupressocyparis leylandii* at 3 ft. apart for this is quicker growing but, strangely enough, it is listed by only a few nurserymen.

G.R.W.

M ANURES AND FERTILISERS: Last month the value of organic manures such as leafmould, compost and farmyard manure was emphasised for soft fruits. These materials do not supply a completely balanced feed however and, in particular. reference must be made to the need for adequate supplies of potash. On poor, sandy soils a deficiency will soon become apparent unless regular dressings are applied. These can be given in the form of sulphate of potash, using it at one ounce per square yard during March. Where a deficiency is actually affecting bushes two applications can be made at a monthly interval. The greatest need for potash will be found in apples, gooseberries and red currants. On many soils an annual dressing of bonfire ash will help to ensure an adequate supply.

Lack of feeding is very often the reason for poor crops and for stunted bushes. Even where farmyard manure is not available good results can be brought about by using fertilisers like sulphate of ammonia and nitro-chalk at one ounce per square yard or fish meal at double this rate. All these are best applied as the trees concerned come into growth. Nitrogen and potash are the two most important nutrients for fruits. Phosphate, although less important, is still necessary and a dressing every third year should suffice.

With fruit, trouble may be caused by indiscriminate applications of lime or chalk. Lime is not necessary for any fruit unless the soil is really acid; in fact, most fruits do best in slightly acid conditions. Excessive lime can cut off the supply of iron and manganese.

STRAWBERRIES: Usually planting takes place in the late summer or early autumn but this can also be done quite safely during early March. Of course, spring-planted strawberries should be prevented from fruiting by deblossoming, a practice which ensures well-established plants for cropping in the following year. In this crop virus troubles are becoming more apparent and it is advisable to plant a certified disease-free stock. Even with such a precaution infection can still occur from diseased plants in neighbouring gardens. Whilst this cannot always be overcome, at least all diseased beds in one's own garden can be rooted-out prior to replanting.

With regard to varieties, the season can well start with "Perle de Prague" followed by the widely-praised "Auchincruive Climax." Both varieties are excelled in some ways however by the sweetest-flavoured of all strawberries – "Royal Sovereign." Unfortunately many stocks of this variety are virus infected.

G.R.W.

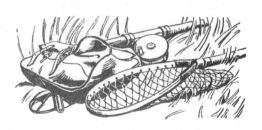

FISHING

March ... aptly named for the fisherman, because this is the month of progression Trout fishing begins; salmon fishing is improving day by day.

Let the trout fisher progress slowly and be not too eager to knock some hungry but lean fish upon the head; thereby depriving himself or others later of a more worthy quarry. Let him not be so progressive that he uses the modern engineering devices of the thread line without thought; for trout are recovering from the exertions of spawning and are easily caught. I often wish fishing had not marched forward so much with the times and the technique of it had stood still twenty-five years ago. I am no purist, but there is more pleasure for me to be had by casting a couple of wet flies down or upstream on some West Country river with little success than the continuous throwing of some gadget-controlled bait which results in a full bag.

Let us be fair to the trout, enjoy the delights of the angler without the lust for catching more than the other fellow by the use of a modern contrivance. Trout are depleted enough by pollution and land drainage, the advent of the motor and over-fishing without new-found weapons of attack. I prefer the worm man to the thread-liner and the fly man best of all; for on his achievements depend his skill alone in wielding rod and line and choosing the feathered imitation to lure his antagonist.

I have seen good hatches of fly towards the end of March and changed to a dry fly, sometimes two flies, both floating. There is an old idea that to fix a small piece of cork behind the tail of a fly is effective. Perhaps the fish imagine it to be a female full of eggs and more succulent. It often succeeds when all else fails.

The temperature of the water is rising and salmon are more likely to take a fly sunk or fished with the line floating. Fish in peaty rivers like purple, claret or orange. One fly I used in the Torridge with success was tied thus: *Tail*: Golden pheasant topping. *Body*: Claret mohair with flat gold tinsel spaced widely upon it. *Hackle*: Claret. *Wing*: Hen pheasant. This tied upon a wide-gaped outpoint hook I fished *à la* greased line and caught several salmon. The *Black Fairy* already described in these notes is my favourite for the West. The late Stephen Gwynn introduced me to it and on dull days of a size appropriate to the conditions I find it hard to beat. To remind you here is the dressing. *Tail*: Golden pheasant topping. *Body*: Black mohair (or seal's fur). Thin silver tinsel twisted upon it. *Hackle*: Black. *Wing*: Hen pheasant. Who would think so drab a fly would catch so many fish? When fishing the greased line I find it indispensable.

R.B.

THE NATURALIST

THE TOAD'S LOVE PARADE

An army is on the march, an army of toads making its slow, laborious way to a nearby pool.

The time has come for them to mate and spawn, and as if at a given word they have all emerged from their hibernating quarters and set forth on their annual spring pilgrimage to the waters where they themselves, perhaps many years since, first began life.

One by one they reach the water's edge and, wading in, push off into deeper water. Some come singly, others are already mated, the males mounted like jockeys on the backs of the females. Throughout the long spring night they come, hundreds of small, warty, earth coloured creatures, pioneers of life upon terra firma, all tramping steadfastly, and with great singleness of purpose, towards the pool where, possibly for centuries, their ancestors came to breed. Ignoring all other pools and lakes that may lie in their path, they march on until by daybreak a great host of them is gathered where a big weeping willow dips its slender fingers in the still, dark waters at one end of the tree-girt pool of their choice.

Once in the water the males begin their singing, a watery,

purring sound that continues night and day whilst breeding is in progress. Only a sharp frost at night will hush the choristers, for the cold makes them torpid and takes away their desire to mate. Sometimes during these early spring nights the frosts are so severe as to form a sheet of ice over the pool. Then the toads will sink to the floor of the pool, burying themselves in the mud until the spring sunshine melts the ice and warms the water.

A warm sun by day sets the business of mating and spawning in full swing, and late arriving males have to search long and diligently to find an unattached female, as there never seem to be enough of the latter to satisfy every love-sick male.

A male on finding an unattached female scrambles hurriedly on to her back, encircling her chest with his sturdy arms in a vice-like embrace that will not be relaxed until after the female has deposited her eggs. Unattached males, unable to find a lone female, will frequently endeavour to obtain a hold on an already mated female, but the occupying male keeps them at bay by kicking out with his long hind legs, which are so flexible that he can actually touch his nose with his toes.

The lone males are persistent, though, and occasionally several males will succeed in getting a hand-hold on one female. They cling to all parts of her anatomy and, burdened by their weight, the hapless female sinks to the bottom of the pool. But, eventually, the surplus males, apparently realising the futility of holding on, release their grip and only the rightful male remains with the female.

During the breeding season the skin of the male becomes smoother than usual and tends towards a greenish colour. A further distinctive feature of the male at this time of the year is the development of patches of hard skin on the three innermost digits of the forefeet. These patches are dark brown in colour and are known as nuptial pads; their purpose being to assist the male in maintaining his hold on the female.

Some of the females that come to breed are quite gigantic in size. One large specimen I took the trouble to measure was found to be no less than 105 mm. in length from nose to vent; and even larger specimens can sometimes be found. The males are usually all about the same size, and they never grow to such large proportions as do the females.

Often there arrive at the breeding waters female toads little bigger than the males mounted on their backs. These are the young females which are, most probably, breeding for the first time.

Comparing the two sexes it will be seen that there are differences, other than size, between male and female, and these differences, slight though they may be, serve as a useful guide to identification of the sex of toads seen away from the breeding waters.

For one thing, the female's skin is coarser and more warty than that of the male. While the paratoid glands, those large swellings behind each eye, are larger in the female than in the male.

Unlike the frog, which lays its eggs in large, irregular-shaped masses, the eggs of the toad are laid in long chains which measure anything up to ten feet in length and contain as many as five thousand eggs. These chains or strings of spawn become wound around water weeds and submerged tree branches as the female moves about during laying, and being so anchored they are unable to drift about the pool or sink to the bottom.

There is not the same mass movement of toads away from the breeding waters as there is towards them at the beginning. As each pair finish spawning they leave the pool and go their separate ways, some returning to their old haunts, whilst others take up new abodes.

The breeding habits of the frog are very much the same as those of the toad, except that the former spawn earlier, usually at the end of February or the beginning of March, depending on the weather. The male frog also mounts the female in the same way as does the toad, although the male frog embraces his partner so tightly that he sometimes crushes her chest and kills her.

The main difference between the breeding behaviour of toads and frogs is that the latter seldom use the same pool each year, and will deposit their eggs in any available water. Water-filled ditches are frequently used, as are other temporary pools of water, which invariably dry up as soon as warm weather arrives. Occasionally a number of frogs will gather at one pool to spawn, apparently drawn there by the sound of each other's voices.

Only once have I seen a really large gathering of frogs, and that was many years ago on a piece of waste ground which was invariably water-logged during the winter and early spring months. Much of the water gathered in a shallow depression among some tall thorn and bramble bushes, and in this small pool hundreds of frogs had congregated. The very air seemed to reverberate with their singing, the sound of which I can best liken to that of a distant motorcycle. The tiny pool was literally filled from brim to brim with frogs and spawn. Never before or since have I seen so many frogs at one time.

Needless to say, the pool dried up after the frogs had left and all the eggs perished. For a number of years afterwards I made a point of visiting that piece of waste ground each spring, but although the pool was usually there, the frogs never came there again.

L.G.A.

THE NATURALIST

A TURNERY OF WORMS

Few people appreciate earthworms at their true worth. Even gardeners grumble at the casts on the lawn when, if sensible, they should give praise and take a firm broom to sweep the valuable top dressing over the whole. Darwin spent a large part of his life studying the worm, and his book on the subject should be required reading for us all. He shows that without worms agriculture and gardening would be in a poor state. Worms not only tunnel and so aerate the soil, they also eat up all kinds of decaying matter (including the actual earth as well) and then pass the residue out as fertile, fine soil. According to Darwin you may find about 50,000 worms in about an acre of ordinary garden soil, and these will bring up around ten *tons* of fine soil to the surface every year. Therefore in fifteen years they will spread a fine, fresh layer, three inches deep on top. The richer the soil, and the more the worms, the better the work.

There is an amazing fund of fertility in worm castings. This is partly due to the digestive processes. Another valuable piece of work is done by the pulling down of decaying leaves to line burrows, thus composting without tears. They will gradually move top dressing down to where it will do most good.

In the United States, you can buy extra worms from worm farms if your garden is in a poor way. Here you may encourage your own earthworm population by making a comfortable compost heap in which they will breed, by spreading manure and compost to make a cool mulch in hot weather and by considerate digging. Try to avoid chopping up worms as you dig (and don't let the hens follow you around until you have a really large worm population and can spare a few). It isn't so serious if you chop a tail off – or a head – because usually a new one grows. Sometimes you will come across a worm with an obvious join by his tail.

Don't confuse these scars of adventure with the large belly-band worn by an expectant-mother worm. Worms are both mothers and fathers, turn about, and when a worm is about to lay her eggs this belly-band exudes a splendid plastic container, also circular. The worm gradually wriggles out of this, laying the eggs into it on the way. Then she pops food from her own mouth into the container, which is sealed up. This capsule remains in a safe spot until the eggs hatch, the baby worms eat their packed lunch and in due course emerge.

E.C.

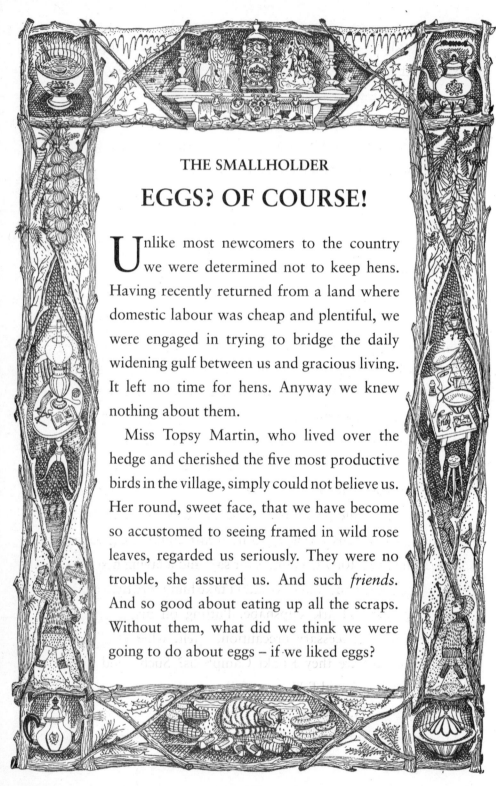

THE SMALLHOLDER

EGGS? OF COURSE!

Unlike most newcomers to the country we were determined not to keep hens. Having recently returned from a land where domestic labour was cheap and plentiful, we were engaged in trying to bridge the daily widening gulf between us and gracious living. It left no time for hens. Anyway we knew nothing about them.

Miss Topsy Martin, who lived over the hedge and cherished the five most productive birds in the village, simply could not believe us. Her round, sweet face, that we have become so accustomed to seeing framed in wild rose leaves, regarded us seriously. They were no trouble, she assured us. And such *friends*. And so good about eating up all the scraps. Without them, what did we think we were going to do about eggs – if we liked eggs?

We said we couldn't eat enough eggs and we'd thought of buying them from other people who kept hens. Topsy appeared to find this funny.

Other people, we soon discovered, were curiously reluctant to part with their eggs. I had two sources of supply – both painfully uncertain. Everybody's Handyman kept a few hens as a sideline, but his priority list was governed by the number of hours would-be customers employed him. A day's work in return for the privilege of buying a few of his fabulously priced eggs was beyond our modest means.

My greengrocer, with the air of one bestowing an undeserved honour, occasionally let me have a few. When other people were in the shop it was decided I should ask for peaches. As I *never* buy peaches confusion would not arise. On a day selected by the Fates I gave my order to his wife, adding "… and half a dozen peaches if you have them." But the understanding one would expect between a greengrocer and his wife, trading as one, did not in this case exist. Next day six costly peaches arrived with my carefully budgeted order.

Five minutes later Everybody's Handyman found me working off my rage in the pansy bed. He'd heard we were thinking of keeping a few hens (Topsy?) so he'd just come along to tell us that he had two forward pullets for sale and a laying hen – lovely brown eggs she laid. And it wouldn't take him more than a minute to make that old ark shipshape. Putting on my country-wise expression – a necessary precaution, I felt, when dealing with E.H., I said: "Are they Khaki Campbells? Such good layers." "Them's ducks," said E.H. scornfully.

Next day E.H., after putting in a good *day's* work on the ark, brought over the hens. (So great was my rage – between peaches and egg starvation – Henry had to restrain me from ordering a couple of hundred.) Looking like a cross between Father Christmas and a conjurer he opened a bulging sack and out jumped a large, dusty brown hen. I was bitterly disappointed. My idea a hen was an elegant all-white bird, modelled on the appearance of a china hen I'd seen in a Bond Street antique shop. However, though her appearance verged on the dingy, her deportment was beyond reproach. She was quiet and poised; the flapping and fluttering usually associated with her kind being amply supplied by Henry and me.

The sprightly, frivolous, forward pullets – delicate cinnamon and charcoal grey – followed her out of the sack. Not wishing to reveal the extent of our ignorance we assumed that forward pullets laid only two or three eggs a week. "Let's not be disappointed if we get only a dozen eggs the first week," I said to Henry as we walked back to the house. Then I pulled down from a shelf a mammoth bowl – to be known henceforth as the Egg Bowl.

A week later we had not collected one egg. "All that farm work for nothing," Henry complained. "All those horrid little pots of garbage for nothing," I cried. Next day we sent for Everybody's Handyman, whom we imagined to be avoiding us. His visit resulted in a declaration of faith and a plea for patience. We *should* have had a brown egg but we hadn't expected the pullets to lay for two or three weeks, had we?

At the end of the second week I put the Egg Bowl back on the shelf and we walked down to the ark with slaughter in our hearts. Topsy Martin was at the hedge to sympathise and advise. "You must talk to them if you want to get the best out of them," she said. Henry turned quite puce – but it was not a new theory to me. I'd been given the same advice when I was learning to ride – but no horse ever understood a word I said. It would be sad if our hens were equally uncomprehending, for obviously Henry, in his present mood, would be the worst possible kind of conversationalist.

I sought out Everybody's Handyman. "Sell me a layer," I said, "it will make the waiting less monotonous." "Right off the nest," he assured me later when he deposited a fiery ginger bird in the ark. I stayed to have a word with them, carefully looking round to see if Henry was within earshot.

Next morning there was an egg in the nest. *An egg!* Down came the Egg Bowl. Out came the record book with heaven knows what on the debit side and one egg – and hope – on the credit side.

In the afternoon we found a brown egg. A week later the pullets started to lay. Eggs in omelettes, eggs in cakes, eggs for breakfast – this is gracious living.

PS. – We've just added two pullets to our collection – white ones with steel grey necklaces and delicious little black and grey tails. Topsy Martin is quite insufferably pleased with herself about something.

E.S.

THE NATURALIST

MAD MARCH HARES

Madness surely means the performance of actions that are irrational or contrary to reason; and I am by no means sure that the spring-time gymnastics of hares should be so described.

In any case, hares are not the only creatures that go in for odd behaviour, particularly when spring is in the air.

The so-called madness of hares in February and March – sometimes even in late January – consists of weird antics on the part of the buck or "jack" hare. These antics take the form of standing straight up on the hind legs, waving the forelegs after the fashion of a boxer sparring for an opening; or sometimes the buck takes crazy leaps forwards, sideways and backwards; or again, he bucks like a broncho at a rodeo. A lucky observer may even see all variations during a short period of time. This posturing and cavorting is part and parcel of preliminary mating behaviour, and is really a mixture of combat among the bucks for eventual mastery over the others and a display of agility and bombastic showing-off for the benefit of the does, a few of whom are often in the vicinity of these gladiatorial exhibitions.

Curiously enough, not much real harm ever seems to result from these battles, though I have several times seen one jack hare kick another one almost head over heels. The whole display is a really wonderful spectacle, and well worth the wait in some secluded corner of a large field – where the observer can be protected from the keen March winds which seem almost to stimulate the rival bucks into more frenzied efforts. Protection from wind is more necessary than cover from sight, for at most times the hares seem indifferent to human spectators. This is not further evidence of lunacy; it is merely a remarkable example of how, in the animal world, the dominant stimulus of the prevailing life-phase overcomes all other reactions. Another possible instance of this is the fact that although normally hares do most of their travelling and feeding by night, in the breeding season night seems turned into day as far as courtship is concerned.

Don't assume, however, that jack hares tolerate humans or other interlopers too far. Years ago I remember lying in some scrub at the edge of a field, watching some hares "going mad." Then, very much to my surprise, a large buck rose on his hind legs a yard or so from me. He sat up, nose twitching, ears cocked, all ready I suppose to join in the fray. I, in my boyish ignorance, thought I would try to catch it, and I launched myself forward in a wonderful rugby tackle. I just touched the hare's hind quarters, and received such a powerful kick that not only did it scare the life out of me but it left me with a two-inch scratch on the back of my hand. This was a practical reminder of the fact that the hare's powers of seeing behind it are first class, and its reactions instantaneous.

On another occasion, in Wiltshire, I saw a jack hare surprised by a wandering sheep, and the sheep received a kick in the ribs that would have done credit to a master of the French art of *la savate*.

It must not be thought that all this aggressiveness is indicative of any family feeling on the part of the brave buck. Still less is it evidence of a paternal instinct; for once the mating is over the jack hare is as indifferent to his spouse as he is to casual observers of his courtship. He not only leaves the cares of rearing the young entirely to his wife, but he is an inconstant fellow and distributes his favours wholesale. Moreover, the wife of one season is most unlikely to be chosen again.

Hares, of course, are inconsistent as well as inconstant. Quite apart from the breeding period they show bewilderingly contradictory temperament. One moment they are brave almost to the point of foolhardiness, the next moment they seem the embodiment of timidity.

No account of eccentric hare behaviour is complete without

reference to the amazing gatherings of hares so often reported. I myself have never seen more than twenty hares in one moderate-sized field. But shepherds in Scotland, where our own brown hare is superseded by the blue or mountain hare, have many times told of hundreds of hares meeting together, usually in winter and at night, to indulge in a sort of game of "touch," punctuated by frenzied leapings and skippings.

I have also heard of such meetings taking place in Southern England. What these mass midnight revels mean I have no idea. I can only say that I should very much like to see them. Are they rehearsals for the more serious business later on, or are they some kind of play? Do such gatherings consist of both sexes, or are they entirely male affairs?

Whatever they are, they have a purpose you may be sure. Hares are volatile, temperamental animals, but they have their own special ways of expressing their feelings and urges. But except to us conventional human beings, I think it can definitely be said that they are *not* mad.

M.K.

THE NATURALIST

MOLES

If one has a garden that touches open country, one must expect the occasional mole, unless the garden is completely surrounded by a wall or a hard roadway; even so there may be an old run under a gate or through a drain tile which moles have used since long before the garden was made.

With us, surrounded by old turf-grown field roads, the catching of the occasional mole has long since become a matter of establishing quasi-permanent trapping points where the main runs are forced near the surface by the hard rubble below; it has proved almost impossible to take a mole in the garden itself or under the lawns, where there is a network of old runways more complex than the Underground system of London with all its cross-connecting passages. A mole can work unnoticed for weeks, or only break the surface here and there, but sooner or later he has to cross one of the buried roads, and there one may take him.

In the last few years we have been experimenting with some success with "mole fences" to exclude them from specially sacred areas and to restrict their movements strategically to the known permanent ways. In its simplest form the mole fence is a narrow trench – the width of the smallest spade – a foot or so deep, or down to a hard bottom, filled in with gravel or rubble, well rammed. The turf soon forms over it again, and only browns in the driest weather. More elaborate alternatives are old slates set on edge, not quite flush with the turf, or breeze blocks, or fine meshed chicken wire. These fences bring to notice an unexpected number of moles where no moles ought to be; they travel extraordinary distances along them in the newly dug soil seeking a way through. An occasional gap should be left, and marked, to allow for a trapping point, or to allow those enclosed by the defences to escape.

It is curious how reluctant moles are to travel on the surface, except in the mating season, for they have so few enemies other than man. Cats are seldom interested in them, owls and hawks dislike them, the weasel tribe will not kill them. Foxes may kill them but do not eat them, so too do some dogs, more for sport or the relief of boredom, perhaps, than anything else. We have one spaniel who catches them alive and unharmed; but she is less enthusiastic since she met a dog-catching mole, who held on to her nose for a hundred yards overland before letting go.

H.D.

WHAT EVERY COOK
SHOULD KNOW ABOUT

PRESERVING GAME

In some towns the municipal authorities have cold storage chambers attached to the market, and, for a small fee, game shot during the season can be kept in cold storage. In America the domestic freezing cabinet, as distinct from the refrigerator, is a commonplace country house equipment, but it is still uncommon here. Actually game will keep in the English winter for an incredible length of time provided a good "cold larder" or cold cellar with adequate ventilation is available.

For many years I used to set aside a tough old cock pheasant shot on the last day of the season to be eaten on Easter Sunday. As this is a very variable date and our climate is also variable it would seem optimistic, but actually the temperature in one of the old "cold larders" is not subject to great fluctuations and I do not remember any occasion when the ritual failed or when the bird was not both tender and not too high, though rather more "developed" than one would suggest for average consumption.

But birds which have been frozen behave differently. They ripen a great deal more quickly and to my mind are never quite the same. In this way one needs to keep rather a sharp eye on birds which have been picked up the day after a shoot in hard weather and which have been frozen solid by a sharp frost. These will not hang as well as others and birds hung in an outside gamelarder where they may get frozen in really hard weather are equally undependable.

An older way of preservation is worth trying. This is the preservation of cooked birds in or rather under fat. It is very successful with fat domestic goose but so far as game is concerned needs added fat. Traditionally, butter was used, and the birds preserved in stoneware pots or wide-necked clay vessels. Large brown stone jars are suitable. The tops are covered with bladder and these are a far better seal than modern cellulose film, which is too porous to keep out condensation of moisture and so moulds.

Birds preserved in this way are used throughout Southern France and Spain but there is this important difference. Usually only some portions of the preserved bird are used as the meat or flavouring element in a mixed stew, a nice dish or a "cassoulet" of beans.

The basic process of making a "confit" of goose or game is to joint the limbs, breast and all meat and fat from the carcase. These are lightly tossed in butter or lard and put into the jar with chopped fat pork, herbs, or chopped ham or bacon and garlic.

The game they use is mostly partridge and distinctly well-hung partridge at that. This strong game flavour is probably more than the British palate would relish but as they use a few small pieces of "game confit" as a flavouring agent, it is a distinct economy.

Cooking is a very long time in a very low slow oven. The warming oven of an "Aga" used overnight would probably be ideal. In some countries the pot is again given another six hours low heat some twenty-four hours later. Now for the essential bit of "know how." The fat must completely cover the contents, no pieces must project and, if there is not a solid inch of fat over all, set aside and when almost set add more melted fat. In Spain the process is simplified. They pour olive oil over the cold fat to the depth of half an inch. This makes a perfect seal and is simply poured off into a vessel when the "confit" is opened.

Portions are used, the jar reheated and when cool and set the oil seal poured back. It is a primitive system of hermetically sealing the jar and works supremely well.

Obviously the meat in these "confits" is rather overcooked, but used as they are meant to be used, as an addition to other less savoury meat or a mixed dish, it is excellent and you can have a singularly rich game dish of chicken or even rabbit adequately aromatised by game preserved in this primitive manner.

Smoking is another method of preservation, which is applied in Germany and Central Europe to goose breasts and in the U.S.A. to turkey breasts. Both are expensive delicacies and the end result is a most delicious sort of mild smoked ham which is eaten raw and in thin slices on toast. I am uncertain of any specific instructions. Probably it is simply the usual "mild bacon cure" followed by wood fire smoking. It seems an ideal experiment for anyone with a Tudor hearth and a wood fire, but the goose fat is very light and would be inclined to run in any mild warmth, so smoking has to be done with care really high up the chimney or in a cool eddy. When smoked they are rolled up into little bolsters and seamed with string rings like miniature versions of the peculiar meat joints butchers now try to force on us.

Why only the breasts of goose and turkey are so treated I do not precisely know. It is probably that boned the joints would be a little difficult to keep together when carved. I believe, however, that they are in fact smoked but appear as "Potted Smoked Turkey." Anyway it appears well worth the experiment and a rather more manageable size of joint than is furnished by the average bacon pig.

Inquiry at a very knowledgeable "charcuterie" suggests that it might be even a profitable enterprise for it is – when obtainable – wickedly expensive, but I am told that it is better value than, say, smoked salmon. "It slices thinner." Personally, after my last plate of smoked salmon at a famous hotel, I cannot conceive of anything being cut thinner and not blowing off the plate on its way to the customer.

H.B.C.P.

WATERCRESS

I think we are rather inclined not to use watercress in all the ways that we might. Not only is it a delicious herb or vegetable, particularly good just now, but for those who look for health-giving properties to encourage them to eat, there is the authority of Culpeper, who, in the middle of the 17th century, spoke of a "pottage" of watercress as a remedy for headaches, consuming the "gross humours winter hath left behind."

In France watercress is a classic accompaniment to grilled meat and to roast birds. Little bunches are just dipped into a sharp French dressing, shaken and set on the dish.

With devilled food, too, watercress is good and for this may be cooked. Allow for four people about four bunches of cress, a good ½ oz. butter and 4 tablespoonfuls of consommé (tinned will do), or *jus*. Prepare the cress by picking over and removing the part of the stem which bears fine white rootlets. Put it in the pan with the water that clings to it and let it simmer gently, lid on, as you cook spinach, for about 10 minutes, until softened. Season well, add butter and stir. Add consommé and heat up. If too moist, cook an extra minute or two with lid off pan. Finish with a dash of lemon juice.

Watercress soup is delicious and there are many recipes. Some call for a soup made with potato and milk with a flavouring of the cress – say one good bunch for a soup for four. Some call for onion and garlic to be softened in the butter, after which the potatoes are softened in the flavoured butter for 8-10 minutes then the roughly chopped cress and the milk are added and cooking continued. The whole is then sieved and thickened with a liaison of egg yolks and cream, and garnished with a few chopped leaves. The recipe which follows for six people calls for 10 oz. cress after it has been picked over and prepared.

10 oz. cress, weighed after picking over and after reserving 2 dozen or so leaves or small central sprigs for final addition:

2 large potatoes

2½-3 oz. butter

1¼ pints water, vegetable stock or potato water

A scant ½ pint milk

A good gill of cream

3 yolks

Seasoning

Prepare cress by removing any yellow leaves and shortening stems to avoid white rootlets, reserve about 24 small leaves or central tips. Gather cress together and cut the bunch in half or in three lengths Melt butter, soften cress in this for about 10 minutes (lid on pan). Add warm water or stock, potatoes cut in pieces, bring to boil. Season, cook for 25 minutes. Put through a fine wire sieve. Return to pan, add milk, bring to boil, adjust seasoning. Add reserved leaves or tips, simmer 5 minutes. Make liaison by mixing cream and yolks, adding a few spoonfuls of the hot soup and then returning all to the pan, through a strainer. Serve at once.

THE SALMON ARE RUNNING

Apart from ringing the changes in March with beef, lamb, mutton, pork and veal, for variety on the table the cook will look, I think, to the sea. But many fish are not yet at their best. With mackerel coming in, skate, smelts, sole, prawns and shrimps pretty good, the king fish is again the salmon. It is a thrill, gastronomic anticipations aside, to think of this noble creature coming in from the deeps, prawn-fed most likely, to be taken in the first of fresh waters with the sea-lice still on him that his fatness has attracted.

A rare and exceptionally fortunate gastronome is he who has the luck to eat of the salmon-fish that has gone to the kettle while still limp from the quieting knock of the "priest." What later will be blackish, oily flesh along the sides and by the fins is here a delicious creamy curd. The dark solidifications appear after the lay-out on the slab needed for the passing of the rigor during which no fish should be cooked. This is not to say that the fish which has stiffened and gone limp again is not good eating. But a new flavour has developed quite different from that in the new-killed, freshly poached beastie.

Just what is the best way of cooking the cut of salmon got from the fishmonger's slab is a much-argued question. It is one thing to poach the new-killed fish *whole* in simply salted water; another to do this with the *cut* of fish that has been on and off the monger's slab over an unknown period. Putting the unprotected piece of salmon into plain, salted water is bound to extract more from the fish than goes into it. I therefore (as a Scotsman, mind ye) recommend a modification of the method given by Mr. William Verral, host of the White Horse Inn at Lewes, Sussex,* about the middle of the eighteenth century. It is in the classic vein.

* *The Cook's Paradise*, a reprint of Verral's book edited by R. L. Mégros (Sylvan Press, 1948, 7s. 6d.), if not completely practical for these days, is historically of much interest.

Verral lays the "preferred jowl," both sides notched to the bone an inch apart, in a marinade of a little vinegar, white wine, salt and water, some green onions and bay leaves, some blades of mace and whole pepper, for several hours before that devoted to cooking and serving. He then puts the piece in a stew-pan "just its bigness" with a fish plate or napkin under it – that you "may take it out without breaking." With it goes a pint of white wine, a dash of vinegar, salt and whole pepper, two or three shallots, a bunch of parsley and green onions, and as much water as will cover. "Let your lid be shut close upon it," says Verral, "and put it over a slow stove to simmer."

Verral, a copy of whose book, heavily annotated by the poet Thomas Gray, is in the British Museum, advises a shrimp sauce to go with his poached salmon. This he makes from a fish Velouté or cullis with a dash of white wine and a little sweet basil, thyme and parsley, "all minced very fine," and finished with the juice of "a lemon or two." Peeled shrimps are added before this sauce is simmered for fifteen minutes. My own preference, however, is for a simple *hollandaise* made a shade more tart than ordinarily with lemon.

One may well dismiss the white wine from the bouillon, but if flavour is not to be given by the poaching-liquid, it is better to steam cuts of salmon peppered and salted and close-wrapped in well-buttered paper. This is certainly the trick, apart from grilling, for the single cutlet. Yet, nothing else being handy, I have myself with excellent results cooked a buttered slice dry in an inverted pot-lid, covered by another lid or the right-sized plate, over boiling water. A cutlet to be grilled should be well brushed with melted butter or oil, peppered and salted, and sealed quickly with good heat each side before turning it about over or under quieter heat until cooked through. In my view a generous pat of *maître d'hôtel* butter made with a dash of anchovy sauce and lemon juice on top of the grilled salmon cutlet is sauce a-plenty.

V.M.

WHAT EVERY COOK
SHOULD KNOW ABOUT

SALMON

The noble salmon is one of the most practical harbingers of spring. The fox-hunter may be looking with a jaundiced eye on "those damn stinking primroses" as closing a season, but the angler on a salmon river is hopefully aware that a new season is already open. Unfortunately a very large proportion of the early-door salmon are "kelts," that is to say, exhausted old roués – "All passion spent!" – and they are completely inedible.

If by any chance you are offered in some slightly monochrome market an obvious salmon fish whose head appears to be too big for his body and the latter lean and shrunken instead of beautifully plump and silvery, avoid this bait!

Incidentally, a mysterious sort of frozen salmon imported from Canada appears sometimes in fishmongers, and sometimes, I regret to say, with the label of "Scots." It is delusively pink and looks like salmon, but under the grill it turns an unpleasing yellowish beige and acquires a sort of flannelette or fibrous consistency like "Hotel Halibut." This expensive deceit should also be avoided.

The cooking of salmon is simple, for it is best as plain as plain. Steamed (not boiled) or grilled, could anything be more simple? Yet a really good cook knows that neither of these operations should be prolonged more than a minute longer than necessary and that it is far better to keep the table waiting than the fish "warm in the oven."

If on the other hand the consumers are unpunctual people, you can gain time by cooking your salmon steaks *en papillote*. This is simply wrapping each separately in good stout white paper – which you have liberally oiled on both sides with olive oil. Enclose the salmon steak with a little butter and no salt or pepper, each steak in its paper bag. As you will have to turn them, it is worth while making a neat parcel and tying it with fine string, otherwise the paper curls up in the oven and turning and opening may be difficult. Simply bake in an earthenware dish. The oiled paper holds in the moisture and you can allow considerably more "tolerance" for time than you can by steaming or grilling, when timing has to be perfect. Nothing is really more difficult than perfect plain cookery!

The two main sauces for hot salmon are *maître d'hôtel* and *tartare*, but *mousseline* is far better and *hollandaise* a reliable standby. Mayonnaise is really best with cold salmon.

Now consider the salmon. It is one of the few fishes with a substantial amount of natural fat – it's a rich fish. So you want a sauce which is not of itself too buttery and it should be essentially a smooth egg-sauce flavoured with herbs and a little dab of lemon juice. Purists prefer a *maître d'hôtel*, which is simply finely pounded parsley, chervil or a mixture of parsley with a little fennel, beaten up with butter and a drop of lemon juice. *Hollandaise* is simply plain, white, thin sauce flavoured with a little herbs and adequately sharpened with lemon juice. To this while hot, but not anywhere near boiling point, is added a little butter in small pieces and the yolks of two eggs to the half-pint. These are well beaten till the mixture thickens. *Sauce mousseline* is essentially the same as the above but in place of white sauce use cream.

While the mature salmon has a magnificent flavour, this is less developed in the "grilse," or undergraduate fish. In the case of grilse one may have to rely rather more on the sauce, and it is possibly worth remembering that when salmon is served with accompanying boiled potatoes, a sauce-tureen full of water the salmon had been boiled in was also put on the table by our wise grandparents. Add to it a little salt and a dessertspoonful of white wine vinegar and it is excellent.

Smoked salmon is not too difficult, as it is really more of a business of salting than a prodigious mystery of smoking. The fish has to be cut up the back from tail to shoulder, cleaned, scaled, and the bone must be taken neatly out and the head economically removed. If it is a very large fat fish it is rubbed with plain salt and left for a day to drain before proper salting. This is done with a mixture of half-and-half kitchen salt and sandy brown sugar with a little saltpetre, not more than one ounce to the pound of mixture. Some modern receipts advocate a heavier proportion of salt and less sugar, but the old Scots one is probably the best for keeping qualities, and variations may be fit only for fish destined for fairly rapid consumption.

The "cure" is thoroughly well rubbed in and the split fish is pressed flat with a weighted board on its back during the process. One skilled treatment is enough, but the amateur will be wise to give a second dressing after 24 hours. Two days' "curing" and pressing is enough. You now have a salted fish and this can, if smoking is beyond you, be simply skewered flat with suitable twigs and allowed to air dry in any free current of warm, dry air.

Usually inquiry will find a "smoke house," for in the days when farmers were allowed to kill their own pigs, home-curing and smoking were common. If none can be found it is not too difficult to improvise one. The point is to have whatever is being smoked far enough away from the source of fire that no accident can cause it to "heat." The traditional Canadian "smoke house" is simply two or three old kegs with the tops and bottoms knocked out. These are piled on top of one another as a chimney. The fish or meat is hung from a stick resting across the open top. Now the smoke fire is not at the bottom of this inflammable contraption but in a simple pit in the earth about two yards away. The connection is a small covered trench, or better still a bit of drainpipe.

The smoke is made by filling the pit with sawdust, lighting up a bush fire on top of it and, when the latter is glowing charcoal, smothering down with more sawdust. A very small vent hole is poked in to afford air to the smothered fire, then the whole is covered with a lid and the smoke allowed to find its way into the barrels. Properly made, the affair works without attention other than adding a little more sawdust daily, and a very few days' smoking suffices for relatively thin objects like fish. Salmon do not require more than two or three days.

H.B.C.P.

LIVING ALONE AND LIKING IT

To live alone is generally supposed to be a difficult business, particularly for a woman. Personally, I'm not sure it isn't much less difficult than to live with other people. Anyway, what I am sure of, and grow increasingly sure of, is that I'm infinitely less lonely living alone in the country than in a city. That's not the popular theory. Most people take the opposite view. Six times out of eight the advice tendered to single persons considering retirement to secluded country cottages is not to risk it – for fear of loneliness, boredom, and the almost certain development of queer, eccentric habits.

I wouldn't advise it myself for the young, the gregarious, or those not born or bred in the country. Nor for those who "love the country" in terms of weekend gatherings, golf courses, shooting-parties, and summer teas under striped umbrellas. To get along by yourself in the country you've got to prefer it to the city in all its moods, even its most vile, when it's blowing and raining, drizzling and damp, or just plain dull and uninspiring. You've also got to prefer it in your own worst moods; when you're low and dis-spirited and you've no one to talk to and nothing that doesn't seem utterly humdrum to do.

But if you can stand it under those conditions, if such setbacks as frozen, impassable roads and blown-down telephone wires not only fail to arouse a sense of panic at being temporarily cut off from the outside world but even induce a rather smuggish sense of satisfaction that now you are unassailable in your ivory tower, if on a drenching day you can take real pleasure in the fact that instead of walking comparatively dry pavements as one of a crowd you are splashing and squelching your way through mud and muck and puddles in splendid isolation, then indeed the bond between you and the country must be a strong one. As you'll surely settle there in the end, I'd advise you to do it now. You can't feel lonely while being entertained. And, to my mind, anyway, the country in any of its moods is the most entertaining and satisfying companion one could wish for.

Hazlitt, in an essay on country-lovers, says that they are almost invariably those who were bred in the country, and that the sense of security which they feel at being surrounded by the sights, smells and scenery which was part of their childhood is at the bottom of their nostalgia for, or attachment to, the country.

I'm sure he's right. For while there are, and always will be, hundreds of country-bred people who prefer city life and vice versa, and though it's certainly not impossible for a city-bred person to be able to rusticate in comparative solitude without reaching for a pistol or the brandy bottle through sheer loneliness and ennui, rustication must obviously be easier for those who, having in early years known no other life but country life, revert to it with much the same sense of relief as that of someone very cold and tired getting into a hot, pine-scented bath.

My own bath began three years ago. I'm still wallowing in it and hope to be able to go on doing so for ever. I grew up in the country, and then, afterwards, there was London and a flat and a job. I went to the country only during weekends or holidays and it wasn't enough. London life was fun and the job interesting; there was always plenty to do but there was no quietude and little sense of reality. Life was restless and crowded and fast and, indeed, one wanted it that way; for to be by yourself for more than a very few hours in a teeming city of eight million souls can easily result in a strong inner conviction that you are the original lost soul. Such feelings probably only apply to those who live alone. Domesticity and family life obviously do much to counteract the artificiality of cities. But, without them, a sense of futility and rootlessness is apt to grow with every new grey hair. So one day I left London and rented a farmhouse, without the farm, in Suffolk. And I've never been lonely since.

Compared to the busy lives led by people like Constance Spry, or Esther McCracken, or any other active country woman, my life is disgracefully un-busy and non-productive. I neither farm, market-garden, nor even keep hens. For my own sake I garden – through trial-by-error methods on half an acre of stubborn soil – and for my bank manager's sake write an occasional article. Of what happens to all the time that ought to be left over I truly have no idea, except that after the twice-weekly household shopping trips are done, and the dogs are looked after, and I have caught up on what goes on in the village, and gone to visit a neighbour or two, and perhaps been through an agony of preparation for a weekend visitor, there doesn't seem to have been any.

Unless, of course, you count all those millions of moments which are wasted – well, I wonder if that is really the right word? – in sheer mooning. In staring into space with a vacant expression and bones turned to water because every bird within miles has "suddenly burst out singing" and you can't believe it's really happening to you. In gaping at the ground (same expression) because there, miraculously are the first green spikes of the daffodils in spite of the fact that you put them in upside down. In peering into the thickness of the night outside your bedroom window because that sudden shrillness that made you jump and took your mind off what you were reading wasn't the telephone, but *your* moorhen scolding its young on *your* pond. And, most of all, perhaps, in endless rapt contemplation of the signposts on the road which, when you first arrived, pointed the way to unfamiliar places and now, by the grace of God, are pointing towards home.

Time wasted? Well, all right; but in that event I'm one of the happiest wastrels that ever got plenty for nothing.

That's another thing about living in the country. If you haven't got much money you not only get more but can give more than if you lived in a city. In the city, to keep in touch, you've got to have money to spend on clothes and food and drink, for you can't do much for people except entertain them, which you probably can't afford, or be entertained by them, which they probably can't afford either. But in the country it's different.

A few minutes' conversation outside a cottage door or in the local bus, a few hours up at the village hall at a Women's Institute meeting or at a village party and, hey presto, you've got treasure. Treasure in terms of strong links in a chain of friendship and interest, in a sense of intimacy, with those who live round you, so that though those lights which twinkle at night across the fields may be half a mile removed from you, they are infinitely more warming than those which shone a bare inch from your door in London, because they are the lights in the cottage windows of Mrs. Appleton, and you and she are pals and in accord because you both live in the same village and like it, and because in small ways you've been able to help each other.

Loneliness? Oh, no; that is the last thing you need fear, living alone in the country.

P.W.

THE ENGLISH FRAGRANCE

"BUY my Sweet Lavender" was a familiar London street cry and our love for this delightful herb is as strong now as ever it was, though in few gardens is it rarely seen at its best and so few of the many lovely varieties are to be found. Like most herbs the lavender is happiest in a dry, sandy soil where it may be thoroughly baked by the sun which will bring out the fragrance of the blooms to the full. The plants may be set out at any time between autumn and spring and the younger they are, the more readily do they become established. They must be given no manure and should be very lightly pruned in the spring each year; especially is it advisable to cut out any old, straggling wood. Planted as a hedge or individually amongst the shrubbery or in the herb garden, lavender is both pleasing to the eye and to the senses. The blooms should be cut just before they are fully open for then is their fragrance at its strongest. Made up into small muslin bags and mixed with the dried leaves of the lemon scented geranium and the leaves of Rosemary, they bring about deep sleep if hung about the bedroom. And do not discard the stalks, for if these are dried and lighted in a room they will permeate it with a rich perfume which is particularly pleasing on a winter's evening. The stalks burn slowly, like incense and are most appreciated in a sick room and yet are so rarely used in this way.

There are many varieties, several of which are little known today, but quite as easily grown as the more common and highly aromatic Old English lavender, the variety most in demand by the distillers. This is a tall variety which makes a hedge of 3 ft. tall and almost as wide. As a contrast the lovely white lavender, alba, is superb. This is the lavender of which Parkinson writes in his Paradisi (1629), "there is a kind that beareth white flowers, but is very rare and seen in few places because it will not so well endure our cold winters." It has a reputation for being tender, but on the cold north-east coast it seems quite happy.

Bearing a very dark flower is the Grappenhall variety, a tall vigorous grower, and equally striking is the silvery leaved Dutch variety, which will reach a height of 2 ft. and looks particularly attractive when planted amongst dark coloured evergreens.

Delightful for making a dwarf hedge to a knot garden or for edging the front of a border is Lodden Pink, which rarely grows taller than 15 in. and makes a very neat bush. The blooms are of a charming shade of shell pink. Of similar habit is the rich, violet-flowered Hidcote Purple, which also has striking silver foliage, the blooms being richly fragrant. Extremely hardy is the dark, lavender-coloured Munstead, which is the most dwarf of all varieties. A place should be found for all these charming shrubs and especially are the dwarf lavenders so useful in the small garden for besides their silvery evergreen foliage, the blooms have so many uses in the home even though they are not so much in demand today as in Parkinson's days "to comfort and dry up the moisture of a cold brain."

R.G.

LETTER TO THE EDITOR

WILDFOWL: I must disagree most violently with Major Hugh Pollard's remarks (January) on the edible qualities of wildfowl. It has puzzled me that a man who knows so much about wildfowl and, indeed, wildfowling should repeatedly make statements such as "the taste of wild geese is fishy" and "that they are tough as old boots." Also it is quite wrong to say that curlew are fishy and oily. Knot are as good as golden plover.

I have just eaten a wild goose I shot a fortnight ago in the north. It surpassed in flavour and tenderness any domestic goose I have ever eaten. Waders, curlew included, if they have been feeding on muddy estuaries, especially where there is "Zos" grass, do taste oily, but where curlews have access to grain fields and fresh grass they are excellent on the table. Brent geese may be "fishy" as they are slob-feeding birds. I have never tasted one. But pinkfooted geese and greylags, which feed almost exclusively on the land and eat more or less the same food as domestic geese, are *never* fishy.

Major Pollard must have been very unlucky indeed in his wildfowl or his cook. If only he lived near me I would ask him to dinner of roast pink-foot or, better still, greylag, which has been hung fourteen days, and has been cooked in the way a wild goose should be cooked, slowly roasted with fat bacon on the breast, and stuffed with herbs.

"B.B.," Woodford Lodge, Kettering,
Northamptonshire.

APRIL

WILD LIFE

Man has written specially about April for 4,000 years or more. And even in these days of scientific nature-watching he's more interested in spring than in autumn. All the county bird reports that arrive on my desk as fast as I can read and file them have lists of arrival dates and (almost as an afterthought) a few departure dates. Human beings are a lot more interested in, and stimulated by, spring than by autumn. Nobody writes to the papers about the last barnacle goose or the last brambling; it's the first chiffchaff or the first cuckoo that they write about. Moreover, it is the first of a species that tends to be noticed, while the main arrival, often much later, may even go unnoticed. Besides, there is no constant relation between the date of arrival of the first and the date of arrival of the main rush. For instance, for the chiffchaff, that scholarly analyst Dr. Ticehurst in the *Handbook of British Birds* gives the main arrival dates between

March 20 and March 30, continued till the third and fourth week in April, while the passage of Continental birds goes on till the third week in May. Yet chiffchaffs are often seen and heard long before March 20, sometimes even in February, and most years a few actually winter in south-west Britain. Any link between an early chiffchaff and an early season is a coincidence.

Although the cuckoo letters to the papers always start in late March (or nearly always) the peak arrival is pretty steady from year to year during the third week of April, and the cuckoo is followed quickly by a collection of birds which seem to go more by the calendar than by the weather (unless the weather is exceptionally bad) – house-martin, whitethroat, whinchat, wood-warbler, nightingale. Nightingales, when they arrive at the beginning of the fourth week of April, are often very tame and obvious. They show themselves openly by day on hedgetops, walls and gates; it is only when they settle in their territories that they become skulkers and disembodied voices.

Main arrivals of sedge-, reed- and garden-warblers come soon after that of the nightingale. In fine weekends in late April the natural history societies get out into the field and begin to pile up the records. Indeed, if you look at the county reports, you might often think that birds only arrive, or move, or do anything, at weekends! But I don't think the average bird-watcher ponders, as he reaches for his notebook and scribbles "heard first nightingale in the spinney" or "four garden-warblers now sing in the forest," or "the spotted flycatchers arrive at last," whether these notes are of scientific value; he is the unconscious priest, I believe, of an ancient cult, the officer of an old pagan rite.

J.F.

———•–•———

Changes in distribution and habits of birds in April in the Northern Hemisphere involve more individual birds than in any other month in the year. In Britain, peak of the passage of the subarctic birds along the coastal flyways – quantities (mostly in breeding plumage) of godwits, whimbrel, snipe, dunlin, sandpipers; some ruff, greenshank, dotterel. Only the high arctic birds – sanderling, knot, arctic tern – delay their main passage until May. Many residents and even some summer visitors already have eggs – on the hills and moors curlew, plover, oystercatchers, stone-curlew. Most of our resident small singing birds start laying in earnest, and so do most of our birds of prey, at least those which live primarily on rodents.

Though it is not yet their egg-time, not until mid-May, more fulmars haunt our cliffs in April than at any other time. But before egg-time comes, many young birds will begin to drift to the ocean.

Most of the small birds which arrive in England before the end of April, with the exception of the swallows and martins, are birds which largely seek crawling insects – grubs, caterpillars and pupae – as their prey. Those which live on flying insects, such as swifts, nightjars and flycatchers, do not come till the big hatch of such insects at end of April or May. But first fortnight of April nearly always sees first swallows. In fifteen years Gilbert White saw swallows first in this period ten times. In second and third week in April expect willow-warbler, blackcap, redstart and main arrival of cuckoo. White's earliest first cuckoo was on April 9 and his latest April 22.

Third week of month brings in first substantial trickle of wood-warbler, white-throat, whinchat, nightingale, house-martin. In sixteen years White heard his earliest first nightingale on April 2, his latest on April 26: his average date was April 14. In fourth week of month sedge-warbler, garden warbler and quail (the expectation of hearing the latter in England just now seems better than it has been for several years). In fifth week reed-warbler, first turtle-dove, sometimes first swift. Towards the end of the month the dawn chorus of territorial song is almost full, and the posturing of aggressive small birds almost universal.

But perhaps the best place to see spring displays is on open waters, where many ducks, already paired, display to each other while on transit to their breeding grounds. Watch particularly wigeon, shoveler, pochard, tufted and the wonderful sawbills. Even Londoners should get a chance to see the display of the smews on the big reservoirs, before they finally depart to breed in the forests of Lapland and Russia.

J.F.

First and foremost April activity for the naturalist is the arrival throughout the month of spring migrant birds. Of course a few will have got here already: willow warblers and chiffchaffs; and their tentative notes, uncertain to begin with, will gather strength and style as the month progresses. A mere list of arrivals makes dull reading; but in addition to swallows and house martins and sand martins which should be with us by the middle of April, the lovely yellow wagtail will be here too – also the redstart, whitethroat, and that curious bird, the wryneck, or "snake bird" – so called from the way in which it wriggles and twists its head and neck.

By the time we are half-way through the month there should be no need for young practical jokers to imitate the cuckoo, for the cocks of this species will be present in some numbers, and will be practising hard. These will be followed, before the close of the month, by the almost identically plumaged hen cuckoos whose normal note is a lovely bubbling whistling call which many people probably hear but do not recognise as such. Our resident songsters will be in full voice, and the dawn chorus is almost monopolised by them until, perhaps, the last week of the month. It is great fun to lie in bed in the early morning and make a mental list of those birds which can be recognised.

Bird song is not the only attraction now. Wild flowers and other blossoms delight the eye; the cuckoo flower appears very early on – before the arrival of its namesake; ground ivy and dog violets will be in bloom, and the flowers of blackthorn and wortleberry too. The spring sunshine and the presence of these blossoms will attract butterflies – the migrant painted lady and red admiral; the bright and frisky orange tip and the delicate holly blue; and of course, tortoiseshells, peacocks, brimstones and the speckled woods.

Toads may not spawn until early April if the last part of March has been cold and dry, and the long chains of spawn will be detected by the keen eye which searches among the pond weeds near the edges of known toad spawning grounds.

The observer who lives in adder country may, on a nice warm day towards the end of April, see one of Nature's more curious spectacles – the adder dance. This is performed by the males only. Two males will face each other and then will rear up until half their length is well off the ground. They will then twine themselves about each other, and push and sway back and forth – sometimes going on like this for quite a long time. This performance is for the purpose of establishing authority over territory

M.K.

THE VEGETABLE GARDEN

April is the busiest month for sowing. The ground has warmed up and germination becomes more rapid. Continue to sow all ordinary crops in rotation. This is essential for a supply of fresh young vegetables. Study catalogues carefully to make certain you have the right varieties for early or late sowings. Main crop peas should be of the higher type – dwarfs are more suitable for early or late work. The first week is the time for a batch of cos lettuce. Be certain to get a true self-folding variety such as Sutton's Little Gem or White Heart. Some are a snare and a delusion and never show the slightest inclination to fold themselves. Late savoys, autumn cauliflowers, leading broccoli, sprouting broccoli and kales should not be sown until the third week, otherwise bolting will occur. A small bed of pickling silverskin onion is useful.

Many beginners fight shy of asparagus. There is no need for this, provided a well-drained and richly manured plot is available. There are two main methods – from seed or from crowns, which are easily purchased. The first method is to be avoided by the amateur; germination is slow and weed control difficult. Wide beds can be used but the single-row system allows for easier cultivation and cutting. The trenches should be three feet apart and four inches deep. Crowns should be set twelve inches apart, covered with soil and well trodden in. Mark rows clearly with sticks. Some varieties may suit a locality better than others but Connover's Colossal is universally popular. It is essential to keep the weeds in check.

Another little-known vegetable which can be valuable during the winter is salsify – popular on the Continent. The culture is simple – deep non-manured soil, seed drilled in rows one foot apart and thinned out later. If the onion bed fails or the thought of isolating the tiny seedlings from a mass of weeds is more than you can bear – dig it up. Buy some frame-reared onion sets, draw shallow drills and lay them in four to six inches apart, covering with a little soil and firming well. This is probably the safest method of getting a good plant and avoids the fly menace.

Dig up leeks that are left and heel in a shady place. To those with little knowledge of chemistry the study of a fertiliser catalogue with all various formulae can be a nightmare. Be content and stick to any well-known complete fertiliser for all green vegetables at about 4 oz. per square yard. This should be well worked in before sowing or planting out.

E.B.

You can go ahead now with the principal sowings for summer crops; with the exception, of course, of those more tender subjects – beans, sweet corn, cucumbers, marrows – which must wait quite another month before being sown in the open. With crops that can be sown either in spring or autumn, such as cabbage or lettuce, it is necessary to get the correct variety for the time of year; this is usually stated on the seed packet or in the catalogue, so it is worth making sure that the seeds are the right kind before buying.

One of the pressing jobs is to provide support for peas, but there is no need to worry if you haven't any pea-sticks. These are not always easy to get, are extremely untidy in use, and encourage pests and fungi when put away. A strip of wire netting, or mesh netting stretched between light posts, is a much neater and more hygienic arrangement. You may even have given up growing peas because they are all taken by birds, and if so here is a still better way: set some bamboo canes or other supports at the end of each row, with one or two at intervals along the row if it is a long one. Make another row 18 in. away. Take a reel of black cotton and tie it to one of the supports, fairly near the ground; then work your way round the two rows of supports with the cotton, bringing it upwards and crossing it until there is sufficient for the peas, which will grow inside the enclosure, to cling to. One or two strands of twine may be necessary to give extra strength, but on the whole the black cotton will serve both as support and bird scarer. The little extra trouble of this method is amply justified when the peas are gathered.

Precautions against potato scab still seem to be experimental, and methods claimed as successful in one type of soil may be completely useless in another. For instance, the practice of planting tubers in peat or lawn mowings is not an infallible scab preventive; it is also very doubtful whether potatoes need be planted any deeper than 4 in. and whether earthing-up is necessary. Plenty of scope, here, for personal experiment. If you still want a good coloured maincrop, try *Arran Victory*, a round, pinkish-purple potato which did very well at many Somerset shows last year.

Leeks are beginning to form the spikes which will later develop into seed-balls. Leave a few plants where they are if you want to save your own seed.

Outdoor cucumbers should have the ground prepared for them with well-rotted manure and wood-ash; a light rich loam suits them best.

C.M.

———

Unless the weather is more freakish than usual, April can be regarded as the busiest general sowing month of the year. The sun should have gained sufficient strength to warm up the soil to ensure quick germination. It is absolutely essential to maintain a regular succession of sowings of such vegetables as peas, beans, carrots, lettuce, radish, etc., if they are to be eatable.

A close study of any well-known seedsman's catalogue will give varieties for production at different times, but, by keeping to the simple rule of planting another batch directly the last shows drill clearly, the dreadful business of solemnly eating through a bed of "gone to seed" lettuce and bullet-hard peas will be avoided. "Onward" and "Gradus" are main crop peas of excellent flavour, and flourish on soil which has had a spring application of hoof and horn meal. Far too little use is made of the dwarf French bean which is a splendid cropper, not too particular about soil and one of the very best vegetables going. "The Prince" is a well-tried variety but there are others well worth a trial, such as Carter's "Granada," which is a stringless, round-podded bean and retains its tenderness when well forward in growth.

There is also the climbing purple-podded variety which has a remarkable flavour but must be treated as a runner. Without doubt "Streamline" is par excellence where runners are concerned. To obtain the best results, these should be well mulched with manure when half-way up the stick to prevent the roots drying out. Another little-grown vegetable is seakale beet, the leaves being the edible part and quite comparable to spinach. The midrib of the leaf can be treated as seakale. The plants should be thinned to at least fifteen inches. A common error is the insufficient thinning of plants when small. Lettuces should be dealt with as soon as they can be safely handled. Cabbage type to at least a foot and the self-folding cos – such as "Lobjort's

Improved" – at a little less. The latter must have good soil and plenty of moisture to enable growth to be quick. Otherwise the self-folding habit is inclined to fail. Main crop potatoes should be in by the end of the month.

E.B.

THE FRUIT GARDEN

After a severe winter it is often assumed that a large number of insects will have been killed. Conversely, after a mild winter such as the one just past, an increase in the number of pests is expected. These theories are not accepted by the experts. They believe that in a consistently cold winter insects remain in a state of hibernation, little harm coming to them. On the other hand, mild spells induce premature development of the life cycle before the food supplies of the insects are available. This, linked with the possibility of further cold weather results in a sharp reduction in numbers.

If Nature could be relied upon to give a helping hand in some seasons the need for spraying programmes would not be so great. As things stand, however, regular spraying is imperative if really clean crops are to be gathered. During April, the majority of spraying is against diseases rather than pests although the Gall Mite causing Big Bud in blackcurrants should be dealt with. This is done with a lime sulphur spray at ½ pint of lime sulphur to 2 gallons of water applied before the trusses of flowers open. At this time the trusses resemble bunches of grapes hence the technical term of "Grape-Bud Stage."

With gooseberries the most troublesome disease is American Gooseberry Mildew which later in the season results in a thick, felty, white covering on leaves and fruit. By spraying in April with lime sulphur (½ pint of lime sulphur to 2½ gallons of water) any outbreak can be checked immediately. Yellow-fruited varieties are intolerant of this treatment and should be sprayed with washing soda at ½ lb. to 2½ gallons of water plus 2 oz. of soft soap. Where the caterpillars of Winter Moth or Gooseberry Sawfly are troublesome derris may be added to the above sprays at the rate quoted in the makers' instructions.

Turning to apples, lime sulphur can be used to check the appearance of Apple Scab. Here it should be applied at both the "green cluster" and "pink bud" stages. Both applications are at the same strength as for Gooseberry Mildew and in this case the sulphur shy varieties include "St. Cecilia" and "Stirling Castle." Here again derris can be added in case of early caterpillar infestations.

Cloching Strawberries: Although it is late in the season for cloching, strawberries can still be forced. The cloches should be put on at once and kept tightly closed until really warm days are experienced. It is not essential to straw plants grown in this way, as the fruit keeps clean and dry.

G. R.W.

191

———◆———

Obtaining the maximum: In many gardens there is the problem of the old tree which does not fruit, although it appears healthy and blossoms quite freely. If the tree is a variety worthy of retention this trouble can often be overcome. Such a tree may be self-sterile and so needs pollen from another variety to fertilise its flowers. Of course, the trees must in every instance be of the same kind, that is apple to pollinate apple and so on. In fixing a pollinator it is necessary to choose varieties which will flower at the same time, and ones which are also compatible with each other. The whole question of pollination is a complex one, and detailed information can be found tabulated in such publications as *The Fruit Garden Displayed* and in John Innes' leaflet *Fertility Rules in Fruit Planting.*

Reverting to our unfruitful specimen, two further points are worth mentioning. Trees planted expressly as pollinators should not be more than fifteen feet apart if one is to ensure complete fertilisation. This point is stressed because it has been proved in recent years that bees tend to confine their visits to one tree until the source of nectar there is exhausted.

Before taking the permanent step of actually planting another tree as pollinator, however, a simple experiment can be carried out this spring. At flowering time secure a few jars filled with water to the tree and into these place some flowering shoots of several other varieties. If one of these is a suitable pollinator then a marked difference in the crop will be noted.

The case also arises of the tree which grows vigorously at the expense of blossom. Where apples and pears are concerned such excessive vigour may be counteracted by root pruning in the dormant season or by the less strenuous practice of bark ringing. The latter can be mentioned now, as it is best performed at flowering time, preferably by an expert, especially if one is not really familiar with the operation. This consists of removing the bark to the inner hard wood in a complete ring around the main trunk to a width not exceeding a quarter of an inch and decreasing proportionally according to the girth of the tree. Immediately afterwards the wound should be covered by two or three layers of adhesive tape to assist healing. Never coat the wound with any form of paint.

Where plums, cherries and other stone fruits are concerned, bark ringing is not the answer. The reason for this is their susceptibility to Silver Leaf and Bacterial Canker, both of which enter the tree through wounds and snags. The recognised way of controlling vigour here is by root pruning during the winter months.

G.R.W.

THE FLOWER GARDEN

Early April affords the last opportunity until the autumn for planting shrubs and herbaceous plants. Evergreen shrubs can be safely moved providing every precaution is taken to avoid undue disturbance of the roots. When in position they should be securely staked and never allowed to become dry, but if a dry spell should follow, the occasional spraying of their foliage will help their rapid establishment. Crowded clumps of herbaceous plants and Alpines may be divided with considerable success this month for the increased warmth in the soil promotes rapid root action, and the shock of moving is soon overcome. Hardy Annuals should be sown and in the milder districts the hardier bedding plants can be put out at the end of the month.

When applying selected weedkillers to a weedy lawn, remember that both weeds and grass must be growing strongly when treated, otherwise the results may be disappointing. The application of a good fertiliser about a fortnight before treatment not only increases the growth of the weeds but also enables the grass to cover quickly any bare patches left after their destruction. For the more persistent weeds two applications may be necessary and these should be about three weeks apart. Great care is necessary where plants immediately adjoin the lawn for untold damage can be done by the drifting of these highly volatile preparations in even the slightest breeze. The grass should not be mown just before or after the weedkiller is applied.

One of the loveliest sights in springtime are the Japanese Flowering Cherries which have become so popular in our gardens and streets. They present few difficulties in cultivation although many prefer a limey soil. They are rather prone to fungoid attack and if any pruning should become necessary the wound should be carefully trimmed and sealed over. One of the very finest varieties is Tai Haku with pure white flowers, and this makes a fine contrast with the ever-popular pink Kanzan. Prunus Sargentii is supreme if spring flower and autumn colour are required. There will only be room for perhaps two varieties in most gardens but if a further selection is required, Shirotae, Ukon, and Shimidsu Sakura can be recommended.

Excepting for Rhododendrons, Camellias are the most handsome of our spring flowering evergreens. They need a lime free soil, a little shade from the hottest sun and some moisture during the summer months. They thrive in a peaty soil in the semi-shade of deciduous trees.

C.P.

———·•·———

Deciduous trees and shrubs can be planted any time from autumn until early spring providing weather and soil conditions are suitable. Evergreens are more difficult, owing to the constant loss of moisture from the leaves, which cannot be replenished quickly enough by the damaged and inactive roots of a plant moved in the winter. Increased root activity this month provides the opportunity to do any necessary transplanting of evergreen shrubs. Lift them carefully with as much soil as possible and after planting water freely for a few days. In fact, they must not be allowed to become excessively dry during the coming summer. If hot weather follows planting, syringe the leaves daily with tepid water, whilst the use of temporary shading on any special plants will help ensure success. Owing to this difficulty in planting it is best to purchase evergreens which have been pot grown.

Sweet peas raised from seed in frames may now be planted in permanent positions which have been previously thoroughly prepared. The seedlings should be about nine inches apart and suffer as little root disturbance as possible. In the early part of the month seeds can be sown where the plants are to bloom if this less elaborate method is employed. An open sunny situation is necessary and a deeply dug soil which has been moderately manured will give the best results.

The full beauty and grace of the water lily is often lost through overcrowding, for a certain amount of clear water is essential if they are to be seen to their greatest advantage. They need to be divided every three years, retaining only the young growing portion of the tuberous root. The soil in the baskets, tubs, or mounds of earth in which they are usually planted should be replaced by fresh fibrous turf. Firm the plants well when replanting, otherwise they will be lifted by the water. Whilst the water is out of the pond keep the plants moist and shaded by the use of damp sacks.

The young shoots of many herbaceous plants afford a ready means of propagation. Cuttings placed in a cold frame containing a sandy compost will soon root, and the young plants can then be transferred to a nursery bed until required in the main borders. Hardy plants which have been rooted from cuttings such as violas and pentstemons can be planted out to take their place in the general summer display. The young shoots of many newly planted herbaceous plants and annuals are often very subject to the attention of vermin, but the new rat and mouse destroyer "Aidrey X77" if used in accordance with the makers' instructions gives excellent results.

C.P.

U NDER GLASS: Pot on seedlings and cuttings as necessary. Sow *Primula sinensis* (Pink Enchantress is an excellent new variety) for next season. Be sure to sow thinly and only cover the seed very slightly. Cinerarias may be sown this month for Christmas flowering.

IN THE OPEN: Continue to plant gladioli and montbretias. Finish planting herbaceous perennials as early as possible in the month, watering freely if ground is at all dry. Delphiniums grow rapidly in April if weather is not too cold and dry. All thin and weakly growths are best removed when about fifteen inches high, cuts being made a few inches above the soil level to avoid damaging the crown. Plants that are very forward may require staking (bella-donnas excepted) – stake when growths are about 3 ft. tall.

Rose pruning should be finished by the end of the first week in April – pruning later often causes the plants to bleed. After pruning give established trees a mulch of hop manure, peat or farmyard manure. Watch for the first signs of greenfly, especially on climbers and ramblers, which are usually more forward than bushes or standards, and spray with "Sybol," derris or nicotine.

Prepare borders or beds for planting out early-flowering chrysanthemums next month. A south or south-east aspect is ideal, as they appreciate plenty of sun. Incorporate well-rotted farmyard manure at the rate of one barrow-load to about fifteen square yards, plus bonemeal at about four ounces per square yard. Soil preparation should be finished not less than three weeks before planting to allow the soil time to consolidate.

Directly *Prunus triloba plena* has finished blooming, cut back flowering shoots fairly hard. Continue to sow hardy annuals such as clarkias, godetias, larkspur, mignonette, etc. Seedlings sown at the end of March may now be thinned. Make a further sowing of sweet peas. Where no greenhouse or frame is available, start dahlia tubers into growth at the end of the month in boxes of light soil outdoors. Keep the soil moist and protect at night, as dahlias are susceptible to the slightest touch of frost. The clumps may be broken into three or four portions, each with an eye. This is best delayed until the shoots are about three inches long. Do not plant out until early June.

LAWNS: Though new lawns may be sown this month, or May, according to temperature, early September is usually preferable, as the soil is warmer and less dry and germination is consequently more satisfactory.

N.P.H.

FISHING

April is a month of variable weather. The fisherman must suit his tactics to its moods. I always associate this showery, sometimes blustery, period with the wet-fly trout fisherman. How delightful to stroll some four miles down a Devonshire stream, flicking a couple of flies beneath overhanging branches into likely eddies, with the knowledge that, if there is no response, about midday the trout should rise.

On a still day the flat at the tail of a pool appears like a mirror and a cast upon it produces a series of waves upstream and at the most a fingerling flung by the recovery stroke past an ear into the brambles behind. But when a strong wind makes waves upon the surface how different the result. Then the best method is to cast well towards the opposite bank and pull in the line in short sharp jerks with the thumb and forefinger of the left hand; it is most effective especially in the mill leat above the mill itself, where on other days only a dry-fly will yield results.

Do not despair if the wind is in the east. On the contrary I have often witnessed a great hatch of fly when conditions are supposed to be "fit for neither man nor beast." The Iron Blue particularly favours cold days, when the nor'-easter sweeps the valley. Try the pulling in method across the big pool below the mill. You will certainly have more rises and pulls than by leaving the flies to fish themselves.

It is strange how quickly even a beginner (if left to himself) will learn where to expect a fish. That tiny backwater below the steep bank under the alder will either hold a big fellow or nothing. There, where the fast water slows up and splits to pass a rock, is a sure take, both above and downstream of the obstruction.

The light seems to play a part in wet-fly operations. The veteran will know that when the surface looks "steely" his success will be limited, while when the water appears black he will catch fish. This certainly applies to salmon fishing. The "steely" appearance is a form of glare caused by the sun, the blackness a uniformity of shadow. For all such signs the experienced angler is ready.

The salmon fisher will suit the selection of his fly or lure and his method of approach to the vicissitudes of the elements. On them he is much dependent and in April often more so than in other months. At an early age I had a poem published:

> "If weather, water, wind combine
> To grant my earnest wish
> And Walton wield my rod and line
> E'en I may catch a fish."

R.B.

———————

THIS is the month for the salmon fisher and wet fly trout man, for Lent lilies and primroses on a Devonshire bank where bushes provide natural bunkers and trees plenty of climbing in search of casts and favourite flies. Here the young angler will learn accurate casting (or lose much tackle). Here he will learn the difference between trout and salmon parr, trout and smolt. Remember – *Eyes*: Parr's larger in comparison; draw, in imagination, a perpendicular line from back of eye downward. Trout: line will pass through maxillary bone. Parr: line will pass behind and not touch maxillary. *Tail*: Trout: nearly square. Parr: forked. *Spots*: Trout: all over. Parr: none below median line. *Adipose fin*: Trout: tinged orange or red. Parr: lacks these colours. *Finger marks* of parr very pronounced and even. Trout: irregular. When hooked parr wriggle much more.

Smolts ready to go seaward are parr in silver livery. Put back parr and smolts (and under-nourished trout). Trout flies for West Country: Blue Upright, Red Upright, Half Stone, Rusty Red and Roy's Fancy (Blue hackle in front of fiery brown hackle, gold body, blue tail).

Go salmon fishing with a thermometer. If river temperature above 45 deg. (and air warmer) try greased line. The warmer air compared to water, the better chance. Bigger difference in temperature, the smaller the fly. On dull days try Black Fairy. (*Wing*: Hen pheasant. *Hackle*: Black. *Body*: Black mohair whipped with silver or gold tinsel. *Tail*: Golden pheasant topping). For April I prefer Anthony Crossley type bug-like flies to bare hooks and little dressing. Devonshire salmon like claret-coloured flies. Try this: *Wing*: Hen pheasant. *Hackle*: Claret. *Body*: Claret mohair whipped gold tinsel. *Tail*: Golden pheasant. When water and air very cold fish sunk fly with sunk line or spin. In very high-coloured water try a plain pike spoon – most effective on Taw and Irish Slaney. I like brown and gold or silver and blue wooden minnows with celluloid or perspex fins. In high water a reflex (flat sided) silver or gold Devon. Gold always a good colour in peaty rivers, where yellow flies such as Torrish and Canary both good in dirty water with sunk line. My Canary I dress like this: *Wing*: Golden pheasant topping cut square at back with scissors. *Hackle*: Yellow. *Body*: Yellow mohair whipped with gold tinsel. *Tail*: Golden pheasant topping.

On some rivers gaffs are not allowed until the end of April. The tailer, the hand or the net are the alternatives. The tailer with its wire noose is a serviceable weapon until when playing fish you make a bad shot and spring it. Then the devil to set it again with one hand and play the fish with the other.

R.B.

———•—•———

THIS is the month which can be heaven or hell, according to how you do your fishing. For the coarse angler it is the start of the long, black ache that lasts until June 16th. For the fly-fisher, April is the rebirth.

The fishing books offer the coarse angler poor consolation in his loss. He is told to varnish his rods, paint his floats, oil his reels. But this is like suggesting to the opium-smoker that he try herbal cigarettes. Might not the float-fisher make it his April resolution to go out and catch a trout? Years of propaganda have persuaded him that fly-fishing is difficult. Bunkum! Any good roach man can learn enough in a day, if not to catch a fish, then, to enjoy himself; and that, surely, is what fishing is about. He may further be told that he needs to be an expert entomologist. Bunkum to that, also. Here's all he need know about flies in April.

On chalk streams (a privileged beginner this) he will see two flies that sit the river with their wings folded vertically, the Olive and the Iron Blue. Hare's Ear or Greenwell's Glory will do nicely for the first while a smaller, darker Greenwell will imitate the second. The little Iron Blue appears very dark on the water and is frequently taken in preference to anything else. For rougher streams, choice of fly is simple. On Exmoor, for example, where local guidance will say Blue Upright or Half-Stone, I have found that you can throw the entire contents of the fly-box at these sparkling brook trout and still catch them. Fish dry with a short line for maximum fun. The newcomer should know that the March Brown and Grannom (end of the month) are much in demand on some streams.

My own trout ambition? To catch a silver Thames monster. By the way, isn't this the perfect answer for the London coarse angler river-starved after March 14th? Chances are slim, but the prize is great; besides, one *is* fishing, and fishing at the crown of the year, too. (Memo to self: renew Thames Conservancy Weir Permit, cost £1). Actually, if I do get my Thames trout, it will be not by spinning from the weir apron but through the good offices of an acquaintance with a riverside bungalow. He will tip me off where and when my fish feeds, and then, at the right moment, I shall float it down a live minnow. Unfair, you say, to enlist a second party? Almost anything's fair in Thames trout fishing.

On salmon and the sea trout rivers that permit its use this early in the year, the fixed-spool reel will be doing its deadly work. A word to new users: no matter who told you that the secret of this reel is to wind *against* the fish and thus tire it, forget it. Nothing is more fatal. Play your fish with the clutch three-quarter tight, and kill him *by finger pressure on the spool*.

C.W.

FALLOW DEER

Sixty years ago there were over 70,000 fallow deer in the parks of England. Their number has since declined to less than a seventh of that total. Deer parks, and the people who can afford to keep them, are growing fewer every year. Yet, far from being in danger of extinction in these islands, fallow are continually increasing – in the wild.

Wild fallow deer were rare before the 1914 war. During that war, and the following one, a great many parks were occupied by the military. The result, more often than not, was that large numbers of deer escaped through open gates and damaged fences.

In greater or lesser numbers they now occur in almost every English county. They are found, too, in parts of Wales. They are common on numerous Scottish estates, and in many parts of Ireland. From the New Forest to Sutherland they range at will in the majority of woodlands which are large enough and quiet enough – apart from the organised drives – to give them food and shelter.

In the woods they behave very differently than their forebears did in the parks. They go about in fives and sixes rather than large herds. Persecution has a lot to do with this, as it has with the fact that wild fallow are much more nocturnal than their tame brethren, especially in summer. Late evening and dawn are the best times of day to see them.

Once they have settled down in the wild, they are not much given to seeking pastures new. A railway or a three-mile stretch of open land is usually more than enough to limit their travels – except in the rut. A buck in search of a harem will sometimes trek as far as twenty miles to cool his ardours. He is normally content, though, with some half a dozen wives. These he will defend against all-comers with more of show than real pugnacity, but it is as well on these occasions to treat him with a certain amount of respect. I know at least one countryman who claims to have been "treed" for over an hour by a bad-tempered buck which he met in a Wiltshire wood one October morning!

The rutting-season is short, and reaches its peak about October 25. The fawns are born in May or June. One fawn at a time is usual, but twins are on record from one or two localities.

The colours of adult fallow vary from herd to herd, and often within the herd itself. New Forest fallow are chestnut brown in winter and spotted fawn in summer. Those of Epping Forest are almost black at all times of the year. In the past many other colours were evolved by selective breeding. There are even some blue fallow running wild in one part of Dorset. Menil is a commoner shade. White fallow are far from rare. They occur as "sports" among herds of other hues, and one or two all-white herds still exist in parks.

Whatever their colour, wild fallow add much of beauty to the woods. If the woods are too small, or their numbers too large, it is true that they can cause havoc among root crops and young plantations. But the damage done by a small herd in a large wood of well-grown timber, where there is plenty of natural food in the form of rough herbage, is almost nil.

P.H.C.

THE SCOTTISH KITCHEN

In the deep country, where it may be difficult to get really fresh sea-fish, it is well to remember that there is one of these which is all the better of having been kept for a day or two in clean conditions. This is the skate. The skate is despised only by those who don't know how much nutriment is in it, or how many ways it can be served up deliciously. If a leaf cannot here be taken out of the book of the French – who even turn skate out baked in pastry – a page about the fish may be lifted from that of the Scots. And let none whisper about Scots plagiary. There are plenty of elaborate recipes for skate in old English cookery-books. Too elaborate. Let us approach the matter simply.

You may, if you choose, bone the fish with a sharp knife, having first removed both skins. This is to lose the sapidity which is in the bones and the white skin. Cut the wing into pieces suitable for serving, and poach them gently for about quarter of an hour, from tepid, either in a nice bouillon previously prepared, or else in plain salted water with a bunch of herbs, some white pepper, and a touch of crushed mace or grated nutmeg. When done, drain, and keep hot.

There are several ways of saucing skate to serve. One is to pour over it roasted (wrongly called "black") butter to which has been added wine vinegar, chopped parsley and capers. Another is to pound the liver (cooked with the fish) with cold butter, adding lemon juice, salt and pepper, and a faint touch of mixed spice, simply placing a pat of this on top of the hot fish. If, however, you can find a few cobnuts or hazels, crush these finely, and gently simmer them in as much butter as is needed for as long as it takes to cook the skate, never letting the butter colour to deeper brown than the nutshells. Add salt and white pepper while cooking, strain, then add cautiously as much lemon juice as will only faintly sharpen the sauce. Serve separately. And, as my old friend Rafael Sabatini used to say when he poured for me a glass of his Cheval Blanc, 1929: "Give me news of that!"

Incidentally, there is no fish better than the skate for filling a case of pastry. All one does is chop up the flesh of the cooked fish, bind it with a liaison of the nut-butter, a little flour. and a little of the cooking liquor with some extra seasoning, and put this mixture cold into patty-pans (or a round pie dish) lined thinly with either short or puff pastry, cover and bake nicely. Delicious for that first picnic of the year.

With rabbit under suspicion, away from butcher-meat there is little to which the home-caterer can turn these days for variety, unless it be to something from cold storage or imported, like the hazel-hen. And that, almost certain to have been chilled, is unfit for roasting. It can only be treated by braising in the pot, or poached as suggested for the guinea-fowl last month. And I'm afraid both chicken and duckling ought still to be left to grow a little.

Choice, then, would appear to rest in the vegetable garden, and that suggests seakale. It ought to be, if unforced, full of flavour at the moment. To preserve that flavour it is better steamed, and then it wants an unpronounced sauce if the flavour is not to be killed. My nut-butter here begs to be tried with it, though honestly I've never used it so myself. Plain nut-brown butter with a touch of lemon, yes. But, as variation is here the theme, I put forward something that I have myself succeeded with. This is to tie the prepared seakale in a bundle and, instead of steaming it for the full fifty minutes needed ordinarily, to give it only about thirty then lay it out, drained, on a buttered baking dish. Using some of the valuable liquor resulting from the steaming with an equal amount of clear, not over-flavoured meat-broth, I made a white sauce finished off with a little grated Gruyere and some thin cream. This went over the seakale which finished cooking in a fairly hot oven, the sauce being nicely browned on top. I can remember nothing that goes so surprisingly well with roast shoulder of lamb.

The thought of pastry for the skate pie brought into my mind one of those Scots "Flory" things that came to us from Florence through the French Court. It is made with prunes. The prunes, stoned, are simmered gently until cooked in a syrup – just enough – of sugar and water with a touch of cinnamon and grated zest of lemon. Towards the last, a squeeze of lemon juice is added, with a good tablespoon of port to the pound of prunes. Finish cooking, and allow to cool. Line a shallow round tart-pan with puff-paste, put in the prunes, cover with a lid of puff paste and pinch orthodoxly to the underpart. Prick slightly, glaze and ornament to fancy. Bake judiciously – it won't take long. The name will be apparent. Prune Flory.

V.M.

IN PRAISE OF NETTLES

Why do we make an enemy of a plant like the nettle that is the giver of abundant health and vitality? And how strange to ignore, from the same source, a free supply of animal fodder said to be higher in food content than the best Lucerne! Not only do we fail to appreciate *Urtica dioica*, we even go to considerable expense to exterminate it. Yet this particular displaced plant (for a weed is merely a plant out of place) has some exceptional merits.

Urtica has the ability, to an astounding degree, of taking up every substance in the soil, thereby passing on to its consumer an extra allowance of iron, copper, sodium, lime and other essentials for purifying and nourishing the human and animal system. No wonder that letters are written to *The Times*, claiming it as a cure for skin troubles – even boils – and asserting its unequalled value as a food-stuff for highly bred stock herds. Cattle relish nettles left to wilt for twenty-four hours, while pigs and poultry can have them simmered to the consistency of cooked spinach. Indeed, this is sometimes how we are told to cook them for ourselves, but the liquid form is much more enjoyable.

Take a glove and a pair of scissors, then search where the leafmould lies thick at the end of the garden, or beyond the garden gate. Find the clear green, vital shoots, as yet not more than a few inches high, snip off the growing tips, take a bunch in your gloved hand, or wrap them in a dock leaf if you left the glove behind. (You will always find docks where there are nettles.) Take them indoors and submerge in cold water for a short while; rinse and shake into a saucepan. Cover with cold water, bring to the boil and simmer until the water has reduced itself by about a third. Now strain into some container which can be kept for this purpose, for the liquid will stain any cup or jug it stands in. Experience will soon result in getting the strength that is liked, but the finished product should be amber and clear as apple jelly, with no floating specks. Drink it freshly made, a wine glass full night and morning, for at least ten days together. Later in the year the make-up of the nettle alters and it has not so much to offer, so make full use of the young ones in early spring.

C.M.

THE ENTOMOLOGIST

First out from their winter hibernation among the bees, wasps and ants of Britain are the bumble-bees, of which we have seventeen species. All are social bees; they make and provision nests and tend their young, an endearing trait, which they share with the honey-bees and the social wasps.

Bumble-bees' nests are hard to discover, for the mother-bee is apt to employ misleading tactics when searching for a site. She will creep into a crevice and spend several minutes investigating the interior, only to desert it, flying away across some hedge where we lose her from sight. The buff-tailed bumble-bee is perhaps one of the bees most easily tracked down to her nest-site which she may choose in a hollow in a bank, shady spots being preferred. Coming out of this cavity she hangs in the air a foot or two away, her wings vibrating rapidly – darts to left, then to right – memorising landmarks so that she may in future recognise the entrance to her home. Then she goes inside for spring-cleaning.

Inside the cave there is a litter of moss and of dry grass which has first to be cleared and flattened into a saucer-like depression. The mother-bee places on this foundation a small circular dish of food – nectar and pollen mixed with her saliva – and on the pottage she deposits her first batch of eggs, fathered by the male bee with whom she paired last autumn before retiring for her winter's rest. Round the eggs she builds, and seals, a wall made of wax secreted in tiny flakes from the plates of the upper side of her abdomen. In the intervals of foraging she sits upon these eggs, and in order that she may not starve on cold days she builds, close to the first, a second cell in the form of an urn or pot, and fills it with nectar.

In a few days the eggs hatch into white larvae, which feed upon the mass of food provided by their careful mother. These larvae are full-grown in about a week. Then they spin upright cocoons and in them become nymphs or pupa; pearly white at first, darkening as they develop and showing, now, the head, six legs, the thorax and rotund abdomen of the future bee. The wings are as yet rudimentary flaps folded flat down upon the body.

The bees that in due course emerge are all workers, sterile females that may never pair, though they may, in emergency, reproduce their kind parthenogenetically, as may the worker of the honey-bee. These first daughters are smaller in size than the sisters that hatch in relays from the second and further batches of eggs laid by the Queen. Egg-laying now becomes her sole business; foraging, cell-building, the care of young, all is now handed over to the worker bees. The daughters run the home; the family being increased, as the season advances, by perfect females – Queens-to-be – and males that fly in autumn and mate with the season's young Queen bees.

Thus the humble-bee colony develops, founded and peopled by the Queen, managed during its first stages by her unaided efforts. Increase by swarming, as evinced by the honey-bees, is a later development on the history of the race.

Bumble shows us some of the first bee homes; she also shows us the ancient stages in the development of polymorphism – that is, the difference in form and in function in members of one colony: the division into castes.

The social bees produce one winged form of the worker in addition to the fertile Queen and the male. All colonies of bees, wasps and ants are more or less permanent families of females; the male representing merely a fertilising agency which is active at the moment it becomes necessary to start other colonies.

V.T.

WHAT EVERY COOK
SHOULD KNOW ABOUT

TROUT

The trout, like its near relation, the salmon, is one of the freshwater fish whose arrangement of bones is fairly simple and provides few difficulties for the consumer with dental appliances. Most of our freshwater fish are not really worth bothering about. Unless you are something of a student of anatomy and have the delicate skill of a surgeon you will find nearly all coarse fish inedible because of their luxuriation of small bones, and if they do not "taste of the smell" of mud they have all the charm of a piece of old and fibrous flannel.

The trouble about trout is that they do not keep very well

and, though really fresh newly caught trout are delightful, trout travelling by our British Railways are edible but astonishingly savourless after the journey. Nevertheless they are a welcome sight in these days! They are also extremely variable in qualities and flavour, which I think depends on the water they live in. The average Scotch or Devon trout is delightful, but I consider some of the Hampshire trout insipid and some lake trout are also disappointing. There is no real standard of taste for trout as they vary so widely, but from a cooking point of view it is rather a nuisance, as the newly caught trout from a good river (in the gastronomic sense) needs no sauce, but some little accompaniment is necessary to help out the larger and more flannelly specimens from waters regarded as holy by anglers and with rather a bleak eye by gastronomers.

There are two simple ways of cooking trout. They can be "steamed," which is best accomplished by putting a pile of saucers into a large saucepan and resting the trout a little above the water level and simmering, or they can be split down the tummy and broiled on a grill. Both these simple processes involve absolutely precise timing and relatively slow heating but, as time varies with the size of the fish and many variables, the best thing to do is to behead your fish and, feeling delicately with a fork, you can tell after some experience when the backbone and other bones are loose.

It's a matter of timing and experience and in the wilds of Devon, where the three-quarter-pound trout is rather on the high side for "breakfast fish," they are fried in bacon fat with a saucepan lid which more or less fits the frying pan dropped over them, so that one side is being steamed while the other is being fried in hot fat. Three to four minutes is enough as a rule. It is quite easy to spoil trout by over-cooking. They are the most sensitive subjects and should be cooked as little as possible.

Some trout are almost salmon pink, others grade through the various degrees of face powders, but I honestly doubt whether the colour has any relation to flavour. A red trout may look better and so approaching salmon seem more desirable, but I think it is an illusion, as rather pale little "Burns Trout" are often sublime in their perfection of flavour where some larger and redder trout is, despite his colour – or perhaps because of it – wholly insipid.

In the Lower Baltic area they smoke a trout, which is delightful, but they also have a custom which would not appeal to our Min. of Health. They allow trout to decay in pots with salt, sugar and spices, and all Finns and Latvians have, so to speak, a cult of extremely decayed trout which is horrible on first acquaintance but rather grows on one as one acclimatises. I think you can do this sort of thing in a reliably cold climate, but I am not at all certain that it could be done in England, where the wrong sort of bacteria might get a lead.

Now the delicate flavour of trout needs really no sauce when prepared, but with flannelly trout a sharpened mayonnaise or hollandaise goes best. Actually a cold mayonnaise with a very little good tarragon vinegar in it will redeem flavourless or even frozen rainbow trout.

To make small trout look important they should be dusted with coarse oatmeal and sautéed in a deepish pan with bacon fat. The bread for the support of these fishlings should be cooked to a light surface yellow in the bacon fat first.

Owing to their perishable nature few people send trout as gifts, but they will tolerate a quick journey if kept cool in very damp paper. If packed in nettles or seaweed they taste of nettles or weed, and the first wrap should be of clean greaseproof paper as otherwise they may "taste of the smell" of printer's ink.

The "Truite au Bleu" is the classic French way of cooking trout and is simple. Make a saucepan full of half wine vinegar (it *must* be wine vinegar, not malt) half water; in this simmer chopped onion, thyme, peppercorns and a bay leaf. When this marinade is powerfully flavoured, it should have at least half an hour's preparation, strain out the solids and bringing it to a brisk boil cook your trout in it at simmering for not more than four to five minutes. The marinade can be kept for further use and a hollandaise or plain rum butter sauce can accompany the trout.

In Spain, trout are cooked in a similar marinade to which is added both olive oil and about half a cupful of honey. The fish are filleted and steeped in the mixture for an hour, then some of the marinade is made into a sauce and the filleted fish, wrapped in paper, is cooked in oil. It is a peculiar dish but a "sweet sour" sauce is rather a help if the fish are of the insipid variety. In Austria, trout are usually served with fat bacon and tomatoes but I have not found it a really happy combination.

On the whole the simplest sauces are the best and with a little rum butter and a slice of lemon you have probably the best of all.

Lastly, cold trout in aspic is a splendid summer dish and no fish is easier to fillet. Very little flavour is needed in the aspic; lemon juice and a little tarragon vinegar and discs of cucumber will provide all that is necessary.

H.B.C.P.

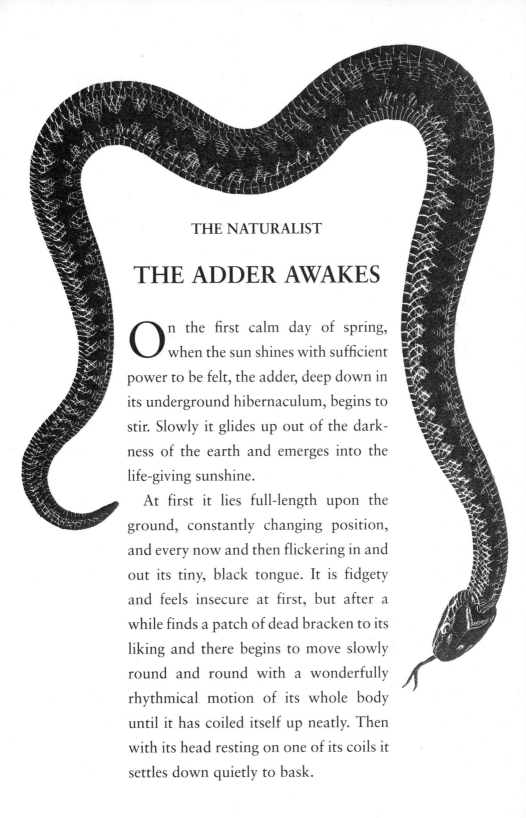

THE ADDER AWAKES

On the first calm day of spring, when the sun shines with sufficient power to be felt, the adder, deep down in its underground hibernaculum, begins to stir. Slowly it glides up out of the darkness of the earth and emerges into the life-giving sunshine.

At first it lies full-length upon the ground, constantly changing position, and every now and then flickering in and out its tiny, black tongue. It is fidgety and feels insecure at first, but after a while finds a patch of dead bracken to its liking and there begins to move slowly round and round with a wonderfully rhythmical motion of its whole body until it has coiled itself up neatly. Then with its head resting on one of its coils it settles down quietly to bask.

For full twenty minutes the adder lies thus without movement, until the sun has warmed its body right through. Now it begins to stir once more, gliding slowly over the bracken for a short distance before stopping again. Its raised head droops again on to the warm bracken as it relaxes beneath the sun's warm caress. But a moment later it raises its head, and opens wide its jaws in a prodigious yawn revealing the two poison fangs which are erected in their white fleshy sheaths. Then comes a second even wider yawn, and as the jaws close the adder's whole body gives a violent, sideways jerk, which lifts part of the body clean off its bracken bed. It is as if the reptile had received a sudden electric shock. The adder itself appears a little surprised by this happening but soon forgets it and settles down to sun bask.

Presently a faint rustling sound is to be heard, and soon a lizard comes creeping jerkily from the heart of a large tuft of dry grass. Slowly the lizard comes over the ground, looking cautiously from side to side, and stopping ever and anon to cock its head on one side like a dog, and all the while drawing closer to the basking adder. Like the adder the lizard loves the sun and it too succumbs to the warm rays. Lying flat on its belly with legs stretched out backwards alongside its tiny body it closes its eyes and gives itself up to the glorious warmth so long denied it. But soon the lizard is wide awake again and, as if it had suddenly remembered the urgency of its journey, sets off on its way.

So still and quiet lies the adder that the lizard does not even notice it. Gradually it draws close to the adder, rustling as it makes its way over the dead bracken. The adder hears nothing, for it is deaf; but its eyes catch sight of the lizard as it passes close by. In a flash the adder's head turns, and it stares hard with its slit-shaped eyes at the lizard, which stares back, the sides of its body heaving quickly in and out. The adder continues to stare, waiting for the lizard to move again, and its black, forked tongue comes flickering out for an instant and then disappears. It is protruded again, stretched to its full length and waved more slowly this time, up over the head and then down under the chin. The tongue is withdrawn and the adder begins to move toward the lizard which stands transfixed as if unable to move. Stealthily, almost imperceptibly the adder glides forward over the rust brown bracken, getting nearer and still nearer to the motionless lizard.

In an instant the lizard is gone, disappearing with a quick rustle into a grass tuft. Immediately the adder dashes forward in pursuit, and it also disappears inside the tuft of grass. Presently it reappears, moving more slowly now and poking about with its snout amongst the grass like a short-sighted old gentleman hunting for his spectacles. It has obviously lost track of the lizard and for a moment appears nonplussed. It raises its head high out of the grass and looks about, but still no sign of the elusive lizard. The adder lowers its head, slides forward over the ground for a short distance, and then freezes into immobility.

Several minutes pass. The adder does not move, and no lizard appears. A rustling sound is at last heard, and the lizard now comes jerkily into view. It comes on slowly, back the way it came, apparently unaware of the adder who appears not to notice it. As if suddenly afraid the lizard makes a quick little dash over the ground, and then stops a few inches short of the adder's nose. The adder's head snaps round and its stony gaze is levelled at the hesitant lizard, which stares back, body pulsing with apprehension.

The adder moves towards the lizard which immediately turns to flee. But it is a fraction of a second too late, and with lightning speed the adder strikes. The lizard is momentarily knocked off balance, but does not pause in its hurried flight, and in a moment is gone from sight.

The adder does not go in pursuit, but waits, remaining quite still, confident in the lethal power of the venom it has injected into the lizard.

Again the lizard makes its appearance, moving very slowly now and obviously with considerable effort. It staggers laboriously out into the open, pausing for a moment to open wide its jaws, from which a drop of blood emerges and falls to the earth. It does this several times before reaching a small clump of short heather, hidden from the adder's sight, into which it disappears.

Meanwhile the adder waits on until another full minute has gone by, and then, at last, it begins to stir. It flows over the uneven ground and disappears into the tuft of grass into which the lizard took shelter after having been bitten. In a few seconds the adder reappears and with its tongue working rapidly, goes in the direction taken by the lizard. On coming to the first drop of blood left by the lizard it stops and presses its snout to the ground like a bloodhound. The head is then raised and the forked tongue oscillated slowly as before, in an attempt to pick up any scent particles in the air which would betray the lizard's whereabouts. On again goes the adder unhurriedly, stopping at every bloodstain on the ground and surrounding herbage until at last it reaches the clump of heather wherein the lizard now lies dead. The adder enters the heather clump, and there follows a continuous rustling noise, and then silence.

Ten minutes have passed before the adder again appears, now with a slight bulge in its armoured body. Still the sun shines, and the adder, after yawning twice, settles down to bask.

L.G.A.

NATURALIST

RATS

There are probably fifty million rats in the country, each needing fifty pounds of food a year; of which fully half comes from our larder. They also destroy five times as much as they eat, for they never make a proper meal of anything, but leave it at once for something identical. In a granary a single rat will bite into a dozen sacks, causing further loss by spillage, and for each grain eaten six are bitten and discarded. Rats will eat anything, including all forms of grain, vegetables, fruit, young trees, meat, including their own dead, eggs and young of poultry and game, garbage, pig food, roots and potatoes in pits, poultry-food left in the runs overnight, and meals set down for dogs and cats. Also, like squirrels, they hoard; ten or fifteen pounds of otherwise useful food being stuffed into some hole or crevice and forgotten.

Damage to inedible property is equally great, as they seek entry everywhere. Even when they are not eating they are driven to commit damage by the irritation of their rapidly growing teeth. This makes them attack lead pipes, releasing water and gas, if the pipe is not old and too impregnated to make it distasteful; and many a rat has been found asphyxiated by the hole it has made. Their attacks on electric cables lead to fires. But much of their havoc seems to be wanton. They will chew along the backs of a row of books, or take a single bite from each one of a pile of a dozen cloth caps. They love paper, and cause ruination among parchments and manuscripts; to say nothing of secret hoards of banknotes under floors and behind skirtings. Each rat is reckoned to eat and destroy annually about one pound's worth of food. With a further pound each for the property damaged, the figure reaches one hundred million pounds.

Breeding at three months, they produce three litters a year, averaging ten a litter. They live singly, in pairs, and in colonies; probably at a density of a rat per acre, though this depends on food. A large dirty pig farm could easily support from five hundred to a thousand. They are tenacious, and though they can be killed by a blow under the forearm with a twig, they can absorb amazing punishment. Once, a gravid doe, already gassed with cyanide, escaped up a crooked stick that pinned her to the ground. Again, another rat also got off without trace, leaving its tail and spinal nerve in the catcher's hand. They will normally bite off a trapped limb, and can resist drowning for two minutes.

But rats have a fatal weakness: clearly defined habits. Thus, all rats use the same runs; all suffer from curiosity and a furtive compulsion to travel behind cover; and all jay-walk; putting their heads down and bolting for sanctuary as wildly as any pedestrian. On this knowledge defence can be based, and traps laid.

P.M.

THE PATTERN OF FARM GATES

A friend living on the outskirts of our market town has decided to replace a pair of garage gates, recently wrecked by gales, with one five-barred, or field, gate; but he received an unpleasant surprise when the carpenter he consulted told him that he would almost certainly need also a new pair of gateposts, no matter how good a condition they were in. The carpenter was right. He knew that a five-barred gate is heavy and would quickly pull away a pair of posts designed for ordinary gates. Oak, a heavy wood, must be used for its making and each of its many parts must be strong and stout.

There is an upright at each end of the gate. The back upright, on which the hinges are bolted, the carpenter surprisingly called the Head, while the front, or shutting end, was the Heel. The top horizontal bar, which must be thicker at the hinge end than it is at the shutting end, he called the Rail and below this the four remaining horizontal bars made the Frame. That was only the beginning of a five-barred gate, however, the would-be owner learnt. It must be strengthened and prevented from sagging by stout oak braces, generally diagonal, although there are other ways of placing the braces.

The type of gate chosen by my friend is a common type in the South Country – the usual uprights at each end, with five horizontal bars between them and with two cross braces, one fixed from the bottom of each upright to the middle of the top horizontal bar, and one from the top of each upright to the middle of the bottom horizontal bar.

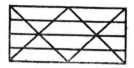

The carpenter pointed out a good old gate of this kind. It had probably worn out more than one pair of posts, though they would be good oak posts too, he added as he examined those now in use and drew attention to the tops of them, which were rounded and well finished. "That's to throw off the rain and not let it lie and rot the wood," he declared. The gate itself was heavy and strong, as well made as the posts, for the ends of the "back" were mortised into the head and the heel, and held firm with strong wooden pegs, while the diagonal braces were also mortised for strength, and not nailed for cheapness.

It was a better type of gate too, than some that you came across in other parts of the country, though not so strong and heavy as the field gates of the North Country, the carpenter considered. Gales were fiercer there than in the South Country and a five-barred gate would have three or more vertical bars between the two uprights to strengthen it, with one long, heavy, horizontal bar over them, going right across the gate. Even six-barred gates were common in the north, while on the Yorkshire moors seven-barred gates, with five verticals between the uprights and one massive horizontal brace across them, can often be seen.

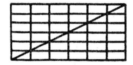

Five-barred gates varied also in other parts of the country. Sometimes two verticals would strengthen one half of the gate while the other half was braced by a short diagonal. Sometimes two verticals placed between the uprights divided the gate into three equal parts and only the part nearest the hinge was strengthened by one short diagonal brace.

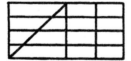 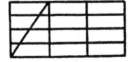

R.M.H.

ANSWER TO A READER'S LETTER

Why do most country people dislike thatch as a roofing material for houses or cottages?

Because – note I am writing of straw thatch not of Norfolk reed – they have learned by bitter experience that thatch is not only expensive but unsatisfactory. I know of no good thing to say about a thatched roof, but its bad points are almost innumerable – here are a few of them.

In theory a good straw thatched roof should give no trouble during the first ten years of its life; in practice it will probably give trouble every year, even during its first. The point is that a gale of wind may rip off a portion of newly-laid thatch, and deposit it a hundred yards away. When this happens it happens everywhere in the district, which means that the local thatcher may take a couple of months before he can get round to your roof. For thatching is hard work, and consequently nowadays few thatchers' sons follow in their fathers' footsteps; so the one remaining aged expert can pick and choose his jobs.

Then a thatched roof harbours mice, rats, sparrows and starlings. If you don't cover the roof with wire-netting, every really wet day will mean a damaged bedroom ceiling because of the holes these vermin have made in the straw; if you do use wire-netting to prevent this trouble, the appearance is awful.

Again, when a thatched roof does keep out the rain, the water drips from the eaves. You can put up metal guttering to prevent this; but this means killing all the beauty of a thatched roof that town sentimentalists rave about. To sum up, if there is anything good to be said about a straw-thatched roof for a house, I have never come across it during my lifetime.

A.G.S.

MAY

WILD LIFE

This month there is such a profusion of bird, insect and other animal life, in addition to a great array of wild flowers, that whatever one's favourite branch of fieldwork there is something to satisfy the most exacting student.

Birds come first, because they draw attention to themselves rather than hide away, as do the mammals which have so much herbage to screen them. Most of our summer bird visitors are here by now, though a few arrive in May – the swifts, the spotted-flycatchers, red-backed shrikes and that curious bird – now rather rare – the wryneck. Bird song seems so continuous and competitive in the early weeks of the month that those who are trying to learn their birds by this means complain that there can be almost too much of a good thing. The lesson here is not to try to learn too many bird songs each season. Six new bird voices recognised in the course of a spring and summer is quite a good total. Do not allow the spell of the nightingale to dominate your interests – he is not the only star songster. The wood lark is beautiful, too, and so is a blackcap in full song; while our own thrush and blackbird take a lot of beating.

Similarly, when thinking of bird watching it is so much better to concentrate on one or two birds and watch them regularly and thoroughly than just to turn one's efforts into a sort of catalogue of birds seen. Select one bird from the garden, one from a copse or open woodland, and one from a nearby stream. Start to study them in all their activities – nesting, incubating, feeding young and so on. In this way the birds' behaviour can be truly studied.

The insect world is also full of activity; and in addition to the usual butterflies of the early summer some very interesting moths appear. The Emperor moth, for instance, may be seen by day as it flies over heathland. This is one of the moths that uses its almost miraculous powers of scent for the purpose of mating. A newly emerged female will bring amorous males to her from a distance of a mile or more. The male's sensitive feathery antennae detect the scent particles that she gives off in order to advertise her whereabouts.

Among the less pleasant insects the maybug, or cockchafer, appears in hordes flying around oak trees in the evening and annoying us by blundering into our lamps. These harmful creatures, however, attract little owls and the larger bats which exact a great toll from the vast numbers of cockchafers. Badgers like these beetles, too, and it is a lucky maybug that survives near a badger sett if it alights on the ground or really low down on a tree trunk or bush.

M.K.

By the stream tall monkshood gleams a deeper blue above the fading primroses. Greater celandine smothers the half-shaded bank where the robin's nest, in an abandoned kettle, already has a second clutch of five eggs. The blue-tits are feeding their first brood, in the hole in the garage wall, upon the new swarms of caterpillars which may later defoliate the oaks.

Buttercups richly gild old grazing meadows. By the pond's edge the silverweed is a soft carpet for the long striding toes of the moorhen, whose red comb matches the scarlet busbies of the amphibious persicaria flowers.

The chaffinch has woven her exquisite nest with wool and lichen and moss, in the crab-apple, whose rosy petals one by one fade and fall in the hot sun. The goldfinch has selected a young horse-chestnut and neatly binds with hair and the down of weeds her shallow nest about the fingers of one fork. The slovenly greenfinch is building in a thorn bush a cradle made entirely of green groundsel stalks, which with powerful bill it has dragged bodily out of the weedy strawberry patch. Each bird has its decorative design. High overhead I saw a buzzard carry to its tree-top nest a flowering spray of mountain ash – what mental process moved it to adorn its home thus deliberately? At my feet a giant bumble-bee queen was rifling the purple honey-filled blossoms of the ground-ivy; she tumbled heavy-laden into the hole in the ground where she established, at first single-handed, her spring nest.

The goldcrests have slung their cobweb-bound nest under the drooping branches of the cedar; as in other years I shall place a net of inch-mesh netting around it to keep out the magpies and jays. The spotted flycatcher has come; last year it fixed its open nest of string and odds and ends upon – of all places, but safe from the local cats – the spiny scales of the monkey-puzzle tree, in the top of which a magpie was nesting; these magpies stormed the nest of the mistle-thrushes in the holm oak, but ignored the flycatchers in their own tree.

The stock-doves which laid two eggs in the hole of the elm tree have been robbed, I think by the red squirrels which have built a new drey in the silver fir; I heard the uproar of scrabbling claws and beating wings two days ago. Now unconcernedly the doves are cooing again from the niches of an old watch-tower. Through the ruined gate of this gazebo march nightly a family of three young badgers foraging for fill of worms in the dew-wet pastures beyond the ever-growing shade of the green beech forest.

R.M.L.

DAWN CHORUS

The sun rises in May at about 5 a.m. British Summer Time (4 a.m. G.M.T.). And this rising is anticipated, greeted and followed by the dawn chorus.

The true dawn chorus begins sometimes nearly an hour and a half before dawn; usually about an hour before dawn. It does not go on for long, for it is usually over by the time the sun has shaken off the horizon. Indeed it is only at its lovely best for a scant half-hour, only in May and early June, and only on those mornings that are fine.

Following gives sample of Northamptonshire dawn chorus in May. (Corner of a wood, by fields with hedges.) Best song experience of self and several bird-watching friends. If dawn is at 5 a.m. (summer time) and we are enterprising enough to get up at 2.30 a.m. we shall hear nightingales at this time, if it is quiet and dry. At 3.30 (B.S.T.) first statements in true chorus made by lapwings crying in the half light from nearby fields, before there is enough light to see the flowers in the hedges; 3.35 the skylarks begin; 3.55 a blackbird, and a minute later a cock pheasant. And then at 4 a.m., an hour before dawn, the song-thrush; 4.05 the male cuckoo, and quickly afterwards a wood-pigeon singing, and the spring song of a male robin. And then quickly in succession the first warblers, chiffchaff, garden-warbler, blackcap. It is now 4.10. A cock wren explodes in the wood-edge thicket.

There, more or less, is the permanent cast of the dawn repertory company. Many other birds do not really belong to it, for they come too late for the full flush of song at 4.30. The crow and the rook vary very much in their calling-time. The great tits and blue tits do not often sing till near dawn or after. Most of the finches, and particularly the chaffinch, are late.

The fundamental purpose of bird song is now generally agreed to be the marking and establishing of a territory, and most (though not all) scientists think that the possession of a territory helps to ensure a good food supply for the young. But if bird song (as seems the case) has a biological purpose, there is no doubt that under good conditions of environment, such as often endure in spring, a large amount of the total song output is beyond the birds' biological needs.

So much happens in May that it is only possible to select a few other private favourites for special mention. If a sycamore is flowering, take tea under it one sunny May afternoon. The little green blossoms hanging everywhere will make the air smell quite strong, and all the bumble-bees from the garden will come for the nectar.

J.F.

THE VEGETABLE GARDEN

There is so much to do this month that it may help to put it under three headings: attention to the young crops already growing; successional sowings of quick-maturing crops; and the first sowing of less-hardy crops, to be made from mid-May.

In the first group we have potatoes, broad beans and young brassicas. Early potatoes are just at the stage to catch frost damage, so keep the earth loosely raked up right to their tips. Broad beans are at their most attractive this month; pick them when they are no longer than 3 inches, slice them whole and cook like French beans. There will be plenty of large mealy ones in the shops but only your garden can give you this delicacy. Cut off the growing tips, too (while they are still free of blackfly) and cook them as a green vegetable. March-sown brassicas of all kinds are growing fast and must have individual space now if they are to make good plants; better to waste some and give the rest a fair chance than have a quantity of overcrowded greenstuff that will never develop properly. Remember, with all the greens family – plant *firmly*. Go over all rows of earlier sown salads, also spinach and turnips, and thin gradually, using the thinnings where possible. Never leave thinnings lying on the ground; they harbour pests. Give the young peas some twiggy sticks.

It is easy to forget about successional sowings now that the garden seems to be in full swing, but it is the small regular sowings which are most rewarding over the whole season; so see that the first early crops are not the one and only. For a different lettuce, try *Salad Bowl*, the all-America prizewinner; it has a loose but tightly-packed serrated leaf, grows quickly and easily and does not bolt.

Now for some first sowings: all dwarf and runner beans can be sown in the open ground about the second week in May; *The Prince* is a good French dwarf, straight and long, but do include some of the coloured ones as well; they add interest to any dish and make very good eating. Sow all beans where they are to grow and place the seeds singly at not less than 6 inches apart. Sweet corn should be sown as soon as possible now, but do not sow in single lines or the cobs will not get sufficiently pollinated to develop; arrange it in groups instead. Marrows can also be sown now, but should have cloche or some other protection until June. This also applies to tomatoes of the compact-growing varieties, such as *Puck*, and *The Amateur*. Both these need very little attention and will fruit well from present sowings.

C.M.

It is time for the perpetual battle between plants and weeds. It is fatal if the heads of the former are not kept above the latter. The hoe must be kept going, not only to kill weeds but to prevent soil cracking and to preserve moisture. Use a Dutch hoe and keep the hoe flat, taking care to cut the weeds below the surface with the forward movement and to disturb them when the hoes are drawn back.

Prepare celery trenches by digging two spits deep, placing manure in the bottom and replacing one spit of soil. Trenches should not be nearer than four feet apart to obtain sufficient soil for earthing up. If you are not prepared to spend a lot of time and trouble growing celery, it is better left alone. Main-crop potatoes should be in by the first week. Golden Wonder has magnificent keeping qualities and is excellent to eat. For those who like potato salad, try a row of Fir Apple, a long pink-skinned variety from the Continent. Sow main-crop carrot, such as Favourite, towards the end of the month. When the foliage is about 3 inches high and the root rather thinner than a pencil they can be sprayed with ordinary TVO which is a splendid weed control.

Carrots should be sown thinly, as drastic thinning gives access to the dreaded fly, especially in dry weather. Put in vegetable marrows towards last week, direct into growing positions. It is much better than transplanting. Bush varieties are the best and most prolific. Try a few of the small Squashes. Treat them as marrows; they are excellent, and even if not eaten are extremely decorative when ripened off. Every garden should sport a pumpkin – delicious in a pie – a great standby for Harvest Festival services and a never-ending source of interest as its girth increases.

Be certain to pick peas before they become ammunition suitable for pea-shooters. The right moment is when the pod is round and the skin shiny. Lettuces should be cut when the morning or evening dew is on them. When wrapped in damp newspaper they will keep fresh for much longer. Pinch out the centres of broad beans when in full flower. At the first sign of black fly, spray immediately with a Derris wash. Sweet corn can go in during the second week. Golden Bantam matures the quickest. Plant just below the surface about six inches apart.

For those who do not use tools regularly, it is a good idea to rub the palms of the hands hard with surgical spirit as a prevention against blister.

E.B.

THE FRUIT GARDEN

Tree fruits are grown in one of two ways; either the ground is grassed down or it is cultivated. Bush fruits on the other hand are grown in the open garden. Whichever method is used orchards will need regular attention when the growth of grass or weeds is at its peak.

Where trees are growing in grass this must be cut regularly if the trees are not to suffer. It should never be allowed to grow more than four inches high, thus preventing the development of flower heads. Moreover, the young growth has high manurial value because it quickly decomposes. So it follows of course, that all mowings must be left uncollected on the surface.

In some orchards perennial weeds such as ground elder and stinging nettles predominate but this condition need never arise if mowing is carried out regularly. The problem of keeping grass short is not as difficult as some people imagine. There are one or two most excellent mechanical appliances on the market which make easy work of such operations.

Reverting to the control of ground elder, it is sometimes suggested that the new hormone weed-killers be used to destroy this and other noxious weeds. This is an interesting theory but their use in the fruit garden cannot be advocated at the moment because a vestige of the spray will disrupt the growth and contort the young shoots of any fruits. Thus the only control for weeds is clean and regular cultivation linked in some cases with surface mulching.

Occasionally a fruit tree is grown as a standard specimen on a lawn and in this case a circle six feet in diameter should be kept cultivated around the tree. This simplifies mulching and above all guards against growth being checked by the grass.

Wall-trained peaches: Most people are at a loss as to the correct treatment for training peaches against a wall. Very briefly the aim is to keep the tree in shape and to retain a maximum of young wood. This is done primarily by "disbudding" and "pinching." Disbudding involves the removal of badly placed and superfluous buds before shoots from these are more than an inch in length. One bud is allowed to develop from the base of each shoot in addition to the one at the tip, whilst growths alongside fruits are pinched back to two leaves.

G.R.W.

There are two kinds of cherry, the sweet cherry which fruits mainly on old spurs and the sour cherry which fruits entirely on the previous season's growth. The sweet cherry is not suitable for the small garden as it is naturally a large-growing tree. Unlike apples there are no dwarfing rootstocks available for the tree and resultant vigour means loss of valuable ground for other uses and also means waiting ten years or more for worthwhile crops. What is more, even when the trees do start fruiting their size makes any reasonable form of bird protection impossible so that much of the crop is lost to our feathered "friends." It might be asked therefore how the Kentish cherries are ever produced and the answer is that there is safety in numbers. Where acres of cherries are grown there is obviously much more fruit than even the birds can account for. If sweet cherries must be grown then the fan-shaped tree against a large wall or fence is to be recommended. This economises in space and also makes netting against birds comparatively simple.

As with most fruits the question of cross-pollination must be considered and with sweet cherries this is all-important. The single tree is useless and no variety will give a crop of fruit unless it has been pollinated from another tree. This, of course, must be another sweet cherry and, even more important, it must be a *particular* variety. Much work has been carried out on sweet cherries and as a result they have been divided into some twelve or more groups. No two varieties from the same group should be planted together as they are useless for pollinating each other. When making selections chosen varieties should be from different groups and their flowering periods should approximately coincide. No question calls for expert advice more than this one.

Acid cherries are a more straightforward proposition. They are normally self-fertile and are only moderately vigorous. On the other hand, to obtain sufficient new wood some of the branches should be cut back each spring.

Timely reminders. May is the ideal month for bark ringing over-vigorous apple and pear trees. This is a tricky operation needing great care and if done incorrectly it can easily result in the death of the tree.

In the cultivation of strawberries one of the problems is the control of weeds. Culturally the important factor is to get the bed clean before strawing down. Once this is done the straw itself is usually sufficient to smother any seedling weeds which may appear.

G.R.W.

Fresh Fruit Out of Pots

Fresh from the tree! This is the way to eat fruit, ripe and perfect. Grow it in pots. In a small greenhouse, or a room with a big sunny window, you can grow apricots, peaches, nectarines, cherries, plums and beautiful unscarred apples and pears with a flavour that far surpasses those grown outdoors.

It is important to take a little trouble to see that great care is taken over potting the trees in the first place. They should be obtained from a reliable nursery, and should be suitable for pot culture, that is to say bush trees, on dwarf stock.

The first pots should be in 8 in. and must be well crocked. Place a big crock over the central drainage hole, and another layer of smaller crocks on and around it.

The compost must be as follows: To each barrow-load of good friable loam: A 6-in. pot of bone meal. Two 6-in, pots of broken mortar rubble with no trace of cement. A 3-in. pot of old soot.

A shovelful of very old rotten manure mixed with the whole. Failing this last, a 3-in. pot of Thompson's Vine and Plant Manure, or of Clay's Fertiliser.

Put in the bottom the rougher lumpy bits over the crocks, and ram it well down. On this foundation place the tree and hold it upright while the rest of the compost is put around it.

Each layer must be absolutely tight fitting, rammed in as hard as concrete to within one and a half inches from the top. The handle of an old spade makes a useful tool for this. It is surprising how much compost it takes.

When the trees are potted, which will be in the early autumn, they should be plunged in the garden with litter or leaves over them, or failing a garden they can be put in a shed, until the beginning of February. Even here they must have a thick layer of protection against frost put over them.

In February they will require pruning which consists of cutting each branch back to ten inches. By May each branch will have made three or four shoots, and each of these except the top one must be pinched back to four leaves. This pinching must be continued at intervals as the tree grows, always down to four leaves from the last pinching, and should be continued up to August.

As soon as there is any colour showing on the buds, the trees must be brought into the house, and from now on the watering is very important. They will need a good drink night and morning according to the weather. A cotton reel on a stick tapped against the side of the pot is a good indicator of the quantity required.

A house full of trees in blossom at a time when there is little in the garden outside is one of the loveliest sights one could wish for, a real foretaste of spring. As soon as there is any free pollen showing, it is necessary to help on the pollination, as there are no insects to do it.

This is done at midday, by means of touching each flower gently with a rabbit's tail or a soft camelhair brush, or by giving each tree a sharp tap on its branches every day for a week or so, until the petals have fallen. The trees must now be sprayed morning and evening with clean cold water when the sun has moved away from them.

The trees require extra food during the summer, and a top dressing of Clay's and Thompson's Top Dressing Fertiliser must be given – alternately two heaped tablespoonfuls well watered in every three days.

Now the exciting thing to watch for is the setting of the fruit. It usually needs thinning, and it may also be necessary to thin the leaves a little, to enable the sun to reach the ripening fruit.

The growing colour of the fruits is as beautiful a sight as the blossom in the spring, and when they are completely ripe the appearance is perfect. They have not been pecked by birds, nor have they been storm-swept and soiled. The crowning glory is the flavour.

It is most important to have very good ventilation throughout, or red spider and other pests will make their appearance. This, in a greenhouse, will mean covering the door and windows with wire netting to keep the birds out.

When the fruit has all been picked and the pots are dry, the trees must be removed from them, and as much soil as possible scraped off the roots. A hooked tool is useful for this. The top two inches of soil is discarded, the trees replaced in the pots, or in larger ones, and the compost rammed in in small quantities as before. Water very thoroughly, then plunge the trees in the garden, covering them well with litter. The second year it may be necessary to move the trees into 10 in. and eventually into 12-in. pots.

By this method I have won First Prize for Cox's Orange Pippin apples at a large show.

C.M.

THE FLOWER GARDEN

The wide choice of colour, habit and beauty of leaf afforded by Rhododendrons and Azaleas make them the first choice amongst flowering shrubs for all lime-free gardens. Their cultivation presents few difficulties providing the site is thoroughly prepared before planting, adding a liberal supply of peat or leaf-soil during trenching. They resent a waterlogged soil but need an ample supply of moisture during the growing season. When planting, it is essential to remember that they are shallow rooting plants and an inch of soil covering the ball is quite sufficient. The removal of seed pods after flowering is beneficial and each winter the humus content of the soil should be maintained by the addition of rotted leaves, peat or bracken.

Visits to gardens and shows at this time of the year will assist in the choice of varieties, and notes can be made of those to be obtained in the autumn. In the case of hybrids every effort should be made to get only the superior forms and preferably on their own roots, especially the named Azaleas. Amongst the taller varieties the blue Augustinii and pink Davidsonianum provide an excellent start for any small garden. A little shorter, the yellow campylocarpum and scarlet neriiflorum immediately come to mind, and for a spot plant the spreading orbiculare with pink bell-shaped flowers. In the middle group the hybrids come to their own, with Fabia, Gladys, May Day, Naomi and Vanessa well to the fore. The dwarfer section are equally at home in front of the border or in the rock garden, and russatum, campylogynum, fastigiatum, chryseum, Williamsianum, haematodes, Blue Tit, Elizabeth, Humming Bird and any of the repens hybrids will form a good selection. In the coldest districts, and for general landscape planting for effect, it is difficult to beat the older hardy hybrids. The colour range of the deciduous Azaleas has been extended by the Knap Hill and Exbury strains, but there is still much to be said for the scented Ghent group. The evergreen Kurumes are well known, and for a dwarf mass effect in every hue they are ideal.

With the prospect of warmer nights the summer bedding plants should be hardened off in frames or sheltered spots ready to take the place of Wallflowers and Polyanthus, which are almost over. If these plants have to be bought, do not be tempted to get them too early, and if they appear to be a little on the tender side harden them off – many failures are due to too early planting of soft plants. Half-hardy annuals in the colder districts should be left until the beginning of June.

C.P.

The staking of herbaceous plants calls for the discreet use of supports, for there should be no distraction from their natural beauty. Brushwood is by far the best material, for it provides ample support yet soon becomes hidden by the plant's growth. Use the minimum number of stakes, fixing them securely around each clump and tying them loosely to avoid any suggestion of bunching. The short branches which are trimmed off can be used for annuals and other dwarf plants. Lightly fork or hoe through the border when staking has been completed.

Hardy annuals, providing that they have been grown in cool conditions and gradually hardened off; can safely be planted in their allotted positions this month. The more tender bedding plants such as geraniums, salvias and fuchsias, together with the half-hardy annuals, are, however, better left until the first week of June. When planting ensure that the site has been well prepared and that all plants are watered before their removal from pots and boxes. Many of these plants will take the place of the early spring flowers and bulbs which are now over. Tulips that have flowered should have their seedpods removed and then be carefully lifted and heeled in a vacant plot so that the foliage can die down naturally. Polyanthus can be divided and grown on for next year's display.

Roses are at their best in June so every effort should be made this month to carry out a regular spraying programme. The addition of a nicotine solution to one of the well-known proprietary fungicides such as "Tulisan" or "Bouisol" makes a combined spray which gives good control over most rose troubles including greenfly, mildew, and black spot. The latter does not show itself until later in the season, but the control of this difficult disease lies in the prevention of the spores entering the leaf, so that even if the roses show no signs of attack spraying should take place every 10 to 14 days. Wet periods should be avoided and also the hottest part of the day otherwise scorching of the foliage may occur.

The removal of the seedpods of rhododendrons and azaleas as they pass out of flower is a tedious task but it is amply repaid by the increased vigour of the plant in future years. It is advisable to remove at the same time any young growths which may have been frosted, so as to allow space for the secondary buds to produce new growths. Other shrubs which also benefit by the removal of their dead flowers are laburnums and lilacs. The hoeing of shrubberies at this time before the first weeds have seeded can save many hours of extra work later in the year.

C.P.

FISHING

This is the month for the dry-fly, when trout should rise regularly at lunch-time or a little earlier each day; when the Iron Blue or Olive should prove acceptable to chalk stream trout, trout that have not yet become wise to the ways and bunglings of the fisherman. At this time they are easy to catch.

There is a myth about this chalk stream angler that places about his head a false halo of prowess; for as soon as an individual has learnt to judge distance, can cast without undue disturbance and is able to recognise the natural insect upon the water, he ought to be successful, especially today when rivers, of necessity, are largely stocked with stew-fed fish. How much more difficult to capture with a floating fly the smaller, yet more wary, inhabitants of the still waters of a West Country stream. An ill-considered move and only waves upon the surface will tell of "puttings down" and the results of poor craftsmanship. Take the crown from the Hampshire, Berkshire or Wiltshire man's head and transfer it to that of the dry-fly exponent of Devonshire or the becks of the North.

The chalk stream man, however, must learn how to strike, learn self-control before he raises his point after a rise at his fly, because his quarry is a more leisurely feeder, slowly but with deliberation opening his mouth to suck in a selected morsel. Count "one, two, three" rather than just "one" and be too late rather than too early when striking; for the fish must be given time to close his mouth.

Why is it that trout in some rivers will not be put down as soon as they have risen to an artificial while in others after one unconnecting attempt they vanish? In the Test a missed fish will go on rising unconcerned. In the Kennet, if he is not hooked when he first rises at the fisherman, he will cease at once to partake of food. In the Test I have hooked and broken in a trout, yet hooked him again within a minute and landed him with a foot of gut and the first fly in his mouth. In the Kennet I have risen scores of fish without touching them, but each at once has put itself down.

Why? Can any reader tell me? The Test flows roughly north and south, the Kennet west and east. Is it something to do with the light, the breed of trout (the Kennet fish are certainly much better fighters) or an hereditary wariness developed from the sore mouths of ancestral survivors of past anglers' endeavours? I wish I knew.

If you find difficulty in obtaining *amadou* (with which to dry your fly) ask your dentist for some. Those who have long sessions in the chair should have no difficulty in obtaining a supply. My teeth are most troublesome, but I get plenty of *amadou*.

R.B.

———•—•———

I must keep close contact with my spies in the lower reaches of the Severn, for this is the month the Shad show up. Not the Allis Shad, of course, but the Twaite Shad, the fine, fighting silver fish that invades some West Country rivers in late May and early June for spawning. Taken on a light fly-rod, the Twaite can give a performance of which no sea-trout need feel ashamed. Sea-trout flies do nicely though red-boiled, white-winged sea flies are better. The most important element for success in Twaite fishing is up-to-the-minute local information. The run does not last long.

With April behind him as a warmer-up for the trout season, with wrist, arm and rod working fluently – or at least as well as they did last year – the trout fisher can concentrate on perfecting finer points in May preparatory to the carnival next month of what might more accurately be known as the June-fly. For me, this year, this polishing process will have nothing to do with longer casting or more exact choice of fly. I am simply going to concentrate *on not being seen*. I believe many more trout would come to a bad end if an angler worried less about fishing technique and more about unobtrusiveness. In another branch of angling, Richard Walker, captor of the famous 44 lb. carp, refuses to blow his nose at the waterside on a white handkerchief, preferring – or imagining the fish prefer – khaki. This is perhaps, carrying things to extremes, but the lesson is there to be learnt.

Even the most bungling of us puts his fly in the right place, in the right way, occasionally. But what use if the fish is already in the next parish? From the angler's point of view, trout – indeed, all fish – are impelled to flee, by two things (1) bank or boat vibration; (2) changed skyline. The latter can be brought about by the following factors, among others: sudden addition to familiar scenery of angler or his accoutrements (a rod tip is sometimes enough); movement: change of light-pattern, as, for instance, the effect of sun flashing on a burnished reel or chromium landing-net handle (a wide selection of such heliograph devices is, alas, offered for sale). The poorest of casters, quietly dressed, taking care to keep his back to a bush, and, above all, leaving the skyline unbroken, can bring his fish comfortably into range.

Talk of handkerchiefs reminds me that this is the hay-fever season. This disease can make fishing torture. I know. I suffer from it. Dark, particularly Polaroid, glasses relieve affected eyes a little, but fail to touch the root of the trouble. See your doctor and ask him for anti-histamine pills. Put them in your haversack. They work almost immediately. They may make you slightly dopey but you aren't likely to become sufficiently dazed to miss a likely-looking rise.

C.W.

Wise owners of chalk-stream water are only now beginning to fish. Olives dark and olives pale and the iron blue are the likely flies and towards the end of the month on Test and Avon the mayfly. Kennet must wait till June for the green drake. Remember olive spinner (really female) is the red spinner, iron blue spinner is the jenny spinner. Houghton ruby is a good red spinner. Watch the swallows, martins and swifts. When they fly low expect a hatch of fly.

In Eire, about the 20th, expect the mayfly on the great limestone lakes. Here you can dap with an eighteen-feet rod, a length of blow line and two natural flies impaled upon a single hook (remember the males are smaller than the females of both species *vulgata* and *danica*). In less float-like manner you can dap an imitation from your trout rod without a blow line as the boat drifts downwind. As night falls you can stalk in boat or waders cruising monsters with an imitation spent gnat (sometimes called the grey drake). I prefer one tied thus: *Tail*: three (correct) hairs from a deer's single or tail. *Body*: stripped quill on tying silk base. *Wings*: deer's tail hair (hollow and floatable). Both wings tied forward and flat. A large wide-gaped hook; for a ten-pounder is safer on a big one. Remember to fish the streams (with a dry fly) that feed the lakes. Leviathans go up them to spawn and sometimes forget to return.

This is the greased-line month for salmon. In fast water hang the fly, holding rod at right angles to your bank. Otherwise I prefer to hold point low and follow fly round (except when mending the line) and, in spite of the anti-slack brigade, hold a yard in the spare hand. I suspect they hold rod point high and drop it when fish takes. I release slack causing most fish to be hooked in corner of mouth and maxillary. Hence I like Martin's outpoint hooks; they have a wide gape for the purpose. Actually the belly on the line causes hold in corner of mouth. If fish very dour put on a dropper and risk a break or like the late John Rennie use a "terror" on two hooks whipped on gut, tandem. Tie two hackle feathers grey or blue along the tandem and whip the hook bodies with gold or silver tinsel. He had great success. I have had none. Some rivers unresponsive to orthodox greased-line. Try *à la* Ernest Crosfield casting far out and pulling in line with hand fast or slow. He had success. I find it most profitable. When you hook a salmon which will not budge remember "sidestrain." Get opposite fish. Hold rod parallel to surface and move point of rod downstream of fish. He must turn his head, the body will follow.

R.B.

HOME HINTS

HOUSEHOLD: This is the month to start your onslaught on house and clothes moths.

All winter clothes and household woollens which are to be stored away should be washed or cleaned first. Failing that, give them two to three hours in hot sunshine followed by a thorough beating and brushing. If you have the time and energy to repeat this treatment every three or four weeks throughout the summer and autumn, you will keep your stored woollens and furs free from moth. Alternatively, here are two protective methods which I have found completely satisfactory.

For things which are to be put away in a closed container – box, chest, airtight bag, etc. – use paradichlorbenzene crystals. These may be bought at most chemists under various proprietary names and are usually packed in small flat containers in which holes must be pierced before they are put into use. The volatile crystals give off a vapour which is lethal to moth and larvae, but not dangerous or unpleasant to humans. The odour soon disappears when clothes are shaken in the air.

For clothes which are to be hung in wardrobes or cupboards, and for upholstery and carpets, I recommend spraying. There are protective fluids on the market which will proof materials against moth for a whole season. The one I have used leaves no odour and is guaranteed not to harm dyes or leave a stain. It is necessary, of course, to use an efficient fine spray and to do the job thoroughly, paying special attention to seams, collars, pockets and so forth.

For blankets washed at home, this month and next give the best and longest drying-days. Contrary to general belief, woollens are not harmed by soaking; if you leave your blankets in warm suds overnight all that remains to be done in the morning is to rinse thoroughly and wring as dry as possible. Choose a sunny day with a slight breeze and by sunset your blankets will be bone dry and will smell delicious.

E.G.

———•◆•———

Clothes and house moths begin their most active period this month. Look inside the piano – a place where unchecked moth can do very serious damage. It is in any case good for the piano to open it up and expose the action to the air from time to time, especially in dry sunny weather, and this can be done to an upright piano almost as easily as to a grand, by lifting away the front panels above and below the keyboard. It is then possible to remove most of the dust from the action with the small brush fitting of the vacuum cleaner, and, if you don't mind the mess, to finish the job by blowing out the rest with a hair-drier.

The key may be cleaned with a cloth moistened with methylated spirit, taking great care not to make it too wet, or drops of spirit may do damage by trickling between the keys or splashing on the polished case. The rubbing should, of course, be done back and forth along each key.

To remove "bloom" from the polished woodwork use a mixture of equal parts of turpentine, methylated spirit, vinegar and paraffin. Shake well, apply sparingly, rubbing in well, and polish with a soft dry cloth.

A quick and unlaborious way of polishing silver is to immerse it completely in a solution of water and common salt – a tablespoonful to a pint of boiling water – in an aluminium vessel and leave it till all stains have disappeared. Usually ten to fifteen minutes is long enough. Rinse in clear water before drying. This method is quite harmless to the silver, but as it does very gradually roughen the surface of the aluminium, I don't recommend using a good saucepan for the job. If you haven't an old one that you don't mind spoiling, you can buy metal sheets made for this purpose and carry out the whole operation in an enamelled bowl.

E.G.

GARDEN PESTS

Many pests and diseases start in late spring from small beginnings. If tackled promptly when the first signs of damage are noticed, a build-up can often be prevented, avoiding considerable losses later in the season.

FLOWERS: Watch for chrysanthemum leaf miner attacks, characterised by white or yellowish lines (usually known as mines). Frequently entire leaves shrivel up and die, weakening the plant. A BHC spray applied at fortnightly intervals to both sides of the foliage is now superseding older treatments like soot and nicotine.

Aphids on roses (especially climbers and ramblers) may also be tackled by a BHC insecticide. Aphids multiply at a phenomenal rate and a further application may be needed a day or two later to clear up fresh infestations from any unsprayed plants and weeds.

If black spot was troublesome last year on your roses, mulch with peat, grass cuttings or similar materials. Though mulching undoubtedly helps, preventive spraying is also essential. I have tried various preparations, the best so far being a thiram spray applied at ten- to fourteen-day intervals from late May onwards.

FRUIT: Though pre-blossom sprays against apple scab probably give best results, it is worth while spraying again with lime-sulphur when about 80 per cent. of the petals have fallen, also two to three weeks later. (Avoid using lime-sulphur on trees which did not have this material before blossoming, otherwise leaf damage may occur.) Alternatively, a dispersible sulphur preparation such as Spersul may be used and this is particularly valuable for sulphur-shy apples.

VEGETABLES: May is one of the worst months for vegetable pests. Two of the most serious are carrot fly and onion fly. Carrot fly is often more troublesome on light, dry soils, especially if the ground has been recently manured. The larvae bore into the roots which turn rusty and may eventually rot in the ground. Seedlings wilt in hot weather and the foliage develops a reddish hue. Thin sowings lessen the possibility of attack but the most up-to-date treatment is to apply the new gamma BHC dust to both sides of the rows during the first week of May and again ten days later.

Onion fly attacks are denoted by yellowing of the tips of the leaves, young seedlings being sometimes killed outright. Calomel dust has long been the accepted remedy but promising results have been obtained with gamma BHC dust.

H.A.

THE NATURALIST

THE BIRD'S GLORIOUS MONTH

"In summer," wrote Aristotle over 12,000 years ago, "the nightingale lays five or six eggs. But from autumn it is hidden from us until the days of spring. Now it is the custom of the nightingale to sing without stopping for fifteen days and nights at the time when the woods begin to be canopied with leaves. It also sings later but not incessantly, and when the height of summer comes, it makes a different sound, not varied above or harshly modulated, but a single note."

What Aristotle went on to say about the nightingale was less accurate; for neither he nor anybody else in the next two thousand years was able to solve the mystery of the nightingale's autumn disappearance.

The earliest reference to a nightingale in definitely British literature, as far as I can discover, is in a Saxon list of animal names of the tenth century, known as *Archbishop Ælfric's Vocabulary*, which contains among about a hundred other bird names the "Lucinia ... nightegale." Most of the birds that creep into early English literature and which belong to the "57 varieties" (which is about all that had been recognised by anybody by the end of the thirteenth century) are so celebrated and familiar as to be the subject of legends and superstitions, to be "developed" in folk-lore. There is a big folk-lore of the robin, the cuckoo and the wren, but the only legend I can find of any importance about the nightingale is first heard of, probably, in a poem of Richard Barnfield, published in 1598.

> *Every thing did banish moan,*
> *Save the nightingale alone.*
> *She, poor bird, as all forlorn,*
> *Lean'd her breast up-till a thorn,*
> *And there sang the dolefull'st ditty,*
> *That to hear it was great pity.*
> *"Fie, fie, fie," now would she cry,*
> *"Tereu, tereu!" by and by;*
> *That, to hear her so complain,*
> *Scarce could I from tears refrain;*
> *For her griefs, so lively shown,*
> *Made me think upon mine own.*

This idea was, of course, taken up by many other poets, notably Shakespeare, Fletcher and Pomfret among the earliest. The remarkable seventeenth-century naturalist Sir Thomas Browne suggested that the origin of the belief might lie in the fact that the nightingale frequently builds in bramble thickets as a protection against enemies, and as late as 1862, somewhat unhumorously, the Rev. A. C. Smith describes as observations of significance rather than of coincidence the "discovery on two occasions of a strong thorn projecting upwards in the centre of the nightingale's nest."

The nightingale has a broad distribution in Europe, west of

the Danube in the North European plain. In Poland and the Ukraine it overlaps over a rather wide band with its bigger cousin the thrush-nightingale or sprosser, and there are races too of the ordinary nightingale from the Near East to Central Asia. All of them migrate in winter to tropical Africa. North-west the distribution of our bird extends into England, and in south-eastern England it can be as abundant, familiar and common as it is anywhere in France or Germany. But west of Devon, and not far north-west of a line roughly based on the Severn and the Trent, it disappears as a nesting species.

This north-western boundary of the nightingale's breeding distribution in Britain does not appear to have changed very much in 200 years. In 1772 Gilbert White wrote, "Nightingales not only never reach Northumberland and Scotland but also as I have been always told Devonshire and Cornwall" (letter to Daines Barrington). A writer in 1791 believed the nightingale had "not been heard in Britain north of the Trent or the Were [Wear]. At the utmost in Scotland, Ireland and Wales he is unknown."

Actually we now know that the nightingale does nest in some of the southern river valleys of Monmouth and Glamorgan, but the excellent map in the *Handbook of British Birds* shows the situation almost exactly as these older writers described it, though in the present century there have been some minor extensions of range westwards into Devon. Until recently the only records for Scotland were of odd birds in the passage months, two on the Isle of May in the Firth of Forth and one in Shetland. Often there have been rumours of singing in southern Scotland, all of which until recently were identified with warblers (usually sedge-warblers) or the redstart. But on May 14, 1952, Mr. C. G. Hendry heard a bird singing in a hawthorn thicket at Stirling Castle, and on May 29 it was still singing and formally identified as a nightingale by George Waterston, secretary of the Scottish Ornithologists' Club. Waterston even found a mate for this bird, which he liberated on June 2. The birds joined up and went on calling to each other till July 22, but there was no evidence that they nested. This was, incidentally, not the first nightingale record for the mainland of Scotland, for on the autumn passage of 1950 the Rev. John Lees caught one in Easter Ross. So far there is no record whatever of a nightingale from Ireland.

In England few nightingales begin to arrive till the middle of April. There is only one authentic March record, and the main arrival is from the end of April until well into May. The nightingales are still moving in the second half of May. When the males first arrive they do not always go straight to their territories and start singing; but some at least (perhaps the young ones doing their first year's exploring) work the gardens and hedges and parks in a desultory way, and sometimes make themselves strikingly conspicuous. But when they find their headquarters in some thickset hedge or bramble patch or bushy wood-edge, the red-brown birds disappear into their surroundings, and only their voice comes forth. And what a magnificent nightingale population England can show, in some suitable places like the Weald of Kent or my own county of Northamptonshire!

In spite of the nightingale's predilection for bramble thickets, and the nests that the Rev. Smith found among thorns, it seems that the site of the nest, which is built entirely by the hen bird, is most often among nettles, sometimes in grass; it is always on or near the ground, and quite big, almost untidy, with a lot of leaves worked into it. Very few nightingales lay before the middle of May, and the hen alone sits, when she has completed her clutch of five, for the usual small passerine period of a fortnight. There is never more than one brood in the season, and the young ones, again like those of most small passerines, take a fortnight from hatching to fledging (or a little less), during which time they are fed by both parents, to a very large extent on caterpillars and spiders.

Contrary to the general opinion, the cock nightingale does not stop singing when the young are hatched. That pioneer nightingale-watcher Dr. N. F. Ticehurst records a cock uttering a burst of song with his bill crammed with green caterpillars; and this particular male went on singing until at least eight or nine days after the young were hatched.

In late June or July there is a dispersal of nightingales about which really very little is known. Indeed, as the *Handbook* says, there is "very little information as to autumn movements in general." There are no signs of real movement apart from local dispersals until late in July, and none appears to leave the country till quite late in August, many in the first half of September. Apart from a curious record from Oxford on November 10, 1836, no nightingale has been seen in Britain after September 30. Sometimes the after-breeding dispersal may restore nightingales to the exhibitionist tendencies that some show in the early days of their spring arrival. Thus, H. M. Bland records the appearance of an adult nightingale in his garden at, Eton on July 13, by which date it could certainly have completed its breeding cycle. It fed quite conspicuously, indeed rather like a robin, about the garden until August 5, even surviving a village fête, though it disappeared on Bank Holiday!

It has become the fashion to suggest that the nightingale has the most famous song of all the birds simply because it gets its audience at a time when there are no competitors. This idea seems quite untenable. When the nightingale sings by day, as it very frequently does, it can hold its own against anything, even any member of the thrush family; not merely the song-thrush but also the blackbird and even the wild missel-thrush. Its consistency, the range of its tone, volume and register, its inventiveness and variety, are unparalleled.

J.F.

THE NATURALIST

SWAT THAT WASP

Now is the time of year when the queen wasp will have woken up from hibernation and be looking for a place to begin her nest. During spring cleaning you may have found a hibernating queen in the house, for they often enter houses in the autumn and get into a protected crevice. A fold in a curtain affords excellent protection. Here they lock their jaws round a few threads and then let go with their feet and hang, since unlike birds their feet have not got an automatic gripping system which allows a bird to sleep without falling off its perch.

As soon as the queen awakens in the spring she will seek food, generally from holly, and then will search for a suitable mouse hole, in a bank for choice, which will make a good entrance for a nest. The queen will make a small nest about the size of a large walnut, entirely by herself, making the paper from scrapings of wood masticated in her jaws and then pasted on, a thin strip at a time. This nucleus will hold enough cells for a few workers to be reared, and as soon as these hatch they can take over the queen's duties of nest making and baby minding. After this, the queen will not leave the nest again; she will be fed by her workers and become an inexhaustible egg factory.

The nest will be enlarged by the workers, who will chew off parts that are in the way and use the same material to build up elsewhere. The early cells remain, and others are built round them until they make a large flat plate of cells. Further layers are added until the nest is as big as a football. These layers have rings of cells in different stages of development. This begins at an early age as the nucleus will hold small larvae at one stage, and freshly added cells round the outside will contain eggs. As soon as one brood hatches to the adult wasp the queen inserts a fresh egg and the cell is used over again.

The mouse hole soon gets too small and the workers who bring in food carry out grains of sand and soil. If you spread a large sheet of newspaper in front of a wasps' nest, you will find it is quickly sprinkled with their earth and rubbish in the form of unsuitable food brought back by inexperienced workers, and an odd dead wasp or so.

The wasps will be unable to move stones and pebbles as they come across them and these sink to the space they leave immediately below the nest. More than one gardener, on excavating a nest while I watched, has indicated the small pile of stones and explained to me the cunning ways of wasps who put these stones in for drainage!

Towards autumn, the wasps build a layer of much larger cells which will contain hundreds of male wasps and queens. These will leave the nest on a mating flight and the males and workers will die as the colder weather approaches.

Male wasps have considerably longer antennae than workers and no sting. They are quite easy to recognise, so you can pick them up and demonstrate your fearlessness to unsuspecting friends.

There are several species of wasp in this country, but only two common ones, the Common wasp and the German wasp. The two species can be distinguished by looking them squarely in the eye, head on. The German wasp has a black mark rather like a lawn edging-tool, blade downwards, while the other has only small black dots. Both make nests almost anywhere from under the rafters to holes in the ground, but their nests are of different colours. The German wasp makes a grey papery and the Common wasp a biscuit-coloured nest, more fragile.

If, in the spring, you come across a small nucleus with a few workers and can pop a jam jar over the lot, you can easily make a most interesting experiment. You transfer the nest to a wooden box with a hinged lid and then snip off the queen's wings, which is quite a painless operation. You make a small exit hole in the box to allow the workers to leave and enter with food for the queen. A tame nest should be pointed away from your house and the wasps fly straight out for quite a distance and forage on your neighbour's land. Should your nest be a grey one, you must now find a queen of the Common species who will want to make a buff-coloured nest. I will explain the difference later, but having found one you snip her wings also and exchange her with the one you started with. This is best done when the nest is the size of an orange and has quite a few workers. The adoption may not succeed, either the queen will resent it or the workers may kill her, but you are likely to be lucky.

Common Wasp
(*Vespula Vulgaris*)   German Wasp
(*Vespula Germanica*)

The new queen will now lay eggs and in due course her workers will appear, having been reared by their step-sisters. These new workers, however, will start making a brown nest and will add their little rings of buff material to the grey nest, which soon becomes streaky. As the nest proceeds, you will have a striped nest where each species has done its best with its inherited ability, but soon the early workers will die off and be replaced entirely by the Common wasp workers. Then the whole nest will turn buff. But you are most likely to be interested in getting rid of wasps rather than cultivating them. The main food of the wasp is not jam but small caterpillars and insect life, and they only enter houses about plum jam making time. If you get pestered at this time, you must search for nests. If a normal search fails, then get up just as the sun rises and choose a hopper's morning with a slight mistiness which will only last half an hour or so. In this light, when the suns rays are low, you can easily spot flies and wasps flying in and out of a nest in a steady stream which is most conspicuous. If this fails, then cook them a small piece of white fish. They are passionately fond of this so you must dice it into small cubes with a sharp knife, each about a tenth of an inch each way. These the wasp should be able to lift in its jaws, but only just, and consequently its flight homewards will be retarded and fairly slow. Watch the white fish in the air, which you can follow some way off. Then leave the house and stand in the track and watch the loaded wasps pass over you. You can soon walk nearer the nest and find it.

Now to deal with it. This depends largely on the situation, and your patience. Chemists sell good wasp-killers for use in the entrances of nests, but don't forget the safe brands all take a little time. The less safe way, but quicker, is to get a little potassium cyanide and dissolve it in a tin lid of water. Approach the nest and just before you operate add a few drops of vinegar. This now makes the fluid really dangerous so you get a garden cane, slightly split one end, and clip in a lump of cotton wool. You then dip this in your tin lid until the contents are soaked up and poke the stick in the nest entrance. The wasps will drop dead as soon as they touch the wool. You then bury the tin lid and wash your hands.

Next day you can burn the wool, or bury it and dig out the nest which will be quite harmless by that time. You will be able to notice that the grubs will all have their heads turned to the centre of the nest (they all hang downwards when in the nest), and the white-capped cells will have wasps in various stages of development, some almost ready to break out. Some of these may show signs of life.

You should now become immensely popular amongst your fishing friends, who will compete for the grubs.

R.F.

I HATE PICNICS

The picnic season in my household starts with the may-fly and extends into wasp-time. At this season of the year a wild and distant look develops in my wife's eye at the approach of tea-time. On a mere wink of invitation from the sun the family moves off, with the impedimenta of a gipsy's caravan, to share a meal with the ants, the coleoptera and the ephemeridae.

Personally, I hate picnics. Most men do. But it seems that every woman has an atavistic instinct to get back to the campfire again. Let a man bring a pair of muddy boots into the house and her sensitive feminine heart is offended. But give her half a chance and she'll jettison all the comforts of civilisation for the primitive joy of feeding her family in the unspeakable discomfort of a wet wood.

I can understand a townswoman wanting to do it. I could be more sympathetic if picnics meant a saving of housework. But far from it. The preparations for a picnic involve a feverish intensity of labour which keeps a man out of his own kitchen from breakfast-time until the last child has been rounded up inside the family car.

In my seamier days as a crime reporter I made the discovery that people who commit suicide show a strong tendency to perform the deed anywhere but in their own home. Maybe the urge to go picnicking is a related instinct. It's a way of escape from everyday reality. But I shall never understand why women who squeal when they find a beetle in the bath, actually welcome the presence of the creatures inside a mustard-and-cress sandwich.

M.H.

IN DEFENCE OF PICNICS

Late May is the most lovely time in the woods at Longleat. Each year their early summer beauty strikes me afresh. The woodland rides blaze with the yellow flame and pinks of azaleas; the air is heavy with the smell of honey. Against a background of the wild pontecum rhododendron, huge "monkey puzzles," sweeping their tails along the ground, assume the proportions of forest trees. It does not seem possible that these exotic monsters, which look as if they belong to the background of a Douanier Rousseau picture, can be the same species as the mangy objects one sees in suburban villa gardens. I collect their discarded tails and dry them, shredding off their leaves; when dried they make magic wands for lighting cigarettes from the fire. They contain an oil which, when the end of the branch is lit, ignites a mysterious gas jet of ice-blue flame.

May and June are my favourite months of the year. With them comes the urge to go on jaunts, which means picnics for me, and here is where I disagree with Macdonald Hastings. In his editorial comment for March he says "To my taste a picnic (the wasps and women sort) is the foulest of all social disasters." Well – I know that one man's meat is another man's poison, and I don't want to force picnics down his throat, but loving them as I do, I am jolly well going to stick up for them. First of all, I think that a picnic should have an object, it must be in hot weather and for me it should be by water and end in bathing.

I was born in July, my Zodiac sign is Cancer – the Crab.* I believe that most Cancerians, who are under the rule of the Moon, have a craving to live beside water. I know that I could not be happy if I lived away from it. Like Water Rat in *The Wind and the Willows* I love "messing about in boats," and unpacking picnic hampers in boats. Can Macdonald Hastings deny the allure of a delicious bottle of sparkling Moselle, anchored to a stone and dropped in the river to cool? I admit that a certain

---

* I was born under Libra, which, to astrologers may explain everything. Or doesn't it? M.H.

amount of trouble is to be expected from insect pests such as the vile horse fly, but that can be warded against by a previous application of "Mylol" (on sale at any Boots Chemist).

Sandwiches are very uninspiring and for a really posh picnic I recommend Roman Pie, which means knives and forks, but never mind.

ROMAN PIE

The flesh of two boiled fowls (chicken, pheasant or turkey) cut into slices, some macaroni cooked until tender, 2 oz. of grated Parmesan cheese, slices of tongue, ham, truffles, white sauce made with cream and cheese. Fill, in layers, a deep pie dish. Add cream sauce and cheese and cover with a rough paste. Bake slowly for an hour. Remove rough paste and when cold cover with chopped aspic jelly. It should be made forty-eight hours before required and allowed to set in a cool place.

I love picnicking by myself, but this does not justify Roman Pie and sparkling Moselle, but bread and cheese and a hard-boiled egg with a bottle of romantically river-cooled beer are a good enough substitute.

Further to Macdonald Hastings's comments on the women and wasps variety of picnic, I must say that men are sometimes very tedious on picnics, because they suddenly become extra bossy. I have suffered from men who will make an over-emphasised point of everything being "Bristol Fashion," i.e. a place for everything and everything in its right place. They insist on unpacking, packing, stacking and sometimes washing up – making a business of the jaunt. They think they are being helpful, but they just look plumb silly doing these jobs.

One of my most memorable picnics took place in northern Wiltshire last summer. The object – crayfish catching and eating.

The night before a sheep's head had been dropped in a shallow part of the river and surrounded by branches to partly dam the flow. Next morning the sheep's head was swarming with crayfish who are voracious bottom feeders, like lobsters.

The company was a mixed one including a rabble of children. The raising of the sheep's head got nearly everyone into the water and afterwards the hunt was continued in a more picturesque manner – the pursuers chivying the crayfish with shrimping nets, gently shaking beneath the weeds and scooping up the sides of the river bank. That night we had crayfish soup for dinner.

MARY CAMPBELL'S CRAYFISH SOUP

Boil the crayfish alive until their heads and tails fall off. (My word! this does sound brutal!) De-gut crayfish – the latter operation consists in removing the intestinal tube, a small black thread to be found in the middle phalanx of the tail. (This really is a barbarous recipe!) Add white wine, shallots, a bouquet of herbs and simmer gently for ten minutes. When dishing up, add more shelled crayfish, which have been set aside. Serve with croutons of fried bread.

Since I am on recipes, I am going to give you one which I consider to be invaluable. It is my husband's secret concoction for a dog's tonic. I have even taken it myself! For many years he has kept this a closely guarded secret and would not tell me the ingredients, but he has at last weakened and has given me the recipe with permission to disclose it to COUNTRY FAIR. Here it is:

2 oz. of reduced iron.
2 oz. of Carbonate of Magnesia.
2 oz. of Flowers of Sulphur.

Shaken up until it is thoroughly mixed in a jar. *DOSE* – A level teaspoon, sprinkled over the food for a large dog and a quarter of a teaspoonful for a small dog. *WARNING*! It has a laxative effect at first, so do not increase the dose.

I am all for dogs being put on a course of the no longer secret pep powder, although I am not always in favour of my husband's experiments on the dogs. The worst one was their day of fasting once a week. Sunday was the chosen day and everyone's life was made miserable by imploring eyes hungrily watching the door, anxiously awaiting their accustomed twice daily meal. One's own eating was ruined and became guilty and embarrassed to the point of indigestion. Thank goodness this experiment soon ceased.

D.B.

THE ENTOMOLOGIST

THE BUMBLE BEE

The bumble-bee has travelled a long way from the ancestor-insect. During countless generations her structures have become developed and modified into the tools and equipment necessary for her particular occupations of cell-construction, pollen-collecting and nectar-gathering.

The joint above the foot on the hind-leg has become flattened and enlarged and bears several rows of stiff bristles that hold the pollen grains transferred to them from the front legs and body-hairs of the bee. The long joint of the thigh, above these combs, is hollowed outside and forms a kind of basin or basket into which the pollen loads are packed for transit to the nest. And so that she may feed, *Bombus* possesses a long and elaborately constructed proboscis, or sucking tongue.

This proboscis is made up of two sets of parts, elongated, but corresponding to the lower lip and lip-like appendage of other insects, such as the grasshopper, and it gives us an example of how an organ, or group of organs, can be changed in form without losing the plan of the original structure, so that it may be used in a new way for a new purpose.

The grasshopper serves as an illustration of the typical insect head because the *Orthoptera*, to which it belongs, is an exceedingly ancient order, the members of which have not changed much in structure since the carboniferous period that saw their development. The primitive insect head has jaws, or mandibles, as well as upper and lower lip. For the ancestor insect devoured smaller insects, or, possibly, leaves and vegetation. The bees and wasps feed both on solids and liquids, consequently they have retained mandibles or jaws of the biting type, while the lower lip has been modified for taking up liquids. The bee uses her jaws for kneading and handling wax, and for biting through the cellulose covering of pollen grains in order that she may eat and digest the pollen that affords her the necessary protein. Her chief nourishment is liquid, and to suck it in her proboscis has gradually developed; a tube, the "tongue" proper, encased in a four-piece outer tubing that can be assembled at will – an organ specialised for her particular needs.

The hindwings of bees are furnished with a row of hooklets or hamuli that engage with a ridge on the forewing during flight, thus strengthening the wing-fabric by welding it into one firm plane. There is some evidence to show that the number of hamuli is related to the flight-range of bees; those that fly farthest having the greater number of wing-hooklets. In the bumble-bee genus, *Bombus*, the Queen always has more hamuli than the male or the worker; she needs them, for she has to forage far afield when founding her colony. The workers of the bumble-bee colony are for ever busy among plants and on the flowering trees. They keep longer hours, start work earlier and retire later than do the workers of the honey-bees.

A field of red clover is the bumble-bees' paradise – a heaven which they have to themselves; for there are few insects with tongues long enough to reach the drop of nectar at the base of each clover floret. The white dead-nettle too is a flower which seems to have been made expressly for the bumble-bees, which forage there from spring to autumn – for the dead-nettle blooms again after the grass is cut in summer. A dead-nettle flower sometimes falls off, and in it the bee, which lies on its back, buzzing angrily. The buzz comes from an apparatus under the wings. Here, just inside the breathing-hole, the windpipe is enlarged to form a sounding box, and the noise is produced by the air expired passing over the edge of a membrane fixed across the mouth of the cavity.

The different species of bumble-bees store their pollen in different ways. The buff-tailed and the red-tailed, and their group, pack it into large waxen vases separate from the brood-cells. But a different domestic economy is practised by the large garden bumble-bee and its kin, and by the carder-bees. Their pollen is stored in small pots built on to the brood-cells which are themselves sometimes lined with pollen. These characteristics betoken differences in the method of rearing the brood. It seems that the buff-tailed bumble-bee and allied species provide pollen in the cells of the first larvae only. Thereafter, the Queen feeds the larvae with liquid food prepared in her own body, after the manner of honey-bee "nurses."

A Queen bumble-bee has been seen to open the wax covering of the brood-cell and to insert therein her tongue. This is an advanced method of feeding and the bees practising it must needs have well-developed and functioning brood-food-glands. The carder-bees on the other hand, with the garden bumble-bee and allied species, have retained the more primitive plan of feeding their larvae with stored pollen and honey. This practice may be a vestige of the methods of the solitary bees, which lay their eggs in cells provisioned with enough honey and pollen to sustain the larvae that they will never see.

V.T.

THE NATURALIST

THE BIRD WATCHER

In the nineteenth century at least nine species of birds dropped off the list of those that nested in Britain. Six of the nine were marsh-birds – Savi's warbler, the bittern, the black-tailed godwit, the ruff, the avocet and the black tern. And these probably disappeared primarily because of the draining of the fens and marshes; that is, because of the advance of civilisation. It is a paradox of our time that nowadays we note with pleasure every stage in the reversal of this process, each bird we regain from those we thought we had lost.

Thanks to sixty years of active bird protection, during which we have learned lot about the habits of birds, we have had five of our six departed marsh-birds back, though not all of them are yet nesting with us every year. And we have had some odd marsh species nesting with us in the present century that we have never had before, though only sporadically, like the moustached warbler, Temminck's stint and the black-winged stilt.

This recovery is the result of a wise and enterprising sanctuary policy, particularly in the eastern counties of England, and of the dedication and intelligent caretaking of our remaining areas of fen. For the first time in history it is possible for the human race to boast that, through the exercise of a bird-protection policy, it can control and improve the number and variety of a country's breeding birds.

In this manner, the avocet has been restored in what is now agreeable strength to our community of regular breeders. Well over a hundred years ago, this lovely wader appeared to be on its way out. That remarkable Norfolk naturalist of the seventeenth century, Sir Thomas Browne, knew it as a summer bird of the East Anglian marshes. Until 1805 the avocet nested in Norfolk, some distance inland up the River Bure; and it bred in the Broads until at least 1819, and in Salthouse Marsh in the north till at least 1822. But they had all gone by the middle 1820s; and probably not as a result of the draining of the marshes (which did not really take place till a quarter of a century later) but as the result of collection and persecution, certainly for human food, and probably also for plumage.

The last observation of the avocet in Lincolnshire (where it was known as a breeder to the naturalists Pennant and Montagu at the end of the eighteenth century) was in about 1837, when eggs were taken on a sandy island at the mouth of the River Trent on the boundary between that county and Yorkshire. It is probable that Kent was the last county in which it nested in Britain. N. F. Ticehurst, the county bird historian, shows that young birds were reared on Dungeness in 1842, and two young birds were killed on it in 1843 which may well have been reared on the spot. Since that date there has been no proof of the avocet breeding in Kent, though there are, of course, still large areas of suitable marshes in the county. Indeed, after 1843 the avocet became nothing more than an occasional visitor to the eastern counties of England, calling at some of its old marshes, mostly on spring or autumn passage. It is true that in Suffolk a pair were stated to have laid eggs (which somebody ate) at Thorpe Ness in about 1882; but this was the only record.

In the second quarter of the present century the number of avocets in the famous Frisian island sanctuaries of Holland began to increase and spread under careful protection. The first sign of what was presumably a spill-over of the Dutch population into Britain was a curious one. In 1938 two pairs of avocets nested together on a coastal marsh in Ireland – the species never having been recorded as breeding in that country before. However, no more breeding avocets have been seen in Ireland since that year. In 1944 an avocet was seen with newly hatched chicks on a coastal marsh in Essex. In 1946 a pair laid a clutch in Norfolk which vanished.

In the following year three nests were occupied in the bird

sanctuary of Minsmere, in north-east Suffolk, not far from Thorpe Ness where the pair probably nested in 1882. In the course of the season, under close guard, the Minsmere colony increased to four pairs, and four or five nests were also discovered on Havergate Island, a large sheet of gravel isolated by two arms of the River Ore, below Orford and close to or identical with the nesting place of 1818. Two young avocets were reared in Suffolk in 1947, but 1948 was an anxious year in the Suffolk sanctuaries; reception committees composed of local landowners and their friends, and officials of the Royal Society for the Protection of Birds, eagerly awaited the return of the avocets. They showed themselves in no hurry to settle down and, though they did so at Havergate, they abandoned Minsmere, and founded another colony some distance along the coast, which turns out to have been a temporary one. At Havergate there was a disastrous episode when rats destroyed no fewer than eight of thirteen surviving eggs. Only three chicks got on the wing on that gravelly island. Fortunately ten others were reared at the temporary colony.

In 1949 the R.S.P.B. guessed that Havergate was the real chosen headquarters of the avocet colonists and was prepared to back this judgment with the funds at its disposal. During the winter of 1948/49 it purchased Havergate Island, and with the aid of the Ministry of Agriculture cleared out the rats. No sooner had the society bought the island than a high tide and high wind in March, 1949, breached the sea-walls, and it was only by hard labour that the R.S.P.B. was just able to repair the breaches and drain the flood to a depth suitable for the returning avocets. But the gamble had succeeded, for seventeen pairs nested that year and thirty-one young were reared.

The R.S.P.B. was not to be caught by floods again. During the winter of 1949/50 they emptied their savings bank, spending £3,500 on repairs, and on a new sea-wall and sluices. When the avocets arrived they found the water level adjusted to their exact requirements. Twenty-one pairs nested, and reared over forty young. In 1951 twenty-four pairs finally nested and reared.

Any bona fide bird watcher who has no evil designs on the avocets and their eggs, and who is willing to observe an entirely reasonable drill and code of rules during his visit, may apply to the R.S.P.B., 82, Victoria Street, London, S.W.1, for permission to see them. The visitor to Havergate will find that when the society repaired the sea-wall it took the opportunity of building comfortable hides from which the avocets can be easily observed. Indeed, a journey to Orford and a contribution to the society's funds secures a real view from the stalls of the nesting of the latest British breeding bird, the rare and beautiful awl-bird, the curious avocet.

J.F.

THE APIARIST

THE NECTAR FLOW

To attract bees, and to barter their nectar for pollen from another plant, the flowers secrete their bait of nectar and put forth their lures of colour and scent. Most flowers yield their nectar freely in warmth after rain, for nectar is a product of the sap of the plant which circulates when the plant is charged with water. This is drawn up by the plant's roots from the rain-soaked earth, and in it, held in solution, are various mineral salts from the soil – potassium, magnesium, iron, phosphorus, sulphur and calcium.

The sap, diffused through the plant, passes upwards to the leaves, there mixing with the carbon that they have absorbed, in sunlight, through the agency of chlorophyll, from the carbon dioxide in the air. This carbon unites with water in the sap to form sugar. Some of the sugar, deprived of its water content, is transformed into starch which the plant stores until required. This starch is broken down again during the night by means of a ferment called diastase into elements which, combining again with water, form sucrose, or cane sugar. A further combination – aerial carbon dioxide separated into carbon and oxygen – forms, with water, carbohydrates. These are converted by the plant into protein, necessary for its growth.

The sap rushes upwards, charged with these various substances. Dispersing, drawn away to feed the growing tissues, some of the liquid fills the nectaries of the flower. Proteins from the sap make their way to the anthers of the flower, whence they are gathered by the bees in pollen taken away to the hive.

When the bee imbibes a drop of nectar she adds to it a small amount of a glandular secretion, or ferment, called invertase. She swallows another drop. Soon her honey-sac is full, but its contents cannot pass to her second stomach because the honey-sac is separated from it by valves. These, when closed, retain the nectar which the bee, on her return to the hive, regurgitates to receiving bees. These receivers add to the nectar more invertase. This ferment breaks down the sucrose in the nectar, and two sugars called dextrose and laevulose are formed. When the surplus water is evaporated, the sweet stuff has become honey and can be sealed and stored in the combs.

In May, during settled weather, the garden resounds with a loud melodious hum. From the moment the morning sun touches each hive until four in the afternoon bees stream in and out of the hives. Each outgoing bee, on leaving her home, describes an aerial pattern of loops and angles. She is taking her bearings. Then one makes off in a straight, mounting line. Another, after preliminary convolutions, soars, then makes off in a different direction. Travelling bees always fly high. Once, standing in the lane a hundred yards from the garden, I realised that I was below a line of flight. Every two seconds from high above my head came the "Zip – Zoom" of a bee passing like a speeding bullet.

How does one bee, when she has discovered a source of nectar, communicate to her fellows the exact aerial route to be followed? That she does so seems evident, for the foraging bees keep to their highways of the air, which seem for them to be traced and recognised, as our terrestrial roads are to us. That the high-flying bees recognise their airways from terrestrial landmarks below seems doubtful, for the vision of the bee is limited to a yard or so.

The bees of my four stocks have a rich field. The Downland is carpeted with nectar – yielding plants – white clover, thyme, vetches, with dandelions by the wayside, and charlock on arable land.

Flowers of different families yield a nectar flow at different times of day, in different weather conditions, and the bees, knowing this, are on the spot at the right moment. I have seen patches of thyme black with bees at seven in the cool morning – this being, presumably, the moment when the sap is circulating after the plant's night-time chemistry. White clover is said to need cold nights, with sunshine during the day, for the production of nectar. The climate of these uplands must then provide ideal conditions, for the temperature always drops at sundown; even in torrid summer weather the nights are cool, and the honey-yield from our white clover is heavy.

When the spring dusk deepens into night, and the bees are all gathered together in the warm darkness of their homes, I hear from all the hives a steady, reverberating roar. The factory is working; the bees are ripening their honey. Phalanx upon phalanx of bees, each with a droplet of nectar held in her mouth, stand in ordered array with rapidly vibrating wings. The resulting draught evaporates the superfluous moisture from the nectar, and the honey, ripened and inverted, is stored in the cells. The bees roar in the dark night, and I listen with a feeling of profound contentment; for within the hive is stored the goodness of the very earth itself.

V.T.

CUT FLOWERS

There are times when lilac in a vase loses some of its clotted richness and the flowers, overwhelmed perhaps by an excess of greenery, have a sparse aspect. Flowers and foliage both have a tendency to soften, wilt and die over-quickly; and yet lilac may be made to last really well indoors.

It is best, I think, to relieve the flowering stems of the whole of their foliage, except possibly the little sprays up close to the flower head (not, of course, abandoning the foliage but keeping it apart from the flowers); then, having bruised the tips of the stems of both flowers and leaves, all may be put into deep water in a cool, dark place for the night.

In the morning the flowers are arranged as lavishly as you may choose with the foliage disposed about them. It is quite easy to arrange them so that no one looking at the vase will realise that the flowering stems have been stripped of the foliage. The flowers themselves will last well.

Earlier in the year, the forced leafless lilac looked particularly good with grey eucalyptus and now one may arrange stems of garden lilac stripped of their leaves with the silver-grey foliage of *sorbus aria lutescens*; I know that I have referred to this combination of flowers and foliage before and it gives me such pleasure that I venture to remind you of it.

The advent of lupins brings to mind another point concerning the care of cut flowers. It is possible, especially with the Russell lupins, the flowers of which open to a high point on the stem, to keep them in condition for four, five or six days, without that lamentable dropping of the buds which may give them a moth-eaten appearance. First, remove as much foliage as you can possibly spare, especially on the lower part of the stem; their beautiful spreading leaves offer a wide area for the evaporation of moisture – that transpiration which exhausts cut flowers; turn the cut flowers upside down, fill the hollow stems with water from a small can or teapot, then put your thumb over the base of the stem and turn the flower the right way up, lower it into a bucket of water and finally push the stem firmly to the bottom of the pail. When I first did this I wondered how the next day when I came to arrange them I should be able to keep the water in the stems because I could not introduce them into tangled wire netting and still keep my thumb over the base, but I cut the stem to the length required and found that without any further precaution the flowers lasted; evidently the filling of the stem with water supplies sufficient water to the buds to keep them going.

Wallflowers massed on a country market stall are irresistible, but they lose some of their glory in the passage from stall to vase. They are not easy to keep in good condition, having woody stems and a great deal of greenery. They, too, need to have the tips of the stems bruised and have the lower foliage completely stripped off. They do not look their best in conventional bowls or vases but, I think, are more appropriately arranged in wooden containers: a wooden work-box containing a tin or a knife or a salt-box or an old-fashioned milk bowl. If, when they are brought home from the market they show signs of wilting they, like other flowers, may be revived by having their stems put into water at once as hot as you can comfortably bear your hand. They should have a preliminary night in water.

I suppose that of all flowers of May, the tulip is most used for the adornment of the house. Tulips are so strong-looking that they are not always accorded the preliminary treatment of a night in water before being arranged in vases, and yet this is advisable even for home-grown flowers, for if the flowers are brought freshly from the garden and immediately put into vases they often wilt, they may then be lifted out, rolled up in paper to keep them straight and put into deep water as warm as can comfortably be borne by the hand. For special occasions, it is wise to arrange them well ahead of time. At first the stems take a slight downward curve, then swing upwards towards the light, curving and branching like the arms of a lovely candelabrum. I particularly like to put tulips in shallow bowls so that the whole curve and strength of their stems may be seen.

One of the best arrangements of them I ever saw was in a large shallow bowl about the size of a wash-basin, but not so deep. Pale yellow and deep purple May-flowering tulips had been arranged in two separate masses of colour side by side, meeting in a soft, uneven line, but not intermingling. In this arrangement the stately stems were properly seen and the architectural quality of the flowers accentuated.

Some of the newer shades of Oriental Poppy are exactly what are wanted by those who arrange flowers. The sombre tones of those known as Sutton's Art Shades and the brilliance of the Cherry Shades are a great asset in painting living pictures. These flowers are not easy to keep alive in water. It helps greatly to singe the tips of the stems in a gas ring, to strip off all the lower leaves and to put them straight into warm water, leaving them all night. They must, of course, be picked in a very early stage of their development after the calyx has split and the colour of the flower shows. I have found it satisfactory sometimes to keep them for a day and a night in water before arranging them. It is worth this extra trouble, for in their grandeur and in the wonderful shades of colour, particularly of those mentioned, there is really valuable material for the flower arranger.

C.S.

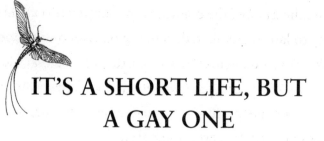

IT'S A SHORT LIFE, BUT A GAY ONE

There are precisely forty-seven species of mayflies in Britain, excluding the Channel Islands, and as a group they have been the subject of more printed balderdash than the significance of Stonehenge or the whimsicality of women. The following facts are intended primarily for the bedevilment of riverside dogmatists for, armed with them, a skilful fisherman should be able to catch no more fish than the village half-wit and probably less.

Any four-winged and two- or three-tailed insect with compound eyes and a sub-imaginal existence is an Ephemerid or mayfly. Fishermen label the three biggest (*vulgata, danica* and *lineata*) as "Mays" and confound the rest with at least 777 names. All forty-seven, however, belong to one family.

From egg to adult the big Mays live as long as three years and cavort aerially for at most three days of that time, in which state they are mouthless and mostly mate-seekers. The grubs, nymphs or larvae are mud-boring vegetarians. Others are climbers among sub-aquatic plants, sprawlers on the bottom, nippy free-swimmers (like the Iron Blues), under-stone clingers (like the March Browns), or waders (e.g. the Blue Winged Olives).

Mayflies, like the ferns and horsetails, are the mere relics of a noble, prehistoric family stretching back 300 million years and are probably the oldest insects on earth.

Despite their name, the big Mays emerge at various times from mid-May to late September, depending on river and temperature. Eggs take eleven days to hatch at 25 degrees Centigrade. In the Little Yellow May Dun (*Heptagenia*) the laid eggs sprout skeins of yellow filaments at both poles for anchoring purposes. Up to 4,000 eggs are laid by certain females.

The love life of the big May (*danica*) lasts four hours, all but three seconds of which is spent in dancing, mostly at night.

Even for insects, the brain weight of the Mays is small and, as Ephemerids, they take their name from certain Grecian ladies of brief repute. One common still-water species (*Chleon*) changes its skin at least twenty-three times before floating up to the surface for a breather.

Lastly, the standard work on the subject (Klapalek's *Susswasserfauna Deutschlands Ephenserida*) makes fascinating reading.

J.H.

THE SCOTTISH KITCHEN

If I were asked this abundant month to cook a dinner for friends of "adoption tried," this is what I would do. Discarding early Scots prejudice, I would look first for mackerel. Away from the sea, I would let eyes and nose tell me if the fish were worth eating. The fresh mackerel is bright of eyes and skin, and it smells fresh. With modern methods of packing, there is no reason why the mackerel should be unsafe.

Dependent on what wine I could give my friends, I would either pickle the mackerel overnight, or cook them for dinner with a butter sauce. But even in the latter case I would produce nothing nobler in the bottle than a little Mâcon.

Pickling the mackerel, I would do it the old London way. A small fish apiece would be cut into slices, and have spiced salt well-rubbed in. The salt would have a third of its weight in coarse-ground black pepper, and another third of grated nutmeg or pounded mace. The pieces would then be well-fried in deep oil, and taken out to cool. When cool, they would be covered with a mild wine vinegar and oil, and left overnight. Alternatively, the well-cleaned fish with their heads left on would be simply rolled in flour, and deep fried. In a double saucepan, fresh butter in generous quantity would be melted, then be added little by little to a good glassful of white wine – a dry Spanish white at 6s. 6d. per bottle would do – which had been reduced with a teaspoonful of finely chopped shallot. The butter-sauce would never be allowed to boil, and at the last would have a dash from the peppermill, plus a dessertspoonful of nicely-chopped chervil and parsley mixed. This sauce would be poured over the hot mackerel just before serving.

Having some consideration even for a Beaujolais, such as Fleury, there would be in the oven (above the chicken that was coming) a number of tartlets made of short paste and filled with a cheese mixture. This mixture would consist of old Gruyère grated and added to butter-flour-milk sauce, seasoned, with a beaten egg added when cold. If time pressed, this filling would go into the tartlets and be cooked overnight, ready to serve when warmed just before the roast chicken.

With the roast-chicken, so good at this time of year and therefore generously basted, there would go new potatoes, small-sized, peeled simply by rubbing with a coarsish cloth. Cooked in hot water, salted at the last two minutes, they would be jumped in butter and sprinkled with fine oatmeal with a pinch of white pepper added. The effect would be a dry finish, rather than a buttery one. Because the new peas, only faintly minty, would certainly be buttered, and so would the alternative spinach. Instead of either, there would be cucumber if that were available. And this would be poached in quarters about 2 in. long – after being peeled and seeded – in liquor obtained from the skins and seeds by ten minutes mild infusion. Just enough of this seasoned liquor would be used to cover the cucumber slices, with a nut of butter added.

Personally, then, I would have looked about for the blackest cherries obtainable. For a company of four or five, a pound and a half would be needed. The cherries, stoned, would be sprinkled with sugar, turned about in it, and left for about four hours. Excusable extravagance would add a wineglass of Kirsch. The stones would be boiled in water for half an hour, and the resulting liquor strained and set aside. The next step is to prepare a batter: 3 tablespoonfuls of flour with a pinch of salt are made into a paste with 3 eggs, and about 1½ pints of milk are stirred in with 3 tablespoonfuls of sugar, all being thoroughly mixed. The cherries, strained, are put into a buttered cake-tin, and the batter is poured over them. Fifteen to twenty minutes in a moderate oven – such as would remain when the chicken was taken out – bakes this. When turned out on to a hot dish it is served with a sauce made from the reduced stone-liquor and the cherry-straining mixed. This can be made in the manner of the old English Sweet Sauce, reducing the amount of cream and egg-yolk to allow for the fruit juice. Or it can be made like a white sauce – flour cooked in butter (equal proportions) stirring in the fruit juices, then carefully adding milk or cream, with sugar to taste.

V.M.

WAYS WITH MINT

There is plenty of mint about now and it is a good plan to preserve it for the winter. Pick young sprigs for this purpose. One simple method is to put the mint in bags, tie the mouths up, and hang them in a dry place. Another way is to gather the mint and to spread it out on a tray in the sun to dry. Then put it in tins and keep them shut down closely. A third method is a little more trouble but gives good results. Pick the leaves from the stems and wash them well in running water. Then pour boiling water over and place in the oven to get quite dry. Finally, rub the leaves to a powder and shut down in airtight tins.

Mint sauce can be prepared for the store cupboard for winter. Choose young sprays and chop them up finely. Allow a gill of vinegar for ¼lb. of mint. Boil it and pour it over the mint, and stir well with a wooden spoon. Leave to get cold and put into a bottle, closing down quite airtight. All that is necessary when this is required for use is to add a little boiling water and fresh vinegar to the sauce. Another preserve for the store cupboard is mint vinegar, much used in the olden days. Pick over and wash some young leaves and bruise them well. Put them into a wide-mouthed bottle, just cover with cold vinegar and close down. Leave to stand for a week or two. Strain into bottles and cork down, storing in a cool place until required.

The plant can be used to make chutney, welcome on warm days with any sort of cold meat. Wash and pick over the mint and pound it in a basin. To a handful of mint allow a similar quantity of sultanas, salt to liking, a chili and two tablespoonfuls of sugar. Keep pounding the whole together until juicy. Add sufficient vinegar, stir, and serve.

As a change from ordinary mint sauce with mutton try mint jelly. It is delicious. Cut up 1lb. of cooking apples and cook them with ½ pint of vinegar. When soft strain off the juice and vinegar. Measure it and for a pint allow a pound of sugar and a tablespoonful of finely chopped mint. Boil the whole fast and test for setting qualities. Turn into little pots and tie down, keeping in a cool dry cupboard.

When making mint sauce it is a good plan to sprinkle a little sugar on the leaves before chopping. It helps to cut the leaves finer. As a guide, chop up half a dozen sprigs of mint and put in a basin with a similar number of lumps of sugar (or equivalent caster). Pour over two tablespoonfuls of boiling water, stir well and leave for a little while. The boiling water helps to keep the bright green colour. Then add ½ pint of vinegar.

E.R.Y.

JUNE

WILD LIFE

The mid-summer month: when wild life of every kind is at its peak. Many birds are still busy with their family affairs though it is true that many species cease their singing during June. Of these the most quickly missed will be the blackbird and the robin and the hedge sparrow, for these are such frequent tenants of our gardens. In this month it is always said that the cuckoo "changes his tune"; though in truth many of them stop calling altogether.

Throughout June, however, young cuckoos in various stages of growth will make their whereabouts known to those who can recognise their shrill *chizz-chizz* call. If such a youngster can be located while still in the nest, there are few more constructive ways of spending a few odd moments than in watching the fosterers ceaselessly trying to satisfy the demands of their monstrous "child." Should a young cuckoo be seen after it has left the nest and is sitting on a branch – in a thorn bush perhaps – it is fascinating to see that, not only will its own foster parents feed it, but also other birds which may be passing by with food for their own brood. The hunger cry of a fledgling cuckoo seems to be almost irresistible.

Butterflies should be quite plentiful, and those who live in districts where the lovely white admiral is still to be found may account themselves lucky. Some of the hawk moths appear; the humming bird hawk and the elephant hawks in particular – the former in the daytime and the latter at night.

June is also a good beetle month, for the stag beetles make their appearance and on the warm evenings they may be seen zooming overhead looking almost as large as small birds. Why are beetles so often looked upon with horror? Admitted some of them are harmful to crops and gardens, but many are harmless and many do much good work. The glow worm (which is a beetle, not a worm) lives on snails; the sexton beetles bury dead animals thus justifying their name; and without the lovely many-spotted ladybirds there might be even more greenfly to ravage our garden plants.

Our lizards are active now, and although the slow worm is the only one of our three species that quite definitely does good – since it eats slugs almost exclusively – the other two, the common or viviparous lizard and the rare sand lizard, take their toll of flies and other insects even if they do also counter-balance this by the number of spiders they also consume.

In the fungus world the foul smelling stinkhorn makes its unwelcome presence known in woods. But even this plays its part in nature's works, for its odour attracts flies that could not breed were it not for the sticky liquid that exudes from the tip of its pillar-like growth.

M.K.

June – month of natural perfection, signalled by dog roses raining in wax-pink loveliness over green hedges. Alive with hovering birds and butterflies, the hayfield is sweet scented with clover, the sunlit bank with wild thyme, the ditch with meadowsweet, the thicket with honeysuckle. Moon-daisies whiten, poppies redden, corn. Tufted vetch splashes its deep blue over unkempt hedges. Water-lilies open, orchids stand like toy soldiers in the stream-side grass where the lofty plume-thistles throw shadows upon the mosaic of marsh forget-me-not, yellow rattle, ragged robin and stitchwort. Upon non-calcareous soils foxgloves flower and upon chalk the lovely mullein and evening primrose.

Late-nesting turtle doves coo in the shade of old coverts as they settle to build a flimsy platform for the two white eggs – innocents which somehow defeat the egg-thieving jays and magpies now overworked feeding newly fledged young. The cuckoo changes its tune and presently is silent: each hen has victimised the owners of more than a dozen nests of a chosen species in the vicinity, and now she is already preparing for the southward flight to the burning summer of West Africa. The starling broods are fledged and appear in small wandering flocks, in plain unspotted plumage, calling "Gee!" to each other like excited children. Young leaf-warblers flit by wood and hedgerow, devouring the summer plenty of insects and larvae, while the adults sing again and build second nests.

The mechanical hay-mower shears away the cover in which pheasants, partridges, quail and the rare landrail have attempted to nest; they and their surviving young and the scarce rabbit slip into the green corn, now in ear, for six weeks' sanctuary. On the coast guillemots and razorbills crowd the steep cliffs and rock stacks growling and gesticulating as each clings to its huge scrolled and painted egg, the guillemot incubating below the breast, the razorbill under one wing. The handsome clown-like puffin broods deep in the safety of its burrow, where the solitary chick is fed with its own weight in small fishes each day. Scavenging far at sea in the wake of trawler and drifter for days at a stretch the fulmar petrel returns to its egg laid on the bare ledge of many British cliffs, and relieves its fasting mate, who sails away on a recuperative fishing expedition. Herring and black-backed gulls hatch on cliff and island, the black-headed gull by mere and mountain tarn: screeching and squabbling and often killing and devouring each other's chicks, these large gregarious but unsociable gulls achieve a low rearing success from the three eggs laid.

R.M.L.

Best approach is to mention those birds which have *not* got young in June. Those still sitting on eggs which they won't hatch till July comprise mostly tube-nosed seabirds – storm-petrel, Leach's petrel, fulmar (only exceptionally do young fulmars, young Manx shearwaters, hatch in the last week of June). Other late breeders which still have eggs late in month:

northern waders such as black-tailed godwit, whimbrel, red-necked phalarope.

Late hatchers among terns are roseate, arctic; do not expect to see first hatched young of great and arctic skuas or common guillemot before last ten days of the month. Other late breeders include hobby, which hatches young not before last ten days of June, when ready plentiful supply of new-fledged (and therefore foolish) young of swallows, martins, larks, pipits and other favoured prey species.

In England, there is a formidable crop of insects of every stage and every size. From it, nearly every kind of land bird chooses its own special selection, its own food pattern, and upon this feeds and rears its young. High above the village the swifts are at the peak of activity of their short four months' visit to Britain. All hirundines (house-martin, sand-martin, swallow) feed young in June. Cockchafers bang at the windows and bombard electric lights, rooks and jackdaws catch and eat a lot of them at the edges of the wood.

Gilbert White's diaries for June are a glorious muddle of animals, events, activities ... mole-cricket's nests, a hatch of mayfly, the shrilling of grasshoppers, the cutting of the sanfoin, hay, the flowering of wheat. "When the elder blows summer is at its height," he wrote on June 11th. Glow-worms. Young ducks. Bees swarming. Young moorhens. Young grasshoppers. Young nightingales ("nightingales are very jealous of their young and make a jarring harsh noise if you approach them").

Most butterfly families have members on wing. Among the "blues," Adonis, brown argus, common blue, large blue, small blue; among hair-streaks, black only; among skippers, chequered, large; the swallow-tail; among the browns, speckled wood, small mountain ringlet, small heath, large heath; among the whites, orange-tip, small white; among vanessids, Glanville fritillary, heath-fritillary, marsh-fritillary, painted lady, pearl-bordered fritillary; also the Duke of Burgundy.

J.F.

THE VEGETABLE GARDEN

This is the planting-out month. Spring-sown brassicas of every kind are growing rapidly; young leeks are ready for their winter quarters; tomatoes, sweet corn, marrows and ridge cucumbers can now be planted out; and the trenches should be ready to receive celery.

The sooner all this is done the better, for June is usually more rainy than the next two months, and planting out seedlings in baking sun makes an already tedious job into hard work, besides giving the plants a difficult time.

If space is limited, look round and see which crops can be cleared to make way for the winter ones; broad beans are not worth keeping any longer, so cut them down to ground level but leave the roots undisturbed. Brassicas need a firm soil, and the bean plot should be just right for these without any forking over.

Give Brussels sprouts and broccoli 3 ft. all round; cabbages and savoys must sit right on the soil, that is, burying the "leg" on which they were previously growing. Where early potatoes have been lifted, rake and firm the ground and give it a dusting of lime, if it is to have greenstuff on it, or sown with turnips.

Choose tomato plants for sturdiness rather than size, putting the stakes firmly in position before planting. Sweet corn also needs a sunny position, but plant this in solid groups instead of rows, leaving 18 in. between individual plants. Marrows and ridge cucumbers will need protection from cold winds for a week or two, and do guard against slugs or the young plants will be completely devoured.

The time to think about saving seed from peas and beans is not in the autumn, but now. Mark off – with cord or stakes – a few feet of each row, and make it clear that nothing is to be taken from this enclosure. Seed for harvesting should be fully ripened on the growing plant, which means starting now if you want your own seeds next spring.

Make a first sowing of runner beans, and a late sowing of peas; French beans should still be sown at two week intervals, also carrots and lettuces.

The most useful of winter salad is land-cress, which only needs slight protection out of doors, and does best in a moist border. Endive is another no-trouble salad; sow this in a sheltered bed and only very lightly cover the seed. Corn-salad is not to everyone's taste, but is hardy during the winter.

C.M.

———

There is nothing quite so good as the first crops; but they will only be at their best if taken at the right time. Most vegetables are left growing too long, then gathered too far ahead of cooking. If peas are gathered regularly as soon as the pods become plump, they will be sweeter to eat and yield over a longer period. Carrots should be thinned as soon as the roots begin to form, going over the whole row every few days and using the small crisp ones that are taken up (always put the earth back firmly because of carrot fly). The first potatoes are ready for digging; they may not have reached their maximum weight, but it is the small, tasty, ones that are wanted now.

Try to plant out the winter greenstuff before it gets deformed through growing too thickly. A pinch of bonemeal in each planting hole will help it to root quickly; remember that these will be standing until perhaps next February, so make quite sure they are going in the right place. All the cabbage family must be planted extremely firmly, and rather deeper than they were in the seed bed. Tomatoes, too, should be planted with a few inches of stem beneath the soil surface, as they always form roots at the base of their stems. Give outdoor dwarf tomatoes plenty of room, as they are so much bushier than standard varieties. Three feet between each plant is not too much for those of the *Amateur* type.

Leeks are most accommodating and will root without being properly planted. You simply make a hole about 6 in. deep with a blunt dibber, drop in the leek with its roots to the bottom, and pour some water into the hole. These also must be planted where they can remain all winter. Marrows and cucumbers being planted out will have to be encircled with slug-bait; the dead slugs should be removed each day.

Jerusalem artichokes will make a useful hedge if they are cut back to the required height, which has the effect of making them thicker at the bottom.

It is better to fix supports for runner beans before the seeds are sown, or the roots may get damaged. Eight-foot bamboo canes are neater and more supple than heavy poles, and will last for years. Some people find that birds peck out the red flowers of runners, but not the white ones; if this has been experienced, try a white flowering one such as *White Rajah*. Other sowings this month include turnips, maincrop carrots, endive, parsley, beetroot; and further sowings of peas, French beans, and lettuces.

C.M.

THE FLOWER GARDEN

Lupins and Delphiniums are the most valuable of early flowering herbaceous perennials. They have much in common and, above all, require good drainage and an open sunny situation to be seen at their best. Lupins due to their profuse flowering often do not have a long life but are easily propagated from cuttings in April.

There is considerable variation in plants raised from seed, and many revert to the common blue but worthwhile varieties do appear and once proved these can be propagated vegetatively. Seedlings often germinate unnoticed around the mother plant, and eventually take its place, this being one of the main causes of the common belief that lupins change their colour. They are especially beautiful when planted in a mass, but if incorporated in the herbaceous border it is best to site them at the rear of a later flowering perennial.

Delphiniums prefer if anything a richer soil, but one of their worst enemies is slugs from which the young growths must be protected. Like lupins they are easily propagated in a shaded frame provided the cuttings are taken before the hollow appears in the base of the stem. Lupins and delphiniums need early and careful staking for their growths are often broken by high winds. In recent years plant breeders have paid particular attention to both these perennials and the advent of the Russell Lupin has increased its popularity tenfold. Delphiniums have advanced in size of flower and spike but there is still a lot to be said for the Belladonna group and some of the older varieties.

The spring bedding will have been removed to make way for the summer display. Polyanthus are often raised from seed each year but the best forms of the older plants may be worthy of preservation for another season. These can be divided and planted in a shady border where they will soon grow away to make good specimens for putting out in the autumn. Spring bulbs lifted from the beds must be heeled in and the foliage allowed to die down naturally before they are stored. This equally applies to those naturalised in grass which should be left long until the latter half of the month.

Once the summer bedding is safely in it is time to commence sowing for next year's display. Biennials such as Sweet William, Canterbury Bells, and Forget-me-nots and also Wallflowers for next spring should be sown without delay. When the seedlings are large enough they can be transplanted in rows in nursery beds where the biennials can remain until next year.

C.P.

ALPINE PLANTS are, in many cases, passing out of flower and this is a good time to reduce any growths which are exceeding their allotted space and are encroaching on their neighbours. Trailing plants such as aubrietias, alyssum and helianthemums are amongst the worst sinners but, with a little care, these may be cut back without disfigurement. Turn the whole of the growths back so that the longer ones, which are always at the bottom, are fully exposed. Cut these out so that the plant is reduced to the desired size, then turn the remaining growths back to their original positions and the plants will show little evidence of having been cut back.

Small branches of shrubs which are overhanging other plants may be cut back to their union with the larger branches so that no stump is discernible. It is surprising what a large quantity of surplus growth can be removed in this way without the pruning being noticeable.

RUSSELL LUPINS flower so freely and set such heavy crops of seedpods that if these are allowed to develop the plants become weakened and therefore short-lived. The named varieties of lupins are so lovely that they deserve every care, and it is very unwise to allow them to bear seeds as, in any case, they will not breed true. Lupins can be readily propagated from cuttings, taken in the spring.

Remove the flower spikes when the last flowers are fading, cutting them just above the uppermost leaves; the plants will then keep fresh and green and produce a secondary display of flowers from lateral growths. On no account should the plants be cut back to near ground level. This ruthless treatment will definitely shorten their lives. Some amateur gardeners believe that these select varieties of lupins are apt to revert to other colours, but this is quite impossible with plants which are vegetatively propagated. The idea must have originated through seedlings, which have germinated from dropped seeds, surviving after the mother plant has died.

BEARDED IRISES are such good-natured plants that it is easy to assume that they will grow anywhere. Consequently they are often planted in odd corners but they rarely flower satisfactorily in these positions, and the modern varieties are so beautiful that they fully deserve a place in the sun. Although bearded irises will grow in a lime-free soil, they prefer a calcareous one. They do not ask for a rich soil, but they like good drainage and a sunny position. They benefit from being transplanted about every third or fourth year, and the best time to do it is immediately after the flowering season, generally about the end of June, as they are then commencing to make new roots and will quickly become re-established. Plant them firmly with the top of the rhizome just level with the surface of the soil. The rhizome will gradually become more exposed but this is quite natural and no attempt should be made to cover it by top-dressing.

Bearded irises are sometimes attacked by a disease which is commonly called "rhizome rot." It is more prevalent on soils which are deficient in lime, and can be easily recognised by the rhizome becoming soft and slimy, and having an offensive smell; the leaves also become yellow at the tips. The best treatment is to lift the plants and cut off and burn the diseased portions of the rhizome. The cut surfaces and the base of the leaves should be dusted with copper-lime dust, and the plants should then be planted on a fresh site. The older foliage of bearded irises tends to die back in the autumn and the dead leaves should be removed so that the rhizomes are kept as dry as possible, but the leaves should not be shortened while they are still green.

SWEET PEAS grown on single stems sometimes suffer from a yellowing of the foliage and I feel certain that this is caused by the main stems being unduly exposed to the sun, owing to the removal of the lateral growths. I particularly noticed this at the Wisley trials two years ago. Each variety was represented by a number of plants grown on the single stem system growing side by side with others growing in the more natural way. The single-stemmed plants had, in many cases, badly yellowed foliage whilst plants of the same variety which had been allowed to retain their lateral growths were perfectly green and healthy. I feel certain that plants restricted to single stems would benefit by the lateral growths being allowed to develop one or two leaves before the points are pinched out.

In nature, the majority of plants have their main stems shaded from the sun by their foliage, even large trees, and it is unwise to expose them by unnatural pruning or defoliation. Clematis often suffer through their main stems being exposed to the sun's rays, and this is no doubt a contributory cause of plants collapsing during the summer months.

It is these apparently small things which often make the difference between success and failure, and it is when we fully realise that our gardens are inhabited by sensitive individuals that gardening ceases to be commonplace and becomes a fascinating study. Through that study we become better gardeners.

C.P.

The cultivation of the common Flag Iris presents few difficulties, and this had led to it being often relegated to a poor shady position where little else will grow. The beautiful modern bearded varieties deserve much better treatment and are ideally suited for a sunny border, with a well drained soil containing some lime but this is not essential. Although the planting season extends into the autumn, the best results are obtained as soon as the flowers are over about the end of June. Existing clumps may be lifted and divided, the older and dead portions of the rhizomes being discarded. The short young growing pieces can then be carefully planted with the top of the rhizome only just covered with soil, so that they soon assume their natural position of creeping along the surface of the soil.

The many shades and combinations of purple, blue, yellow, white, pink, and copper offer an ample choice for everyone, and although the season is on the short side, they form a most colourful feature of the garden in late May and June. Amongst the well tried favourites, Golden Hind, White City, Blue Ensign, Great Lakes, Sirius, Shot Silk, Ann Marie Cayeux, and Mrs. Valerie West cannot fail to please. For the enthusiast there are countless new varieties raised both here and in America, of almost every hue, and in future years the increased popularity of the iris is assured.

It is a great temptation at this time of the year to remove the leaves of many of the spring bulbs before they have completed their function of producing next year's flowers and new bulbs. Where they are naturalised in grass the early cutting of the leaves leads to a considerable reduction in the quantity of flowers in the spring. Allow the leaves to die away naturally if at all possible, for a little patience will be amply rewarded in years to come.

The blue Gentiana acaulis is one of the most popular of all alpines, and the countless blue trumpets forming a lovely carpet is one of the sights of the garden in April and May. In many places, however, it has proved rather difficult to flower although making rapid growth. It needs a sunny position and should not be allowed to become a crowded mass. After flowering lift and divide the clumps, adding a little fresh leafsoil and loam to the soil and replant the small divisions firmly, repeating this process about every three years. When division is not necessary work in around the plants a good topdressing, and clear the leaves by watering in with a fine rose.

C.P.

THE FRUIT GARDEN

Raspberries respond handsomely to generous treatment. This should have started with a liberal manuring of the bed before planting and continued with annual applications as a mulch thereafter. Excellent alternatives for a mulch are peat, leaf mould, or garden compost. Whatever material is used, it should be applied generously and sufficiently early in the spring before the soil has dried out, for the raspberry is naturally a plant of damp soils with a cool root-run.

The value of the annual mulch cannot be overemphasised. Essential plant nutrients can most certainly be applied in the form of well-known fertilisers, but the effect of these is lost if the bed becomes at all dry. Where manure is used the need for fertilisers is reduced; where the mulch is of some other material it must be supplemented as necessary by fertilisers.

Something frequently overlooked is that by June the spring mulch has often become so thin through weathering and the activities of birds that it has lost much of its value. The point to remember is that during this month the plants have the coming crop to carry as well as the production of new canes. Dryness at the roots in June therefore can have telling results – that is, stunted canes and a mediocre crop. When the mulch has become thin it should be renewed and, if necessary, the ground soaked by watering with the garden hose.

There is only one major pest of raspberries and this is the Raspberry Beetle. The grubs which cause the damage hatch out from eggs laid in the blossom by the adult beetle and feed on the ripening fruits. Berries that are seriously affected fail to develop whilst many grubs are not discovered until they are seen floating on the top of the bottling jar. Fortunately control of this pest is simple and straightforward. It merely entails spraying with Derris (according to makers' instructions) as the first fruits commence colouring and possibly again ten to fourteen days later where the infestation is serious. Derris is best applied as a wash although a dust can be used.

The scourge of virus affects raspberries as well as strawberries. This scourge, unlike Raspberry Beetle, cannot yet be controlled. The effects of virus in raspberries can be seen frequently in small gardens by the characteristic yellow mottling of the leaves and in the later stages by stunted canes and meagre crops. When this happens it is time to destroy completely such beds and obtain fresh certified canes for a *new* site.

G.R.W.

June is the month for strawberries and no plant gives a richer or a more enjoyable harvest. They are one of the easiest fruits to grow, provided one or two important points are watched in the selection of plants and their cultivation.

The practice of strawing down is a general one and is done when the fruit starts to weigh down the trusses. The straw used must be dry and clean and should not be put down too early as this increases the risk of frost damage.

Trouble from birds is bound to occur unless the bed is protected. The material normally used is ordinary fish netting which will last for many years if it is used properly and thoroughly dried before storing. Old pea sticks and the like do not make suitable supports; the best ones are stout stakes linked by cord or plastic-covered wire. By this means the netting can be rolled back without being damaged by any snags and picking is made a lot easier. The permanent enclosure of strawberries, and indeed all soft fruit has lost the favour it once enjoyed and is not recommended.

The strawberry can be affected by several troubles. One of the most widespread is Botrytis or "Grey-mould" which is most troublesome in dull, wet seasons, particularly where plants are too close. Fruits when almost ripe, become soft and rotten and are soon covered by thick, grey fungus. As a crop can be infected by rain splashes from the soil the value of strawing down is all the more important. In conjunction with this, rotting fruits should be picked and burnt.

In some gardens the strawberry is a difficult plant to grow; it is found that growth and crop are both poor and that plants tend to die out prematurely. These failures are mostly due to the spread of the virus diseases "Crinkle" and "Yellow Edge" the chief vector of which is Strawberry Aphis. "Crinkle" causes leaves to develop a wrinkled appearance whilst "Yellow Edge" as the name implies, shows as a yellow margin on the leaves and gives plants a stunted, flattened appearance. Such symptoms show during certain periods of the summer. The method of overcoming the problem is to burn infected plants and where this involves a large percentage, to make a fresh start. Certified virus-free stocks of some varieties are available and it is preferable to plant up a completely new bed on fresh ground than try to patch up an old one. In any case the carrier aphides must be controlled by dipping runners in a strong solution of nicotine and soft soap and by spraying established beds with H.E.T.P. in summer.

G.R.W.

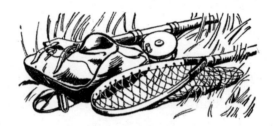

FISHING

Two events this month keep my mind pleasurably off my work: the mayfly and the opening of the coarse season on the sixteenth. Of the two I know which, for me, is the greater occasion, and it is not the emergence of the grey drake. I mean no disrespect to the great chalk stream festival. The choice is based simply on the fact that by early June one has already had the opportunity, if not the satisfaction, of catching trout regularly every day for two months whereas the unmatchable joy of float fishing has been denied to the angler for ninety long, lean days.

There can be no doubt how, or at what hour, to greet the great day. Tench are the fish: dawn is the time. And let your first fishing be done, if possible, by a lake. There is nothing quite like the right sort of June morning, about 4 a.m., by the side of a still water, when the mist rises, and the rabbits and wood pigeons are so surprised to see you that they almost forget to be cautious. One other important requirement: see that your chosen swim is one where the reeds and bank grasses stand intact and untrampled. There is powerful magic in being first man there.

I do not think that the best and biggest tench are to be caught with float tackle. The antics of the fish as it stands on its nose to feed inevitably interfere with a cast rising vertically to the surface (hence the shy shiggling movements of the "typical" tench bite). Light ledger tackle or, better still, fishing, as for carp, with no weights save the bait – a generous lump of paste – these are the most effective methods with what is, after all, an extremely timid fish. But this morning of all mornings let a light quill float with a red tip be used. This has a vast ritual significance.

If weeds are thick at your chosen swim, arrive not later than dawn and drag the bottom, using a garden rake attached to a length of rope. It is a strange fact that the wary tench will often start biting just as soon as this awful commotion is over. The reason, I suspect, is that the rake stirs up several thousand chironomid larvae. So, if dragging is to be done see that a redworm is used on the hook.

The rough-stream trout fisher will not take it kindly if I forget to say that his "mayfly" too is still active the first half of this month. On Exmoor I rummage among the pebbles for live stone-fly creepers, impale either the creeper or the fully-fledged fly on a small hook and lob the bait up-stream to the trout with a gentle side-cast.

C.W.

SHOOTING

The best way to eliminate rabbits from the garden is to rise early and see what can be done from a window with a .22. This is quite all right if you live far from neighbours, but the .22 can kill or injure at a distance well over half a mile. If you live, say, on the outskirts of a country town, rather too close to neighbours and public roads for safe use of a .22, the .410 shotgun may be safe in a walled garden but what one really wants is the lowest possible lethal load for rabbit. This is the old "No. 3 Saloon" or garden gun.

They used to be one of the cheap Belgian or German exports and could be bought at any country ironmonger for less than a pound. The calibre is 9 mm. and the cartridge is a longish cylinder with a copper rim fire base which holds a pinch of powder.

It is probably the best of "garden guns" as it will kill rabbits up to about twenty yards. It does no serious damage to fruit or vegetables and is as safe as it is possible for any gun to be.

As grass gets high the difficulties of rabbit shooting with the .22 increase. To avoid fiddling with sights, the Ommundsen "Negative Angle Battle Sight" principle is useful. You sight the rifle accurately for sixty yards and then, whatever the range of the target from twenty to a hundred yards, you aim two and a half inches below the "bull."

Few of us have looked at our guns since we put them away at

the close of the shooting season. They should go to the maker for overhaul and interior cleaning. The expert eye detects things like unnoticed dents in barrels, incipient looseness of the joint, all small matters easily set right and adding years to the life of the guns. Incidentally it is wise to give the baize lining of guncases a good spraying with insecticide, for baize and gun oil seem to be a favourite diet for some clothes moths. In the same way cartridge bags can be well washed, then dressed while wet with neatsfoot oil. This will re-waterproof them, but I do not know of an oil soluble fungicide and leather may mildew if hung in a damp room. This does not so far as I know affect the lasting quality of the leather.

For ordinary cleaning and lubrication I always use Three-in-One oil and for the stock and fore-end woodwork artists' linseed oil. This must never be used for locks, etc., as it literally gums up the works. It is this slow oxidisation to a gun which fills the grain of the stocks and makes them perfectly waterproof and which eventually takes a lovely polish.

H.B.C.P.

HOME HINTS

Green gooseberry jam makes a pleasant breakfast variant to marmalade and is very quick and easy to make: cook three pounds of gooseberries in one pint of water till soft; add four pounds of sugar and boil hard for five minutes exactly; put into pots and cover at once. Green gooseberries also make an excellent base for mint jelly.

Elder-flower wine is a refreshing occasional drink and does not take very long to mature. Pick the flowers on a dry sunny day and choose those that are just open; on to a pint of flowers pour a gallon of boiling water and add either one ounce of crushed root ginger or the grated rind of a lemon. Leave to infuse for four days; then strain into an earthenware bowl, add three pounds of sugar and when it is dissolved half an ounce of yeast mixed to a cream with a little of the syrup. Cover with a sheet of greaseproof paper in which you have pricked one or two holes. Three days after fermentation has stopped filter the liquid (white blotting-paper in a funnel if you have no filter-paper) into bottles or earthenware jars and store in a cool dark place. It is a good idea to cork lightly at first and inspect frequently. As soon as you are sure there is no further fermentation cork tightly and leave for six months. It is better if kept for a year.

Elder-flower water, made by infusing the flowers in boiling water and straining when cold, makes an excellent astringent face-lotion shaken up with witch-hazel – one part to four of elder-flower water – and a dash of perfumed cologne.

Any time the oven is cooling down after baking slip in a few trays of herbs. Parsley and mint, in particular, have a better flavour if dried early in the season. Similarly, if you salt down green beans, choose the young ones rather than the end of the crop.

E.G.

OLD-FASHIONED ROSES FOR ME

June is an exciting month and the major pleasure for me lies in the flowering of the old-fashioned roses. In his book *Roses as Flowering Shrubs* Mr. G. S. Thomas says that the old roses are, like wine, an acquired taste. It would seem that many are acquiring it, and rapidly. If I were pleading a cause, which I am not, and sought to win adherents, which I do not, I might cast the first spell by setting in an old and small goblet a few blooms of the delicious pink *Rose de Meaux*, a miniature cabbage rose not larger across than a florin, but perfect in form. The bush itself, four to five feet high, is of slender growth and the leaves small and in proportion to the flowers. Another pink old rose of enchanting form, a trifle larger, is *Petite de Hollande*, also of the old cabbage or centifolia group. With either of these roses there are pictures to be made, pictures reminiscent of old china and half-forgotten chintz.

It seems odd, when one considers the prejudice against blue tints in modern roses, to feel so passionately the beauty of the purples, wines, plum tones and grey and slaty shadowings of certain of the old roses. You have only to put together a handful of these for someone who does not know them to find how immediate is the pleasure and appreciation of their deep beauty. Perhaps the most beautiful of them is *Cardinal de Richelieu*, plush-like and purple with tones and shadowings of grey. Once I came on a bush of it in full flower in the evening light when its grey quality predominated and it had an almost unearthly look as of a ghost of a rose bush. The purple moss rose *William Lobb* also has something of this grey quality as it matures, though the large velvety flowers when first open are rich mauve in colour. *William Lobb* is a very vigorous bush growing up to eight feet and bearing its large roses and lovely buds in well-mossed sprays and in quantity.

There is a much smaller purple moss rose which delights most hearts, its bloomy petals have almost black tones and it is called *Nuits de Young*. This is a smaller flower and a smaller bush, but very free flowering. I have an oblong vase made of mirrored glass, not sparkling but grey and watery in aspect, and into this go the purple roses in great profusion. Profusion indicates no extravagance, no robbing unduly of the garden, for although these roses have not the advantage of the moderns of being "remontant" when they are in flower, they riot with bloom. To those already named I add in this vase the old velvet rose *Tuscany* and long richly flowered sprays of *Hippolyte*. There is endless pleasure here, especially if there is some place in the garden suited to their gentle charm, not in formal beds, for these roses are not pruned each year as are the moderns and they look best in an informal setting. I have to admit to one large bed of them in my own garden, where at the end of a lawn is a broad stretch patterned with the grey of Stachys Lanata and planted with such lavender, lilac, mauve and pale purple roses as *Du Maître d'Ecole, Tour de Malakoff, Belle de Crècy* and *Reine des Violettes*.

I always had in the back of my mind the idea that the old roses and the moderns did not associate well together and on the whole I think this is so, but last autumn I was given some long sprays of *Madame Ernst Calvat*, a flower of lovely pink with richly tinted foliage and of strong growth. This proved a perfect companion to the fine yellow modern *Peace*; and the two together, arranged with warm foliage of outdoor vine, made a glowing autumn arrangement. Of course I am not being quite logical anyway, because the term "old roses" ought perhaps to be confined to the gallicas, damasks, albas and centifolias, and *Madame E. Calvat* is I think a Bourbon of later date, although by no means a modern. But whatever the logic of it may be the association of the flowers was delicious.

C.S.

You Grow Them Like This:

Modern hybrid teas and hybrid polyanthas usually flourish and, equally important, look right in almost any surroundings. The old roses are less accommodating. Though in some respects easier to grow, they must be in the right situation to show their full beauty, which is of quite a different order. The old-timers are more suitable for planting in mixed borders of herbaceous plants and roses – the beauty of the individual flower being less important than with the modern hybrid teas – or treated as specimen lowering shrubs where height and width make this practicable. They often demand plenty of room. For example, where space permits, planting of species like *Rosa Moyesii* in isolated beds in grass is most affective. I suggest that you prepare the ground just as you would for the moderns, digging deeply and incorporating well-rotted manure in the bottom spit, compost, peat and bonemeal in the top. An occasional top dressing of manure in late spring will help established plants to maintain their vigour. Damasks and mosses are perhaps more partial to land in really good heart than to thin, dry soils. It is usually sufficient to remove spent wood after flowering. Even this is not essential every year. Established trees may be cut back where they occupy too much room, but it would be foolish to recommend pruning to a specified number of eyes.

Pests and diseases give comparatively little trouble. Greenfly attacks are always possible and for some reason which I cannot fathom these pests nearly always infest the Rugosa hybrid Conrad Ferdinand Meyer in my garden, often in preference to the hybrid teas. You may also encounter mildew, especially if the trees are in a draughty position – that fine old hybrid perpetual Mrs. John Laing is very susceptible. Black Spot is less likely except with *Rosa foetida* and its varieties, likewise the Penzance hybrid sweet briars.

The high-centred formal blooms of the moderns are absent. The flowers are informal, often somewhat flat, as in the exquisite Maiden's Blush, but their lack of form (judged by contemporary standards) is outweighed by the great freedom of bloom. The period of flowering is usually short compared with the moderns – four to six weeks at the most. On a very dry soil the period will be shorter. There are, however, some old-timers which give a second crop or bloom intermittently from late spring to early autumn. These include the Chinas, Bourbons, Teas, Noisettes and Rugosas.

By no means all are scented. The following are usually considered among the most fragrant of all roses: *Rosa alba* Maiden's Blush, the White Banksian Rose which smells of violets (the yellow Banksian is scentless), *Rosa bourboniana* Boule de Neige, Souvenir de la Malmaison (give this a hot, dry position) and Zephirine Drouhin, also the majority of centifolias, damasks and gallicas.

N.P.H.

THE APIARIST

SWARMING TIME

June, the month of splendour, is also the month of swarms. The bees feel an urge to found colonies, to perpetuate their race by sending out swarms that will become established in far places. This tendency to swarm can seldom be completely stifled, but it can be checked.

Some strains swarm hardly at all, preferring to supersede their Queens when the necessity arises. But my bees are not of this disposition. They are quick, prolific, tremendous workers, apt to be possessed, in June, by a fever of swarming. By thinking and acting quickly I have so far been able to frustrate the plans of my bees, or to take, without loss, the outgoing swarms, either returning them to the parent colony or hiving them in new abodes. I would not have my bees otherwise, for the movements of a swarm are an unforgettable experience. I had formerly seen the bees as exemplary housewives, kind nurses, skilled mathematicians, chemists carrying with them the secret of an ambrosial food. Now I behold them in a different guise: they are individuals compelled by the power of an inexorable law; a race on the move. It is a prodigious spectacle.

For several preceding days the bees have been restless. They gather in groups on the alighting board and creep up in front of the hive. Foraging for nectar has ceased. Suddenly, before noon, without warning, the swarm rushes out. Its outgoing can be heard from a distance and there is no mistaking the sound; for its roar has a melodious, sustained overtone like the deep note of a violin.

The bees swirl about high in the air, descending like a stinging hail on any onlooker who approaches too closely. The swarm drifts across the garden.

When watching bees I have often been puzzled because when I expect them to be busy at some job or other they appear to be doing nothing at all. In fact they are doing things their own way – which is a way not immediately apparent to humans. So it is with a swarm. It is impossible to foretell the settling of the Queen, and it is at first hard to see the flying bees settling round her. But then I perceive, on the upright bole of a small apple-tree, a small quivering knot of bees. The knot becomes enlarged by settling bees. Soon, the whirling cloud is absorbed into an enormous mass.

Holding an inverted skep under the swarm, I jar the tree as violently as I can. The bees fall with a hiss into the skep. A few are left behind; these will in due course return to the hive. I tie a piece of coarse-meshed cheese-cloth over the mouth of the skep and leave it propped upside down in the shade of the tree until the evening.

Before sundown I arrange a board covered with a white cloth, sloping up to the entrance of the spare hive. I untie the skep and shake the bees out on to the board. They fall in a heap, leaving behind them, in the top of the skep, a small, oblong piece of wax comb with cells; the work of an evening. All is at first confusion. Bees crawl over the cloth, hither and thither. Groups form. The bees touch one another with their antennae as if conferring. One bee, then two bees, three, four, crawl away from the others up towards the hive. They have found the entrance. The news spreads. Order is re-established. A thin, steady stream of bees moves upwards, like a trickle of molten lava. A squadron detaches itself from the crowd. Its members station themselves at regular intervals, one behind the other, in two lines on the alighting board. Each bee spreads her legs, raises herself high, and with her head down and vibrating wings, exposes the scent-organ on the fifth segment of her up-tilted abdomen, thus wafting behind her a stream of scent that directs the oncoming crowd.

The trail is blazed, the road is sign-posted. In troop the bees, faster and faster, tumbling over each other in their anxiety to enter their new home – but all the time keeping to the narrow bottleneck, the appointed road, which is flanked on each side by the line of fanning bees. Some drones blunder along. The Queen runs in with quick movements distinct from the steady crawl of the workers.

I make a fold in the muslin, a ridge that impedes the progress of the crowd. The bees on its peak link their hind feet to the front legs of the bees behind, which do the same to the bees behind them. The first bee drops over, dragging her companions after her. A living bridge is thus formed for the oncoming bees.

A contented hum comes from within the hive. The new home is satisfactory. Dusk falls; a few exhausted stragglers are all that remain of the swarm. This stock consolidates its position, and, helped at first with sugar syrup, becomes at the end of the season a productive community, providing me with fifteen pounds of surplus honey.

V.T.

THE BIRD WATCHER

GOLDEN ORIOLE

I'm afraid there is no doubt that the majority of golden orioles that are "seen" in the British Isles are green woodpeckers. It is true that both sexes of the green woodpecker have distinctive crimson crowns, and nobody who has once heard it is liable to mistake the green woodpecker's yaffling laugh for anything else. But there are many occasions when quite experienced observers have disturbed a green woodpecker sweeping up ants on a lawn; and have seen little else but the bright green-yellow flash of its rump and its undulating flight as it fled, and have put two and two together and made five. Common though the green woodpecker is, its colour in some lights is so exotic as to make it hard to believe it a native bird. Moreover, the fabulous golden oriole also has an undulating flight and can flash bright yellow or yellow-green as it makes away.

June is the month in which we are most likely to see or hear the golden oriole in England, and if the climatic amelioration continues, we are likely to have it a little more often, and the chances of its nesting must become slightly greater. So let me recount the facts about this handsome bird, this temperate-country member of what is, primarily, a tropical and subtropical bird family, the Oriolidae – and the only member of it, incidentally, that nests in Europe. It is a bird of old open woodland, of parkland, particularly in its European range, of orchards and vineyards. It's never found in conifer forests except in open, dry pine country. It's purely a summer visitor to Europe; most of the European birds seem to winter in East Africa. A great many go to the area Kenya, Uganda and Nyasaland, though some go on to Madagascar. Only the birds from Spain and Portugal go to West Africa. Possibly this means that the bird's breeding-range has spread west into Europe since the Ice Age, while it has remained more conservative about its winter-quarters.

In a very fine recent analysis of marking records Dr. Erwin Stresemann, the famous German ornithologist, has shown that the eastern group runs its autumn passage on a really quite narrow front, through Greece and its islands and then up the Nile. But on the way back on the spring passage, the East African winterers seem to cross the Mediterranean on a quite broad front, with its left wing through Tunis and Sicily. South and East England (particularly Norfolk) have some summer visitors somewhere every year, but so far most of them appear to be non-breeders. If a pair of golden orioles are going to breed in Britain they must arrive in late April or early May. Quite a lot of birds arrive, it is true, in June, but no one has ever proved that any of these June birds have attempted to nest. The song has been heard at any time from the beginning of May to the end of July. In August the golden orioles leave their English territories and disperse; in September they depart, and none has ever been seen after October.

It's rather odd that the golden oriole should be so rare in Britain, and quite irregular as a breeding visitor. It nests in the whole of mainland Europe, except for some rather isolated peninsulas like Greece, Brittany and Jutland – Europe, that is, south of the Baltic, for with the exception of the extreme south of Sweden and south-east of Finland, Scandinavia north of the Baltic is beyond its range. Through this breeding range it is a tree bird, hiding through the summer in the foliage, hardly ever seen on the ground – hardly seen at all, indeed, for both sexes are most secretive and wary.

In the hand, or in the museum, the contrasting coloration of the golden oriole is most conspicuous; but into green natural foliage, the leafy canopy of open woodland, even the unique yellow and black of the cock blends and disappears. It has black wings and tail and the rest of it is bright yellow. The hen and the young are more sober yellow-green with dark wings and tail and grey-white underparts; and both sexes have pink-brown, robust bills. Golden orioles do not get full adult plumage until the second season after that in which they are hatched. The first-year birds tend to be as dull (comparatively) as the adult females: but the young males have more yellow and the young females more olive upper parts.

These descriptions, however, are not quite as important to the field naturalist as the cock's song, which is by far the most usual characteristic by which the presence of the bird can be recognised. Once heard, it is never forgotten; a low fluty, fruity, melodious "deedaleeo, deedleeo."

Towards the end of May both members of the pair build a nest of stems and grasses in a special way which is, as far as I can detect from the abundant Continental literature, consistent for the species. It is always in an angle of a largish horizontally-forking branch of a large tree pretty high up. From the arms of this Y the beautifully-woven nest is suspended; it is lined with moss, wool, spiders' web and so on. There are usually four eggs, quite white with a rash of small dark spots at the big end. Many Continental observers believe that the birds occasionally rear two broods, though none has ever even tried to do so in England. The incubation and fledging periods are more typical of a small than of a medium passerine bird, about two weeks each.

The data on the attempts to breed of the golden oriole in England are rather surprisingly incomplete. Although scarcely a year passes in Norfolk without Anthony Buxton or some other member of the coterie of experienced county naturalists hearing a singing male, there seems to be no well-authenticated record of one with a nest in Norfolk in the present century. Indeed in all Britain since 1900 only about ten pairs have occupied territories before June, and there is only one certain breeding and one certain attempt at breeding. In 1930 a pair nested in Surrey and reared a brood which left the nest safely. In 1940 Mr. P. A. Adolph saw a pair at Chiswick in Middlesex, first on April 27. By May 4 they had half completed a nest, which was constructed in typical oriole fashion on the horizontal fork of an oak tree. Unfortunately the pair were not seen again and the nest was not completed.

Apart from these records of the present century, the golden oriole nested in the 1890s in Hampshire, Kent, and Buckinghamshire, and before the '90s also in Norfolk, Suffolk and Northamptonshire. It is probable that towards the end of the nineteenth century a pair bred at a village near Haseley in Oxfordshire, but the event was kept so quiet that it did not get into any important records, and was only brought to light in 1929. It thus became the kind of record that our careful county recorders put in square brackets, a "probable but not proved."

I would not be surprised if the golden oriole does not try to nest rather more often in the rest of the present century. It is always rash to make predictions about the behaviour of birds; and I think that any extra efforts that the golden oriole may make will come to nought unless the species is specially undisturbed. The trouble with nearly all the best golden oriole country, such as parks, formal gardens and orchards, is that either the public owns it or is freely admitted to it. Golden orioles do not like human disturbance very much. Still, we must hope for the best.

J.F.

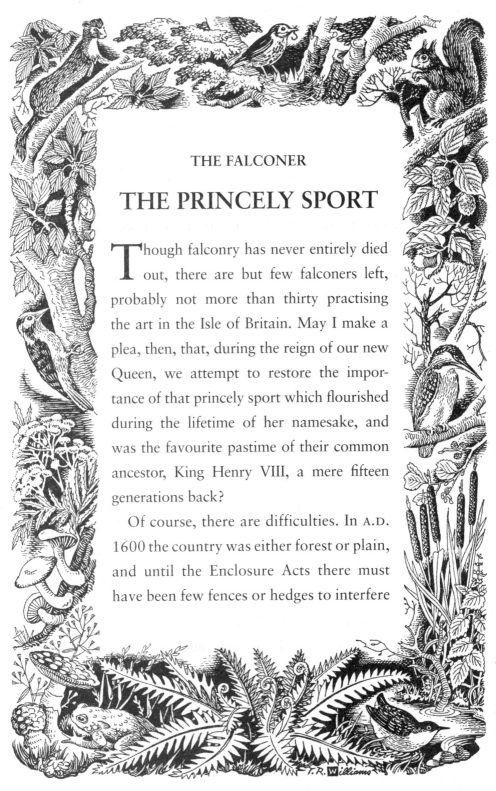

THE FALCONER

THE PRINCELY SPORT

Though falconry has never entirely died out, there are but few falconers left, probably not more than thirty practising the art in the Isle of Britain. May I make a plea, then, that, during the reign of our new Queen, we attempt to restore the importance of that princely sport which flourished during the lifetime of her namesake, and was the favourite pastime of their common ancestor, King Henry VIII, a mere fifteen generations back?

Of course, there are difficulties. In A.D. 1600 the country was either forest or plain, and until the Enclosure Acts there must have been few fences or hedges to interfere with the sport. For it was the enclosures which dealt a nearly mortal blow to falconry – the enclosures and the development of the "too frequent gun," plus, of course, the increasing ignorance of the rural population. In the seventeenth century, a lost hawk was rarely lost for good, or indeed for more than a few days. Everyone knew the procedure for taking it up and there was a more or less recognised scale of rewards. Nowadays it usually falls victim, in spite of legislation, to some idiot with a gun, or, even worse, to the keeper, who should know better.

One hundred and seventy years after the death of Elizabeth of England, an anonymous author, writing an introduction to James Campbell's treatise on *Modern Falconry*, lamented the decline of the noblest field sport ever practised by man. "It was," he says, "when hounds and hawks were the only means whereby the recreations of the field could be enjoyed with dignity, that the reputation of falconry was highest. It was then practised and studied by men of rank and distinction in every country of Europe, where anything of civilisation existed. Game was to be found everywhere in the greatest plenty, without the interposition of the legislature for its preservation – hawks being adapted to give much sport without much slaughter. But firearms were improved, and introduced as remarkable an alteration into sporting as they did into the art of war. The sportsman had hitherto drawn his pleasure from observing the various surprising turns of the chase or flight, and, when he obtained it, he was little mortified that the hare or woodcock made its escape at last from his hounds or hawk. This is the true idea of the pleasure which the sports of the field are qualified to afford; but this idea was gradually lost after guns were made of easy carriage, and pointers trained to find out game. Sport came now to be confined entirely to the act of putting the game to death; and a man measured the liveliness of his diversion according to the number of birds he had slain.... This new idea, however, of sport, made hawking decline; because, a good marksman could procure more of this amusement from his gun than from a hawk. It also helped very much to bring the latter into disuse, that the former could be kept with less expense and without any trouble.

"Though the pointer and gun were of considerable detriment to hawking at their first introduction, yet they did not triumph over this diversion till the dexterity of the French lighted on the knack of shooting on wing, and taught it to their neighbours. This knack enabled every man to act up to his idea of sporting by the ease and certainty with which it enabled him to kill game. And thus it reached a blow to falconry which has proved almost fatal to it."

Well, the wheel has reached nearly full circle. Never again, I imagine, will we see the battues fashionable around the turn of the century, with pheasants released from under flowerpots, and hand-reared mallard so fat that they had to be thrown into the air. Your keen shot today demands quality, not mere quantity, and, if it is a question of quality, then the hawk should once more come into her own.

In any case, I should hate to appear pessimistic. If, two hundred and fifty years ago, a falconer, well mounted, would have had no difficulty in following the flight of his bird almost as far as he wished, there are still some places, even in the South of England, where the sport is still possible, and still some enlightened landowners who will give leave to fly over their estates. In the South, though, the abominable American invention – barbed wire – makes of a horse a liability rather than an asset, for while even thirty years ago it would have been possible to have chased a field-mouse for twenty miles along the Wiltshire Downs, most of them now are under the plough and wired.

It cannot be too strongly emphasised, for the benefit of landowners and game preservers, that a falcon does *not* drive away game. Some persons with whom I have discussed the sport were convinced that either every partridge and/or grouse would be driven over the marsh, or else had visions of the falconer returning with a veritable holocaust of carefully preserved game. In fact, of course, it is a very good falcon indeed which will attempt more then six good flights a day and a bird with more than a hundred kills to her credit at the end of the season is a wonder.

There is nothing like the difficulty in manning and training a falcon that most people imagine there to be. Six weeks should be plenty long enough for an eyass to be killing game for her owner's delight, and the only problem facing the average falconer must remain the question of time. A good game-hawk must be flown as regularly and often as weather conditions allow, otherwise she will not wait on; but for the impecunious, occasional, or weekend and therefore average falconer the rook will always provide a suitable quarry which requires no waiting on, and which, on occasion, will afford as good a flight as is nowadays possible.

Herons, I fear, except in very few places, are quarry of the past, but the rook makes a passable substitute and has the merit of being ubiquitous. A *good* rook, though he is not all that common, will tax the powers of the best falcon and will ring up until both hawk and quarry are but specks in the sky. And it is then that you will see something worth while, my masters. Once above her prey, the falcon turns over, and, with her sails to her sides, rips down the sky at the black flapping thing beneath her. But the B.F.T. is both faster and more clever than he appears; with a last-second twist he evades the stoop and the impact of the hind toe. The falcon immediately throws up again to reach her pitch – it would be interesting to estimate the amount of "g" she must endure – and the process is repeated until the rook makes his point in cover or the falcon manages to kill. Mr. Patrick Chalmers has put it better than I can:

> *The lightning's child – where the hill shower shifts,*
> *She strikes her quarry a-wing, she lifts,*
> *Where the great winds roar in the granite rifts ...*

but not even (in the days when I still shot geese) the great skeins flighting out of Rockcliffe on an October evening could give me such an enduring prickling up and down the spine as the sight of my own, my very own falcon putting in a dozen stoops and knocking her rook out of the air with a thud that can be heard half a mile away.

I have never kept short-wings, and so am quite unqualified to discuss the merits of the goshawk and sparrow-hawk. I would suggest that they are more difficult to manage than the falcons, but they can be flown in any country, and, if not so dramatic, are, on their day, more ruthlessly efficient than their long-winged cousins. Flying a goshawk is, in any case, very much more fun than mooching round with a gun with nothing more than the pot in view. I am not suggesting that flying hawks should compare or compete with shooting, but, for those who live in the country, and have a little spare time (for, nowadays, not many of us can shoot more than twice a week, if that), the keeping and flying of hawks can provide us with an unmatched pleasure.

To train a hawk requires skill and patience. To see a falcon stoop is one of the most breathtakingly beautiful things in nature, and, when she performs under command, one of the most fascinating examples of man's dominion over the really wild creatures of the world. Furthermore, once bitten with the fever, there is no giving up. I know of no falconer who has abandoned the game in disgust, though I know a few who, deprived of opportunity, have pined, themselves like sick hawks, until the time when they could again take the creature they have "made" and fly her down the winter sky.

Her Majesty was pleased, recently, to spend a singularly cold day watching hawks being flown at Sandringham. May we hope that some of her loyal subjects may be encouraged to take up the art, so that once more the falconer's cry may be heard in the land – HOLD FAST!

J.R.J.

DOG MAN
THE PARSON'S TERRIER

When someone says "I've got myself a grand little Parson Jack Russell terrier, a real nailer, come and see it!" I know what stamp of dog I am going to be shown.

Seldom am I wrong. There it is, head held on one side in the manner of all intelligent dogs, legs straight and rather short, coat not quite smooth yet not really rough – "broken" I would call it – ears half-pricked. I act as I do with most terriers after we have been introduced, gently turn back their lips so that I can look at their front teeth to see what sort of a grip they have. After all, it is only fair when a dog is going to be asked to kill rats and catch rabbits, that it shall have the right equipment to do so. I am less interested when the owner of this so-called "Jack Russell" proudly points out the spot near the root of the tail and reminds me that this is the hall-mark of the breed.

For there is no such breed. The Reverend John Russell, who was born in 1795 and lived to be eighty-eight, had a wonderful eye for a working terrier and kept a number of "good 'uns" at his Devonshire parsonage of Tordown. The duty of these terriers was to bolt foxes when they were run to ground by his own pack of hounds. They were expected to run with the hounds, too, so they could not have been short on the leg, not nearly as short as many of the dogs which are now named after that sporting parson.

Parson Russell was always on the lookout for terriers of the right sort and, when he found one, he would not rest until he had begged or bought it. His ideal of a perfect terrier was a bitch named Trump which he found when a student at Oxford. Trump belonged to a milkman who was persuaded to part with her to young Russell who, it seems, was not disappointed for, when he became a Devonshire parson, he bred several litters of pups from her.

From the description of Trump which is available, it seems that she had legs in about the same proportions to body as had the modern fox-terrier, but she was certainly smaller. Jack Russell's idea of the right size for a terrier was that it should be about the same as that of a vixen, and his were all expected to go to ground. Also, Trump's head was not too long or too pointed. She had a thick, wiry coat and a tan patch, about the size of a penny piece, at the root of the tail. It is similar spots which some breeders of terriers are so fond of pointing out as proof that their dogs are "genuine Jack Russells."

Now, I can easily understand that length and straightness of leg, nature of coat and shape of head can be passed on to succeeding generations, but I am not going to accept a chance freak of marking, like a spot in a certain place, as proof of ancestry.

One of Parson Russell's terriers, Juddy, helped in founding the present day fox-terrier, but I can only guess at the unclerical remark which he would have made at the appearance of some modern show specimens of that breed were he alive to see them. It may be that others of his dogs are among the ancestors of the Sealyham, although they, too, were very different.

If direct descendants of Russell's strain of terriers exist today with the character and appearance of his Trump, I imagine that they are to be found somewhere in his own West Country, perhaps in foxhound kennels or in the homes of men and women who know a good, varminty tyke when they see one. Some day I must go and look for them.

I know several people who breed and work "Jack Russell terriers"; I have had them myself, short-legged, game little bounders who will tackle rats, chivvy rabbits and which have enough sense to do their job without getting damaged when they go to ground to fox or badger. I love such dogs and, when nobody is looking, I go on all-fours and play at badgers with them under chairs, but I know that they are not the same stamp of terrier which the famous West Country parson kept. They are all too short on the leg and most of them too small to have pleased him.

Does it really matter? Nowadays, few masters of foxhounds expect their terriers to run with the pack and those who do can find Borders or Lakelands in the districts which produce those grand types of terriers.

However, if I am choosing a dog with the label "Jack Russell" attached to it, even if its legs are a trifle short according to that gentleman's ideas, I make sure that they are *straight*. I see no virtue nor advantage in crooked legs even in bulldogs or dachshunds and certainly not in terriers, whatever the show-bench people may say. My dogs are expected to travel far and sometimes fast on their own feet and, to do so, good action is necessary and they can't have good action without straight legs. Nor must it have a body which is too heavy in proportion to its limbs.

To lovers of the right sort of terrier, the name "Parson Jack Russell" still means everything that is right about a dog, even though some rather peculiar animals change hands under it. Actually, it describes a *type* of terrier, not a breed, but do let us be sure what this type is, especially if we are buying one.

J.I.L.

WHAT EVERY COOK
SHOULD KNOW ABOUT

THE EARLY RABBIT

In February and March you could swear that there were hardly any rabbits left about the place; but by April, if spring has been mild and dry, the first litters make their appearance. Those who survive of these will be grandparents.

The basic way of preparing young rabbits is to skin, empty, and remove the head and neck. Set aside the liver (as it is invaluable in forcemeat and stuffing) and remember to detach from it the small gall bladder. Joint into four main limb quarters and two sections of saddle or back. In general, young rabbits are accompanied by appropriate young garden produce, which is cooked separately and added to the rabbit and its appropriate sauce or gravy just before serving. This is very necessary as young rabbit needs long slow simmering, where the vegetables need a short sharp boil of length suited to their individual needs.

Taking "Laperau aux Fines Herbes" as a basic dish the procedure is: Let the joints take colour to a light golden brown by sautéing with bacon fat or butter in a pan. Take a good handful of parsley, chives or onion trimmings, chop it fine and add plenty of the leaves but not the twigs of thyme. In France a little chopped garlic is also added. The herbs are mixed and mashed up with a little butter. Having browned your joints sprinkle them with a dessertspoonful of flour and put back on the fire. The moment the flour begins to take colour, draw the pan to the side and add a glass of water and a glass of white wine (half water, half wine vinegar can replace this).

Now add your mixed herbs and stir to blend until the whole has begun to thicken, never letting it do more than simmer. Now you can add the livers, and at the end of three minutes – no more! – draw the pan to the side and with a wooden spoon break down the livers smoothly into the thickened gravy in the pan, which is best poured into another pan for this operation. Return the mixture to the joints and cook for another five minutes, adding such vegetables as small new potatoes, onions, etc., which you have cooked separately just before dishing up.

There are endless slight variations to this process, but they all come to much the same. You "brown" to a very light colour and you *simmer* in a sauce which thickens to the consistency of light brown. You can replace butter by olive oil and *fines herbes* by tomatoes and call it "laperau Marengo" and you can to some extent replace wine by lemon juice. You can keep your "sauce" or, rather, gravy thin, pour it off through a strainer and thicken with yolk of egg, not allowing it to boil, and call it "Poulette." You can use cider – dry hard cider – and produce

"Normande," or beat in cream, in which case the rabbit gravy should be strained and run off to make a "white" sauce, to which the cream is added.

Young rabbits are even better cold than hot. The preliminary processes are the same, but the joints are then preferably deboned and the flaked meat presented either in aspic, with a thick mayonnaise, or a Sauce Ravigotte which is easier and is simply hard-boiled yolk of egg pounded up and rubbed down in olive oil, to which is added a little tarragon vinegar and French mustard. Served with an undressed lettuce salad and mayonnaise or any of the foregoing the rabbit may well pass as chicken, and can indeed be mixed with chicken, when it is unlikely to be detected if boned.

It should be noted that even if the traditional "Boiled rabbit and onion sauce" is not the best way of doing rabbit, it can be made a good dish by treating basically as suggested – browning first, then simmering, and finished off in a well-flavoured white "soubise" onion sauce. As a change, I can recommend young rabbit with a good caper sauce, which is a mildly onion-flavoured white sauce to which capers are added at the last moment.

To expand young rabbits, if there are insufficient for an adequate family meal, they can be helped out with forcemeat balls made of crumbs of bread, chopped bacon, onion, herbs, and the rabbit liver poached for three minutes and crumbled into the mixture. Bind with white of egg and bake lightly and separately. As an alternative young rabbits can be stuffed and sewn up and roast with careful roasting. They should be smothered with a fairly thick sauce before appearing on the table, as they lack the appetising appearance of a finely roasted fowl.

Later in the season, when field mushrooms are often available in quantity, basic young rabbit served with mushrooms stewed in milk, drained and then added to a plain white sauce of the rabbit gravy sharpened with lemon juice is a superb dish. The milk in which the mushrooms have been cooked is not suitable, as it will produce a grey to brownish colour, so a small separate white sauce must be prepared.

H.B.C.P.

THE NATURALIST

IT'S SPRING IN THE HIGHLANDS

A day's journey from England to the Highlands of Scotland at the end of May or the beginning of June pays the naturalist most agreeable dividends. When he reaches the pine-forests of Inverness or the lochs of Wester Ross he finds spring waiting for him, and he can enjoy it all over again.

Moreover, June, of all Highlands months, has the most stable weather. On the mountains all kinds of alpine flowers shine, some rare and all beautiful. The midges and mosquitoes and cleggs have not begun their worst. The country is all fresh, with plenty of water in the rivers and new leaves on the birches.

The birch-woods are exceptionally beautiful when the late evening sun shines through the leafy canopy and throws its yellow light on the old knotted trunks. Most of the natural birch-woods of the West Highlands are old, and many are dying away; for the nibbling sheep check natural regeneration. But in cattle country they are growing and creeping to new sheltered places on the hillsides.

The old birch-woods of the Western Highlands have fascinated me ever since I first explored them ten years ago. The landscape of Wester Ross is composed of extraordinarily ancient rock, the Lewisian Gneiss, which forms a maze of lochs and little hills – the hills rounded, almost polished, by the action of the ice ages. In the valleys, running quite high up the neighbouring hillsides, the birch-groves shelter; and on quiet days the rock-climber can hear the song of their many birds from his perch on the sandstone precipice above – a perch he often shares with ring-ousel and merlin, sometimes with ptarmigan.

Round about the turn of the century, these birch-woods of the North-West Highlands were fairly thoroughly explored by the famous Scottish faunist J. A. Harvie-Brown and some of his friends. They published several accounts of the birds they found in these woods, and it is interesting to compare them with what we find today. It seems pretty certain that during the last fifty years these woods have been gradually colonised by species coming in from the south. Zoologists are not surprised at this, for throughout Northern Europe as a whole there has been a marked northward advance of many species of small birds in the present century, and it is generally agreed that this is a consequence of the amelioration of the climate.

If you walk to visit one of these birch-woods you may meet a fox trotting along a shepherd's track; wild cats and even pine-martens still inhabit this country. On a big loch near by a black-throated diver makes a reverberating barking shout, and a greenshank sings its piping, lilting wader-song overhead. By the banks of a big burn a common sandpiper utters its insane, dithering titter. Just at the edge of a wood a disturbed roe deer bounds into cover and completely disappears behind some low birches.

Round the edges of the main birch-wood are many isolated groups of stunted trees – birch, rowan and sallow – often under the shelter of rock outcrops. From each one of these sings the commonest small bird of the Highland valleys, the willow-warbler. Only the meadow-pipit of the moors outnumbers it, and often as we listen we hear the descending little air-song of this bird mixing with the flowing lilt of the willow-warblers. This sweet delicate little song is the real voice of the Highlands in June. There are more than twice as many willow-warblers as any other species of bird in these Highland birch-woods. The next commonest is the chaffinch, that ubiquitous creature which is probably more numerous in the British Isles as a whole than any other kind of small singing-bird. Chaffinches, as everybody knows, show a marked geographical variation in their song, and the Highland birds have a distinct northern accent, a different tone and rhythm and song-pattern from those in England.

The robins of the Highland birch-woods also sing in June and often their song is the first indication to us of their presence; for these Highlands robins are shy birds, much more like Continental robins in behaviour than the robins of our gardens. And besides willow-warblers and chaffinches and robins there are wrens and blue-tits, coal-tits and great-tits, long-tailed tits and tree-pipits and redstarts.

One day in 1944 I was walking through one of the biggest, oldest and darkest of all the Ross birch-groves, the Doire Dhubh, under the sandstone mountain Cul Beag, when I heard the cry of a great spotted woodpecker. This was a newcomer, the first in Wester Ross of a bird which seventy years ago was confined to England, which reached the Lowlands by 1900, the Eastern Highlands by 1920, and the Central Highlands by 1940. The tree-pipit, though it is the fourth commonest bird in these birch-woods, may be a newcomer, for it was rare fifty years ago.

Another little bird which is spreading to the North-West is the wood-warbler. Quite recently it has been singing in West Sutherland for the first time, and not many years ago I found a large and unexpected group of ten singing males in a large and straggling birch-wood near the Ross-Sutherland border. Its shivering song is an agreeable addition to the Highland scenery. Another pleasant embellishment is the redstart; the russet flash of the cock shifting from one birch stump to another gnarled trunk is now a common sight in the Highlands, though rare fifty years ago.

In a birch-wood near the gorge of the Polly river in Wester Ross I found a family party of willow-tits in 1942. Though it was too late to prove formally that the tits had been reared on the spot, it is worth pointing out that the normal limit of the breeding-range of this species in Britain was nearly a hundred miles to the south-east. Later my friend Dr. T. G. Longstaff saw willow-tits in the same district, and moreover, 30 years ago, the late J. Gordon found a nest by Loch Maree, also in Wester Ross. There is no doubt that there is a scatter of odd pairs of this interesting species of tit miles beyond the normal edge of its breeding range in the Lowlands. They have been seen not only in Wester Ross, but in Easter Ross, Inverness, Argyll and Aberdeenshire, and sometimes proved to be breeding.

I know few better refuges in June for the naturalist who likes to live among interesting animals and plants and avoid his fellow-men. On the borders of Sutherland and Ross there are areas up to a hundred square miles in which no man sleeps – a maze of hills, lochs, valleys and woods, some of which are not visited from one year's end to another, and in the next year only by some bird-watcher or fisherman or stalker. This country is not virgin country, and man and his sheep have made important differences to it; but it has suffered fewer changes than any other large area of Britain.

J.F.

HERBS AND THEIR USES

Today we tend to neglect those herbs so highly thought of in mediaeval days. We prefer to purchase a bottle of artificial spray, or a packet of herbs so long dried as to have lost almost all flavour. In my garden, pride of place is given to the herbs for they are so much used about the home throughout the year.

Rosemary we love best, possibly because of its historical associations or because in our garden overlooking the North Sea it flourishes. So it should do, for it is found in its natural haunt along the shores of the Mediterranean and because it loves a dry soil and a salt laden atmosphere it is called the "dew of the sea." It is evergreen, loved by bees and about the home may be used in numerous ways. In olden times it was said to "gladden the spirits" wherever its richly aromatic leaves were pressed, and it has the same effect today. Several sprigs left to partially dry in a warm room will do much to relieve the most stubborn headache if pressed and inhaled.

Distilled oil of Rosemary is still one of the chief ingredients of eau-de-Cologne water, whilst the water from simmered leaves acts as an excellent hair tonic, and as a freshener and purifier of the face. The ancient Greeks simmered the leaves in white wine with which to beautify their faces. But it is the freshly gathered foliage that is most valuable, for if placed under the pillow case it will bring about rapid sleep. Bancke's Herbal, the first complete herbal written in English, mentions that "the leaves laid under the pillow deliver one from evil dreams," which I suppose is the same thing as sleeping well. That great herb gardener, the late Miss Sinclair Rohde, has told us how in the same way the potent seeds may be gathered in September, dried and placed in muslin bags and hung about the bedroom for encouraging sleep.

Though hardy, the plants should receive protection from drying winds, which is why they do so well in a walled garden; and do give them some lime rubble to get their roots into.

Mint. Parkinson tells us "where Docks are not at hand, the bruised leaves laid upon any place stung by bees and wasps, is to good purpose." In olden times mint had other important uses apart from making sauce. Gardeners and even city folk, carried with them metal boxes containing the dried leaves of peppermint, the Black Peppermint, which almost takes the breath away when carelessly inhaled. To "gladden the spirits" it was sold in the streets of London from earliest times along with Pennyroyal, which was believed to be capable of purifying rain water so making it suitable for drinking.

Pennyroyal has the power of bringing relief to the most exhausted body and in our garden we have a small bank planted entirely with creeping Pennyroyal and Chamomile. The plants have completely covered the ground and on a warm day if one would lie stretched out over the plants, their aromatic fragrance will not only revive one's mind, but will revive tired limbs equally well.

Southernwood or lad's love, as we called it in earlier days, is a most charming plant with its pale green feathery foliage and rich pungent smell. We use it in the home about clothes for it will keep away moths and keep cupboards sweet and fresh. With Bergamot it possesses a more pungent smell than all other herbs and for that reason the leaves of these two plants were used first to strew about the floors of churches and later were carried with the leaves of Rosemary as small posies by the children to relieve the musty atmosphere of the church.

To place amongst clean bedding, sprigs of Marjoram, Rosemary and eau-de-Cologne, mint and the flowers of lavender will give to it the most delightful fragrance, and when put on the bed will retain its potency for several days. The same concoction may be placed in muslin bags inside a pillow, which will, on being pressed with the head, emit a most soothing perfume, especially appreciated in the sick room. Those who frequent the hop gardens of Kent and Worcestershire know the value of a pillow stuffed with hops for encouraging sleep. The hops, like the herbs, should be renewed twice each year.

Sage has many uses apart from its value for stuffing. For indigestion, an ounce of the fresh leaves simmered in a pint of water and a wineglassful taken after each meal will not only help the digestion but will tone up the system whilst to cure a sore throat the same infusion to which has been added a small cupful of vinegar and used as a gargle will work wonders.

There are numerous forms of sage, a red leaf variety; one having a variegated leaf and the more common broad-leaf variety.

The Thymes could well have a book devoted to their many uses and attractive forms. Still grown in our garden for rubbing on beef, though scarcely the baron of beef from which it takes its name, is T. *Herba Barona*, of prostrate form and possessing the scent of carraway seeds. Delightful for drying and hanging in small bunches about a room is T. *micans*, a native of Spain and possessing a rich pine fragrance, particularly refreshing in a bedroom. For adding spice to pot-pourri nothing is more valuable than the Lemon Thyme, in both the golden and silver forms. Dried and mixed with the lemon-scented geranium leaf, put into tiny muslin bags for one's handbag or pocket, this will give a most refreshing perfume and be most appreciated when taking a long journey by air, car or train. It needs to be crushed in the hand to bring out its full fragrance. Smelling almost of peppermint is the rare T. *membronaceus*, which bears dainty white, tubular blooms and is a lovely plant for an edging to a lawn or path. For curing a cough this is an excellent plant and should be mixed with lemon thyme or the juice of half a lemon. An ounce is boiled with a large teaspoonful of whole linseed and the half lemon. When cool, it should be sweetened with honey, strained and a tablespoonful taken whenever the cough proves troublesome.

To obtain the greatest benefit from all herbs with the exception of mint, they should be planted into a position where they will receive the maximum amount of sunshine to encourage them to build up in their foliage as much natural oil as possible, for only then will their fragrance be most potent.

R.G.

STARTING A ROCK GARDEN

The site for a rock garden should be chosen with care. It need not be large, but it must be away from the drip of overhanging trees and it ought not to be in narrow, draughty passages, nor should it be densely shaded, although a trifle of shade on one side or the other will be an advantage. A gentle slope to the south-west is the ideal, but do not despair if it is not available. My own rock garden faces due north and is open to the east and grows a wide collection of alpine plants very successfully. Nor is a slope essential; flat ground may be used as long as the drainage is good. If the soil is heavy and does not drain rapidly it will he necessary to excavate a good depth and fill in with rough material before starting on the construction.

If there is a local stone to be had it should be used, both for reasons of economy and fitness. Westmorland limestone is very lovely, but it looks out of place in a sandstone district, and vice versa. For general purposes sandstone is the best stone to use as most plants like it, it weathers quickly and attractively, and it is reasonable in cost and easily obtainable in most districts. A good rock garden can be built by using about two tons of stone, in pieces varying from half a hundred-weight to one and a half hundredweight. Very small stone is not advisable, and large stone is difficult to handle.

A good heap of prepared soil should be in readiness. If the ordinary garden soil is of good quality it may be used, mixed with half leafmould or granulated peat and quarter sharp sand or grit. If the available loam is not first-rate, a supply should be obtained. It is important to start right. From two to three tons of mixed soil will be required with the two tons of rock. Make certain that all stones dip slightly backwards into the ground, and that they are rammed very firmly around and beneath.

What to plant is the next question, and here the choice is so vast that I can do no more in this limited space than to indicate a dozen or two plants which should be on every rock garden. None of them is difficult or expensive and they form a good nucleus which can be added to with growing experience.

For early spring bulbs and very early alpines you must wait until the autumn before planting, but any of the following planted in the spring may provide at least a few flowers the first year. *Campanula muralis,* deep blue. *Gentiana acaulis,* blue. *Dianthus caesius,* pink, *Gypsophila fratensis,* pink. *Sedum spathulifolium purpureum,* yellow. Phlox Temiscaming, crimson. *Geranium subcaulescens,* carmine. *Saxifraga lingulala,* white. *Saxifraga* Winston Churchill, pink. *Erinus* Dr. Hanelle, deep red. *Primula auricula alpina,* deep yellow. *Primula marginata,* lavender-blue. *Helianthemum*

Watergate Rose, port-wine-red. *Hypericum polyphyllum,* orange-yellow. *Penstemon cristatus,* rich amethyst. *Thymus serpyllum coccineus,* crimson. *Veronica pectinata rosea,* pink. *Zauschneria californica mexicana,* scarlet. *Iberis* Snowflake, white.

W.I.

READER'S LETTER

A BADGER IN THE KITCHEN

Your recent article on rearing a badger prompts me to send a photograph of my own Bill Brock. He is three years old, weighs over 40 lb. When he was dug out he weighed 1¼ lb. and was naked and blind. I started him off with Lactol on a fountain pen filler. He had 4 meals a day and took 45 minutes a feed. So I fed him before breakfast, when I got home from work at 6 p.m., and again before I went to bed. My wife fed him midday. We kept him warm with a 15-watt bulb in a cigarette tin covered in a sock.

By the time he was six months old he was well grown and strong and as rough as a bull terrier pup.

Never one day in his three years (except when away on holiday) have I missed handling him and playing for at least fifteen minutes and he is as docile now as ever.

He sometimes comes to the "local" with me and it's worth taking him to watch strangers' faces when they notice him. They look hurriedly away until they think nobody is watching and then furtively peep again to see if it really was a badger they saw.

PHIL DRABBLE, Ashlyn, Bloxwich, Staffs.

THE NATURALIST

CALLING WILD CREATURES

In Britain there are many animals and birds that will come to one call or another. In order to ensure success it is necessary to keep out of sight, or at any rate perfectly still, and use the wind intelligently.

The squeal of a rabbit will draw animals and birds. During their breeding season, which is a long one, rabbits display a marked lack of the instinct of self-preservation, in coming to this squeal. Stoats take a great interest in it and will come surprisingly close; on one occasion one touched my foot.

Weasels do come to it, but not as readily as they will to the shrill squeak of shrew or vole.

I have twice tried the rabbit's cry on a fox and on both occasions it acted, one fox coming to within eight paces of me.

Listening to the Red Deer belling, one October evening, my children and I found ourselves between a dog fox and a calling vixen. The wind was blowing our scent towards the dog and I knew it would not be long before he was silenced. When he stopped I decided to try my version of his bark on the vixen. She answered, coming nearer all the time, till my younger daughter whispered frightened protests.

Red deer hinds and Roe deer does will come to a noise produced by blowing on the edge of an elastic band, stretched between a short length of split nut stick, grooved slightly to allow the rubber band to vibrate. Neither hinds nor does are interested after the young are three months old.

It is not easy to copy a Red Deer Stag belling. My first attempt silenced the stag, except for the sound of his grunting as he drove away his bunch of hinds. I tried again the same night, moving up the combe below another stag. After listening to him for some time, I cupped my hands in front of my mouth and copied his roar. The result was alarming; the stag charged down the steep wooded face of the combe, crossed the water just below and stood quite close to me. His eyes looked like red-hot half-crowns, when I shone my torch on him. He soon realised this was no challenge to combat and retreated, turning to look back at the torch.

Early one June morning, while sitting in a car by the roadside, a leveret came along a field track on to the road, close to the car. I wondered how he would react to a hare's cry. At first he sat up, ears erect; after a moment or so he began to squat down very slowly, until he was flat on the road. The noise evidently got on his nerves; without any warning he made a leap, enormous for one so small, on to the heather-covered verge and vanished over a bank into a field. The leveret had just disappeared when a full grown hare, the mother, appeared. Following the scent of the little one, she examined the place where he had squatted, then she accelerated, at an incredible pace, for twenty yards up the road, and back again. Her claws were plainly audible as they gripped the road surface. Turning down the field track, for a few yards, she made a flying jump at right angles to the path, and described a big circle, ending up in the same field as the leveret.

Barn owls cannot resist the squeak of a mouse and come very near provided one is motionless. Many brown owls are easily fooled by an imitation of their hoot.

Some people may express surprise because animals often do not recognise the difference between genuine and counterfeit calls, but the average human mother would be quite as easily hoaxed by a hedgehog's cry if it came from the nursery.

H.E.

JULY

WILD LIFE

Whether July is a really silent month or not, silence certainly applies to August. Among small birds practically the only voice is that of the robin, which always seems to be trying out its autumn song well ahead of time. This is also the month when some of our summer bird visitors start to get restive as the return migratory urge makes itself felt. In the vanguard of those that are to leave us comparatively soon are the swifts – though of course a few will be about much later just to give bird watchers something to write about to their local papers. The young cuckoos, so vociferous in July, have mostly started on their unguided and mysterious journey to the South. Peewits and missel-thrushes are gathering together in flocks – another sign that the summer is on the wane.

In the insect world there is plenty to see. The beautiful hawker dragonflies are at their busiest, and their regular flights to and fro over ponds or in gardens or up and down woodland rides are fascinating to watch. The regularity of their progress being interrupted at intervals as they dart aside to pounce on some passing fly. Why were these lovely and harmless insects ever called "horse stingers" I wonder? I have never seen one near a horse, except by chance. The noble caterpillars of some of the hawk moths – privet and eyed hawk, for instance – should approach the peak of their growth; and that of the famous death's head hawk may possibly be discovered in potato fields. Wasps worry fruit growers and picnickers alike.

Adult reptiles are rather more noticeable as they bask at intervals in the sun, and children and dogs should beware of adders. The young of the harmless slow-worm and the grass snake appear, the latter are more likely to elude the eye owing to their protective coloration; while the former is seldom seen except by those who know where to look – under large uneven stones or old logs. Young slow-worms are beautiful little creatures, smaller than a decent-sized earthworm, and a lovely pale golden colour with a dorsal stripe of very dark brown running from the back of the head to the tail.

Fungi are becoming more plentiful and one of our best edibles, *Boletus edulis* may be gathered in woods, particularly in beech woods. While it is true that there are many more edible fungi than there are those which are deadly poisonous, the wise person learns to identify his species accurately before experimenting. With one or two species, the notorious death cap for instance, one never finds out one's mistake until too late!

M.K.

Weed-month and hay-month is also a month of crop production in the animal world. Much of this hard to observe, as under cover. Among mammals, the young come for the first time into relation with the external world. Many leave home, or prepare to do so. Wild cats wean their kittens, and play games with them round their cairns; fox-cubs are still learning, in play, from the experience of their parents; young otters have already learned to swim, but are still full of play. Young moles, hedgehogs and dormice leave the nest; calves of fallow- and red-deer are active on their young legs.

Some beasts have a later breeding season; in July their young are born, not weaned. Most bats need the abundant insect supply of late June and early July when suckling new-born young. Grass-snakes lay eggs in manure-heaps. Occasionally in the last week of July the first young adders are seen.

For some, July is time of mating; all month the pairing of badgers; from July 25 onwards the rutting of roe-deer. First foolish young woodland and garden birds disperse from neighbourhood of nests, and pay heavily for their inexperience; many die to feed animals of prey; many blunder into fruit-nets.

Most birds of prey rear young in June, but one Southern England species, the hobby, rears them in July; it lives mostly on swallows, martins, larks and pipits, whose easy-to-catch fledglings are not commonly available before.

Many sea-birds – cormorants, shags, gannets, petrels – are slow breeders with a long nesting-period, and have young in nest through July. Most fulmars hatch early July, also storm-petrels. Rare Leach's petrels do not hatch until mid-month. Other sea-birds – gulls (except kittiwake), terns and auks – usually get their young down from cliffs during month, the auks (guillemots, razorbills) before they have grown their flight-feathers. Big dispersal movements of gulls and terns usually start about July 20.

On the lonely remote lochans of Shetland, young phalarope; on the high Cairngorm tops, among the fringe-moss, young dotterels. After third week, a beginning of the great passage of waders to the south; our own common sandpipers, dunlin, redshank, greenshank, golden plover; from the Arctic the first sanderling; from Scandinavia the first ruffs.

July often decides game-crop. Young partridges take first flights; many die in droughts, as many in floods. If July be warm, and fairly settled (but not *too* settled) game should do well.

J.F.

THE VEGETABLE GARDEN

Continue with the routine jobs of hoeing and thinning. In dry weather, watering must never be neglected, especially for crops such as runner beans, marrows, celery. Being fleshy types they need a great deal of moisture. Flood the celery trenches every four days. Drag the earth away from the marrows to form a shallow saucer and prevent the water running away. Runner beans should be sprayed lightly as well as thoroughly flooded.

Pick all vegetables regularly. If dwarf and runner beans snap in two easily they will be tender to cook. The moment they bend and break with a string attached, give them to the pigs. Do not wait until the bean has bulges. Pick when flat.

During the first week risk a sowing of dwarf peas. It is a gamble, but worth it. A good method of growing tender heads of cabbage for October and November cutting is to sow a spring variety such as Wheelers Imperial, Harbinger, etc., in the first week. Sow thinly and thin out to about 12 inches. Do not transplant. In sheltered districts another sowing of stump rooted carrots and globe beet can be tried for pulling as small tender roots. A good bed of Batavian endive should be planted in the second week. Thin out to 15 to 18 inches. They need space. Continue to sow Cabbage lettuce, but it is too late for Cos.

Ground which has been cleared of early crops provides an excellent site for broccoli, kales, savoys, etc. The ground should be really firm.

Leeks should he planted 6 inches apart. Make a hole about 8 inches deep with a dibber, push the leek in and knock a little earth in to keep the roots from drying out. Do not firm like a cabbage plant. Do not forget another batch of spinach beet. Remove side shoots of tomatoes, pinch out top of main stem when four trusses have set. Gather herbs for drying when they are in full flower and consequently in full flavour.

Dry off shallots and garlic. Celery plants showing signs of rust can be sprayed with Bordeaux mixture. Read directions most carefully. Blistering can result if insufficient care is used.

Keep an eye on the raspberry canes and remove nets directly the fruit is finished. Clean nets before storing. A good soaking in a weak creosote solution followed by a thorough drying will act as a preservative. Take extreme care not to damage the tips of the young canes during removal.

Give thought to storage for fruit and root vegetables when harvested. It is essential that it should be frost and vermin proof.

If you intend to plant a new variety of strawberry, order now from a reliable firm.

E.B.

<hr />

If you are going away during dry weather, first give a good soaking to crops which need plenty of water – tomatoes, marrows, cucumbers – then mulch them loosely with something which will not settle into a solid mat. (Lawn mowings often do unless they are shaken up every few days.) Marrows for storing or exhibition can be kept unblemished by laying them in hammocks of muslin slung between two sticks. Watch the bush tomatoes, too, for slug damage, as the weight of the fruit sometimes pulls them to the ground and makes staking necessary.

Standard tomatoes will need almost daily inspection to keep them to one main stem. Outdoor ones seldom ripen more than four trusses, so pinch out the growing shoot when these have set; they will ripen more quickly if cloches are stood *behind* the plants so that the warmth of the sun is drawn round them. When mulching tomatoes, leave a space round the stem for feeding;

give them liquid manure, or a liquid fertilizer, but too strong a solution will do more harm than good, and whatever is used, dilute it well. Rhubarb can also do with the same kind of feeding just now, as it is building up its crowns for next spring; keep it well watered, too.

Potato lifting need not be hard work if it is done when the ground is dry, and the haulms cut down with a reaping hook and removed before attempting to dig; lay the tubers in the sun for an hour or two before taking them in. Young plants of Brussels sprouts and other winter brassicas can still be bought if the earlier sowings were missed. When planting out has to be done in dry weather, soak some small flower pots in a bucket of water and invert one over each plant during the daytime; remove them at night, and the plants will be crisp and upright instead of collapsed. All young greenstuff, also leeks, will root more readily if a pinch of bonemeal is put in before planting.

The most important sowing this month is spring cabbage, but it must be the right variety to stand through the winter. *Ellams Dwarf*, or – for a larger cabbage – *Early Offenham*, are two that can be sown now. Lettuce, too, must be the right kind for present sowings. *Imperial* is probably the most satisfactory for winter cultivation out of doors, or *Attractie* if it can be grown under cloches or in a cold frame. Turnips can be sown between the leek rows; they will be out of the way before the leek foliage gets too big. Make a final sowing of globe beetroot and stump-rooted carrots, and sow endive in a bed that is sheltered enough for it to stand through the winter.

C.M.

THE FLOWER GARDEN

O ne of the most satisfying of all garden operations is the successful propagation of favourite plants. Cuttings afford an easy method of increase for many of the trees and shrubs, and those who are lucky enough to have a heated frame will be able to make a start this month.

A suitable rooting medium is one part of leafsoil or peat to two parts of sand. Ensure that there is ample drainage and then fill the frame with the mixture to a depth of four to six inches and well firm. The exact time when the wood is in the best condition varies from year to year and with the different varieties of plants. Half-ripened shoots of the current year's growth should be selected, and removed, wherever possible, with a heel, for this often leads to easier rooting. Heel cuttings need only to be trimmed, but other cuttings must be cleanly cut with a sharp knife just below the node. Shrubs with very large leaves may have these shortened back by half to save space in the frame. The cuttings should be inserted with a dibber and firmed, given an initial watering, and the frame kept closed and shaded.

Each morning the moisture collecting on the glass must be wiped off and care taken to remove any fallen leaves. The cuttings need to be kept moist, but it is better to give a good watering when needed rather than a little at a time.

Although the quicker-growing hedges such as privet need two or three clippings a year the slower-growing yew and box can be kept in good condition by an annual clipping at this time. Clean the bottom of the old-established hedges and remove any dead branches from the base. A good mulching with well-rotted farmyard manure or compost, is most beneficial and will ensure that these permanent features of the garden are kept in good health. Newly planted hedges should be well watered during dry periods. Laurel and holly hedges should be trimmed with a pair of secateurs.

The many new varieties of iris have brought renewed, popularity to these most accommodating plants despite their rather short flowering period. To be seen at their best, iris need a sunny, well-drained border, but they appear to be able to grow in almost any situation. One of the chief errors in their cultivation is deep planting, for the top of the rhizome should be left just visible above the surface of the soil. The best time for any necessary transplanting is as soon as the flowers are over.

C.P.

—·—

Garden pinks are such good-natured plants that they are generally left year after year with no thought of renewal, yet smart young plants from one to three years old are more effective. July is a good month to propagate them from cuttings. These may be taken in the ordinary way or as pipings, which are growths pulled out at a joint instead of being cut. They will root readily if inserted in sandy soil in a shaded frame or a sheltered border. The hybrid pinks which are known as *Dianthus Allwoodii* may be propagated in the same way.

Alpine plants may be propagated this month and if a shaded frame is available there should be no difficulty in rooting the cuttings if they are inserted in a bed composed of three parts silver sand and one part fine peat. Campanulas, Saxifrages, Cyananthus, Dianthus and, in fact, most alpine plants which can be propagated vegetatively, may be rooted from cuttings at the present time.

Roses are flowering freely and it is very necessary to remove the faded blooms so that the plant's energies are not wasted on the production of seedpods. If a light dressing of one of the proprietary rose manures is applied, and well watered in, after the first flush of flowering is over, it will assist the plants in providing a further display. Mildew and "black spot" often assert themselves at this time and it is advisable to spray the rose bushes frequently with a good fungicide such as "Tulisan" or "Bouisol" as a precaution. A pneumatic knapsack sprayer is a good investment.

Pyrethrums will soon finish their first flowering, but if the faded flowers are promptly removed the plants will produce a few more flowers in the early autumn. If it is desired to increase the stock the present is a good time to divide the clumps as they resent disturbance in the autumn. Lift the plants carefully and divide them into comparatively small pieces and replant. Water them well in and keep them moist until they are established, they will then make nice clumps for flowering next year.

Evergreen hedges such as box and yew should receive their annual clipping; holly and laurel hedges should be trimmed with secateurs to avoid undue disfigurement of the leaves. The chief beauty of a garden hedge is its symmetrical outline. It is quite easy to keep the outline of a hedge perfectly correct by setting a few stakes in a straight line and at the desired angle along it. Levelling lines may then be stretched from stake to stake, and with these as a guide the hedge may be clipped in perfect shape.

C.P.

My Blue Border

I think it was in the Botanic Gardens Regent's Park, that many years ago I, saw a herbaceous border in which every flower was of varying blue shades from lavender to purple. I was at that time designing and making my present garden out of an acre-and-a-half of ploughed field and was on the hunt for ideas. "*And one of those!*" I promptly murmured; and thus, in 1934, my blue border came into being.

It was about 85 feet long by 12 feet deep, backed by the six-foot brick wall which surrounded the kitchen garden beyond, and into it I put every blue flower I then knew, violas, catmint, delphiniums, anchusa and so on. It was a success from the start, except for the fact that the first year all our blue Canterbury bells came up pink and were such beauties I hadn't the heart to pull them up. At least they provided a talking point whenever I announced proudly to visitors, "And this is our blue border" but next season I was firmer. Anything deviationist was ruthlessly removed the moment it declared its politics and for the last twenty years the border has been defiantly true-blue.

The edging was for some years *Nepeta* (Catmint) but the soil was too damp and it kept dying off. So now it is *Campanula carpatica* which I think is not as well known as it ought to be. It grows about nine inches, with lovely blue saucers which seem too many and too large for the tiny parent. It flowers from June to August, but planted a foot apart leaves room in between for the earlier-flowering forget-me-not, *Myosotis* Sutton's "Royal Blue," dwarf strain. Being biennials these latter have to be replaced each year, but it merely means transferring some of the many seedlings to their proper places.

Behind this used to be the fifteen-inch gentian-blue spikes of *Salvia patens*, but it was a mistake. The flowers were too sparse and moreover it is not very hardy: a cold winter, unless you cover the roots with ashes, will do a lot of damage. There are only a few left of the row now, which has been remade with two new discoveries, both pentstemons – *prunosus* and *heterophyllus* "Blue Gem." The former, though a lovely clear pale blue, is also somewhat unsatisfactory, as it seems to resent moving. Though grown from seed quite easily and carefully pricked out, half of the plants promptly died when planted in the border and others during the winter. The other pentstemon though is quite a find – slow-growing but establishes itself well. Besides growing from seed I took about a dozen cuttings with great ease off one plant.

Behind these is a long row of a most delightfully showy plant with fat purple-blue heads about eighteen inches high – the kind of flower that visitors are asking about long before they actually reach the border. This is *Campanula glomerata dahurica* and is well worth it. It spreads outwards from the roots and so it is easy to divide and fill out any bare patches in other places.

I have two more campanulas in my border *persicifolia* "Telham Beauty," two foot six, which I am thinking of getting rid of as the clumps travel underground too much and won't stay put; and *pyramidalis*, the "Chimney Campanula," a most showy affair which reaches four foot. Though a perennial it pays to grow a few of these every year as reserves; for it can't be relied upon not to die off suddenly.

Scabiosa caucasica, once established, is a godsend and so are *Erigeron* (blue daisy-like flowers, 18 inches) and *Polemonium* or "Jacob's Ladder"; but the blue flax, though known as *Linum perenne*, is not so perennial as its name implies, though it always leaves its little feathery seedlings all over the place as understudies. A new discovery, with which I have replaced it largely, is the "Chinese Bellflower" – *Platycodon grandiflorus* – with big bells, opening into cups. The dwarfer variety *Mariesii* is the best. *Geranium Ibericum* is another good standby: *Salvia virgata nemorosa* was included for its rich purple flowers, but when they go, little russet leaves – bracts – appear at the flower-base, and the spikes become dull red, and wrong for a blue border; so it is now banished.

The mainstay of the back part of the border is of course delphiniums, blue lupins and monkshood. I also have *Anchusa italica* ("Dropmore" variety, a wonderful deep blue), but at one time I nearly discarded it altogether. It is a brute for flopping over, half-splitting its stem and then lying along the ground, to provide vicarious false blooms for some smirking stranger five foot away. To tie anchusa up properly requires a forest of stakes and cordage like a three-masted schooner. However, after a year or two I moved them back against the wall. This wall, being thin, has bastions every eight foot projecting four inches out, and on these I have fixed two wires right along – one at two foot up and one at four foot, which have solved my tying-up problem. For as the anchusas and the Michaelmas daisies already there grow up they are simply tucked in in the four inches behind each wire in turn and the job is done for the year.

On the wall also, as an ultimate backing for the blue border, are, at one end, a *Clematis patens* "Lasurstern" – lovely deep blue flowers twice a year, up to eight inches across; in the middle a *Ceanothus floribundus*; and at the other end a wistaria, one branch of which is slowly being trained right along; its present length is thirty-five feet.

As a final touch all along the front half of the border I once scattered seeds of love-in-a-mist and *Cynoglossum amabile* which year after year seed themselves and cover all blank spaces with a haze of blue. There are, I know, many other blue "subjects" I have not brought under my sway, but then what is the fun of discovering everything at once?

A.A.

———————

What actual names should you give the flowers in your garden, when asked? I don't mean when asked by another gardener. That's easy: you just sling chunks of Latin at each other and everybody's happy. But when, for instance, you're escorting a charming young lady round the garden, that's when trouble starts. Listen!

VISITOR: Oh, what *are* those mauve daisy affairs?

HORTICULTOR: Erigeron.

VIS: A rigger-what? What's its *real* name? The English names are so much *nicer*, don't you think?

HORT: That *is* its real name. Unless you want to be absolutely English and call it Flebane.

VIS: Oh! (*She takes a count of nine; then:*) What's that crimson thing with the silvery leaves?

HORT (being kind): Rose Campion.

VIS: What, no Latin name?

HORT: Well, really it's a *Lychnis*....

VIS (smartly on to it): But you said that bright scarlet thing back there with flat heads was *Lychnis*.

HORT (she has asked for it): That was *Lychnis chalcedonica*. This is *Lychnis coronaria atrosanguinea*, though it's also called *Agrostemma coronaria*.

VIS: Oh! (*Suddenly defiant.*) I think all these Latin names are silly – why not let everything have good old English ones that we all know? Like – well, like delphinium and dahlia!

Well, you see what I mean. Your garden flowers have Latin names which describe them with botanical accuracy; they have Latin names that have now become practically English, and they have also the accepted English names, vague, open to confusion, and usually medicinal. It's quite impossible to be consistent. Adopt Latin names, and where are you? Calling saxifrage *saxifrage*, and lupin *lupinus*, and acquiring a general reputation for being pedantic and toffee-nosed. Besides, would you really dare refer to a rose by any other name, such as *rosa*?

Nor is there any excuse for turning the lovely name Golden Rod into *Solidago*, yet you might get away with it; it is known. But I doubt if you would if you called a hollyhock by its true name of *Althea rosea*, though you'd have every aesthetic excuse for this.

So you eschew the Rosa-Lupinus school and go all English. At once you'll find visitors backing away from you and looking pityingly at each other behind your back, for you'll now be talking about "Beard-Tongue" and "Blanket Flower" when showing them your pentstemons and gaillardias. They'll be expecting you soon to break out into sandals, morris-dancing, and home-weaving. Besides, what are you to do about delphinium? That, after all, is Latin; and its English equivalent is "Larkspur," but once again the heel-and-toe gardener uses the latter to denote the annual variety.

And that's nothing when you come to mallow. Do you mean Sidalcea or Malva or Lavatera? All are alternatively called Mallow in the catalogues, and you've got a grand battle on your hands – especially if you're pointing to *Malva setosa*, which is practically indistinguishable from a single hollyhock. Aesthetically, too, you're again in a fix. Rose of Sharon, Fog Fruit, Golden Drop, Clover of the Gods, ring bells beside which their Latin names, *Hypericum, Lippia, Onosma and Parochetus* are but tin pans; but the boot is on the other foot with pleasantly harmless appellations like *Linaria, Silene, Alyssum* and *Acanthus*, which have to be transformed into Toad Flax, Catch-Fly, Rock Mad-wort, and Bear's Breech.

Any attempt at consistency, you see, lands you in a proper mess, and the only solution is compromise. Use the names which can easiest be understood and yet express your meaning. *Digitalis* will now be foxglove and *Nepeta* catmint, but Leopard's Bane will have to be *Doronicum*, and "What's that lovely sweet-smelling bush with the little purply-white flowers?" will have to be answered – if they really want to know – with "*Philadelphus purpureo-maculatus.*"

I'm afraid that to this, and other similar Latin tongue-twisters, the inevitable retort, trying to make you look snooty, will be: "And what's that, when it's at home?" But they'll find eventually you've given the only possible answer, and they'd far better have left it alone, because all you can further reply will be: "Well, it's a kind of mock-orange, but more delicately scented, and instead of being pure white, every flower, like most G.I.s, has a purple heart."

And they'll say: "Mock orange? Oh, you mean a syringa?" And you'll say a trifle loftily: "I don't mean a syringa – syringa is really *lilac*," and they'll look at you a little disbelievingly and say: "Oh, is it? *I* always call lilac, lilac." And you'll say pettishly: "So do I, but it's not. Its generic name is …" And they'll say hastily: "Well, I like that thing anyway. What's its name again?" And that's where you both came in.

A.A.

369

THE FRUIT GARDEN

SUMMER PRUNING: Although there is much to do summer pruning should not be overlooked. The simplest form was mentioned last month and it is appropriate now to consider the underlying principles. In the first place the removal of surplus growth ensures that the maturing crop is given the maximum amount of sunlight to improve its quality. It is also said that indirectly it encourages the development of fruit buds. Another point is that the practice helps to check the spread of certain pests and diseases.

Similarly, with gooseberries, summer pruning can check the spread of American gooseberry mildew. The severity of this disease is well known and both fruit and foliage are often covered with the symptomatic, white powdery mildew. This badly checks the growth but it does not affect the eating qualities of the fruit, which after wiping, may be cooked or even bottled, although it will be marked with a brown stain. The important point to bear in mind is that the spores are lodged on the young shoot tips and the cutting away of these forms part of the control. This should be done by mid-August before spores have any chance of acting as a source of re-infection the following year. Here, as with all types of summer pruning only side shoots should be pruned, leading shoots being left intact. In small gardens this disease is often to be found, although the measures outlined together with periodical sprays in late spring and summer, will control it.

PICKING FRUIT: Early varieties of apples and pears are now coming into season. The best test for picking is to lift the fruit slightly and give it a gentle twist. If it comes away easily it is ready for picking. With early pears, however, particularly "Laxton's Superb" and "William's Bon Chrêtien," the fruit should be picked while still green and hard. It is better to pick them a little too early than too late. If left they will ripen unevenly and go "sleepy" in the centre while the outside remains comparatively hard.

REMINDERS: From the abundance of blossom in many gardens earlier this year, heavy crops seem likely. Such a state of affairs is welcome but provision must be made for supporting heavily laden branches; broken branches can so easily ruin a shapely tree. When propping boughs, stout supports should be used with a piece of sacking between them and the branch to prevent chafing the bark.

G.R.W.

———•·•———

A new strawberry bed: with a healthy bed of strawberries a few new runners should be taken every year to ensure a good annual crop. It rarely pays to keep plants for more than three years; this is often done but after the third season vigour usually deteriorates and cropping suffers.

Fortunately the strawberry is easily propagated. Ideally a few healthy plants should be kept at some distance from the fruiting bed solely for the production of young stock. This reduces the chance of young plants becoming ridden with virus and other diseases should the fruiting bed be infected. The best method is to place four plants in a square three feet apart. Then, as runners are produced they are pegged down into the square leaving the surrounding ground clear for other use. Contrary to general belief, there is no limit to the number of runners which can be taken providing the stock plants are completely healthy. Indeed, only the healthiest of plants should ever be used for propagation. Whether the runners be taken from the square or a fruiting bed it is a good practice to peg selected runners into small sunken pots filled with good soil. In dry weather the pots may need watering but later there is the advantage of moving plants with a minimum of disturbance.

Success or failure with strawberries is largely governed by the choice of site and its preparation. The surface rooting nature of the strawberry demands a high humus content. A *slightly acid* soil is best; in fact, practically all of our well-known fruits prefer slightly acid conditions and lime should not be used except in rare instances where acidity is *proved* to be excessive. The finest strawberries are grown on soil that has been well manured for a previous crop. Further dressings of organic matter such as well-rotted compost or peat may also be applied prior to planting as it is virtually impossible to make these additions once the bed is established. For soils that have not been previously manured some sort of humus forming substance must be added. On heavy soils this should be of a coarse and bulky nature whilst on light soils well-decayed matter is preferable.

The site is best prepared several weeks in advance of planting so that the soil has time to settle down. In the West Country planting can begin as early as July and in less favoured areas during August. The plants should be set 18 inches apart in the row with 30 inches between rows and if the soil is dry they should be watered in. It is important that they are planted at just the right depth with the base of the crown at soil level.

G.R.W.

HOME HINTS

POT POURRI: This is a good time to gather red roses, past their prime, and to strip them of their petals and spread them out to dry for pot pourri. The old-fashioned French roses have the sweetest smell. Gather rosemary, marjoram, lemon verbena, thyme and the sweet-scented balm too.

DEATH TO THE MOTH: Clothes moths dislike being disturbed almost as much as we dislike them and their nasty habits. Use any moth-destroyer you fancy, by all means, and at the same time make a practice of taking out all your woollen garments, your furs and your silk dresses and blouses too, and giving them a good shake once or twice a week. Beat them lightly now and again with a cane, and spread them out in the sunshine, whenever there is any. This discourages breeding and it freshens the garments and gets rid of the smell of moth-killer too. Don't forget your knitting and embroidery wools, if you have any in store.

TISANES: Warm weather makes many people wakeful; so do the birds, who wake up earlier than we do. For keeping you sound asleep I know of nothing better than *tilleul* – dried lime-flowers made into a tisane. *Tilleul* can be bought from some chemists, but it is better and quite easy to dry the flowers for yourself. Strip the flowers from a branch or two of lime and spread them out on an old sheet or a newspaper to dry in the sun. If the weather is determinedly ill-tempered, the top shelf of a heated linen cupboard or the bottom shelf of a cool oven, with the heat turned off after cooking is finished, will do. Tisanes can be made, too, of lemon verbena, or of the scented mints. Made from the fresh leaves, these are very refreshing, but *tilleul* has a more soothing effect on the nerves for anybody who finds after-dinner coffee a menace to sleep.

To make tisanes put a small handful of dried lime-flowers, or of the leaves of lemon verbena or scented mint, into a teapot, fill the pot with boiling water, cover, and stand in a warm place for 5-10 minutes. A tisane of *tilleul* is greatly improved if you add a teaspoonful of orange-flower water and a lump of sugar – some like a squeeze of lemon juice and a little sugar with mint.

Apple mint, pineapple mint and eau-de-Cologne mint all make a delicious tisane, scented and refreshing. Unless you have a very sweet tooth they need neither sugar nor extra flavouring. These scented mints are easy to grow in the herb garden. A sprig or two looks cool and pretty in a fruit drink, and the added flavour they give to it is subtle and unusual.

M.B.R.

SHOOTING

VERMIN DESTRUCTION: This is best month to destroy young magpies, jackdaws and carrion crows. A stuffed cat is a deadly lure. Grey squirrels are the greatest pest in the woods, as they steal eggs and will kill poults if they can catch them. Rate them as public enemy number one. Trap, shoot and poison, especially now that game chicks are cut out in mowing grass.

Place all poisoned baits out of reach of domestic animals.

PIGEON SHOOTING: Quite a good month for pigeon shooting as they come to newly mown fields. A little observation will tell which trees are most favoured. *Ivy-clad ash trees* standing alone are much frequented. A hide close by will yield   big bags, and at this time of year you will get single shots all day as birds will keep coming, especially if you set decoys out on the field.

RABBIT STALKING: Rabbits provide good sport in early morning and evening if you use an accurate .22 rifle. Hollow point ammunition is essential for stopping rabbits. Even this type of bullet must be accurately placed in head or shoulder of rabbit, or it may get back to its bury. Take care of "background" when shooting with .22.

COVERTS AND MARSHES: Don't let dogs off lead in coverts, as it is wise to keep woodlands quiet. This applies especially to pools and marshes where duck breed. Mallard must be given a sense of security. Don't go near the water unless you are putting down "feed." This should be done in middle day. Rats and moorhens must be kept in check.

CARE OF GUNS: Don't leave annual overhaul of guns too late. They should be sent to the gunmakers as soon as season ends. Average price for overhaul is two guineas. Check trigger pulls (3½ lb. right barrel, 4½ lb. left). Dents in gun barrels *must* be rectified. A dented barrel, if neglected, will ruin the weapon. If wildfowling is contemplated later in the year, order your big shot now; it is sometimes hard to obtain from provincial gunsmiths.

Rides need a certain amount of "cutting back" and wood-land stands, if cleared now, will have put on fresh growth and look natural when covert shooting begins. In the same way, favourite stands on the partridge side need looking over and can usually stand a very thorough cutting back or topping. The ideal stand is high enough to conceal the gun beyond it, yet rather an attractive "low spot" when seen from the partridges' point of view. A few days' light hedging enormously improves the chances of birds "going where you want them" when driving begins.

DISTURBANCE OF GROUND: A good deal of nonsense is talked about "disturbance." It is more important that things should be quiet before birds have gone down hard on their nests than after this, and admittedly penned birds who have been caught up are all too easily scared; but, in general, a great deal of the legend of the evils of disturbance is more due to the fact that the keeper did not want to be disturbed by visitors than to any odd or disastrous effects produced on the wild inhabitants of the woods. As to the reared game, although far shyer than poultry, they are not paralysed by the sight of man. Dogs, on the other hand, especially yellow ones, are a cause of serious alarm and all dogs ought to be on the leash when in the woods.

JAYS AND VERMIN: If your garden is near woodland it probably has attractions for both jays and grey squirrels. The jay, which leaves your new pea pods hanging deceitfully but ripped open and deprived of their contents, is a vile brute. As for the iniquities of grey squirrels, they seem to include all possible forms of malignant damage, from polishing off the warbler's half-fledged brood to the theft of incredibly expensive tulip bulbs. There is only one way to protect the garden, and that is to eliminate the invaders. This involves a good alarm clock, for very early morning is the chosen time for raid – and for reprisal. Always use cartridges loaded with the smallest possible shot – No. 8 snipe shot or even No. 10. The pattern of an ordinary game cartridge is too loose for a small-bodied bird – but with small shot you may get two or more at one discharge. A .410 is perfectly adequate.

B.B.

FISHING

July should he dedicated to the sea-trout and the big brown trout who appear in the late evening from the depths to seize a Blue Winged Olive. In the West Country, sea-trout by night, but in Scotland and Eire they can be caught in river or loch by day. In low water try a dry fly. A Tupp's Indispensible is the best but give plenty of time before striking. Sea-trout take a dry fly best in bright sun.

Try also the estuary, close in to the seaweed from a boat with a blue and silver Terror as tail fly and any bright, single-hooked artificial as the bob (the Terror is tied on a tandem of hooks). Cast to edge of seaweed and pull in line in sharp jerks with hand. I find the hour before high tide, slack tide and the first hour of the ebb the best. Remember to wash your line immediately after operations. Salt water will soon rot it. You will probably hook a few mackerel which will dive to the bottom and give your light rod a proper bending. I find the Argyll coast profitable for this sort of fishing, but Newburgh on the east is well known for it. The sea-trout take the Terror for a sand eel and an artificial can be trolled or spun with success, but I prefer the fly amongst the seaweed, it demands accuracy and is akin to dry fly fishing.

Dapping for sea-trout in a loch has become popular. A humbly, grey heather moth with a black Zulu as the bob will do. Big fish are caught by this method. On windless days do not despair. Cast a long line from the boat and pull in quickly with spare hand. Remember, the brighter the day, the brighter the fly. At night use a black fly whatever your friends may suggest. Tie it thus: *Tail:* any tag you fancy. *Body:* black mohair whipped with silver tinsel. *Hackle:* black. *Wing:* black. The sea-trout move to the tail of a pool at night. For a torch I recommend the type that hooks on to the coat button; it should have a movable shade. You must fish by touch and with the experience of knowing where your fly is at any moment. You must strike quickly and be not too hard on a fish; for night-caught sea-trout are often poorly hooked.

There is a good evening rise on most chalk streams, beginning with the Pale Watery and ending with the Blue Winged Olive especially towards the end of the month. Trout take the latter with a splash and a heavier boil and are easy to catch. I recommend a large hook size 1 or 2 and a 2x cast. You can break off the last foot or two in the gloaming because the big fellows need strong tackle. If the fish disdain a Pale Watery change to Lunn's Particular.

R.B.

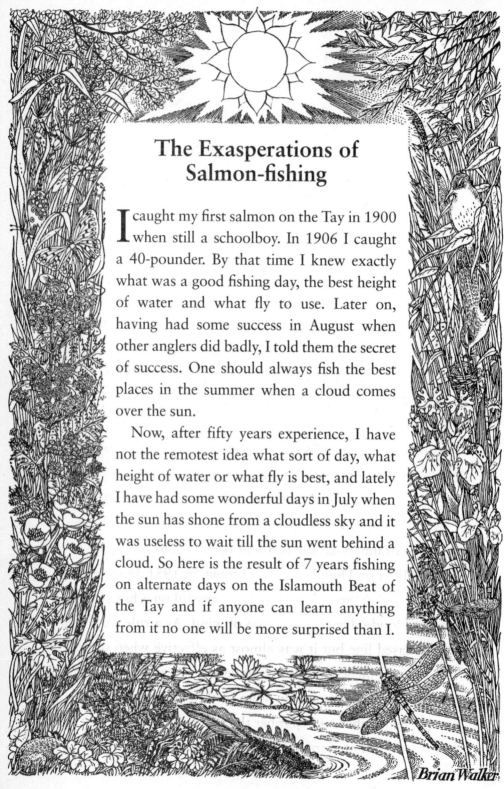

The Exasperations of Salmon-fishing

I caught my first salmon on the Tay in 1900 when still a schoolboy. In 1906 I caught a 40-pounder. By that time I knew exactly what was a good fishing day, the best height of water and what fly to use. Later on, having had some success in August when other anglers did badly, I told them the secret of success. One should always fish the best places in the summer when a cloud comes over the sun.

Now, after fifty years experience, I have not the remotest idea what sort of day, what height of water or what fly is best, and lately I have had some wonderful days in July when the sun has shone from a cloudless sky and it was useless to wait till the sun went behind a cloud. So here is the result of 7 years fishing on alternate days on the Islamouth Beat of the Tay and if anyone can learn anything from it no one will be more surprised than I.

Brian Walker

In these years, 1945-1951 we caught: 90, 86, 75, 74, 43, 81 and 73 salmon.

The best months were:

1945	June:	17 fish	October:	17 fish
1946	March:	21 fish		
1947	July:	16 fish		
1948	Sept.:	14 fish		
1949	April:	11 fish	August:	11 fish
1950	Sept.:	25 fish		
1951	July:	32 fish		

The best catch in a day was 7 fish on March 4, 1946, October 14, 1947, September 20 and October 13, 1950.

In 1950, 55 were caught on bait, 26 on fly.

In 1951, 22 were caught on bait, 51 on fly.

In other respects 1950 and 1951 produced totally different results though weather conditions were identical. In July and August 1950, 19 fish were caught and in September and October, 37 while the same months in 1951 produced 56 and 2 respectively.

Another remarkable feature of 1951 was that although in previous summers all the fish had been caught on a Jock Scott, Dusty Miller or Thunder and Lightning, in 1951 38 were caught on a Black Doctor. It was equally successful on a hot sunny day or on a cloudy day and in a gale of wind. As a rule we fished it on a greased line but it was almost as effective when sunk. The July run commenced on July 5 in very low water and continued till the end of the month in spite of the fact that there was no rain. In September and October the river was always fairly high, fishing conditions were ideal. There were more salmon showing in the pools than in anyone's living memory and in spite of all our efforts only 2 salmon were landed in those two months and other beats had more or less the same experience.

In 1946 I opened the season's fishing on March 4. There was a cold easterly wind with mist and a drizzle of rain or sleet. No fish had been caught by my neighbours who had the fishing on alternate days. On such a day nothing as a rule would induce me to go fishing but I had a new boatman and arranged for him to have a lesson so I decided to brave the elements, With my first throw of the sprat I caught a salmon and by four o'clock I had caught 7 including 2 on a fly. We were all too wet and cold to go on but I had had my record spring day and lost an illusion that fishing on misty days was useless.

In the years that have passed since then another illusion, that it is a waste of time fishing in the heat of the sun and low water, has also gone, and I am glad of its departure. Such a day was July 24, 1947. I had to go to a distant wedding that day but my friend R. H. was anxious to fish. As he wanted someone to share the boat with him, Col. B. was pressed into the service. It was a wonderful summer day and I did not think I was missing much, but they returned with 5 salmon. To this day I have never been able to find out how many others they rose and hooked.

Since then R. H. and I have had many successes on similar days and I have come to the conclusion that there is only one essential to a good fishing day and that is to have some fish in the river and to fish for them. Though it is easy enough to fish for them on a hot sunny day, it requires considerable fortitude when a north-easterly wind is driving sleet or rain down the Tay as not infrequently occurs even in the early days of May.

I am a strong believer in luck. At Islamouth that elusive goddess undoubtedly favours the ladies. From the moment she started my daughter Penelope always caught more fish than I did, but my friend J. B. was perhaps the luckiest of all. The first years she fished with me she never had a blank day. She was an excellent fisherman but not better than other people. There is a stone which sticks out of the water which we call J. B.'s stone. Salmon often lie round about it but there is no current so all we can do is to harl it. Often I have harled this place and once I hooked a fish there and often I caught the bottom, but when J. B. was in charge of the rods she constantly caught a salmon there.

The ladies have had far more than their share of big fish of 30 pounds and over. Penelope has had one of 32 pounds, Mrs. B. two of 32 and 24 pounds and Mrs. C. two of 30 and 32 pounds. Brigadier G. has caught one of 35 pounds and I have just succeeded in getting on to the list with one of 45 pounds caught in September 1950.

I learnt lately not to boast about my captures. Before dinner at my club I met the other day a famous Eton master of other days. He used to be a keen angler so I asked him if he still fished in Norway and he said he had been there this summer. I said I had been lucky last year on the Tay and had caught the best fish of the year, the above mentioned 45-pounder and he was duly appreciative, whereupon J. C. who was standing near said that I would be interested to hear that C.M.W. had caught his eightieth 40-pounder this summer on his eightieth birthday! Incidentally it weighed 56 pounds. I felt very small.

No account of Islamouth fishing would be complete without my telling the story of Good Friday 1948. Friday was our day on

Islamouth. The alternate days were let to a local farmer. I asked him if he would exchange days and I would fish on Saturday. He did and caught 8 salmon.

On the Saturday we did not get a bite until 5 o'clock when we caught a small fish of 8 pounds. I went with my family to church on Good Friday and felt I had been duly virtuous. When I heard of the 8 salmon I was slightly shattered, but expected that I should be duly rewarded on Saturday.

What is the lesson one should learn from this? If the late Bishop of London had been alive I should have asked him for an explanation. The first time he ever fished for salmon was on the same beat of the Tay. He caught 5 salmon, broke 2 rods and all the salmon before they were landed got mixed up with the boat and oars. At the end of the day his boatman assured him he had the luck of the devil.

A.M.

WHAT EVERY COOK
SHOULD KNOW ABOUT

THE HARVEST RABBIT

The rabbit is a profligate and prolific little beast, but he is at his best in the harvest months, as the earlier generations of this year's rabbits are almost at full growth and in the height of lazy summer condition.

No beast more repays rather better cookery than is usually bestowed on him, for where plain roast or boiled rabbit is often mediocre or worse and, if served whole, rather repulsive, properly cooked he is really most excellent eating, and by ringing changes on a variety of accompanying sauces and accompaniments, the usual monotony which too often is associated with the rabbit period of the year is most cunningly moderated.

Essentially the rabbit is a lean animal and his native flavour varies considerably according to his surroundings and his food. In the chalk counties, where aromatic herbs are common, rabbits taste different and better than those from heavy claylands or sandheaths. On the whole, rabbit is best with rather strongly and contrastingly flavoured sauces.

The first operation is to skin and clean carefully, first cutting away carefully the portion between the hind legs and trimming away the flaps of the chest cavity. Then put to soak in salted water with a little vinegar. This will blanch the meat.

Now the basic way of cooking rabbit is to brown or seal the meat by cooking it in fat or preferably butter for about ten minutes. This should not be too hot, and frequent stirring and turning is essential. If the rabbit has not been marinaded, pound up thyme, tarragon and pepper in modest amount with some flour, producing a seasoned flour. Withdraw the joints from the butter, sprinkle well with this, and return to the butter, allowing the seasoning to brown. Finally, grated shallot or onion *can* be used in this seasoning, but will probably require egg to bind it.

If possible, always joint the rabbit a day before and leave overnight in a marinade. This is:

1 glass of olive oil

½ glass wine or Orleans vinegar (if malt vinegar has to be used one tablespoon is enough)

6 bay leaves

3 onions cut in rings

2 sprigs of thyme

1 shallot in rings

2 sprigs chopped parsley

In this marinade the joints should be turned at intervals. The flavours will penetrate the meat and the marinade itself later made to a sauce by reduction.

To your butter in which the rabbit is browning add a little flour to thicken. When this is amalgamated, add ¾ pint of plain stock or even meat extract and water and a glass of white wine or a very little wine vinegar. Add three onions cut in fine rings and allow to simmer for at least an hour. It must *never* boil or the rabbit will be tough. Lastly draw aside, strain off the sauce and remove any excess fat. Taste and possibly season with a squeeze of lemon. Serve hot on toast squares.

If red wine is used, brown the onions lightly. If mushrooms are used, colour your rabbit in butter as above. Then simmer in equal quantities of white wine and boiled milk. Separately cook the mushrooms chopped in milk with a chopped shallot or a trace of garlic. The rabbit will take an hour's simmering if large, the mushrooms half this time. When the rabbit is cooked pour off the liquid from rabbit and mushrooms, beat in the yolks of two eggs mixed in a tablespoonful of water and a little chopped parsley. In this replace the rabbit, bring cautiously *almost* to the boil to thicken and serve hot. Portions of fried rabbit with Tartare sauce made separately are excellent, as is cold rabbit with Hollandaise or Béarnaise. In the same way rabbit can be done in olive oil in place of butter and accompanied with tomatoes and onions made into a *gratin* with grated cheese and just coloured under the grill.

H.B.C.P.

Country Quiz

1 Who wrote of "the coloured counties," and whence can they be viewed?

2 What are *(a)* Old Man's Beard; *(b)* Aaron's Beard; *(c)* Codlins and Cream?

3 What is a "nidicolous" bird?

4 What familiar insect is closely related to the domestic Cricket?

5 *The Natural History and Antiquities of Selborne* appeared in 1789. Where is Selborne and who wrote this celebrated book?

6 Some plants consist of an alga (seaweed) and a fungus growing together, and each dependent upon the other. What are such plants called?

7 In what counties are to be found these characteristically named villages?: *(a)* Bourton-on-the-Water; *(b)* Yardley Gobion; *(c)* St. Endellion.

8 Can you name three companions of the hound Bellman?

9 What is the better-known name of the star Sothis?

10 What have these three flowers in common?: the Common Poppy; the Heartsease; the Scarlet Pimpernel.

11 "I like the weather, when it's not too rainy; That is, I like two months of every year." Whose comment on our weather is this?

12 What have these three names in common?: Bottle Nose; Coulterneb; Pope.

13 For what purposes did our forefathers encourage the cultivation *(a)* of the mulberry; *(b)* of the yew?

14 Bog Asphodel; Solomon's Seal; Fritillary; Crocus; Garlic. Which of these belongs to a different family from the others?

15 "Hark! hark! the lark at heaven's gate sings "And Phoebus 'gins arise...." Who is the author of this lyric and where does it occur?

16 What is a xerophyte?

17 In the old days many birds had their "nouns of multitude," e.g. "a gaggle of geese." What birds were known collectively *(a)* as a "watch"; *(b)* as a "murmuration"?

18 Who, according to G. K. Chesterton, made the "rolling English road"?

19 How many snakes are native to these islands?

20 What has the Nightingale in common with the Nightjar and the Swallow?

COUNTRY QUIZ ANSWERS

1. A. E. Housman; from Bredon Hill. 2. *(a)* The Wild Clematis or Traveller's Joy; *(b)* the Rose of Sharon (*Hypericum calycinum*); *(c)* the Great Willow Herb. 3. One which, emerging helpless from the egg, must remain in the nest for a comparatively long time. 4. The Grasshopper. 5. In Hampshire; the Rev. Gilbert White. 6. Lichens. 7. *(a)* Gloucestershire; *(b)* Northamptonshire; *(c)* Cornwall. 8. Ruby, Ranter, Ringwood. 9. Sirius, or the Dog Star. 10. They all grow abundantly on waste ground and in corn fields. 11. Lord Byron. 12. They are all popular names for the Puffin. 13.

(a) For the rearing of silk-worms; *(b)* for the manufacture of the longbow. 14. The Crocus (the others all belong to the Lily family). 15. Shakespeare (*Cymbeline*). 16. A plant adapted to living for long periods without water. Our best-known xerophytes are the Stonecrop and the Houseleek. 17. *(a)* Nightingales; *(b)* Larks. 18. "The rolling English drunkard." 19. Three: the Grass Snake, the Adder, and the Smooth Snake. 20. All three come to us in spring and leave for warmer countries in the autumn.

THE NATURALIST

THE ARISTOCRAT OF THE WOODS

To "take" a Purple Emperor butterfly is perhaps the dearest wish of every entomologist; it had certainly been mine from boyhood days until the summer of last year, when that ambition was fulfilled.

It is a rare insect but it may not be quite so scarce as many people think, for it is not easy to identify on the wing and its appearance is brief. The last fortnight in July is the best time, and much of its short life is spent playing around the tops of the forest trees. Nor is it found in small woods, for it is an insect which delights in the great oak forests of the Midlands and the South. It is found in Sussex (where it is perhaps most plentiful), in certain large woods in Suffolk, Oxfordshire, Lincolnshire and Northamptonshire, and again in those lovely oak woods which flank the Wye.

I have lived all my life in Northamptonshire, and though this county is mentioned in all the butterfly books as its chief haunt I never identified it for certain until July 1951. This is strange, as every July I visited all the great oak forests in the county, summer after summer, without seeing a trace of it. Yet as I now know, I was often within half a mile of its favourite locality, and that was one corner of a large wood. I always had the idea that where *Iris* occurred it roamed the tree tops and might be seen anywhere. This I find is not the case. It seems to like one certain locality and is as partial to it as is the Marbled White to its own territory. Though odd adventurers may sometimes be found outside their area these wanderers are few and far between. Hitherto I have always looked for it in the centre of the woods where the trees are tallest. I now have found that it prefers the outskirts of woods, especially where sallow is abundant and the trees are spaced well apart, allowing plenty of light and air.

The female is one of the largest of our butterflies and is only rivalled by the lovely Swallow-tail of the fens. She has no purple sheen at all, but for all that is a most handsome insect of a soft, dark, velvety brown with the inner wings patterned with transverse bars of ivory white. The outer wings are perhaps even more beautiful, as they are a pattern of ivory whorls and chestnut markings with a peacock-like eye on the tip of each forewing. The male is slightly smaller though with the same outside pattern and the bars on his wings are smaller. In place of the velvet brown he has a glorious purple sheen which in some lights is quite dazzling. This purple does not show when the male is in flight, and he appears to be black and white, very similar to a large edition of a White Admiral. Both species are found together, as both are woodland insects.

All the butterfly books mention an "Emperor tree," invariably the tallest oak in the forest, on which the male rests, very rarely descending to the ridings, and remaining out of reach of the longest net.

In a measure this is true, but from my observations last year it is by no means the tallest tree he selects, nor does the same butterfly "stay put" on the highest leaf. The tree is, I believe, more of a tilting ground for the males. Many times I saw half a dozen males at a time sailing round and round the topmost leaves in pursuit of each other, sometimes ascending together, fighting as they went.

This warring of the males soon destroys the purple sheen upon the wings, and unless you can net a freshly emerged insect it is very hard to obtain an unspoilt specimen.

Along the particular riding of my favourite locality there was a long line of widely spaced oaks and when the sun shone with power the males were continually passing up and down these trees, sometimes circling each tree top *en route*.

Below was a line of dense sallow and on the other side of the riding a strip of woodland where the larger trees had been felled but where dense sallow had grown up among the underwood of hazel and briar. Beyond this was open country. The females were continually flying over this lower growth with great speed; indeed they travel very fast, as fast as a High Brown fritillary.

The only chance to net them is when they come racing along the ride or when they circle the sallows. Occasionally they will settle on the topmost sallow leaves, but never remain for more than two or three minutes.

On July 23, 1951, I saw twenty in this particular riding. On the 25th I saw thirty and again on the 30th I saw even more, taking one beautiful female from the top of a sallow bush. This insect must have only just emerged as it was in mint condition. My companion, a deft man with the net, had amazing fortune. He was not five yards from me, standing in the riding by the sallow thickets, when two *Iris* came by me "head high." I was too late to try for them, but he slipped up his net and caught both of them, two *newly emerged males*! They were chasing each other and were, I suppose, so engrossed that they were too late in avoiding the net. As a general rule *Iris* is very hard to catch and is perhaps one of the shyest and most wary of our butterflies.

That afternoon both my friend and I took five or six more females, which we liberated again.

The ordinary short-handled net is of no use whatever. Even the females prefer the highest leaves of the sallow, where they sit for a few moments basking in the hot sun, opening and shutting those wonderful wings. And your only chance to net a male is when they come down from the oak tops in pursuit of other males or females. Once I very nearly caught both male and female which rose fighting in the air just in front of me down the ride.

One interesting thing I saw was a large female with a torn wing being pursued down a ride by a dragonfly. The dragonfly, a large green one such as the rustics know as "horse stingers," seemed bent on catching the fleeing *Iris*, but she eluded him. Then to my amazement the dragonfly came back and in turn was pursued by the Purple Emperor!

Three years ago I found *Iris* occurring very sparingly in an Oxfordshire oak wood, and the very first one I ever saw came flying low just above the surface of the ride. When it reached me it circled me twice and settled on my knee!

It was a very worn specimen and was no doubt near the end of its life.

The single eggs are laid in July and August on the under (sometimes the upper) surface of the sallow leaf. The caterpillar hatches in about a fortnight and spends the winter in hibernation on the bare sallow twigs, sometimes making for itself a little house of a dead sallow leaf, though this is not the invariable rule.

In the spring when the sallow buds begin to break and the leaves turn silvery green the little caterpillar begins to feed, changing its colour to match the leaf. It is rather an odd shape, slug-like, with two little horns on its head like a snail's, the only caterpillar of our British species which has these strange decorations.

I found it sometimes easy to confuse *Iris* with the White Admirals, for both are on the wing together.

One last interesting point. Standing under the Emperor tree I noticed the males going to rest. Soon after four o'clock on a July afternoon, however hot the sun, the Purple Emperors went to bed. With powerful glasses I could see them crawling about well inside the tree, some choosing the under side of an oak bough and others resting with closed wings against the actual upper trunk.

Zero hour seemed to be from 11 a.m. to 2 p.m., after which they appeared to become less active. One can wait for an hour or more without seeing any sign and then suddenly you may see a dozen or so, all in the space of a few minutes. I believe this is when a newly emerged female leaves the sallow and the males scent her.

Many of our large forests are fast disappearing and it may well be that *Iris* will soon become extinct, like the Large Veined White or the Large Tortoiseshell, which insect is, for some reason, becoming very rare indeed.

B. B.

COLOURS BIRDS DISLIKE

There's an old rhyme in Lincolnshire that goes:

Coome yar off yon turnip tops,
Coome yar off yon gaete, maete:
For if yar doante, I'll git me gun,
An' then yar'll be too laete, maete.

Instead of shooting and "hollering," however, W.H. Hudson advocated coloured streamers to frighten birds. He found scarlet the best. Used in large masses and combined with a device for reproducing the scream of a hawk it would keep whole orchards clear.

I happened to mention Hudson's advice at a Lincolnshire village gathering and got the following observations. When a swallow's nest fell it was noticed that the lining consisted entirely of feathers from Rhode Island Red fowls. Yet feathers from Plymouth Rocks, Leghorns and Orpingtons had been just as accessible. It was also remarked that the first flush of purple bloom, in violets, violas, aubrietia, crocus, polyanthus and primula, was always taken by birds, whereas the yellow buds were left alone. An invalid chaffinch and a sparrow, which were kept indoors as subjects for study, showed similar taste in colours. If a scarlet tie was worn their feathers would rise and their behaviour clearly denoted something amiss. As soon as the tie was removed they became easy again. While a blue dress was being embroidered with purple silk, however, the birds perched close by to watch.

So fruit growers and others might be advised to try *both* colour effects: lures of purple to attract birds elsewhere and, in the garden or orchard, scarlet to scare them off. What a red rag is to a bull in a field, it is even more to a bullfinch among the damsons.

A.W.

THE APIARIST

BIRTH OF A QUEEN BEE

Bees make their queen cells in batches, timed to produce a succession of virgin queens, after the outgoing of the old queen with her swarm. Her successor emerges about a day after her predecessor's departure. In due course she is mated and lays. About nine days later, another princess will hatch, perhaps even two or three. If not slain by the reigning queen, these virgins fly from the hive with another swarm, or cast.

My black bees had thrown a swarm which I have hived with the intention of re-queening it. This was eight days ago. The princesses should be ripe for emergence. I creep up to the hive after dark, and listen with my ear pressed to the wooden wall. Sure enough, I hear the royal voices. The imprisoned princesses pipe from within their cells with a shrill note: "Teet-teet, teet-teet." Another voice, that of the young queen, answers with a deeper note: "Toot-toot, toot-toot."

Next day, the cast leaves. I catch it and at sundown I tip it out on to the white cloth in front of the old hive, intending to return the workers without their queens. In the cast I find two virgins. One I kill, the other I place, with a handful of retainers, in a prepared box. This box, with its inhabitants, I place on the window-sill of an upper room. The queen wanders about the inserted bit of comb, thrusting her abdomen into the cells, but without laying eggs, and making trampling movements with her front pair of legs.

The workers settle down for the night, clustered round their sovereign. Next morning they are going in and out of the flight-hole. At noon, I hear coming from the upper room a roar like that of an aeroplane. The window-sill, the curtains, outside of the box are black with hundreds of bees. They crawl about on top of the box, waving their antennae; frantically trying to get inside. They have come to the call of the imprisoned princess. What is this call? It is apparently her scent. The workers have smelt her out, and at some distance from the hives, which are separated from the house by the garden and a barrier of trees. From their colour, I surmise them to be the workers of the colony from which the queen came.

The bees show no desire to sting. They are as creatures obsessed or under the influence of a drug. I sweep them into a skep, together with the inmates of the box. Tied in, they are placed in the shade until the evening, when I shake them out in front of the hive. I cannot find the princess, perhaps she has been suffocated. Most of the bees go into the hive; but the weather has been hot, the adventure was exhausting, and the ingoing bees leave behind a heap of inanimate bodies.

There is a pause. Then from within the hive, the rescue party rushes out. Swiftly they run from body to body, tapping each with their antennae. Most, it seems, are dead. Two rescuers halt by an apparent corpse. For twenty minutes they tap and massage the injured bee with their antennae, their tongues, and their front legs. The casualty struggles to its feet, and on to its legs. But it cannot walk. One rescuer lies down on her side, and in this posture slides round the injured one, tapping her with quick movements of all her six legs at once. Revived by this treatment, the sick bee shakes herself; pulls herself together, and crawls slowly up, up into the hive.

Another body evinces a spark of life. Two rescuers are working on her. They work for twenty-five minutes. But their ministrations are in vain. One on each side of the moribund bee, they carry her to a far corner. There, one rescuer stings her twice between the first and second pair of legs. It is apparently a small injection of poison. The sting is quickly withdrawn, but it does its fatal work. Then the rescuers comb out their antennae and go home to the hive. They have done what they could.

Night falls: the adventure is at an end.

V.T.

THE ZOOLOGIST

THE DISAPPEARING DORMOUSE

For the past three years I have been keeping an unsuccessful lookout for dormouse nests. But I have had no luck, and my experience has been shared by others. It is, indeed, becoming generally recognised that the dormouse has become a rare animal, within the last 20 or 30 years, even where it was formerly abundant. Yet there is no obvious reason for this. Usually, such a reduction is the result of persecution, because the animal is a pest or because it is useful for food or for its pelt. It may even be due to changes in environment – new methods of agriculture, the extension of arable land, draining of marshes, pollution of rivers and the like; or even to the increase of a natural enemy. None of these applies forcibly to the dormouse.

The natural food of a dormouse is seeds, berries, acorns and nuts, according to season, with, at all times, a partiality for insects and grubs. This presents no menace to the farmer or gardener. Its home is typically in the hazel copse, especially where there is mixed oak and hazel, and in the hedgerows. Possibly, reduction in the size of hedges may have acted to its disadvantage. In many places, too, copses have been cleared, but even in those that have not been interfered with, and where dormice were previously plentiful, they are now absent or present only in very sparse numbers.

The dormouse is a skilful climber, having well-separated toes and a good balancing organ in its hairy, somewhat bushy tail. Its habit is to keep well to cover. The nest, a ball of grass, leaves and, often, the fibrous bark of the honeysuckle vine, is slung well up in the bushes. Moreover, it has no obvious entrance. The owner merely pushes aside the fibres to enter or leave, pulling them back into position again, so that retreat into the nest or flight from it can be made at any point. Hawks, owls, foxes and, occasionally, cats are the only natural enemies, and except for the last of these we cannot invoke an increase in their numbers to account for the disappearance of the dormouse. The little owl, introduced at various times and places in England during the latter half of the last century, has become increasingly widespread from about 1910 onwards. It must, therefore, come under suspicion; but examination of numerous pellets and stomach contents has failed to reveal dormouse remains among the wide range of food taken.

It has been suggested that changes in climate, with milder winters, disturb hibernation and lead to a higher mortality. This could be a prime cause, for in an animal producing only a small yearly litter of three or four there is little margin of safety over normal hazards. A change in climate could reduce this margin below the safety limit. However, dormice enjoy a fairly wide range of distribution, both in area and altitude, and it is unlikely that climatic changes can be held responsible for their decline.

Perhaps by tracing the yearly life-history we may be in a better position to make a guess. The dormouse emerges from hibernation in March, much reduced in weight from its fasting – and sleeping – period. After a short period of feeding, it embarks on nesting, mating and, for the female, bearing the young. In July the litter is born and from then until the end of August family cares

must weigh heavily on both parents. It is not until late summer that feeding on a heavy scale can be embarked upon. Then the rate of feeding in all hibernating animals is phenomenal, and the weight of the body increases in the short space of two to three weeks by 50 per cent., the equivalent of a 12-stone man reaching 18 stone. The increase is due to the laying down of fat reserves in the body, and clearly the best food for this is nuts and acorns.

Those two to three weeks in late summer are therefore crucial. If the nut or acorn crop fails, or for any other reason is not available, high mortality must result, either during hibernation or after, for if the stored fat is insufficient the animal will emerge from hibernation more wasted than normal. In that case, the heavy strain imposed by nesting and mating will be intolerable. It is not unreasonable to imagine, moreover, that under such circumstances the dormice might fail to breed; or, if they did, would produce smaller litters. The young also would have less stamina.

It is significant that squirrels feed heavily on nuts and acorns – and during these crucial days of late summer. Years ago, when we had only the red squirrel, there were probably enough nuts for all, but since the grey squirrel has become so numerous in the last 20 years or so matters have changed drastically. It is a common experience to see a crop of ripening nuts stripped by a few grey squirrels in a matter of hours.

The grey squirrel has received many black marks from farmers and gardeners. This alien squirrel may be a nuisance, but it is not without its charms, and we must hesitate to accuse it of another crime. Nevertheless, it does look as though the loss of dormice may be another instance where the introduction of a new animal has upset the balance, to the detriment of a native.

M.B.

WHAT EVERY COOK
SHOULD KNOW ABOUT

CRAYFISH & PIKE

In Victorian times, and perhaps even later, most of our rivers contained the common freshwater crayfish. They were abundant and could be found in all English rivers and streams whose waters had adequate chalk in solution. Full grown they were about the size of one's thumb and when boiled went a most brilliant scarlet. I can remember them being offered for sale cooked and reposing on cushions of green moss in strawberry punnets.

It would require a good many to make a meal, but they were popular as one of the courses at boating picnics. Then, one year, there was a mysterious disease and it was generally held that all the crayfish in the country had perished. Whether a small remnant did survive or whether they were (as is possible) reintroduced by waterfowl is not known, but apparently the crayfish is once again abundant.

Small boys used to grope those endless underwater bolt-holes of the water voles and drag out the crayfish that hole up in them by the tips of their long feelers. Some dexterity was involved as they can inflict quite a powerful nip. The more serious way of catching them was with fine-meshed hoop nets which were baited with butcher's offal and lowered in the shallows. These were left for a time, then lifted and the catch removed. Dusk and evening was, I believe, the best time, as I can remember seeing punts with flares or torches and lanterns. Whether the light helped to attract the crayfish to the baited nets or was simply in order to see the result of the haul I cannot say.

Crayfishing was one of the minor riverside employments, for they were not only in demand for the larder but were widely used in biological laboratories as specimens for dissection.

In England I have only seen these boiled and eaten cold with salad and mayonnaise, but in Spain they eat them as the Venetians do their "scampi," which are simply what we call "Dublin prawns." The tails are skinned and dipped in a batter of egg, flour and a dessertspoonful of olive oil. It needs to be whipped really stiff and left to stand for an hour or so before use. The batter-dipped crayfish tails are best fried in oil – cooking oil will do but olive oil is preferable. A fairly good imitation of "scampi" can be made with the conventional ready-boiled Dublin prawn, but the return of the freshwater crayfish affords an opportunity to use really fresh material.

The river lamprey used to be much appreciated and is much more common than is recognised. In fact, they are often not recognised but mistaken for waving streamers of weed. These lampreys or stone-suckers are easily caught by hand, and where you find one you will probably find others. One lamprey is not worth bothering with, as it is like a very thin eel some eighteen inches long and about as thick as a fountain pen. Traditionally potted lamprey was a Worcester delicacy, but they can probably be well accommodated by any recipe appropriate to eels. The lamprey pie of Bristol is, I think, made with the large sea-going lamprey, which is a substantial fish as thick as a cycle tyre. These enter estuaries and even ascend river mouths, but do not, I think, go far upstream. They are reputed to be even better eating than the small river fish.

A coarse fish which does not enjoy the benefit of a close season is the pike, and in France it seems to be very permanently on country menus, but I believe that the roe of pike is held to be dangerous, if not poisonous. Whether this is fact or superstition I do not know, but the French waste very, very little.

Now the young angler often wants to eat his trophy and a pikelet of some three pounds is a fish which looks attractively edible. The French method produces something edible but involves considerable labour. The pike is cooked in a court bouillon of herbs, fish stock and white wine and allowed to partly cool in this. It is then skinned, and if it has been cooked for just the right time the larger part of the meat can be separated from the bones without too much disturbance of the flakes of muscle. All fins and small bones are removed and then the fish meat is lightly blended with a good stiff mayonnaise or similar sauce – seldom innocent of garlic – and the whole reformed to the shape of the fish.

Sometimes a glaze or aspic based largely on the court bouillon in which the fish was cooked is used as a border. Properly made it is quite impossible to taste the pike, but it is not possible to disguise the rather woolly texture.

H.B.C.P.

TAKING THE PIG FOR A WALK

At six o'clock on a dark and stormy winter's evening, I was faced with the realisation that one Sissy must go, forthwith, to the boar. The farm where the boar lives can be reached either by the road or by a short cut across fields. By the latter route the distance is no more than a mile. I find it simpler, under normal conditions, to let our sows do the trip on foot, through the fields, than to load them, protesting, into the trailer and drive them by the road. However, Sissy has a violent aversion to trailers. Any attempt to load her immediately resolves itself into an all-in wrestling match.

My companion, Paddy, due no doubt to his Irish blood, fancies himself as something of a hand with pigs. But even so I couldn't see us carrying twenty stones of highly resistant Large White up the ramp. From the warmth and shelter of the farrowing-house we had a final growl at the elements, and then accepted the inevitable.

Collecting a rope, a stick and an electric torch, I tipped some meal into the sow's trough, slipping the rope on to her leg and adjusting the knot whilst she ate. As soon as she had finished the meal, she let out a hilarious snort, and shot through the door like a greyhound out of a trap. With me in tow, she did the first hundred yards of the field at a gallop. Either her eyesight, or her memory, was better than mine, for at the crucial moment she swerved to miss the barrow which earlier in the day I had left standing out in the open. Just in time, I let go the rope and jumped, getting off lightly with a crack on the knee.

Having won the first round, the sow pulled up and began to graze, whilst we found the torch. The procession then continued, at a more leisurely pace. Our way lay along the headland of some plough, through a slip-rail, and across three or four grazing-fields. It was heavy going, through rich mud. Rain was running into our eyes, and visibility just about nil.

Suddenly the sow swerved violently to the right, and headed for the plough. I checked this manoeuvre by an exasperated wallop on her starboard beam, just as Paddy dived round to turn her. Our combined efforts were too much for Sissy, who promptly swung round and crashed through the hedge and down into a ditch on the other side. The hedge, which looked flimsy enough by daylight, felt like a barbed-wire entanglement as I was towed through. Sissy was now up to her belly in water, and blowing bubbles happily as she pushed her snout into the ooze. I clambered down, filling one gum-boot in the process, and heaved against her with all my weight. She might have been the Rock of Gibraltar. After five minutes of alternate coaxing and coercing she was still a fixture, and the situation was beginning to look desperate.

Paddy, like myself, was now in a vile temper, and he suddenly seized her by the tail – presumably with some idea of pulling her out backwards. At any rate, it worked. With a startled squeal, she shot up the bank and bulldozed her way through the hedge once more.

Across the grazing-land we followed the line of an electric fence, which hissed merrily in the rain. Not being able to see it, we gave it a fairly wide berth. When barely fifty yards separated us from the lane which represented the last lap, half a dozen beef-cattle came gambolling up out of the darkness to see what was going on. With terrified snorts, Sissy went plunging away from them. Paddy followed with his outflanking movement. They hit the electric fence together, and it was anybody's guess as to who made the more noise. Paddy bounced off, like a featherweight using the ropes, his hair fairly crackling with current.

Charged with new energy, he hustled the sow along to such effect that she retaliated and turned the tables on him. He got through the gate into the lane a bare two lengths ahead of her. We splashed up the lane in chastened silence, until the welcome light, shining over a half-door, revived our spirits. I slipped the rope off as the owner of the boar opened the door wide.

The boar came forward to greet her. As she walked past him, she nicked a piece smartly out of his ear. Paddy cocked a golden-brown eye at me, and wagged his tail. After all, a Setter, even an Irish one, isn't brought up to herd pigs. And he had done his best.

J.K.H.

THE ENTOMOLOGIST

5,200 FLIES

When the entomologist speaks of flies he means the flies with two wings. This rules out the caddis flies, dragonflies, sawflies, scorpion flies and the rest. Yet, curiously enough, some of the flies have no wings at all. The notorious Sheep Ked, or Sheep Tick, is a fly, yet is wingless. Other wingless flies are parasites on swallows, house martins and bats.

More than 5,200 species of flies are found in this country, although most of them are known only to the specialist.

Flies multiply with great rapidity. The housefly lays a batch of about 120 eggs and in a favourable season the life cycle may be as short as twenty days. Obviously, a pair of houseflies might be the parents of a vast progeny, but fortunately they have many enemies that keep their numbers down. Many of the mosquitoes produce egg batches of more than 300, and the female of the common blowfly, or "bluebottle," may lay about 600 eggs. On the other hand, the large black Noonday fly lays only six eggs during its entire lifetime. And there is one group, the common Flesh Flies, that does not lay eggs at all, but produces living young.

It is in their larval stages that the flies show a truly astonishing variety, and there is one foreign species that spends its early life in pools of petroleum. Life in the water is attractive to larvae of many species, including the gnats and the bee-like drone flies.

Others spend their early stages in decaying vegetation, in the excreta of animals, or inside tunnels made in leaves. A number pass their larval period as internal parasites of caterpillars, keeping down numbers of insect pests.

Perhaps the most curious life history is that of the large bee-like flies of the genus *Volucella*. These flies spend their larval stages in the nests of social insects, one species being found in the nest of bumble bees, another in that of the wasps and yet a third in the nest of the hornets. At one time it was believed that these larvae were parasites, but more recent research has proved that their purpose in the nests is to act as scavengers, feeding on the debris that accumulates. It is certainly strange that the flies are allowed free entry and exit to the nests and are never interfered with.

The wingless Sheep Ked is another insect that produces living young. Only one larva is produced at a time, and this is retained in the abdomen of the female until it is almost full grown. Then it is deposited among the wool of the sheep, where it pupates almost at once. The Sheep Ked larva leads a sheltered life and is not subject to the hazards of most larval existence, so it is perhaps not surprising that the female Sheep Ked produces only about ten larvae during her lifetime.

Among the vast hordes of flies are many garden pests, some of the most notorious being the carrot fly, the onion fly, the celery fly and the daddy-long-legs, which in the larval stage is that odious creature the leather-jacket. Many flies spread diseases, a well-known instance being the part played by the mosquito in the transmission of malaria. On the other hand, there can be no question that flies play a most important part in the pollination of flowers. Moreover, they render great service as scavengers, ridding the earth of much noxious refuse.

The powers of flight possessed by the flies are truly remarkable, and everyone must have seen hover flies remaining quite still in the air, while their wings vibrate so rapidly that they seem to be surrounded by a tiny halo. A moment later they dart away with a speed that the eye is unable to follow.

Yet perhaps the most astonishing of all are recent experiments made with the common blowfly. These seem to indicate that this insect has the power of both smelling and tasting with its feet.

C.T.

AUGUST

WILD LIFE

August is hot summer's breathless height when vegetation reaches its limit of growth, tree canopies are darkest, corn falls beneath the reaping knife, mushrooms appear, nuts and blackberries are ripe, heather blooms, and fleabane and agrimony shine forth in golden light among the dowdy seeding heads of lush hedgerow herbs.

Animals are wandering away from nurseries and nests. Young bats leave the breasts of their dams to which they clung for many days while the laden mother hunted through twilight after moths and beetles. You may catch species new to the district now when inexperienced migrating bats enter houses in search of roosting quarters, often when they come to snatch moths from around the lamp beyond your open window.

Shrews are but annual creatures; the old ones are now worn out and die, leaving only their children to survive the winter. Moles are biennial at least, and wander miles after leaving the nursery mound, until they find a wormy winter retreat. Hedgehogs produce second litters in August, while the first stroll into dangers on the road or meet their fate under the badger's strong claws. Cats and foxes cannot undo hedgehogs; perhaps that is why hedgehogs are numerous in suburbs where badgers are scarce.

For the rodents harvest is not what it was. Instead of being carried in the sheaf comfortably to the barn, harvest-mouse nests are threshed out by the combine, and the contents dumped as fatalities with the beaten straw; they are dying out save in fen country where they live among the uncut reeds. For a while rats and mice and voles batten in the cut corn fields; under the deposited straw their burrows are safe and food is plentiful until the baler – or fire – takes off this convenient thatch. Then they must run off their fat in a perilous hunt for new quarters. Fattest of all is the young dormouse, which begins to centre its affairs around a new nest low down in dense woodland vegetation.

Roe deer, present in more counties in Britain than is generally known, run in their rutting rings, the significance of which is not altogether clear; but it is a form of play which they enjoy to such an extent that they are utterly exhausted at the end, and their ecstasy may even end in death.

Birds are moulting or migrating. Chaffinches flock, swallows gather on wires, the willow-wren recommences his charming scales, but the chiffchaff takes this month off from his two-note song. Flying at the speed of an express train, the all-but-aerial swifts suddenly depart, screaming a last farewell as they sip water over the village pond where the stay-at-home moorhen is still plodding with her third brood.

R.M.L.

For many mammals, August is the height of mating season and community life. Many hedgehogs have second litters; if grey squirrel's litter found in nest, as is occasionally the case, this may be second or even third; more evidence about third litters of grey squirrels desirable.

Much breeding among the reptiles, though breeding season of amphibians is over. Grass snakes lay most eggs in August, and if weather is stable and moist, some early ones may even hatch. The ovo-viviparous reptiles – those whose eggs hatch immediately they are laid – reproduce themselves this month: smooth snakes, slow-worms, common lizards. Vipers, being truly viviparous – i.e., young born alive without short egg stage – also born this month. Discount legends of vipers swallowing young to protect them.

Among the birds, much gathering for the autumn dispersal and passage; perhaps not yet the main passage of most Arctic waders, but many advance parties of godwit, whimbrel, turnstone, sanderling, wood-and green-sandpipers, spotted, redshank. Our native curlew, dunlin, redshank, greenshank flock up and start to pass. So do some ringed plovers, some oyster-catchers.

A quiet month in the woods, but noisy over the village, with the perpetual screaming of swift families hurtling wildly over the steeples. By the end of the month all will have gone, or nearly all; a September swift is worth a note.

August a better butterfly month than most think; the schoolboys on their holidays know this. A month for second broods of some species: large white, peacock, red admiral, wall; on the chalk hills and railway cuttings the second broods of Adonis blue and brown argus. Round the garden the second brood of the holly blue which lays on ivy, but which has itself been reared on holly blossoms. For other butterflies the main hatching: rare Lulworth and silver-spotted skippers, the rarer purple emperor, the Scotch argus, the chalk-hill blue. Round the hedges fly new brimstones in the woods new gate-keepers. On wood edges and moors green fritillaries; over the dunes graylings.

Quite a month for immigrants, particularly clouded yellows, painted ladies, red admirals, though some of these last two arrive in the spring and have already given rise to an autumn brood. In some exceptional migration seasons we may even get great rarities, especially on the south coast; Camberwell beauties, long and short-tailed blues, Queen of Spain fritillaries, pale clouded yellows, Bath whites. Many are the eager lepidopterists who throng the chalk cliffs of Sussex at this time.

J.F.

THE FRUIT GARDEN

WEEDS: It is not long since the control of weeds was mentioned in these notes but the matter is worth bringing up again as many small growers are faced with this problem. The matter is not as serious as some people think and with regular cultivation the majority of weeds can easily be eliminated. In neglected orchards ground elder and the perennial nettle are the two weeds commonly seen. Both of these plants build up a food supply in thickened roots during the summer, but if the foliage is cut at regular intervals this process is interrupted. As a result, growth becomes weak and the weeds gradually die out. Where small patches are involved methodical forking out of the roots or smothering of young growth by heavy mulching with straw or other coarse material will quickly establish a control. Whichever method is adopted it should be carried out thoroughly or else the weed will quickly re-establish itself.

SOUR FRUITS: Although not often practised, the best time for pruning blackcurrants and raspberries is immediately after the fruit has been gathered. The removal of old wood or canes allows a maximum of light and air to reach and ripen the young growth well in advance of the onset of winter. With blackcurrants the aim should be to cut out as much old wood as possible, without sacrificing an excess of young growths. Ideally the majority of these should originate at the base of the plant although a few varieties are tardy in this respect. In the case of raspberries it is a simple matter to remove the old fruiting canes from ground level and to tie the young ones in their place. Opinions vary as to the correct spacing for these young canes but the writer's experience leads him to advocate a 3 in. spacing along the whole row. If they are thinned too drastically this appears to have a generally weakening effect particularly on the lighter soils and may be one cause of failure with raspberries. Of course, these remarks apply only to summer-fruiting varieties, the pruning of autumn-fruiting kinds being left until early spring.

Two other cane fruits requiring attention are loganberries and blackberries, thornless varieties of which now exist. Both produce long and vigorous new growths which must be tied in if they are not to be damaged or broken. There are various methods by which adequate space can be left for those. One such is to train the first year's growth along the lower supporting wires reserving the top ones for the next season by which time the lower wires will have been cleared for the process to be repeated.

G.R.W.

THE FLOWER GARDEN

UNDER GLASS: Schizanthuses will make a charming display in a cool greenhouse during the spring if the seeds are sown this month. Sow them very thinly, in pots or pans filled with sandy soil, and as soon as the young plants are large enough put them singly into small pots. They may be grown under quite cool conditions provided that they are not exposed to frost. Pinch out the point of the leading shoot when the young plants are about three inches high, to induce bushy growth.

Cyclamen seeds may now be sown for flowering next year as they should be allowed at least fifteen months to flower from seeds. Sow the seeds in well-drained pots filled with good loamy soil and space them about an inch apart so that the young seedlings need not be disturbed until the corms have developed and are fairly firm. They can then be potted into small pots without danger of injury.

Freesias, which have been resting, should now be re-potted as a long season of growth under cool conditions is necessary to produce the finest flowers. Place eight to ten bulbs, according to their size, in a five-inch pot, using a good loamy compost. Stand the pots in a cool frame and water very carefully until the new roots have taken possession of the soil. Ventilate the frame freely.

Cuttings of many half-hardy plants which are required for next year's display in the greenhouse and flower garden will root readily if they are inserted during the present month. Fuchsias, heliotropes, etc., should be rooted in a close frame, but zonal pelargoniums may be rooted in pots stood in a sheltered place out of doors.

Lavenders are rather short-lived plants, as the older branches are often split by winter storms and snow. They may be easily propagated from cuttings taken this month. Take the cuttings with a heel and insert in pots filled with sandy soil or, better still, in a bed of sandy soil in a cold frame.

IN THE OPEN: Narcissi growing in beds and borders will benefit by being divided about every third year. The bulbs are now dormant and they may he lifted and transplanted. Plant them about three inches deep and vary the distance apart according to the size and strength of the variety.

Climbing polyantha and Wichuraiana roses will soon finish

flowering and they should then receive their annual pruning. Cut the old growth to the ground wherever possible and train the young growths from the base of the plants in their places. If there is insufficient of these basal growths to cover the desired space, retain a few of the best of the old ones but shorten them back to a strong young leading growth.

C.P.

———•+•———

It is only too easy to criticise books on any subject in which one is really interested. I think, however, it is true to say that many writers on roses, whether in books or magazines, neglect, or at any rate only partially cover, some of the most interesting aspects of rose growing.

For example, the question of the supposed loss of fragrance in present-day roses is seldom discussed properly. On the one hand, there are those who state bluntly that the moderns are mostly scentless and, even when they are fragrant, are not to be compared with the old-fashioned varieties. Others will tell you that contemporary roses smell just as strongly as their forebears.

August is a very suitable month to examine this question from a practical angle, though I must warn you at the outset that there is no hard and fast answer. Indeed, one of the fascinations of rose growing is that so much room exists for individual opinions (dogmatism in horticulture is always a sign of lack of experience). There's no right or wrong way of pruning, as it depends largely on circumstances; no general agreement on the best manure or fertiliser; no single universal remedy for pests or diseases.

Forty or fifty years ago fewer varieties were grown, and it is probably true to say that most people remember only the best of such roses. Taste is, I think, easier to recall than smell. Some people have a comparatively poor sense of smell, and are unable to detect the subtle scents present in many modern varieties. Roses are usually more fragrant in a warm, humid atmosphere than in very hot or excessively wet weather. Thus, many varieties appear scentless unless you smell them when temperature and weather are ideal.

We are often told that the old Damask Rose is unsurpassed for sweetness, but the plant I grew in my garden at Cambridge was virtually scentless in all weathers, though I am certain I had the correct variety. It is therefore interesting to find that Francis Bacon, writing over 300 years ago, remarked: "Roses damask and red are fast flowers of their smells; so that you may walk by a whole row of them and find nothing of their sweetness."

Modern roses have a far wider range of scents than their predecessors, and many different comparisons have been employed by compilers of rose catalogues and others to define them. Some appear very far fetched (cowslip, geranium, and nasturtium, for example); but to me they are all intriguing, especially the French variety which is claimed to smell like new-mown hay.

Or take the new American hybrid tea Mirandy (incidentally, a poor variety for the garden, as the blooms blue badly even in wet weather). In this case we are assured that the fragrance resembles caramel toffee. When I first saw this novelty at the Southport Flower Show I immediately went over to smell it, and even in the heated atmosphere of the large marquee I could detect an unmistakable aroma of toffee.

For testing the fragrance of your roses, the early morning and evening are probably the best times, as the maximum degree of perfume is never apparent when the sun's rays beat down on the plants. It may also be true that roses grown in country gardens are often more fragrant, as the hot, dry atmosphere one associates with the confined area of many town and suburban gardens is less noticeable.

What of varieties? It may be helpful if I mention a few newer ones, as everybody knows the older scented varieties like Dame Edith Helen, Lady Sylvia, Ophelia, and Shot Silk. Two Irish hybrid teas must come first, the salmon-pink Admiral which is good in both wet and dry summers, and the more recent Hebe. The latter is china pink and salmon, with plentiful coppery-green foliage. I saw Hebe on the raiser's nursery at Newtownards, Co. Down, last September in torrential rain. If all I've said about atmospheric conditions is correct, there oughtn't to have been a vestige of scent in that rose, especially as I'd just been smoking, which temporarily ruins one's sense of smell. It was, however, richly perfumed, which only proves the inconsistency of the rose.

The glowing crimson Red Ensign, the cerise pink Tallyho, and the warm madder pink Eden Rose are also notable for scent. Very few yellow roses enjoy a pronounced perfume, but Sutter's Gold, an American novelty, has a strong tea fragrance.

Lastly, a word about cutting roses. No amount of attention after cutting will revive blooms gathered carelessly, or at the wrong time of day. Cut your roses, if possible, in the late afternoon, when they contain more sugar than in the early portion of the day. Plunge the cut stems up to their necks in water *immediately* after cutting, and leave for several hours before arranging, to ensure the maximum absorption of water.

Remove any leaves on the lower part of the stem, as they decay in water and encourage the growth of bacteria which block the cells. The addition of substances such as aspirin, alum, camphor and quinine to the water to extend the life of the cut blooms is of doubtful value, a continuous low temperature being probably more beneficial than any chemical treatment.

N.P.H.

THE VEGETABLE GARDEN

The first earthing up of celery needs special care, because the roots want moisture but the stems do not want wet earth against them. First, give the trench a good soaking, remove any basal suckers and loosely tie the heads, then rake dry earth from the sides of the trench a few inches up the stems – not more at present.

Peas and beans reserved for seed should he left on the growing plant until they are fully ripened, but watch them from now on and keep the pods away from slugs. Garlic is ready for harvesting when the leaves turn brown; dry the cloves in a sunny place out of doors for at least two weeks, then hang them in a warm place indoors. This is a good time to divide chive clumps, replanting the bulbs at 6 in. apart.

August sown turnips usually do better than summer ones, but they must grow quickly to be successful, and if sowings can be arranged during rainy periods they will get ahead more rapidly. This is the sowing that provides turnips during winter, and should not be left out if the summer ones were disappointing; the ground where potatoes have been growing is a good place.

Parsley takes a long while to germinate and should be sown in good soil and kept watered. To always have a fresh supply it must be sown at least twice a year; thin the previous sowings to 1 ft. apart. French parsley is claimed to have a finer flavour than the ordinary variety; it has large, smooth leaves and can be sown this month.

If you are sowing onions in the spring, prepare the place now by working in manure; but if they are being sown this autumn be careful not to use anything that is not already well-decayed. It is important to get the soil just right before onions are sown, and it is worth giving some time to making it firm and level. The best means of doing this is first by raking, then laying two boards on the surface and treading on each alternately. Make a second sowing of spring cabbage such as Wheelers' Imperial or Flower of Spring.

This is the best time for green manuring, while the soil is still warm enough for the soil bacteria to break it down when it is cut. Mustard seed can be bought in quantity for the purpose, and any kind of beans that were left over can be used; before the seed is sown give the ground some nitrogenous fertiliser, as a shortage of nitrates often makes green manuring a failure as far as next season's crops are concerned. Water the green manure crop if necessary, to encourage a quick, soft growth. Cut just before the flowering stage, chop it up and fork very lightly into the surface.

C.M.

August is an awkward month for gardening. It is often very dry and vegetables are apt to have a tired and dried-up appearance and taste. If you are going to take a holiday, now is the time to do so. There are, of course, many jobs that must be done. The all-important spring cabbage should be sown during the second week, followed by another batch a fortnight later. Harbinger is one of the earliest heading cabbages but Early Giant is invaluable for cutting as greens during May.

Choose a sheltered spot for a bed of White Lisbon for pulling as spring onions. Sow thickly to allow for casualties. Do not be later than the second week, otherwise the seedlings will not be strong enough to stand the winter. Celery should have side shoots removed and the first earthing up. Tying is simpler and quicker if done with a continuous string, wound once round each stick. Take care not to pull it too tight, otherwise the stick will grow like an Indian club. When earthing, no soil should enter into the heart. Soot is an excellent fertiliser and keeps the fly in check. Finish planting leeks. These can be earthed up later to assist blanching higher up the stem. During the last week, winter lettuce should be in. Sutton's Imperial is *par excellence*. It is best not to thin out before the spring. Good, rich ground is absolutely essential. There is no doubt that the method of spraying carrots with TVO against weeds is a labour-saving idea that should not be disregarded by even the smallest grower. Only the best quality oil should be used and must be sprayed at the rate of one pint to ten square yards, after two true leaves have formed and before the root is pencil thick. Weeds are controlled for about a month. The same treatment can be applied to parsnips.

It is an excellent idea to scatter mustard seed over blank areas. This can be dug in when six inches high and provides invaluable humus and checks weed growth.

When the onion leaves have died down, the crop should be harvested and the bulbs left on the ground to dry off. When the operation is done, it becomes obvious that the best and most even crop is obtained by planting out box-grown plants. There is no risk of fly and weeding is infinitely easier, as the plants can be put into ground which has benefited by three weeks extra cleaning.

E.B.

SHOOTING

August 12th Grouse Shooting begins. Game Licences to be renewed.

It is not as a rule possible for even experienced keepers to form a very reliable estimate of grouse prospects until guns and beaters get out on the moor. The changing economic conditions of our time have affected conditions on many moors, and on many too heavy a stock was left from last season. If the breeding season conditions are favourable and the batch good, this all too often means overcrowding, and as "coccidiosis" and "gape worm" are always latent infections in a grouse stock, disease may wipe out the promise of the year. Immigration, which is less understood, may repair the damage of a disastrous year more rapidly than natural increase, for where a seven-year-cycle from bumper year followed by catastrophic disease and a negligible bag in the following year seems to be the natural time cycle, it is quite clear that moors often pick up and return to a clean bill of health in far shorter time.

Heather tries the feet of sporting dogs sadly, despite weeks of conditioning before the journey north. The local dogs, on the other hand, seem to suffer no inconvenience. It is not outside one's experience to see the season started with dogs of unblemished pedigree and the most expensive and aristocratic connections. But towards the end of August, or, if it is hot, even earlier, one finds the real business of the shoot being conducted by the local dogs. Some are retrievers, but in a high proportion of the locals, collie or sheep dog alliances are very obvious.

It is a matter of regret that the tender mouth of the Labrador or the spaniel is so seldom transmitted to the cross-breeds. The "nose" apparently is, the retrieving instinct is – but in general they are astoundingly efficient but about as soft in the mouth as a pair of pliers. For the human "tenderfoot" a foot lotion of ordinary surgical spirit to which 10 per cent. of formalin is added saves a lot of wear and tear. It might be good for dogs, too.

LIMBERING-UP PRACTICE: The country man who never really lays away his gun throughout the year begins the next season with no sense of "being out of practice." The townsman, less fortunate, less exercised and more harassed may well be out of practice – or what is equally distressing be suffering from an inferiority complex about his shooting. A visit to a shooting ground is indicated and will probably restore confidence and self-reliance.

Shooting, like swimming, is never forgotten, but one does lose that sense of timing. A refresher drill and a series of "clays" at a "shooting school" will put things right.

H.B.C.P.

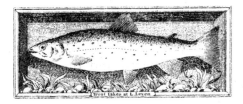

FISHING

In these warm and sultry August days, with a very high air and water temperature, the early salmon are lying "doggo," well scattered in their favourite places – in most of the middle, and in many of the higher reaches of the river.

The Treweryn, a most important spawning tributary of the Welsh Dee, is an example. On the "flats" there, and in the level stretch of deepish water, extending for some three or four miles – an absolutely safe abode from poachers – salmon can lie hidden safely for weeks. Also on a rocky river like the Lledr, with underwater caverns and caves (the same applies to the Upper Wye in some places), salmon can lie safely tucked away, in danger only from the expert poacher.

The poacher's usual weapon is a wire with a triangle fixed on the end, and a thick length of cord tied to the eye of the triangle. With this, hidden caverns can be searched in the hope of finding some unsuspecting salmon or big sea trout.

But enough of illegal methods, and to come down to the almost impossible feat of fairly killing salmon in August. There is no need to emphasise that small sizes of fly are most suitable. But there is a new method about which little at present is known, and about which less has ever been written. It consists of floating a prawn or shrimp with little or no lead at all, down stream on a twelve-pound-strain French nylon line and a small No. 6 Triangle. One hook is inserted below the eyes of the bait, and either a couple of half-hitches of nylon round the tail, or else a couple of strands of fine copper wire or silk matching as closely as possible the colour of the bait used.

All one does is to stand at the head of a pool and let it drift without any check at all, absolutely naturally – and the success following this method is astounding. The bait must almost always pass directly over the fish to be taken. I have dropped a shrimp down at least ten times in one pool on the Upper Lledr (and a small pool at that), and had a solid pull on the tenth or eleventh trial owing to the current taking the unweighted bait along a different course. The most killing way of all is to see your prawn or shrimp disappear under some overhanging ledge, or into some underwater passage between two rocks.

Always remember this: if you know the pool you are fishing, in August especially, carefully fish "First," with a capital F, the most likely lie. Do not start at the head of the pool, or your special fish may see the bait coming some way off and get accustomed to it, be it fly or shrimp or prawn. But throw and let drift right on the best lie *first*, and you will often kill a potted fish that has refused the orthodox way of watching a bait coming many, many times and will fall to the unexpected.

It is necessary, first of all, to straighten out your prawn or shrimp, and the light, curly, slightly twisted women's hairpins make a first-class straightener. They will easily bend in a fish's mouth, and will not make the fish raving mad as often as an ordinary spinning needle will when it penetrates upwards, in some rare cases paralysing the fish by touching some nerve in its head. For hot weather, this is a most fascinating form of fishing.

Let us pass on to the esturial waters. In these, August is, perhaps, the most enjoyable month of all. Generally there is a really good show of salmon and sea trout – and bass and mullet, too – all drifting in with the tide and often out again as the tide falls. In many cases they stop in the deeper pools as the tide falls, especially in estuaries like that at Malltreath, in Anglesey, and at Llandanog, near Harlech, where one can see salmon, sea trout and bass all jumping at the same time.

Esturial fishing is terribly tricky work, and seldom pays good results for the effort used. Firstly, I think, because the tackle used by the average fisherman is far too heavy and coarse, and, secondly, because most estuaries are very local in "where," "when," and "how" to fish with success. Here again, I think the new idea – to me, anyhow – of drifting a prawn downstream without a float, and fishing it almost like a greased-line fly, will be found a most killing way. For bass it is deadly, especially with a newly caught fresh prawn just bound on the single hook and still alive.

There is really only about two hours' fishing-time on each tide, and if this falls at from 4 a.m. to 6 a.m., fishing the last good tidal pool from a boat can be almost as exciting as any form there is; when the tide turns, one can see salmon, sea trout, and bass passing within a very few feet of the boat when anchored in the right spot. But to catch these, except for the occasional one, with fly or bait or anything else is no easy job. But when once you have found the right spot and the right bait, it well repays the hours experimenting.

Four Axioms for Anglers

First and foremost the most important thing of all in fishing, whether it be for salmon, trout, coarse fish – pike especially – and all sea fish, is *sharp hooks*. Always carry a file or whetstone, and sharpen the points of your hooks every few minutes, not just once a day or so. Secondly: never be in a hurry. Thirdly: keep your temper under all and any provocations. Fourthly: fish alone if possible, emptying your mind of everything but the job on hand; keep out of sight; and concentrate on fishing either close to the bottom or close to the surface – not halfway down.

J.H.P.

THE NATURALIST

THE FAMILY OF FOX CUBS

Avixen does not hesitate to remove her cubs to safer quarters if she suspects danger. I once watched such a removal from a small meadow where, so far as I know, foxes had never dwelt before; but this particular vixen appropriated a rabbit burrow, and maybe intended it to be only an emergency home. It had no advantages of secrecy or seclusion to commend it, and I fancy that she had gone there to drop her litter only because she had been driven from another earth.

However, into this meadow she came, enlarging the interior of the burrow to meet her needs, and it was while I was searching for a pheasant family in an adjacent spinney that a flash of golden brown passed beneath the trees, and I saw her slip over the hedge into the meadow. I immediately followed and there, on the freshly dug soil at the entrance to the burrow, were her neat, dog-like footprints.

I made a hide, and waited. After a few minutes I saw the vixen's sharp, pointed features peeping out of the burrow. She stood there without the flicker of an eyelid, then sank back. But the evacuation of her cubs was in progress and she soon emerged carrying one of them in her mouth. She held it by the skin of the neck (as a cat does her kittens) and crouched so low that her stomach almost touched the ground as she moved silently along the hedgerow.

She was absent exactly ten minutes and when she returned every nerve in her body was quivering, and her eyes glared with fiery determination. Without any hesitation another cub was removed and then she returned for the third. The youngsters, not more than three weeks old, were warmly covered in blackish-brown wool.

After waiting an hour I cautiously moved back into the spinney, where a few trampled-down primroses betrayed a little track. It was the way the vixen had taken her family, and the route along which I first saw her returning. It terminated beneath a clump of willows, and although I saw no more of her on that occasion, on subsequent visits I met her again and was able to watch and photograph the cubs. They were four in number, suggesting that one had been removed before I discovered the vixen.

As they grew and developed they exchanged their baby wool for coats of chestnut-brown, with white cheeks and a conspicuous white spot on the tips of their bushy tails.

One evening, as I crept to my look-out, I saw two of them playing at tug-of-war, using a sun-scorched rabbit skin (the relic of an earlier meal) as a rope. With vigour and glee, each pulled in opposite directions until the rabbit skin slipped from the jaws of one of them, sending the other rolling somersaults down the slope. That these four cubs had enjoyed many gambols near their nursery was evident from the many runways through the grass, but my happiest memory of that family was when, one night, I saw the vixen return carrying a rabbit.

At her approach, the youngsters literally jumped for joy, immediately leaving their frolic to greet her. With maternal pride she carefully pulled the rabbit to pieces, giving each cub its share and not partaking of the smallest morsel herself.

As the owls hooted and a nightjar "churred" its evening hymns, she sat down with her quads, presenting a beautiful picture of family life. But the vixen must not always be given all the credit for rearing the cubs, for at this particular earth the father also shared the family responsibility. Dog foxes vary in this respect, some of them taking no interest whatever in their progeny. But this one was a model father.

B.M.N.

THE ZOOLOGIST

THE POOR PERSECUTED CRAB

Crabs are out of joint in the scheme of things. They are heavily armoured and heavily armed, yet are preyed upon without mercy. As free-swimming larvae: they die by the million, swallowed with other plankton to nourish shoals of herring and other fish. Even when, later in life, they have developed an armour, they are beset by enemies. Wrasse eat them. Conger eels smash them on the rocks. Octopus feed on them. Sea-birds hunt them. And at night, at low tide, rats come down on the beach to thin their ranks still further. As if this were not enough, crabs indulge in cannibalism to a degree rarely attained in other species. Truly, crabs must hide to live.

You may often walk across the shore at low tide and fail to see a single crab, until you really get down to it. By which I mean literally getting down to it, stooping and bending to look more closely and turning over rocks and seaweeds. Then it soon becomes clear that the beach has its full share of crabs.

The ordinary shore crabs when well grown are coloured brown, green, or reddish, the colours of seaweeds. When young they show an even greater range of colours, with marblings and mottlings that render them extremely difficult to see against the vari-coloured background of rocks and weeds. The shape of the body, once the legs and claws have been tucked in, is similar to the rounded pebbles. And added to this the animals themselves have an antipathy to light, and habitually insinuate themselves backwards under pebbles, sand or weed when they come to rest.

It is most striking that everywhere in the world the native species of crabs tend to look like the background against which they live. Crabs living among coral rock look like coral rock, in shape and colour. Crabs living on a muddy shore are mud-coloured, and so on. And examples of the same kind are seen on our own shores. The fluted crab, the circular crab, the angular crab, all look like pebbles – when at rest. The tiny porcelain crabs, with flattened bodies and claws, look so like the muddy surface of a rock that if only they keep still they just cannot be seen. Turn a rock over and see the muddy under-surface begin to bubble up, and before long a dozen porcelain crabs, looking like daubs of mud, are scuttling over its surface.

Although most kinds of crabs, especially those of small or medium size, have this natural camouflage, some have not. Of these, a few burrow into sand or mud. Among the others, the most remarkable are those that deliberately cover themselves with living camouflage; in fact, they plant sea-gardens on their backs. They include the various spider-crabs. One kind decorates only its legs and claws with bits of seaweed and sea-firs, so that the small, rounded body at the centre looks like a pebble surrounded by patches of weed – as long as the animal keeps still.

The spider-crab most commonly seen is the more heavily built kind, and this one decorates the whole of its back. It clips off pieces of seaweed and sea-fir with its claws and sticks them on to the minute hooks decorating its shell. So garnished, it can lie among the minute growths on the rock surface with complete invisibility. Take such a crab and place it on sand, or on any such other surface with which its decorations do not harmonise, and, immediately it is free, it will scuttle away. Moreover, it will not settle down again until it is on a surface that matches its particular camouflage.

Hermit crabs, as we know, shelter their soft bodies in the empty shells of sea-snails and whelks. And there are some hermits, the larger ones, that go so far as to carry a sea-anemone perched on the top of the adopted shell. All sea-anemones are armed with stinging-cells, so that the hermit gains not only a disguise but a formidable defensive weapon. This association is not accidental, for the hermit actually strokes the anemone to entice it on to its shell. Perhaps even more remarkable is the association wherein an anemone has one side of its body folded in, forming a cavity into which a hermit crab can insert its soft defenceless body. This anemone is not fixed to a rock, as in the more usual anemones, so the hermit can move about, taking its living shelter with it.

The prize in this series of defence methods goes to the sponge-crab. It cuts a lump of sponge – of which numerous different kinds grow round our coasts – and places it on its back, the last pair of legs being specially shaped for holding the sponge in position. The extraordinary thing about this crab is that it cuts the sponge with its claws, to the right shape and size to fit exactly over its back. Yet, like ourselves, it never sees its own back – and it cuts this novel overcoat correctly at the first attempt. Sponges, not the commercial kind, of course, grow in abundance in the sea, so a crab sitting on a rock and looking like a sponge stands a good chance of deceiving its enemies.

The art of hiding has reached its highest expression, perhaps, in the pea-crab, so named on account of its size. It lives within the gills of a living mussel, and in view of the millions of mussels clustering the rocks it never lacks a hiding-place. What is more, it feeds on the same minute forms of life which the mussel draws into its shell for its own nourishment.

Finally, the masked crab may be mentioned. It habitually buries itself in the sand by day, coming out at night to feed. Although seldom seen alive, between tide-marks its shell is often found on the shore. Its name refers to the resemblance to a human face caused by irregularities on the back of its shell.

M.B.

THE SHOOTING MAN

AUGUST THE TWELFTH

The other day I was discussing with a friend the difference between grouse and partridge shooting. When I maintained that driven grouse are easier than driven partridge he was in violent disagreement.

When I told him that not only did I believe this but that I intended to say so in print, he exclaimed:

"Then you will have everybody who knows anything about shooting laughing at you. Of course, driven grouse are more difficult."

Though the grouse flies faster than the partridge, due to its weight and larger wing span (the black grouse flies even faster than the red) it is easier to see, not only because its plumage is much darker than the partridge, but because one's first shot is usually taken as the birds top the rim of the hill. Most butts are below the tops of the higher ground and you have a clear background of sky.

In partridge driving, your normal position will be behind a hedge and in most cases the top of this hedge is far from level, saplings and trees grow in it, and often there is a distant background of trees to further confuse the eye. A target coming over a clear-cut rim is always easier to shoot than one which is against a confused background. Moreover, the partridge coveys have a habit of suddenly appearing in gaps between hedgerow trees and there never seems to be so much warning of approach. In grouse shooting from butts on the lower grounds you can very often see the grouse pack coming from some distance away, and you have ample time to be ready to give them a reception.

I suppose that neither walked-up partridge nor grouse are difficult; certainly the walked-up grouse is one of the easiest of targets in the early part of the season. I consider dogging on the moors is a splendid sport and quite equals the driven grouse; sometimes I prefer it.

I wish very much that a scientific enquiry could be made into the speed of game birds. As far as I am aware this has not been done (though I stand to be corrected) and the only experiment I know of is one that took place some years ago in the New Forest.

Pigeons, pheasants, and partridges were made to fly down a long covered corridor. Two screens of cotton were placed in the line of flight, two and a quarter yards apart, and the time taken to cover this distance was recorded by an electrical device and converted into yards per second and miles per hour. Amazing as it may seem, the pigeons and the pheasants made identical times for fastest flight, both registering 33.8 m.p.h. Partridges clocked in at 28.4 m.p.h. I should imagine the speed of a grouse must be near that of the pheasant, though in the field it appears to travel very much faster.

Speed in birds is very deceptive and large birds like wild geese and herons, though they appear to be travelling slowly, are flying at a considerable speed. In normal windless conditions a wild goose is estimated to travel between 40 and 45 m.p.h. Professor J. A. Thompson has estimated that the crow and finch travel at

30 m.p.h. and the starling at 46. This seems to be a very high rate. I have seen starlings keeping pace with geese.

It has always been something of a puzzle to me why both grouse and partridge become so wild towards the end of the season. I do not think it can be explained entirely by the fact that they are persecuted by man, rather I think it is a sense of insecurity engendered by the lack of cover.

Game birds must feel very "naked" when the summer growth dies down, as they rely so much on camouflage. This applies much more to the partridge than the grouse, for there is always cover in the heather. Game birds are certainly more alert at the end of the season and take more care to keep well beyond range, though during the nesting and breeding season they lose much of their fear of man and even of their more formidable enemies of the wild.

There is another interesting subject which can be studied with regard to red grouse, and that is the great variation of the plumage.

The most handsome, and I think the best, is the white variety, where many of the flank and lower breast feathers are tipped with white. But variations range from black to red, white and buff-spotted and buff-barred – these variations are more pronounced in the hen grouse. The white variety is common in Sutherland, though it is found also in Westmorland.

It has been noted that on certain moors the grouse tend to pack by sexes, some packs being composed of cocks and others hens, but these are usually younger birds. The old stagers tend much more to lead a solitary life with perhaps only their mates for company.

It is strange why red grouse will not perch on trees, and not very often have I seen them on walls, though they will readily alight on boulders among heather. The black grouse is quite different in this respect and perches readily on trees, like the pheasant.

The special fascination of grouse shooting resembles that of wildfowling; it is the environment which means so much. And what variety of scenery, of colour, lights and shades! Those long waits in the butts ... how enjoyable they are, how much better than sitting on a shooting stick staring at a shabby autumn hedge waiting for the partridge coveys! The very air you breathe is a delight, unsullied essences of miles of moor, glen, bog, and burn. There is the hint, too, that summer is almost spent and in eight weeks' time there will be a different scene from this butt where you are now standing. Gone will be the vivid purple of the moors, that brilliant bloom will be replaced by deeper, richer tones of madder, buff and ashy grey. I suspect the bee, as it explores the drooping heather bell close by, senses this hint of summer's end, for he works urgently at his task.

In the sheltered air inside your ambuscade the midges dance, about your feet lie the trampled empty coloured cartridge cases, fragrant with powder.

A curlew passes and in its clear fluting call is all the wildness and beauty of these solitary Northern hills.

Then comes the faint shrillings of a whistle and you are jerked out of your reverie, pulses quicken on the instant. Yes – only the lonely vigils of the fowler can match these moments.

B.B.

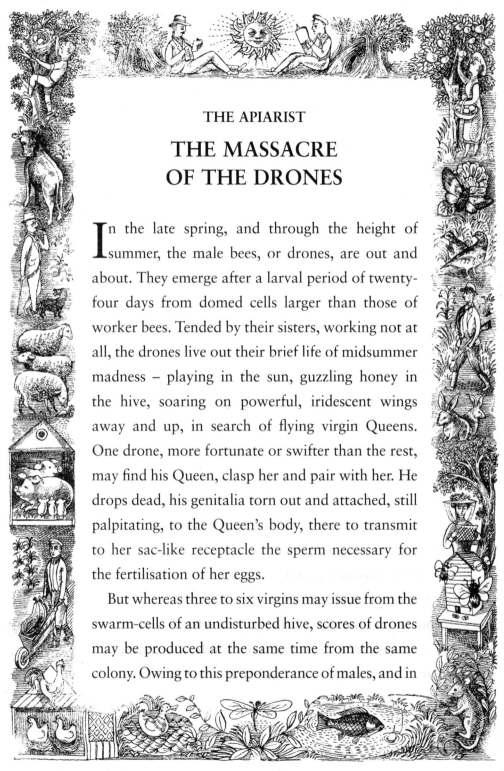

THE APIARIST

THE MASSACRE
OF THE DRONES

In the late spring, and through the height of summer, the male bees, or drones, are out and about. They emerge after a larval period of twenty-four days from domed cells larger than those of worker bees. Tended by their sisters, working not at all, the drones live out their brief life of midsummer madness – playing in the sun, guzzling honey in the hive, soaring on powerful, iridescent wings away and up, in search of flying virgin Queens. One drone, more fortunate or swifter than the rest, may find his Queen, clasp her and pair with her. He drops dead, his genitalia torn out and attached, still palpitating, to the Queen's body, there to transmit to her sac-like receptacle the sperm necessary for the fertilisation of her eggs.

But whereas three to six virgins may issue from the swarm-cells of an undisturbed hive, scores of drones may be produced at the same time from the same colony. Owing to this preponderance of males, and in spite of cross-pairings between drones and virgins of neighbouring apiaries, there will remain – at the end of the summer – a superfluity of drones. These carefree and lazy bachelors continue for a while to be tended by their industrious sisters. But when the time of the young Queens is over, when the hot summer days shorten and the honey is stored, then the doom of the lazy ones is sealed. No longer do the sisters pamper and feed them, allowing them the freedom of the hive. Suddenly savage, the worker bees set upon the drones, chivying them about, nagging at them, biting their wings, turning them out of doors.

Little heaps of dead or dying drones litter the ground in front of each hive. Some, escaping the furies, seek shelter in houses, where a frantic buzz from windowpane or curtain betrays their presence. But the shelter even of human habitation avails them not at all. Homeless, starved, and chilled, the unfortunate ones perish, and the hive, free of its encumbrances, constricts its cluster, re-orders its life and prepares for winter.

The drone has become a byword: we bestow his name on those who are useless, or lazy, in our human race. But it may be that in doing so we malign the insect. There is, in the scheme of Nature, nothing haphazard or uselessly ordained; and it may well be that the drone has functions, unknown to us, but useful to the bee community. His antennae bear a greater number of sense-organs than those of the worker bees; his eyes are larger; it is probable that he and his kind maintain, round the combs of brood, an even temperature.

Some beekeepers make a practice of cutting out the drone cells from the combs in summer, considering that their presence induces in the bees a desire to swarm.

A Norfolk countryman told me that he was wont to stupefy his bees with smoke from ignited cardboard soaked in vinegar and saltpetre. He would, he said, go round his hives on a summer night, smoke each colony in turn, pick out the drones from the stupefied mass, and leave the workers and Queen to revive, unharmed, next morning.

The drone is the father of the race; but the father of females solely. For the mated Queen, when laying, has the power of fertilising those eggs only which are deposited in worker cells or cells destined to produce Queens. On these eggs, by an anatomical, valve-like, muscular contrivance, she bestows a drop of the sperm given by the drone with whom she mated. Stored in the spermatheca, or inner sac, this sperm can be squeezed out on to eggs passing down her oviduct.

Motion photographs taken in an observation hive reveal the slow perambulations of the Queen when ovipositing. Followed by a train of attendants, who caress her unceasingly with their antennae and mouthparts, the Queen mother moves slowly, in concentric rings, round the chosen area of comb. On reaching each cell, she tests it with her antennae and forelegs, then, passing over it, grasps the edge of the second hexagon from it, arches her body over the intervening cell, inserts her abdomen in the tested cell and lays her egg. The length of her body necessitates this mode of progress; were she to lay eggs in adjoining cells, her abdomen would be uncomfortably doubled up.

Moving on, she tests the next hexagon, leaving always the empty cell between each tenanted one. The intervening cells are visited by her on her return journey.

A village beekeeper has likened these movements of the Queen to the slow-motion of a sewing-machine needle: the precise spacing and careful timing of her progress suggesting this apt comparison.

The Queen has, it seems, an accurate sense of the size of the cells she visits. For when she reaches a patch of hexagons that have been built to a larger diameter than the "worker" cradles, she lays, in these bigger cells, eggs from which she has withheld the fertilising sperm. These eggs are identical with those already fertilised; but the valve-like contrivance now being shut, they pass down her oviduct into the waxen cells untouched. From these eggs drones only develop.

A drone has no father: but he has, on his mother's side, a grandfather and a grandmother. The intricacies of the honey bee's family descent are studied by scientific beekeepers with a view to the improvement of our strain of bees. For, should a certain Queen show outstanding merits, her qualities will be transmitted more completely to the daughters of her drone offspring than to the offspring of her daughter Queens. The drones of the first filial generation, having no father, inherit their mother's characteristics – on her side; for one generation, their descent is true.

The temperament, good or bad, of worker bees is said to be inherited through their drone parent. Scientific beekeeping has now advanced to the point at which it is possible to effect artificial insemination between chosen Queens and drones. Through this, and other experiments, research workers exploit the curious facts of this virgin birth, the insect parthogenesis.

V.T.

THE BIRD WATCHER

MIGRATION & NAVIGATION

Readers of the *Ibis*, the official journal of the British Ornithologists' Union, will have found a recent issue almost entirely devoted to the visible migration of birds. It is a subject which has been rather remarkably neglected since the beginning of the present century; largely, one suspects, because of the preoccupation of the ornithological world with the study of migration by means of marking.

Those of us who were at the International Bird Congress in Sweden in 1950 will remember the way in which this kind of study swung back into favour, and how speaker after speaker told us of observations made with new eyes on an old subject. Now, with the network of migration observation stations, directed by men who have had several years of experience in new methods of observation, we can expect great strides in our knowledge and a fuller understanding of the reasons for migrations and the methods by which birds navigate.

Already we understand very clearly that in migration almost anything is possible. It is extraordinary how slow the human mind has been to admit that slight birds can, and do, migrate from one end of the world to the other, and that even slighter birds – frail, small land-birds – can, and do, make sea-crossings of 1,500 to 2,000 miles. As I explained in a recent article, the fact that small land-birds can cross the Atlantic has been so incomprehensible to all but the most recent generation of ornithologists that many suitable candidates have been rejected from the British list because previous list committees could not believe that they were capable of getting to us from North America under their own steam.

As I have hinted, this kind of attitude is rapidly vanishing. Within the last few months we have been able to read of a juvenile Arctic tern of the year, ringed in West Greenland on July 8, 1951, which was recovered, newly dead, in Durban Harbour, Natal, South Africa, on October 30 of the same year. It had flown over 11,000 miles in less than three months after first taking wing, and had made the longest journey of any bird ever recorded by ringing. There have been several other similar recoveries of Arctic terns from Africa, birds which had been marked in Greenland, Labrador and the eastern United States. It would seem that many of the Arctic terns that breed in the north-west corner of the Atlantic, and round the Arctic waters that communicate with it, pass on their autumn migration on a slant to make their great southward passage on the east side of the Atlantic. We know that quite a number, on reaching the Cape of Good Hope, turn northwards up the east coast of Africa to reach Natal and in some cases also Madagascar. We also know that some do not cross to the east Atlantic but pass south down the east coast of South America. We are now also sure that large numbers continue from Cape Horn and the Cape of Good Hope across the sea to the Antarctic.

Now there are two southern breeding species of terns, usually known as the Antarctic tern and the South American tern, which are very similar to the Arctic tern in the field; indeed, even specimens have been confused. Until recently ornithologists have been hesitant about accepting Arctic tern records from the Antarctic. However, the fact that this extraordinary bird does reach the Antarctic continent is now accepted by such critical authors as Dr. Murphy of the American Museum of Natural History, and this was absolutely proved not long ago by Dr. Bierman, an ornithologist, who was the surgeon to the Dutch whaling factory-ship, *Willem Barendsz*.

The Arctic tern in the Antarctic lives as it does in the Arctic. It inhabits the pack-ice in the neighbourhood of icebergs, and feeds in the open water in the splits or leads between the floes and near the bergs, living on the big planktonic crustaceans or krill which the great whales live on. The Arctic tern makes a round trip from one Polar region to another which, in the case of some individuals at least, must add up to 22,000 miles a year. If we suppose that the species occupies two-fifths of the year in its actual migration, it must average about a hundred and fifty miles a day. Clearly it must do more than that on some long sea passages, but only a few miles a day in some areas in order to stoke up with fuel.

I have dealt at some length with the case of the Arctic tern because it is so obviously spectacular. But it is a sea-bird, capable of taking in fuel at sea, so we cannot feel quite as astonished at its ocean crossings and sea miles covered as we would if it had carried all its own fuel on such crossings. Actually the longest known land-bird crossings between fuel-stations appears to be about 2,000 miles. There is the oft-quoted case of the Pacific golden plover, which migrates across the sea south from Alaska to find points on the long, strung-out Hawaiian archipelago. Wherever it makes its landfall, it has made a crossing not far short of 2,000 miles.

But an even more spectacular crossing has recently been illuminated by D. W. Snow of the Edward Grey Institute at Oxford, who has analysed the migration of the Greenland wheatear. I am sure he is right in his belief that this species makes the longest regular migratory ocean crossing of any passerine bird. The distance involved is at least 1,500 and probably 2,000 miles, for it certainly flies from South Greenland directly to Europe between Britain, Ireland and Portugal; and probably some individuals may fly direct to this coast from Labrador. Some, of course, use the stepping-stones of Iceland and the Faeroes, but it is quite certain that an important number make the crossing direct, and a significant group of observations at sea between August 6 and October 4 is quoted by Snow. The breeding range of the Greenland wheatear is wholly Arctic, though it nests south of the Arctic Circle in Greenland and the Canadian North. In autumn the birds put on a great deal of fat before leaving their breeding-places; and we now know why. It is possible that more birds may make the direct crossing in autumn than in spring, since the prevailing winds favour a passage from the west, and the spring records do seem to indicate that the wheatear is more inclined then to use the Faeroes and Iceland. But some spring birds have turned up at weather ships, indicating that they make the direct journey.

I have deliberately chosen, in this article, the most spectacular migratory journeys that we know about. Acutely these affairs raise the question of bird navigation and orientation. Through recent work, both experimental and observational, great strides have been made in our understanding of bird navigation, particularly by D. W. Griffith in North America,

G. V. T. Matthews in Great Britain, and G. Kramer and others in Germany. We are beginning to find that birds may be able to put up these extraordinary performances without magic but with something resembling the aids that humans use for navigation-maps and charts (or a visual memory that serves in their place), dead reckoning, a knowledge of the time and the observation of the sun. I shall be devoting an article to this fascinating business very soon.

J.F.

THE HOLIDAYMAKER

A ROUND OF THE LOBSTER-POTS

It was five o'clock on a July morning when I leaned against an old cannon on the quay, one of six originally mounted on the cliffs to protect our little harbour against "Boney." I had fixed up with "Uncle" Harry Penruddock and his son, "the boy Harry" (aged 50), to go the round of their lobster pots in their 23-foot open motor-boat *Diligent*.

I noticed that there was "Musick," that is low mist, rising from the water in the inner harbour; sure sign of a fine day. The boat came alongside, her bow space piled with spare lobster pots, and I was given the tiller with instructions to steer for "Black Head," where our first pots were set.

Father and son immediately got to work cutting up bait, and preparing the wooden skewers or "pitchers" with which the bait is fastened in the pot. Bait for lobsters and crabs must be fresh. Any sort of fish will suffice, with gurnard first favourite.

We made a bad start for we could not find the corks, or "cobbels," which marked the position of the pots. Probably they had been cut off by the propeller of a passing craft, or, as sometimes, but rarely, happens, a Monkfish may have come to the surface and swallowed the corks in mistake for a young gull. To find our missing pots the "devil," a length of chain to which strong hooks are attached, was brought into play. After some delay the lost gear was recovered, pots reset in another place and we proceeded to the next "string."

The two Harrys used pots which they made during the winter months from withys cut from the local willow moor. They preferred them to the wire pots which are now coming into more general use. These, they owned, were lighter to handle, but did not "fishy so well."

They set a maximum of 200 pots, usually in "strings" of 20 spaced about 12 fathoms apart. Should the weather be bad the loss in gear may be heavy, for much of it has to be set near rocks close inshore; a gale may uproot them and wash them ashore, where they become a total loss. The "crabbing" season here generally lasts from April to September. Consequently a reserve of pots and gear has always to be kept in the loft ashore. Uncle Harry said he could make and stone (they are weighted with flat stones) two pots a day, working "real hard."

When we had completed our inshore round, and set the new pots brought with us, we steered for the offshore ground some five miles from land. In the event of rough weather these distant pots have to be left unvisited for several days. Consequently there is a risk that the inmates will find their way out.

Uncle Harry recalled that, some years ago, on a distant "mark," he hauled a pot and found tied inside a golden sovereign wrapped in canvas. He concluded that a yachtsman had hauled the pots and had thus made payment. "I bet they ain't all as honest as that," he chuckled. He owned that on the whole pots were rarely tampered with. The worst robber is an octopus.

When hauling a pot, Uncle Harry had to call to his son to lend a hand to get it aboard. Inside was a 30 lb. conger, which conveniently slid out of its prison. It was given the K.O. by a blow on the vent (it is useless to knock a large conger on the head) and put under the bottom boards, in due time to be cut up for bait. In another pot we found a huge crab, which the men could not get out. The pot was taken ashore where the side would be cut to release the captive.

We had completed the course and now headed for home. The men said we had a "fairish lot." At times we hauled a dozen pots in succession containing nothing but starfish, sea-cucumbers and small hen crabs which were put back. The hen crab, even if a large one, is of little value, for it is very "watery." They are at times sold to visitors and the unsophisticated at the price a cock crab should fetch. When seen right side up there is no apparent difference in size, colour or shape, but if turned over it will be noticed that the cock crab has a narrower flap.

Crabs and lobsters in this locality are, after each trip, placed into partially submerged boxes, each crabber owning his own, which are moored in the inner harbour. The catch is removed from time to time to be sold alive to the fish buyers. Before being placed in the store box the tendon of their large claw is cut or "nipped" to put it out of action, otherwise the inmates would kill one another. Lobsters are usually packed alive in barrels, with a covering of oak sawdust. Crabs are packed with straw – sawdust would kill them.

While "Uncle Harry" was carrying out the "nipping" operation I noticed that he wore a few strands of blue worsted around his wrist. I asked the reason for this adornment, he replied that he wore it "against sprains and rheumatism," and added that the worsted must be blue.

G.E.B.M.

WHAT EVERY COOK
SHOULD KNOW ABOUT

GROUSE

The arrival of a gift brace of grouse is always an event, and although one should not look a gift horse in the mouth it is necessary – so far as the kitchen is concerned – to come to a decision on the probable age of grouse. There are several indications.

The easiest is to press the skull. With young birds it is relatively soft and yielding, while older birds' skulls are resistant to normal finger and thumb pressure. Another good way is to hold the full weight of the bird by the lower mandible of the beak. If this bends or breaks, the bird is young. These methods are all right with gift game, but not so easy to practice at the poulterers. There one can pull out the third primary wing feather. If the quill is moist, and holds a squeezable drop of blood, it is a young bird.

Another less embarrassing aid is to examine the claws. Grouse shed their claws annually, and the old claw fits like a sheath over the new one. At its base is a small groove, and, if this groove is visible, it is an indication of an old bird.

The essential kitchen difference between the old grouse and a young one is that the former cannot be roasted. No art will prevent him being tough and stringy. Young grouse are really best as a plain roast, but it is always best to let the birds hang some time to develop their special flavour. This depends on the temperature and weather, and the place where they are hung; but they should not be drawn or plucked until they are ready. The nose will inform you, and the soft skin of the abdomen will appear thin and greenish when they are really ready. In general, they can hang at least a week in warm weather and up to three weeks if kept cool.

The grouse is by nature a leaner bird than either partridge or pheasant, and requires additional fat. Pluck, truss and prepare as for chicken, but insert in the bird's inside an inch cube of butter, and rub it well round the cavity. Have your butter or fat melted in the roasting pan, and baste the bird thoroughly with this so that all the skin is covered before fastening on a "bard" or apron of fat bacon rashers.

Grouse are not easy to roast to perfection, and the secret lies in turning and infinite trouble in basting, otherwise the outside will get dry. A grouse also generates little gravy, and, unless you have a good supply of grouse, one cannot prepare a concentrated "Fumet," or grouse gravy, which can be kept in the refrigerator from the carcases of previous birds. Fried bread crumbs, bread sauce, and, for vegetable, French beans accompanying Rowan or cranberry jelly is also advisable. Grouse should not be overdone. Twenty minutes is about right with a good oven.

Another excellent way of doing young grouse is to spatchcock them. Split them down the back, open out, press perfectly flat and skewer across. Heat plenty of fat in a sauté pan wide enough to plunge the bird in, and seal it thoroughly. Drain and transfer to a grill, basting with butter.

Old grouse needs long cooking. Probably the best way is to make him into a grouse and steak pudding. Cut the grouse into chunks, bones and all, seal in butter or fat, and add in place of kidney to a steak suet pudding. To get the approved colour in the suet, add a teaspoonful of black treacle to your suet mixture. Use a good rich stock and cook for at least three hours, refreshing any evaporation outside or inside. All the steak will taste of grouse and the dish is excellent.

Old grouse *en casserole* is easier. Make a good stock of a calf's foot, and flavour it with plenty of onions, carrots, and a good bouquet garni of herbs. Truss the old grouse as for roasting, and cook it in the stock for twenty minutes. Remove and keep hot, strain off the grouse-flavoured stock, and add it to a roux of butter and flour. Thicken carefully and taste, adding, if necessary, a little lemon juice or red wine. Pour this back through a strainer over the grouse and keep hot, but not boiling, till served. A casserole is fairly flexible, and mushrooms are a valuable addition if the season is still too early to sacrifice celery.

A simpler but no less delightful receipt is to cook the old grouse as above but with a big savoy or cabbage, which you have previously quartered and blanched in several boiling waters to abate too strong cabbage flavour. Lemon juice or a little white vinegar can be used to finish the flavouring, but it is worth a glass of wine.

Lastly, cold grouse is held by many folk better than even hot grouse. It is the best of shooting breakfasts, and the basis of a marvellous salad of plain lettuce, grouse cubes, and a faintly tarragon-flavoured mayonnaise. For a picnic lunch, weight of china ware can be saved by putting this admirable confection inside small, hollowed-out half-loaves. Thus packed, it stays moist and cold, and the dogs will clear up all remnants.

H.B.P.C.

WHAT EVERY COOK
SHOULD KNOW ABOUT

THE STILL ROOM

There is a great attraction about "homemade" preserves, pickles and even "wines" or various drinks, some of which are quite successful and acquire an astonishing degree of potency as they age. In older days these activities were usually the task of the younger ladies of the house and they often had a small still or "alembic" used in the preparation of "cordials" which, judging by nineteenth-century receipts, must have been about twice as strong as the 70 per cent. brandy or whisky of today.

These pleasant excursions into the preparation of liqueurs and cordials were possible with "eau-de-vie" or raw strong brandy at about one and fourpence a bottle, but impossible today. It is, however, possible to make a very generous supply of "cherry gin" at the sacrifice of one bottle of gin. The process is simplicity itself but it requires the suitable cherries. The best for the purpose is the dark Morella, but, failing this, the dark well-flavoured cooking cherry – the one that requires a lot of sugar when cooked – is a good substitute.

The method is simplicity itself. Fill a couple of ordinary preserving jars, the glass-stoppered rubber ring kind, with ripe dry selected cherries. Add to each a tablespoonful of granulated sugar. Fill up with gin, stopper and set aside. At the end of a week the cherries will have shrunk and possibly risen in the jar. It is as well to open up and add a "topping up" of more cherries and a drop more gin, but it is not essential.

By the end of three weeks, much of the colour of the cherries will have transferred itself to the gin and at that stage the liquor tastes delightfully of the fresh fruit. It can be poured off at this stage for fairly prompt consumption and the jar refilled with sugar and gin. This "fruit-tasting" liquor does not, however, keep its ambrosial flavour long and it is better to let it stand until Christmas. Then the liquor can be poured off and the jars again refilled with sugar and gin. During the next six months this will produce a second and rather different liquor, for it extracts more of the kernel flavour.

I have known the big fleshy Morellas stand three or more "extractions"; and, lastly, you have the cherries themselves. They are now happily impregnated with weak alcohol. You pour over them a thin light sugar syrup which has been allowed to cool and again put the lot aside for a few weeks. They thus finish an inebriate life as the familiar "Cérise a l'eau de Vie."

The expenditure of gin is very moderate for the yield of liqueur. What you get back is, of course, a mixture of gin and the fruit extract of the cherries, but you will find it decidedly potent. If an extremely "dry" cherry cordial is desired, the sugar can be reduced or omitted but it will probably be found too astringent for most palates. Provided it is well sealed down it appears to keep indefinitely and to mellow and improve with age.

An even more inexpensive "cordial" can be made in the same way but using more sugar and substituting one of those "English wines" which have a really high alcohol content. I used "Segavin," a Seager product, with complete success, and a friend found boiled cherry juice, sugar added cold to the same quantity of Segavin produced a "wine" or "Cherry Bounce" which looked like Ruby port, had a delightful fruit flavour, but was too sweet for the adult palate. It is, however, the most excellent stuff for filling larger children's flasks, as it has plenty of sugar in it and probably only enough alcohol to make the liquor "keep" without fermenting.

Of "wines" fermented with yeast in an earthenware bread bin all countrysides have an endless variety – parsnip, elderberry, rhubarb, etc. They all really depend basically on the added sugar which puts them rather out of court in these days. Mead which is made from honey is an exception. It is a worthwhile drink and simply made. Boil equal parts of honey and water with relentless ferocity until the density of the mixture is such that a new-laid egg floats one-third out when laid on the surface of the still liquid.

Cool to blood heat, then float on it a slice of old toast spread with ordinary yeast, cover with a cloth and it will bubble happily away for about three weeks. When you think it has stopped "working" pour off carefully into *strong* bottles. Those for bottled beer with screw stoppers and a rubber ring are excellent, and pints preferable to quarts. Do not screw the stoppers home until you are sure they have stopped working, then bed them in a box of sand in a quiet cool cellar.

Mead can be drunk in three months but should not really be touched for a year. By then it will have developed potency and a wineglassful at a time is enough for the inexperienced. It is not powerfully alcoholic – leaving the head clear it affects the legs, but only temporarily. A weaker variety about one of honey to two of water is called Metheglin, pronounced "Thiglum," and is a wildly fizzy, honey-tasting lemonade, not a "strong drop" like mead. It can be stored in quart bottles, but these should be opened with care over a basin. It is ready in six to eight weeks but if left in bottle some months becomes sensibly more powerful and approaches a mild mead.

In a good honey season "mead" is well worth making, but it is wisest to keep it in very thick, strong bottles; old champagne bottles recorked and wired are best. Otherwise you may be astonished by explosions in the cellar, as mead is undoubtedly "a strong drop."

The real function of the modern equivalent of the still room is to make use of and accommodate surplus. When eggs are plentiful "lemon cheese" is an excellent thing to make provided you have a double saucepan. Potted like jam it is a welcome change and keeps indefinitely if sealed.

Then there are pickles. Many of these are far better prepared cold than by any of the usual receipts which boil pickling spice in vinegar (to the loss of both) and the cold vinegar process does not perfume the house for hours. Into a bottle of white pickle vinegar put an ounce or so of pickling spice from which you have removed most of the red chilli peppers – if you like to taste your pickle rather than pepper. Let it infuse and it will be ready for use in a week, better in a fortnight and can be left infusing indefinitely.

Pickled shallots are the best of country pickles – and the older in bottle they are the better they become. When dried out they are tailed and husked, plunged into boiling salt water and left for the moment or two it takes for the water to come to the boil again. Withdrawn, drained, pressed into preserving jars and covered with the ready prepared spiced vinegar.

In the same way a flush of mushrooms can be pickled. Wipe, but do not skin, blanch in boiling water for three minutes, drain and pack fairly tightly in small preserve jars, cover with spiced vinegar. These mildly pickled mushrooms look rather like oysters and can be used instead of oysters in an "oyster cocktail" made of tomato juice, a little Worcester sauce and a dash of lemon juice. Served cold from the "frig" they are surprisingly good.

Lastly, one of the best and simplest pickles I know is pickled limes. These little green fellows often appear at greengrocers when lemons are scarce. Buy some at sight and simply put them into a preserving jar, rammed fairly tight, and cover them with a brine made of as much salt as will dissolve in water. Add to each jar half a tablespoonful of dry salt, this will dissolve later, and not more than two red pepper pods from a "pickling spice" packet to each jar. The limes will take six months to pickle and become translucent, but they are then one of the pleasantest condiments of a cold meat and it is hard to think of a simpler pickle.

For "sweet" pickles like gherkins, pumpkin, etc., cold spiced vinegar, plus a little saccharine, ten or twelve tablets to the jar, is perfectly satisfactory; but for a really delightful sweet pickle about one-third honey to two-thirds spiced vinegar is the best basis. The honey should be dissolved with thorough stirring in the spiced vinegar which can be warmed but should not boil.

H.B.P.C.

THE BOTANIST

FLOWERS BY THE SEASIDE

This is the month when many of us will be taking our families to the seaside. I propose, then, to say something of the more interesting plants which are normally to be found around our coasts.

Such plants have not necessarily anything more in common. Seaside plants – like those that grow anywhere else – form many distinct communities. Consider, for example, the vegetation of the chalk cliffs: those dazzling ramparts which confronted Caesar when he came from Gaul. This is markedly different from the opulent vegetation of the Devonshire sandstone, or from that of the more primitive rocks which give character to the coast of Cornwall. And how different, again, is the vegetation of those craggy heights from that of the Cornish coves: Lamorna; Kynance; Polperro. One could produce an indefinite number of such contrasts.

But it isn't possible, in one article, to discuss plant-communities. The best I can do is to say something of such maritime plants as are, for the most part, widely distributed round our shores.

The cliffs, as I have mentioned, have their own flora; its variety, and its gaiety, add much to the pleasure of walking round the coast. But many of the flowers that I have in mind are not, in the strict sense, maritime. They are inland plants which thrive also in the sea air, but, because of their exposed situation, tend to become stunted, and to adapt themselves in other ways to the rigours of the climate. So one finds what are almost miniature varieties, with their own distinctive appeal, of many familiar flowers. I have in mind, among others, Harebell, Centaury, Milkwort, Bird's-foot Trefoil. There are cliff walks, all along the South Coast, where the turf is more or less carpeted with these tiny blossoms. Particularly attractive – as I remarked last month – are minuscule editions of the sweet-smelling herbs: Thyme and Marjoram.

These plants are, morphologically speaking, indistinguishable from those which grow inland. But there are also a number of plants which have developed distinct characteristics as a result of their maritime habitat. They are only of interest, however, to the critical botanist.

Now descend to the seashore itself. Some soil formations (such as chalk) support a comparatively limited flora. But, taking them by and large, there are representative species which are very widely distributed. Some are of interest only to botanists. Though technically flowering plants, they hardly produce flowers in the sense in which Botticelli would understand the term. But there are plenty of quite striking blossoms which can only be found around the coast. One of the most conspicuous is the Yellow Horned Poppy (*Glaucium*). It is called the Horned Poppy on account of its elongated seed-vessels, so different in shape from the censer-like organs normally met with in this family.

The great James Sowerby, writing in 1790, discusses "whether this be the true Glaucium of Dioscorides." He thinks not. "The whole plant," he adds, "is foetid and of a poisonous quality. It is said to occasion madness."

Another fascinating seaside flower is the Sea Holly (*Eryngium*). This is common around our coasts – and, indeed, all round the coast of Europe. Its Latin name derives from Theophrastus. This plant is not a true holly, but one of the umbellates – differing, however, from most of its relatives in that its heads of flowers are globular in form and in colour a pale blue. At first blush, it looks more like one of the composites. It has stiff smooth leaves, armed with formidable prickles; hence its English name.

Several other umbellates grow, usually, by the sea. One of these is the Fennel, a handsome plant with yellow flowers.

The name Fennel is an old one, and probably it was a different flower – perhaps Hedge Parsley? – which the distraught Ophelia distributed:

There's fennel for you, and columbines: – there's rue for you;
and here's some for me: we may call it herb of grace o'Sundays.

Other members of this prolific family are the Hog's Fennel, which also has yellow flowers but is comparatively rare; the Sea Carrot, which has white flowers; and the quite unmistakable Samphire. This last plant can he spotted at once by its fleshy leaves. It is said to be edible and country people used to pickle it.

The more correct name, incidentally, is Sampire: a corruption of the French *Saint Pierre*.

Fleshy leaves, like those of the Samphire, characterise a good many seaside plants. Such leaves are necessary to the survival of species which have not ready access to fresh water. I might instance the Stonecrops; the Houseleeks; and the gay Mesembrianthemum – not uncommon round our coasts, though it is of Mediterranean origin.

Other maritime flowers which, if in bloom, can hardly fail to catch the eye are the Red Valerian (*Kentranthus*), which is also of Mediterranean origin; the Marsh Mallow; and the not very common Tree Mallow: a handsome shrub, with rose-coloured flowers, that may grow to a height of seven or eight feet. Mallows are closely related to that cottager's stand-by, the Hollyhock. Nor must I forget to mention the Sea Lavender (*Statice*) and its cousin, the Thrift. Both these flowers have an "everlasting" quality. They can be used as decoration, dried, for an indefinite period. The Thrift is familiar for another reason. In tribute to its name, a conventionalised representation appears on our dodecagonal threepenny-bits.

I have said nothing of the plants which are, in the strictest sense of the word, maritime: the Seaweeds. This is partly because so few of them – the Bladder-Wrack is one exception – have other than "scientific" names. They are not, of course, "flowering" plants at all, being much simpler in structure and aeons older in the evolutionary scale. Many species are very beautiful, and our grandmothers used to collect and press them – caring nothing at all about their names, their affinities, or the processes by which they reproduce themselves. Such artless diversions went out of favour when the horseless carriage and the motion pictures came in.

H.P.

THE CHATELAINE

I dined the other night with the well-known cooking expert, Elizabeth David. Eight of us sat down to the meal, which was served in the kitchen. The walls round us were festooned with bunches of onions and strings of garlic hanging between culinary implements; and the long narrow table covered with a red-and-white checked cloth was just the right shape and size to facilitate and encourage conversation, the person sitting opposite being as easy to engage in talk as one's neighbours.

Before going in to dinner we drank dry sherry, and instead of the usual assortment of cocktail biscuits and nuts there were dolmades – rolled vine leaves stuffed with savoury rice (these leaves can be bought at several of the Soho shops, including Parmigiani's).

The meal started with a fish soup which had the consistency of a *bisque*, with mussels and pieces of conger-eel floating in it. This was followed by the best cold pork I have ever eaten or am ever likely to eat: ribs boned and parcelled so as to form a single oblong of meat, larded with truffles and surrounded by crisp fingers of golden crackling and small pyramids of delicious brown jelly naturally yielded during cooking. There was a noticeable lull in the conversation as we did honour to this perfect dish.

With it we drank a velvety burgundy; but when I asked our hostess for the address of her wine merchant, hoping to buy a few bottles for myself, she told me that I would find no more of this particular vintage, since over a number of years she had herself consumed it all.

After the cold pork there was a very interesting salad, which I have since copied successfully at home. Finely sliced raw mushrooms are soaked in an oil and vinegar dressing with herbs and a little garlic, and are then added, with more dressing to a green salad. The meal ended with my favourite cheese, *tomme*, which has a purple crust of dried grape-skins – the residue of the winepress – and is thus impregnated with a faintly vinous flavour.

Elizabeth David is an extremely busy woman; nevertheless she entertains frequently – much to the pleasure of her many friends. This particular meal seemed to have entailed no effort on her part, and the menu was so planned that it could all have been prepared in advance. Yet that cold pork must have required many hours of expert attention, and in appearance and taste it was clearly the creation of a genius.

D.B.

SEPTEMBER

WILD LIFE

Nature is called to account in September; the month of hard work, good living, stocktaking and change. The last swifts have gone. The swallows and martins gather. Occasional spring reminiscences; a snatch of song from a passing warbler in a hedge. The autumn song of robins, male and female, and the cooing of wood-pigeons and laying of their autumn clutch. Cosy smell of compost and cosy sound of wood-chopping.

Dispersal of many sea-birds from their cliffs and breeding-grounds. The young gannets and fulmars work off the remains of their fat on the sea below the cliffs, until they can fly. Petrels and shearwaters – stormy, Leach's, Manx – make their first journeys. The great and sooty shearwaters (Britain's only summer visitors which nest in the Southern Hemisphere) are at their peak of numbers round our shores, usually some miles at sea in the western approaches or the northern North Sea.

At the peak of their passage, the waders whose advance units passed in August – godwit, whimbrel, phalaropes, turnstone, knot, dunlin, curlew-sandpiper, stints, sanderling, golden and grey plovers, some gulls, the skuas. Early movement of woodcock, snipe, foreign lapwings. The purple sandpipers from the Arctic haunt the rocky shores. Glaucous gulls and Iceland gulls arrive on our northern shores from the Arctic, and set bird-watchers the perennial problem of distinguishing them from each other.

Iceland gull has bad vernacular name, for it has never been proved to have nested in Iceland. Its breeding-distribution is confined to the southern two-thirds of the Greenland coast, and it is no more than the race of the herring-gull belonging to those parts of the Arctic. It would certainly have been called the Greenland herring-gull had its true refuge been known when its identity was first learned in 1822.

This month's quotation from Gilbert White comes from his *Journal* for September 12, 1774:

"Great hail at Winton. Wasps abound in woody, wild districts far from neighbourhoods: how are they supported there without orchards, or butchers' shambles, or grocers' shops? *Footnote.* – Wasps nesting far from neighbourhoods feed on flowers, and catch flies and caterpillars to carry to their young. Wasps make their nests with the raspings of sound timber; hornets with what they gnaw from decayed. These particles of wood are kneaded up with a mixture of saliva from their bodies, and moulded into combs."

J.F.

———•·•———

Advance guards of swallows and house martins are congregating on overhead wires and roof gutterings, and may even depart should the weather turn suddenly cold. Don't be deceived into thinking that all have gone – even when these eager ones have disappeared. It was on October 8 two years ago that a young house martin – not yet fully feathered – was brought to my house after having fallen from a nest. I hand-fed it for nine days before handing it over to a friend who successfully introduced it into a very late colony.

Apart from the twittering of the swallows and martins there is not much in the way of bird voices, though the robin gives us a taste of its plaintive autumn notes. Chiffchaffs, too, often indulge in a final burst of their very typical notes.

Among the mammals there is a great variety of activity. Badgers have in all probability finished their mating, but an odd pair here and there may leave their nuptials until early in September. Dormice are attending to the construction of winter nests, and have also started to fatten up on nuts and berries. Hedgehogs are feeding greedily in anticipation of the chill nights to come, but they will not hibernate properly until well into October, or even later than that, unless these months be unusually cold.

Writing of berries reminds me that the berry season is at hand, and even as early as this some birds are reaping this kind of fruit harvest. Elderberries are ripening, and many birds show their taste for these juicy morsels. The more substantial mountain-ash berry is also to be had; and among others, mistle-thrushes will be found at work on them. The various berries which are ripe at this time come in handy for some of the migrants which are still with us, as these can stoke up on such food before their departure. Blackcaps and white-throats will eat elderberries, as will any tardy nightingale which has not yet left.

The butterfly lover can still feast his eyes on many species in September, and appreciate at the same time the late-flowering plants that attract them. Red admirals, tortoise-shells, commas, speckled woods and brimstones can all be seen now; and the evenings, if warm, will bring many moths to lighted windows or to garden borders: the lovely angle shades for instance, and the humming-bird hawk, and the large but sombre herald.

M.K.

September comes in new-born like a lamb, and goes out at the equinox like a roaring lion. In the early calms nature is still fresh, rich and warm in her maturity; if the days be cloudless a spring-like re-birth of wild life occurs. Chrysalids hatch instead of hibernating and a second generation of butterflies flutter through woods and fields, mating and laying eggs, although the caterpillars may not all pupate in time to escape the first frosts. Stimulated by the abundance of insect food and the sunlight, swallows and house-martins often embark on third clutches of eggs; the resulting young birds may not be fledged before October, when occasionally the urge to migrate, hastened by a cold spell, causes the parents to desert them prematurely.

Blackberries are now the general food of many mammals, birds and insects. The hips and berries of wild rose, hawthorn, rowan, guelder, elder and spindle are ripe, and summer birds linger to enjoy this vegetarian diet. Acorns fall on hot days or when gales thresh the oak boughs; as soon as they reach the moist ground they begin to germinate, and are greedily eaten by pheasants, wood-pigeons and small mammals, which fatten on such bounteous bulky fare. Bullfinches feed in exotic family parties, led by the salmon-pink-breasted cock, and pipe from the riot of seeded umbellifers, garden weeds, and rushes. Fat greenfinches glean in stubbles with flocks of chaffinches, goldfinches and linnets.

Silent for a month the skylark softly recommences his rich song, soon to be followed by the song-thrush shouting his repetitive phrases, matin and anthem, morning and evening, from lonely woodland tree-top and suburban chimney-pot alike. Male and female robin sing defiantly at each other, each separated in its winter territory in corner of garden, field or wood. By the end of the month only the chiffchaff is left in song of all our summer warblers.

The vagabond young hares, no longer to be called leverets, are settling to regular territories each of perhaps a hundred acres in range; untroubled by epidemics they are all the happier for the disappearance of rabbits and rabbit-fences. Never has the rabbit in Britain experienced such a catastrophic decimation since its introduction in Norman times; many countrymen look optimistically to myxomatosis to free the country of this rodent, and believe that hares and other ground game will thereby increase. Whatever the outcome Nature automatically adjusts the balance without too much interference by man; foxes do not altogether depend on rabbits, nor do badgers—both are easier to control than the rabbits. Stoats and weasels may actually increase in the absence of rabbit-trapping.

R.M.L.

THE FLOWER GARDEN

Although most of the deciduous shrubs transplant comparatively easily during the winter months, the majority of evergreens present a more difficult problem. When transplanted their roots take some time to recover, and the constant loss of moisture from the leaves, even in winter, cannot be replaced quickly enough, consequently the danger of loss is greater. There are two periods in the year when planting is best carried out – April to May and September to October. The operation should take place during a dull moist period, the evergreens being well watered before lifting is attempted. As large a ball of soil as possible should be the aim, and once planted they must not be allowed to become dry at the roots. It is necessary to stake them securely, otherwise the swaying of the plant often leads to the tearing of the roots. The danger of drying winds after planting can be reduced by the erection of a temporary shelter, whilst a mulch will do much to conserve soil moisture. It is the attention given to evergreens after planting which brings success.

There is no substitute for a well-kept lawn to show off the rest of the garden – its restful green ensures that the other brighter colours are seen at their best. If a new lawn is planned this is one of the best times to sow, the grass having an opportunity to become established before the winter. No expense should be spared in the preparation of the site, for this will be amply repaid in future years. It must be thoroughly cleared of weeds, and where new soil is introduced it is best to mix this well with the existing soil, otherwise patchy germination often takes place. The site, having been levelled, needs a good raking, incorporating at the same time a balanced fertiliser until the necessary fine tilth has been produced and the surface then consolidated by rolling. The normal rate of sowing is one to two ounces per square yard, and to ensure an even distribution the site can be divided into yard strips. The seed needs to be lightly raked in and the site rolled. When the young grass is about three inches in height it may be cut, if possible with a scythe, but failing this the blades of the mower should be set high, and providing they are sharp little damage will be done. Any fallen leaves from overhanging trees should be removed, otherwise the young grass soon becomes yellow and dies.

C.P.

A utumn flowering Gentians are most valuable plants in the garden, for they provide a welcome mass of colour until the severe winter frosts arrive. In the southern half of the country they need some shade from the hottest sun, and an ample supply of moisture in the growing season is essential. A well-drained lime-free soil containing a liberal supply of peat or leafsoil is most suitable. About every three years they need lifting and dividing, taking care when re-planting to allow the pronged roots ample room so that they are not bent. They are easily loosened by the winter frosts and the crowns should be firmed and given a light top dressing in the spring. After flowering the dying growths often become a tangled decaying mass and should be removed.

The most popular and easiest to grow is G. *sino-ornata* which soon multiplies and forms a wonderful carpet of royal blue. Deeper in colour G. *Veitchiorum* is also a favourite but the beautiful Cambridge blue of the true G. *Farreri* is now unfortunately seldom seen, although some of its charm has been captured by its stronger growing hybrid, G. *Macaulayi*. Other good hybrids are G. *stevenagensis*, *Farorna* and *Inverleith* whilst for the enthusiast there are G. *ornata*, *gilvostriata*, and *saxosa*. The August flowering G. *gracilipes*, *lagodechina*, and *septemfida* are suitable for gardens with limy soil.

Paeonies are most accommodating plants and present few problems. But they resent disturbance once established, and before planting it is as well to trench the ground and incorporate a liberal supply of farmyard manure or compost. This is the ideal time to plant, making a large hole, deep enough to allow the crown of the herbaceous varieties to be about two inches below the surface of the soil. In the case of Tree Peonies the union of the graft and stock should be two to three inches below the soil, so as to encourage the variety to produce its own roots. As soon as suckers are produced from the stock they must be removed, otherwise they take away all the strength from the plant. Plant in groups and allow each ample room.

The majority of evergreen trees and shrubs can now be safely transplanted. Every care should be taken to disturb the roots as little as possible and after planting they need to be well watered and the foliage sprayed over on hot or windy days. Stake securely to prevent tearing at the roots, and any extra attention will be rapidly repaid by the quick establishment of the plant.

C.P.

The cool nights of September are a reminder that we must make preparations to return to the greenhouse those tender plants which have been standing outdoors during the summer months. The interior of the greenhouse should be thoroughly washed down, and the dirt which has accumulated between the laps of the glass should be loosened with a thin piece of zinc or tin and then washed out with a syringe. It is important to keep these laps clean so that condensed moisture can drain away.

The walls should be lime-washed, and all odd corners thoroughly cleaned. Wash the pots and see that the drainage is clear before taking the plants into the greenhouse. Cinerarias, calceolarias and primulas which are growing in frames should be allowed to remain there until there is a danger of frost. Chrysanthemums should be left outdoors as long as it is safe to do so.

Violas will now be making young growths which are suitable for cuttings, these may sometimes be taken with a few roots attached. The cuttings should be inserted in a bed of sandy soil in a shaded frame or hand-light where they will soon develop roots and make nice plants for planting in the open ground in early spring. Cuttings of the garden varieties of penstemons and shrubby veronicas should also be rooted and wintered in frames, as the mature plants rarely survive a severe winter in the open ground.

Violets intended for winter-flowering should now be lifted, with a good ball of roots, and planted in frames so that they may become established before the cold weather arrives. The frame should face south so that the plants may enjoy the benefits of any sun which occurs during the winter months. Make up a good bed in the frame so that the plants are near the glass. Plant firmly, allowing sufficient room between the plants for a free circulation of air. Keep the frame fairly close and shaded for a few days until the plants have recovered from their move. Then give free ventilation and remove the lights whenever the weather is favourable.

Herbaceous paeonies rank amongst the hardiest and most beautiful plants in our flower borders, they are also very effective when planted in open positions among shrubs. They do not mind whether the soil is calcareous or lime-free, but they dislike root disturbance and it sometimes takes them a year or two to become fully established, so the planting positions should be carefully selected so that they are permanent. Although paeonies may be successfully transplanted from September until March, I would choose late September as the best time for planting.

C.P.

THE VEGETABLE GARDEN

This period is well described as the gardeners' New Year; and it certainly gives us plenty to do. Most important just now is the checking over of crops for a winter supply, and filling the gaps before it is too late. Cabbages can still be sown, but it will be too late to transplant them so drop the seed in very small pinches at 9 in. apart and thin the seedlings to one each. Sow spinach also, but be sure it is the prickly seeded, winter variety. Turnips are a good winter stand-by, both for roots and tops. *Green Top Stone* is a rapid grower, and sown now provides a double-purpose vegetable for winter. For salads, it is still not too late to sow land cress, corn salad and winter radishes in the open. Endive and winter lettuces will stand in the open but are better under cloches. There is now a plastic cloche on the market, unbreakable and claimed to be slightly more transparent than glass.

If there is any fish waste from the kitchen – heads or bones – tie it tightly in a cloth bag and suspend it in water. Renew the water every few days and give it to autumn-sown onions and lettuces; also to leeks and celery before these have been earthed-up too much.

By the end of the month green tomatoes will be a problem. Do *not* remove a lot of leaves in the attempt to assist ripening;

the green leaves are contributing food to the plant and if they are removed, the fruit (being a food store) will suffer. When they have to be brought in pull up the whole plant, or bring whole trusses, and lay them in drawers or closed boxes. A close atmosphere is more important than light for ripening, and the inside of a window is not the best place for them. If tomato seed is wanted, take a fully ripened fruit; from one of the lower trusses. Watch the dwarf tomatoes now for slug damage.

This is a good time to start a new compost heap or reorganise the old one, while it is still warm enough for it to heat up. There should be plenty of vegetation to put on it now, but keep away plants that have gone to seed, or roots that reproduce themselves too persistently.

The stalks of leek-heads that are being saved for seed are getting brittle and will easily snap off if they are not staked. Haricot beans that are ready for storing should have the whole plant pulled up and hung by its roots under cover. Keep all runner and dwarf beans gathered before they get tough; alternatively, leave them until they can be shelled and eaten as beans.

C.M.

September marks the end of the growing season and is the time to review the successes and failures of the past year. It is much wiser to grow the things that do well and leave the others alone. The fact becomes obvious that money spent on manures, both farmyard and artificial, is well spent. Quantity and quality are increased and the land finishes the season in good heart. Quite one of the best general fertilisers is hoof and horn – applied in the spring; suited to all types of vegetables and the results of an application showing for at least three years. Superphosphate will also have proved its worth.

Finish sowing winter lettuce by the first week and plant out the spring cabbage bed. Harbinger and Wheeler's Imperial can be relied on. Give slight earthing up when plants are established to provide shelter and drainage. Planting should be finished by the second week to allow time for establishing good root before the hard weather.

Endive should be blanched in batches. A tricky operation, as rotting occurs so easily. The simplest method is to lift the plants in dry weather, with a good ball of earth, pack tightly in a covered frame, which should be light-proof but allowing air to reach the plants. The hearts should be quite white when eaten to avoid a bitter taste. Blanching takes approximately three weeks.

Finishing harvesting root crops. All these keep better when stored out of doors, but potatoes and beet must be kept frost-proof. At least six inches of earth on top of straw is necessary for this. Carrots can remain in the ground, but this is not a good practice as it prevents the soil being dug over at the right time. Dry sand scattered over carrots and beet in clamps keeps them moist.

When the foliage of haricot beans has turned yellow, pull the plants up, tie them in bundles and hang them up, heads downwards. The pods dry off better by using this method. Fully developed green tomatoes should be picked off when frost threatens and wrapped in newspaper to ripen off. Ripening will be quicker and more even than when merely laid out on racks.

Late peas should not be discarded simply because the pods are discoloured. This may merely be the result of the weather and the peas themselves are perfectly edible. Cauliflower should be looked over daily and the curds covered with the outer leaves if frost threatens.

E.B.

THE FRUIT GARDEN

Of all the soft fruits the blackcurrant is probably the most popular; it is easily grown on the majority of soils and its fruit is nutritious and can be used in a multitude of ways. Like other fruits, however, it must have proper cultural attention if really good crops are to be gathered each year.

Without doubt the commonest mistake is incorrect pruning. There are those who do not prune at all and are content with a poor crop of small berries, while others merely trim back old growths instead of removing them completely. Blackcurrants should be grown on the stool system, the object of which is to encourage the production of a maximum of young wood at or below ground level. Wrong pruning defeats this object as it results in weak young wood arising well up the old stem, thus ruining the shape of the bush.

Because blackcurrants are grown on the stool method all the buds are left intact on prepared cuttings. As these are planted three-quarters below ground level the buried buds will produce the young shoots from below ground level, already referred to. Cuttings are best taken early in the autumn using well-ripened one-year-old growths – that is, those which have just fruited and are about to be pruned off. At this time of year, the foliage is still green and leaves should be carefully cut from that part of the cutting which will be below the level of the ground.

The taking of cuttings in September has the advantage that a certain amount of root is made before the winter, giving them a better start the following year. A most important point is to ensure that cuttings are taken only from bushes known to be free from "Big Bud" and "Reversion" and those which are known to be good croppers.

To go back to pruning, the large majority of people are afraid to prune their bushes hard enough. All old fruiting wood is removed, the majority of it from ground level. Good commercial growers leave all the young shoots coming from the base unless any are weak or badly placed. In most cases, however, these have to be supplemented by young growths arising from old wood to provide a properly furnished bush. Such growths should start from as near ground level as possible and certainly no more than a foot above it. One word of warning; some varieties such as "Boskoop Giant" are shy at producing basal growths and so need to be treated accordingly.

G.R.W.

———•——

Seedling fruits. From time immemorial gardeners have tried their hand at raising new varieties of fruit from seeds as opposed to the orthodox methods of budding, grafting and taking cuttings. The exciting thing about seedlings is that the resultant fruit will almost certainly be different from the parents and there is always the chance that a "winner" will turn up. It is these winners of the past that are propagated in such a way (by budding and grafting) as to obtain trees that are identical with the original seedling which itself may have been raised two hundred years ago.

On the other hand, for every noteworthy variety produced there have been a host of "also rans" which have fallen by the wayside. The natural laws governing the behaviour of such seedlings were investigated by Charles Darwin for a number of years, but he was unable to explain them. The problem remained until 1900 when the world learnt that Gregor Mendel had been able to tabulate certain definite principles of inheritance. Being deprived of the knowledge of these rules, the work of the early raisers was purely a matter of chance but they can always claim the production of such highly prized varieties as "Cox's Orange Pippin" and "Bramley's Seedling." Nowadays these rules of inheritance are embodied in modern scientific plant-breeding and increase the chances of success in producing seedlings with the desired characteristics.

Some fruits offer more scope than others for the chance breeder and of late years a number of particularly fine peaches have been introduced. This fruit is easily raised from seed and in a few years it is possible to obtain a tree producing heavy crops of good fruit in the open garden. The same can apply to apricots but like the peach – or any other fruit – there is the chance that the tree will remain vigorous and unfruitful for many years only to produce poor fruit when it does start cropping. Then again, a seedling may lack vigour never to develop into a worthwhile tree. In such cases the keener raisers may surmount this difficulty by grafting on to selected rootstocks ... but this is another story.

At the present time breeders are following definite lines of thought and for those gardeners who fancy their chance it is worth noting the following example. There already exist ample first-class varieties of apple covering the period September–January. It follows, therefore, that a very early or a very late dessert apple will stand a greater chance of being recognised than one which has to compete with, say, "Cox's Orange Pippin."

G.R.W.

Lush Flavoured Strawberries

For long we have been inclined to look for size and crop-ping qualities with our new fruits and vegetables rather than flavour, until we seem to have almost lost the art of appreciating a fruit bearing a distinct flavour or fragrance. But many of the old varieties found in cottage gardens may still be obtained and though they may not come up to the market grower's require-ments, their flavour is outstanding when compared with modern varieties.

The first to fruit is Leader, which may be enjoyed from mid-May if cloches are used. It was raised by Laxton Brothers in 1895, and was well planted up to the 1914 war. Next to fruit are two superb varieties, Hautbois, the fragaria elatior of the old gardening books; and Black Prince, raised in 1822. Hautbois possesses almost a raspberry flavour, whilst Black Prince carries the fragrance and flavour of old wine. This, to my mind, is one of the finest strawberries ever introduced, for though the fruit is round and small and needs eating quickly, it carries the most delicious flavour of all strawberries, whilst the plants are compact and ideal for the small garden. It also fruits abundantly under forcing conditions. Only the lack of size has brought it to the point of extinction. It makes the most delicious jam, as also does Little Scarlet, which bears rather acid but deliciously fragrant fruit. Those who, by way of a change, appreciate an acid flavour will find the new autumn fruiting American Red Rich an excellent variety.

Carrying the distinct pine flavours the greenish-white-berried White Pine, still to be found in old-world gardens and which fruits late in summer. Not all are old varieties. Two new remontants are Gabriel d'Arbonville, which produces no runners and can be grown in the border. It is divided by root division in November after fruiting non-stop from June. The other is Liberation d'Orleans, which crops in June and again in autumn. It bears a fruit of a rich musky flavour but it is only a light cropper. I have not yet tried the new Docteur Morère, which is said to bear the richest flavoured fruit of them all, but which crops badly on a chalky soil.

R.G.

FISHING

This month trout fishermen can have their last flick with wet or dry fly – a more profitable flick than in August; for lethargic fish seem to come to life again and take their daily meals at hours more convenient for the angler. Five o'clock to seven-thirty in the evening is often the best time, with a Blue Quill or a Silver Sedge as the best flies. Why? Trout must tire of the daily round of Iron Blues, Olives, Blue Winged Olives and Pale Wateries. What heresy I write, especially as the Blue Quill is a fly of fantasy unless it represents an Olive with a dash of Iron Blue about it!

Salmon cheered by the prospect of spawning and journey's end are more gullible, but it is bad policy to kill red hen fish, heavy with ova, though the old, now ugly, cocks can be spared, as there is rarely a dearth of husbands. They can be smoked to good purpose. I have seen a red cock caught in time of spate on a piece of orange peel, which shows up well in peaty water. I always think it strange that at mating time cock salmon should have so unattractive an appearance, but perhaps the great neb and dull red hue is enchanting to the hen. I am now convinced that a salmon can (if the fisherman is patient enough) be so annoyed by continuous appearance of a bait or fly just above its nose that in desperation it will seize the proffered lure.

I know of a gentleman who spent all one day pestering one fish. In the morning and the afternoon the fish used enough self control, but at five o'clock it succumbed and in fury snapped up the plug which had been hurled at it hour after hour. The extra-wise will say the temperature changed or that the oxygen content of the water had altered, but I would not agree. Try sitting in a chair all day with a boiled sweet on a string continuously swinging an inch or so from your mouth. If you make no attempt to rid yourself of it by sundown I shall be surprised.

As a boy I was fishing for trout in the Taw. In the pool a salmon would throw itself out of the water every five minutes. For an hour I cast two trout flies on a 3X cast over it. Finally it took the bob fly with a mighty boil, but after one glorious minute the cast broke. This fish had been worried into action. A trout is usually put down by such tactics, though when fishing dry I have "splodged" the fly several times a couple of feet to one side of a disdainful fish with beneficial results, but curiosity not rage has been the cause of seizure.

R.B.

———

September is the last month of the season for the brown trout fisherman, but often a very good one. Trout rise better than in sultry August, and in the evening the Blue Winged Olive causes fish to guzzle *à la Mayfly*. Get some on large hooks 1 or even 2, and as the light fails fish on wherever you hear a rise. Lethargic monsters will take a fly when at other times they remain incognito. Blue Quill and Dark Olive are good day flies. Remember towards end of month to be on a chalk stream at tea-time. Trout often decide to have a snack between five and six. In Scotland, troll for big brown trout.

Salmon are red except where there are late runs like Tweed. A pity to kill hens heavy with ova. You'll regret it three or four years hence. If you catch some "kippers" (red salmon), smoke them. It's easy.

Get two tea-chests. Take out bottom of one and make a chimney one on top of other. Six feet or so away dig a small pit connected underground to chimney by drain pipe. When ready, light fire of oak or birch chips in pit (covered). Keep heaping on chips and allow to smoulder. Take fish, split it along back and de-bone it. When opened out, rub in saltpetre and molasses for three days. Insert two sticks at shoulder and tail to keep sides apart (like a kipper) and hang up in chimney. Smoke according to taste. I found six hours enough.

While salmon and trout men and women prepare to close down, the coarse fisherman is getting under way. Perch should be moving. A ledgered minnow is very effective, and a perch tastes like sole. Too many weeds in the river to spin for pike. Dace and chub will oblige. Rather satisfying to catch a chub with an elderberry and the elusive dace with a fly. Try to get access to a carp lake.

Don't forget the crayfish, found only in pure alkaline waters (e.g. Kennet, Gloucestershire Coln). Make a hoop. Fix to it muslin. Suspend it from cords like a bank balance (slender). Bait with herring, rather high, and in evening lower into river on end of stick. Have about a dozen of these going at the same time.

Keep hauling in. Then a *Krefta* feast, washed down, if possible, with Swedish Punch or Schnapps.

Crayfish are the sign of a healthy river. First sign of pollution shown by disappearance of crayfish and grayling. You can keep the children quiet by day. Arm each with a tiddler net. Remove shoes, stockings – better still everything if sunny – and allow to hunt crayfish in shallow stream. They will be quiet all day. Can be tried in streams where no sign of fish life, but liable to be unsuccessful.

R.B.

In thirty days at the outside, most fly-fishermen will be hanging up their rods for another six months. This brings home to one with a jolt the fact that a most frightful and far-reaching caste system has gripped the angling world during the past half-century. For the truth is that much of the year's best fishing lies ahead. The ancients knew this. When September came they turned to chub, roach, and pike. Why! Bickerdyke, Francis Francis, Cholmondley-Pennell and their like thought far humbler fish worthy of their consideration. In proof of this, the Piscatorial Society to which most of the great men belonged fished an annual gudgeon match.

If you must stick to the fly-rod, then grayling should now occupy your thoughts. There are those who would root the grayling out of their streams in favour of stew-bred trout. Personally, I believe they are a little touched in the head, for is not all-the-year-round fishing for medium sized grayling and medium sized trout far better than half a year's fishing for cosseted, spoon-fed, highly protected, and consequently slightly larger trout?

With September the roach comes into his prime. The roach is without doubt the most popular fish in England. Do not be deluded into thinking that roach are easy to catch; not big roach, anyway. There are several stuffed fish on the walls of my house including an 18-lb. pike, a 3½-lb. perch and a 1 pound dace. But I would gladly exchange the lot for the single 2 lb. roach which so far has eluded me.

If you would catch big roach you must first narrow down the waters that hold them. Chalk water is your best bet: the Hants Avon has them in large numbers, so have the smaller chalk streams like the Wylie; the tiny Hertfordshire Beane breeds them; two-pounders are fairly frequent in the Kennet, and the Suffolk Stour last season produced a record batch.

How should you seek your glass-case roach? The answer is quietly, stealthily and, for preference, in a boat. At this time, the fish will still be in the between-weeds runs and a gentle trickle of fine groundbait will bring them up to see what goes on.

If fishing chalk stream water, do not attempt any close range work. Fifteen yards is the nearest you dare approach your swim. Trot the tackle down, well-weighted beneath a stout cork float, the hook baited with either a bunch of gentles or a cube of bread crust. Strike at the merest hint of unorthodox behaviour on the part of the float. Even habitual trout men have been surprised at the fight a two-pounder can give.

C.W.

SHOOTING

Organised shooting again: the individual becomes one of a party when partridges are walked-up or driven. So much depends on organisation – both success and safety – that poor planning by host or keeper can irritate the guests, and bad behaviour by a single gun may well hold up the proceedings, endanger another gun or beater, spoil sport and lead to that emphatic decision, "never again."

The good shot is invited to shoots while the poor shot, however pleasant he may be as a companion, may be left off the list for the simple reason that on controlled and limited shooting days birds are to be killed, not missed or maimed.

Early errors are natural enough, especially when the gun is taken up for the first time after the summer. Try not to be surprised by the covey which bursts from the stubbles under your feet; wait for the birds to get well up and away and pick your bird. Do not check your swing at the crucial moment; sustained swinging and trigger pressing can be practised at home with dummy or empty cases in the breech. Take oncoming birds well in front of you, giving yourself more time to turn and pick a second shot behind. However thick in the air they seem, control that instinct to "brown" a covey: you are sure to find the holes if you fire at random.

DOGS: Forward puppies can now be introduced to game and encouraged to work in water. However, be careful of overstrain and dry your dog, particularly the loins and belly, however warm the day and the water may have been. Use the check-line until you are absolutely sure of your puppy's steadiness. Running in is a deadly fault and hard to cure once a dog has met a hare.

FERRETS: Young ferrets should be trained now that some small buries have been cleared of cover. Work the young entry with an old ferret and ensure that there is water available for them. Let us put the old idea of starving a working ferret right out of court; a good meal on the night before work, milk in the morning and milk or water during the day will produce the best results, especially if you are able to take a team with you and rest an animal as soon as it shows lack of keenness.

THOUGHT FOR THE MONTH: Walking-up was the old way of things; modern farming allows us to walk again on many shoots. So, walk in September and do not press the birds too hard late in the day. As he walks the owner of a shoot can study the reaction of the coveys and plan his stands and drives for the later season, when cover has gone and partridges are wild.

M.S.

--- · · · ---

September 1st: Start of the Partridge Shooting Season.

Prospects: A remarkably fine early spring and summer should give something like a bumper year, but against this must be set the early hay harvest and considerable sacrifice of nests. In addition many parts of the country had really heavy thunderstorms in early July and in some areas broods of young birds were quite literally drowned out. Still, these local storms were not for the most part followed by long periods of cold winds, and experience suggests that a prolonged very wet spell with cold winds is far more disastrous than early July thunderstorms. The general increase in arable undoubtedly favours the partridge, though to what extent this is offset by modern mechanised farming methods is still difficult to assess. It is never really easy to estimate the prospects except for local areas where one is familiar with conditions, and even then, so long as crops are standing, one's estimate may be wide of the mark. In general most areas do not seem to have suffered grave disasters.

THE FRENCHMAN: The red-legged partridge seems to have become rather more common; that is to say, these birds account for a higher relative proportion of the bag than was usual in prewar days. It may be a definite increase or it may be that the modern short stubble and quick re-ploughing of land induces the Frenchman to rise and come over the guns. In the past he had a reputation for running and skulking in corn, but I confess that today the imputation seems out of date. In one respect he is wholly inferior to the English partridge, and that is as a table bird. Despite the bright beauty of his plumage he is not half so good to eat as the more sober British bird.

GAME CARTS: On the larger shoots the traditional game cart was a very practical affair specially fitted with proper racks so that birds could be hung neatly by their necks. A brace would be tied together and hung on a nail in the racks. This avoided all bruising and disorder and allowed the game to cool properly. Today we rely in the main on "the van" which is probably a utility of some kind. All too often the bag is somewhat casually dumped on the floor and suffers abuse in the process. It is worth while extemporising racks with appropriate nails – a few boards will suffice or even a couple of hurdles. Game treated respect-fully in this way, and allowed to cool naturally, travels a good deal better, and I think its keeping qualities are improved. In any case it looks better, and if it is sold it fetches a rather better price than "rough looking" game which has been piled in a heap on the floor of a van.

H.B.C.P.

THE DOG MAN

ALL HONOUR TO THE SHEEPDOG

The International Sheepdog Championships are being held at Blackpool on September 20th, 21st and 22nd. Thirty-six dogs, twelve from England, Scotland and Wales, will take part in the qualifying trials, and by sundown on the second day they will have been reduced to the dozen which go forward to compete for the Supreme International Championship, the "Blue Riband of the Heather."

Present holder of the title is a Scotsman, James M. Wilson, of Innerleithen, who at Ruthin last year had his eighth victory in these contests. This is a record unsurpassed by any other shepherd or handler since these trials were first held in 1906. Altogether Scotsmen have won the championship at four of the five post-war trials, Wilson having three victories and a fellow-Scot, J. Gilchrist, one. A Welshman, W. J. Daniel, won at Ayr in 1949.

The road to a Supreme Championship is long and arduous. Each of the three countries has its own national trials, and only the first twelve dogs can go forward to the international. Before a dog can enter a national it must have won a prize at some local trial.

Although international championships began in 1906, only English and Scottish dogs entered, but in 1922 the Welsh shepherds entered the international field. It was Wales, however, which held the first sheepdog trial ever to take place. That was at Bala in October 1873, and the winner was a Scot, William Thomson, resident in Wales and using a Scottish-bred dog, Tweed. A contemporary report describes Tweed as "a small black and tan dog, with a white forefoot, very compactly built, with an intelligent 'foxy' head and fair coat." He also won the prize for the best-looking dog on the field. Brains and beauty often go hand in hand in the sheepdog world.

Sheepdogs have not altered a great deal since this 1873 trial, and the breed seen at the trials and on the hill farms is the Border Collie, a type probably evolved in southern Scotland and most probably introduced into this country during the great droving days of 150-200 years ago. Prior to that the Old English Sheepdog, that woolly-coated breed of great ancestry, was mostly used in England, but the greater speed and intelligence of the newcomer enabled it to gain premier place.

Wales, too, has ancient breeds of sheepdog – the Welsh Hillman, the Black-and-Tan, and the old Welsh Grey – but these have mostly had to give way to the Border Collie. Border Collies are probably descended from an older Scottish breed, the Bearded Collie, which many claim as having similar origin to the Old English Sheepdog.

There is one dog, however, that can be regarded as the foundation sire of the Border Collie as we know it today. That is Old Hemp, which was bred by a Northumbrian, Adam Telfer, in 1893, and whose blood runs right through the modern strain. Hemp was soon recognised as a type apart, and before he died in 1901 he had sired over 200 puppies. These, in turn, were mated, and fifty years afterwards it would be difficult to find a Border Collie at home or abroad whose ancestry cannot be traced back to this Northumbrian dog.

Not only is the Border Collie the recognised working dog of the British sheep farms, but is to be found in practically every sheep-farming country in the world. Farmers and breeders in the United States, Canada, Australia, New Zealand, the Argentine and Eire all purchased dogs from this country. Before the war the

Japanese not only bought dogs, but engaged Scottish shepherds to go out and give instructions in the art of working them. In South Africa they are being used on the ostrich farms. The United States, Australia, New Zealand and Kenya Colony have progressive sheepdog societies and promote trials on similar lines to those held over here.

Although sheepdog trials are held in all parts of the country, and sheepdog exhibitions are included in the programmes at agricultural shows and other outdoor events, the Border Collie still remains a working dog. The International Sheepdog Society has always been keen on keeping its trials for working dogs, and strongly discourages any tests of a "stunt" nature as unlikely to prove the ability for everyday work on the hills. Hence, the best trials' dogs are often enough the best working dogs, and perform feats on their home farms requiring more brains than going through a trial.

One noted trial winner, Bright, belonged to Joseph Relph, a Lakeland farmer, and once, unknown to its owner, set out to rescue sheep fast on a ledge of a Cumbrian mountain. That dog worked for five hours entirely on its own initiative to bring off a rescue which no human being could possibly have accomplished. The slightest wrong move would have caused the sheep to panic and probably crash to death.

Fly, with whom James M. Wilson won his first international, once brought a sheep, whose lamb had died, from the moor to the farmyard, a distance of about a mile, without the owner knowing anything of what was going on. Other dogs, detailed to guard a sheep brought out from a flock, have, when the animal has eluded them and got back among its fellow creatures, gone in and brought it out from a flock of 100 or so. Incidents like this are happening every day on the great sheep runs of this country.

It must be realised that the desire to work sheep is inherited in these clever creatures. Training is mainly a question of instilling obedience to commands rather than to any teaching of the tasks to be performed. The late Mark Hayton, former international champion, put it neatly when he once said: "The great qualities and powers of the sheepdog have been taught by dogs to shepherds, not by shepherds to dogs."

Go to a sheep farm and watch the puppies in the yard. See them rounding up ducks or chickens just for the fun of the thing, and driving them into a corner of the yard. Most likely many of the dogs that will compete at Blackpool did this kind of thing. They are born with brains – and they know how to use them.

S.M.

———

Sporting Terriers

Last week, Fred Fowler, who ought to know better, paid eight guineas for a nine weeks old terrier pup. And cheap at the price, he said, with a pedigree as long as your arm and the breeder asking ten guineas each for the rest of the litter. Not many years ago many a good pup changed hands in a pub for the traditional "bob and a pot." The cost of a pot of beer, in those days, was round about sixpence, so particularly promising pups might fetch as much as a "bob a leg."

My own dogs are expected to work, so I object to paying out several guineas for a pup which may die of hard pad or distemper, or chase a cat into the road and under a car before it has grown up. Even if it reaches the age of eight months and can be shown a rat, or eighteen months and can be entered to fox, the thought of those hard-earned guineas would haunt me. What if it won't look at the rat, or yelps and runs away when it gets nipped? What if it refuses to go to ground or, nearly as bad, rushes in and is mauled.

I would rather take a chance on the pup for which I have paid no more than the modern equivalent of "a bob and a pot," which is one or two guineas.

Crab was such a one. She was short of leg, rough of coat and small, with bright, beady eyes and a powerful jaw. She taught me a liking for ratting by demonstrating just how the job should be done. Afterwards, she carried a corpse home and showed it to a committee meeting of the Women's Institute.

Owning Crab was not all honey. On one occasion she followed a rabbit into a long field drain at dusk and stuck fast in a broken pipe about twenty yards from the entrance. I dug her out (and the rabbit too) at midnight. Crab, too, was a bitch of sudden and unexplained dislikes. Without warning, she would leave my side and go into the attack. Often it was another dog, twice it was a "best laying pullet," and once it was a parish councillor.

A sporting lady who breeds dachshunds for work as well as for the show bench offered me a dog pup as a gift. Well, Toni, my wife's old dachshund, had proved his worth in the field and he was growing a little long in the tooth, so I accepted. The nine weeks old Hollyhill St. Honorat came by train. He was carried through our station and spent the night at Euston. Altogether, he put in nearly twenty hours in his travelling box without food or water, but he came out with stern wagging. I was wondering how on earth I could take him along hedgerows crying "*Leu in Hollyhill St. Honorat!*" when my wife remarked that he looked a "real rasper." So Raspa we called him. He took a long time to mature – nearly two years – but all dachshunds do. When on a lead he had a playful habit of ignoring other dogs until they were in exactly the right position to receive a nip on the rump. This he administered so quickly and quietly that it was a long time before I realised why dogs yelped as we passed them and why their owners were annoyed.

Raspa played with his first rat. The second went to ground under a thick hedgerow and he and I crawled after it. While my head was held fast by thorns, the rat, a big buck, came straight at my face. Raspa put himself between us and the rat fastened on his nose instead of mine. Since then, he kills rats with one quick nip in the right place.

When Raspa caught his first rabbit, in the middle of a briar patch, he stayed there until he had eaten the last tuft of fur, while I fumed and swore and jumped on my hat. I ignored him for the rest of the afternoon – punishment indeed. The next rabbit he caught he brought to my hand as cleverly as a spaniel. His most spectacular act was when he and Ginny, the terrier, climbed up into the crown of a pollard willow and, between them, bolted a rabbit, which jumped into the river. The dachshund jumped at the same time, and when he surfaced he had the rabbit between his jaws. He swam with it to the bank, clambered out and gave it to me.

Ginny, who is now two years and six months old, was not a gift. In fact, by my standards, she was quite costly. She came to me after Tipsy, a wire-hair, had dropped dead in the tracks of a rabbit which she had been hunting. I can never understand people who when they lose a favourite dog say that they will never have another. That same evening I rang up Bill the Vet.

A few days later Bill walked into my den and pulled a mite of a bitch pup out of his inside pocket. "How about this?" he demanded. "If you don't want her, I'll have her myself." When the two dachshunds went to investigate the new pup her hackles bristled and she made quick snaps at both. We agreed that this was not bad at six weeks old. It seemed that one of Ginny's grandmothers was bought from the gipsies and the other was a corgi. On the male side she was all hunt terrier. I asked about price. "Oh, argue it out with Claude," said Bill the Vet.

Now, Claude is master of a pack of foxhounds and I felt sure that I could beat him down over the price. But he was clever enough to put his charming wife on the other end of the telephone and I agreed to pay three guineas – the highest price that I have ever paid for a pup, but Ginny is worth every penny of it and more. To date, between them, Ginny and Raspa have caught thirty-two rabbits, one stoat, a hare and innumerable rats. If they present us with a litter, I shall ask more than a bob and a pot for any one of them.

J.I.L.

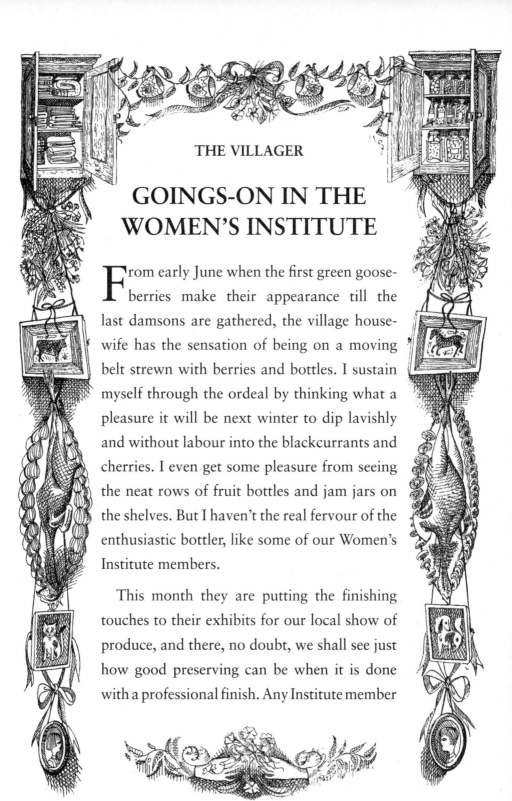

GOINGS-ON IN THE WOMEN'S INSTITUTE

From early June when the first green goose-berries make their appearance till the last damsons are gathered, the village house-wife has the sensation of being on a moving belt strewn with berries and bottles. I sustain myself through the ordeal by thinking what a pleasure it will be next winter to dip lavishly and without labour into the blackcurrants and cherries. I even get some pleasure from seeing the neat rows of fruit bottles and jam jars on the shelves. But I haven't the real fervour of the enthusiastic bottler, like some of our Women's Institute members.

This month they are putting the finishing touches to their exhibits for our local show of produce, and there, no doubt, we shall see just how good preserving can be when it is done with a professional finish. Any Institute member who cares to take the trouble can get the guidance necessary for a professional finish by attending the classes and demonstrations arranged through the movement. The fees are small; the great trouble is to find the time.

We were discussing all this at our last Institute meeting, when we were planning our activities for the autumn and winter. The Women's Institutes are doing a great deal to keep alive the old crafts of the countryside which are in danger of being lost in our machine age, and the list of subjects which can be studied for a few shillings – in addition to various kinds of cookery – includes weaving, patchwork, quilting, traditional embroidery, basketwork, rug-making, glove-making and much besides. Almost everyone at the meeting wanted to take up one or other of these activities, and then came the general chorus, "But we haven't time!"

It's a most puzzling thing that nowadays when almost every routine job in the house can be done in a fraction of the time it took our grandmothers, we all seem to have less time to make and do the things they accomplished as a matter of course.

But in spite of these difficulties several of our members are already busy on their special handcrafts for the big exhibition. This autumn there will be displays in various parts of the country of the best work from the Institutes of each region; and in the spring of next year the cream of these shows will be on view at the Victoria and Albert Museum. The Institutes feel highly honoured to be showing their crafts in such a setting, and of course it is going to be an exciting day for the Institute whose work is represented.

Our own gifted needlewomen are very reticent about their

efforts, and we haven't yet been given an official preview of what is being submitted for the first selection, but I have seen two pieces of work in the making which I would back heavily for a place in the finals. One is old-English blackwork which, in spite of its name, is really Spanish and was brought to this country by Katherine of Aragon. It is restrained, conventional and extremely elegant. The other is an entirely modern picture which is created out of almost anything that can be sewn on to fabric.

Handwork is a luxury nowadays, even when you do the work yourself, because the materials are expensive. When you start paying for other people's work as well the price soars nearly out of sight. Recently we needed some thatching done to one of our outhouses. There are no thatchers left in our village, but we heard of one a few miles away and asked him to come and see us. He was quite a young man, and he drove over in a black saloon car. He took a look at our barn, did some measuring, and then said: "It'll cost you a lot, you know. Of course it's not in my interest to say so, but in your place I should roof it with corrugated iron."

We didn't take his advice, and now a huge pile of straw is sitting on the Michaelmas daisies, and I keep stopping my work to wander out into the garden and watch him at his. First he wets the straw and combs it all out straight. Then he puts neat bundles of it into a wooden rack, swings it over his back and goes up the ladder on to the roof. He works very quickly and soon has his load pegged into place and is down the ladder for more.

He is rather a silent young man and not much given to gossiping, though he did tell me that his people have been thatchers for many generations. He also said that his chief difficulty – and expense – is getting suitable straw, not only because modern methods of harvesting spoil the straw for thatching purposes but also because nowadays farmers don't grow the kinds of wheat which produce long stout stems. In fact, we've got to face it – our thatching doesn't fit into the economics of the countryside.

E.G.

HOME HINTS

Time to think about storing fruit. Some apples and pears are ready to pick, others will be ripe by the end of the month.

APPLES AND PEARS: Will experienced readers forgive me if I give here a few hints for novices? Not everybody knows what a knowledgeable fruit farmer once told me – the test for an apple or pear that is ready to be picked for storing. Lift each sound ripe fruit up in your hand. If it comes easily from the twig with a slight pull it is ripe and ready to pick. But don't attempt to pull hard; fruit that is still firmly attached to the twig may be left to mature. It is not quite ready yet. Another piece of advice from the same source: go over your trees several times, picking each time fruit that is ready for storing, and lay on the top of your store those early ripening sorts that should he eaten first. *Lay* each fruit in a basket or box – don't ever throw apples or pears down and bruise them.

STORING: A good place to store fruit is a loft, airy, cool, fairly dark and not too dry. Remember though that if there are windows in the loft birds may fly in as soon as the weather becomes stormy or cold. Protect windows or openings with wire-netting or old curtains. Apples and pears keep better if each one is wrapped in paper – newspaper will do – and in no case must one touch another. Lay them on shelves, or in boxes, or on trays made to hold a single layer, made so that the trays may be set one above the other so that air may flow freely all around the fruit. These trays are quite easily made by nailing four pieces of wood to form a square and covering the bottom with wire gauze, chicken wire or butter muslin, nailed on.

DRYING: The same trays are useful for drying apples, pears and plums. Fruit should be ripe and sound. Discard wasp-bitten pears and bruised apples if the bruising is bad; if the fruit is bruised only on one side, the bad part may be cut away, and the fruit then cut in rings ¼ inch thick. Pears are quartered, or halved if they are quite small. Apples and pears should be thinly peeled (a potato peeler is useful), cored and laid on trays for drying. Or apple rings may be threaded on canes or wooden curtain rings that will fit inside an oven or airing cupboard.

Drying in the sun is not practicable here. Much better to do it in a cool oven, not more than 150 deg. F., above a stove (though that takes longer), or in an airing cupboard. If a steady temperature of from 120 to 140-150 deg. can he maintained drying should take about six hours.

M.B.R.

THE ARCHERS OF ENGLAND

Britain's oldest sporting trophy, the Scorton Silver Arrow, instituted on May 14, 1673, shot this year at Harrogate, was won at the 1951 contest by archer Frank Newbould, of Knaresborough, he being first to pierce the gold in the traditional double-ended shoot. Thus, on the village green of Scorton, near Richmond in Yorkshire, an ancient sport is still being practised, and the sob of the longbow evokes the yeoman archer "whose limbs were made in England." The Scorton contest, although the oldest and with rules peculiar to itself, is only one of many to be seen almost anywhere in England at the present day. There are no fewer than five hundred archery clubs devoted to target shooting in this country. In the U.S. and Canada, toxophily has boomed since World War II; there are probably close on a million engaged in the sport over there, of which about one-quarter are now hunting big game with the bow and arrow. Using the razor-sharp and silent broad-head arrow, with ranges of roughly 60 yards, they find these ancestral weapons as lethal and as accurate as the gun in hunting deer, moose, wild pig and the grizzly bear. One of these arrows, propelled by a 65-lb. hunting bow, will go right through even a grizzly, unless stopped by heavy bone. And after all, the bowmen of yore were not exactly playing "a kid's game" when an arrow shot 160 yards could pin to the saddle the thigh of a horseman wearing a coat of mail.

But it is not an easy sport. The steel bow, over 5 feet long, has a pull of 45 lb. at full draw. A hundred yards away is a target 4 ft. in diameter with a bull's eye (known as the "gold") of only 9.6 in. diameter. There may be a cross-wind, gusty and variable, from 8 to 15 m.p.h. And the arrow is perhaps too stiff, making it flirt a little to the left in its flight, besides yawing slightly to the right in the wind. Both tendencies must be nicely offset one against the other.

If you are a beginner you stand facing the target, and are promptly told you should stand at right angles to it; and anyway, you're not likely to hit the *right* target with your eyes closed. In confusion, you step on a rival's arrow and are promptly fined seven and six according to ancient statute. Thoroughly unnerved, you begin to introduce a little profanity, and again by ancient statute you are mulcted of one shilling. Between the draw and the loose you forget to shout "Fast!" – as you would have called "Fore!" if playing golf. Had you done so, you would (again by ancient statute, never repealed) have been absolved from murder. As it is, your sin of omission has fortunately done no more than outraged several members crossing your line of fire.

The Royal Toxophilite Society, founded in 1781, began to organise the centuries-old traditions of English bowmen. It is today the autocratic body, the M.C.C. of toxophily. Rules laid down by George IV through the "Royal Tox." still prevail. By these it was determined that the concentric-ringed target should replace the ancient marks such as hazel rods, rose garlands and the popinjay. Each concentric ring is 4.8 in. wide, and the colours and values from the centre are gold 9, red 7, blue 5, black 3, white 1. These are known as the "prince's reckoning."

Men's championship shooting consists of two York rounds and two American rounds. In the ancient York round, one gross of arrows are shot to "prince's lengths," i.e. 72 arrows at 100 yd., 48 at 80 yd., 24 at 60 yd. In the American round, 90 arrows are shot: 30 each at ranges of 60, 50 and 40 yd. Highest score wins; if a tie, the highest number of hits.

If you ever decide to go in for this fascinating sport, you will hardly become a marksman until your bow is matched to your arrows, and both these matched to yourself. First then, decide on the length of your arrows by measuring from your left arm-pit to your outstretched fingertips. This arrow length then determines the length of your bow; and your bow-weight, measured by the number of pounds pull required to draw it fully, depends on your own strength and height. Men using 28-in. arrows need a 5 ft. 6 in. bow, weights 35–45 lb. Women using 24-in. to 26-in. arrows do well with a daintier version – a 5 ft. 2 in. bow, weights 25–35 lb. Anything above this is usually pure swank.

The old-fashioned English Tournament longbow with horn tips is on the way out. Best choice for the novice is still the wood bow, usually of yew, either "self" or backed with other woods. These at £5 or more give a sweet cast and a very fast loose, and this performance is even bettered by bows of laminated yew. Top performance is given by the steel bow, anathema to the old guard, and nothing like the six-foot yews with cloth-yard shafts and staggering weights used at Crécy and Poitiers. But the steel bow, at anywhere round £10, is here to stay.

You'll need six arrows, in a set, matched for weight and spine. The shafts or steles are of pine. Usually they have hardwood footings, brass piles or points, and are cunningly fletched with grey goose, turkey or peacock feathers. Their weight, by the way, is still expressed in shillings, as they were when coins were used for weighing. Women, therefore, generally flight a three and twopenny arrow; a man's shaft might weigh four and ninepence or five shillings.

Toxophilists are noted for their fantastic costumes. Certain items are essential. The leather arm-guard or bracer on the left forearm protects you against painful backlash when the string is loosed. A leather quiver and belt hang round your middle. At one hip you have a tassel to wipe your arrows. And on your shooting hand you wear horsehide tabs or thimbles to encase your first three fingers. For you don't just hook the bowstring with finger and thumb. You adopt a complex fingering called a Mediterranean loose. And you don't "draw" your bow like the effeminate feudal French; you "bend" it, laying your whole body's strength between the horns, like the Englishmen who won at Agincourt on St. Crispin's Day.

E.P.D.

THE FALCONER

THE REVIVAL OF HAWKING

Falconry is probably more popular in Britain today than it has been for upwards of a century. Indeed, the tinkle of the hawk's bell may be heard the length and breadth of Britain. Peregrines are flown at the duck of the Romney Marshes and the Fens; each August they accompany the "guns" to the grouse moor, and they are flown at rook and pigeon wherever trees are not too plentiful – in the Isle of Wight, Salisbury Plain, the Weald, the Downs, and the Dales.

There, too, the trim little merlin is flown at lark. Where woodland predominates, the great goshawk is flown at pheasant, hare and rabbit. I know one falconer whose trained eagle has killed as many as six foxes in one week, and several who delight in the rattle of a sparrow-hawk's pinions, the quarry being hedge birds and an occasional partridge.

My own idea of an autumn day's sport is to take a peregrine on to the hills or a goshawk into the fields; preferably both on the same day. I am satisfied even if the hawks fail to make a kill; the purposeful and deadly flight of the mighty goshawk, and the battle between peregrine and rook, or grouse, is ample compensation for the long hours of training.

The first problem is to secure a hawk. Goshawks and the mighty Arctic gyrfalcon must be imported. The sparrow-hawk is easy to come by, and is not protected under the bird preservation laws; but the merlin and the peregrine have enjoyed the protection of the law for upwards of nine centuries. The trained hawk is also protected by law.

At one time, anyone who pilfered a peregrine's cliff eyrie risked going to gaol for as long as seven years. The penalty has now been whittled down. In extreme cases it can still carry a gaol sentence, but ten years ago I was fined only a pound for taking young peregrines (called "eyasses") from a southern cliff.

Of course, one's choice of hawk must be dictated by the neighbouring country. The peregrine is useless in woodland, where the lumbering gos is at its best; the sparrow-hawk excels along hedgerows, and the dainty, deadly merlin in open country where its stoop can be used to best advantage.

There is little to choose between the various hawks in the matter of sport. There are falconers who favour the gos. They stress that in Shakespeare's time the gos was called "the cook's hawk" because it kept the larder so well filled, and that it can still be relied upon to kill half a dozen rabbits and pheasants in a day. The bird is difficult to handle, for periodically it shows signs of madness, when the falconer should look to the safety of his eyes and keep a firm rein on his temper.

One moment the gos snaps her beak with pleasure in your company; the next, her eye is wild and madness is her prompter. Fly her and she settles on a haystack and ignores the lure. Coax, swear, rant, bribe her with tit-bits – all to no avail. A yard beyond your reach she preens herself, wild eyed. Perhaps in an hour she will return and be as sweet tempered as a pet canary. But there is a thrill in carrying a gos, and also in the ruthlessness with which it drives upon its quarry to kill it with one convulsive grip of yellow talons.

On the other hand, the supporters of the peregrine tend to be contemptuous of the gos, and of the falconer who would allow a hawk's ability to supplement the meat ration to sway his judgment of its ability as a trained bird. And with the gos they class the eagle: "A lumbering great bird, lacking in guile, and inferior to the peregrine in flight and ferocity." And the merlin they class with the peregrine – a "lady's" hawk, to be sure (it was the favourite of Mary, Queen of Scots), but almost without peer in flight.

Never, they say, would a gos or an eagle (which gives excellent sport when flown against such as pheasant, hare and fox) emulate the peregrine which, on becoming separated from a falconer following a flight of many miles, returned to the lure after nine years of free flight.

To most falconers, the training of a bird offers as much pleasure as flying it. Fractious as a spoilt princess, the falcon must be taught to sit unafraid on the fist, take off after quarry at bidding, and return to the fist on sight of the lure. It is accomplished with soft words and the brushing of a feather against the trainee's feet while he (or she) sits huffed with a hood on her head; with the aid of tit-bits and an even temper, even if for no apparent reason the bird topples from your fist and hangs by her jesses (leg thongs) like one dead and, on being replaced on the gauntlet, again pretends she has lost the power to use her feet, and falls off like a stuffed thing, apparently with the sole purpose of maddening the falconer.

Only one thing in the world of falconry is calculated to be more infuriating than a " bating" falcon, and that is a gos which, suddenly afflicted by "the madness," takes off into a high tree and ignores the lure. The lure, usually a stuffed pigeon with meat attached to it, is produced only when the falcon has learned to sit quietly on the gauntlet, and then on the block on the lawn. She is taught to fly to the lure for food – first a few feet, then anything up to 100 yards, first with a thong attached to her block, then free.

When she "answers to the lure" readily, you call her from a

distance, and as she takes off to strike at the lure you toss a live pigeon aloft – and away the falcon speeds. Now is the moment when the worth of the training is to be proved. Should she make a kill, no more is required of the falconer than to watch where she drops and pick her from her kill. But if she fails to kill, swing the lure above your head. Rising into the heavens, as the unsuccessful falcon is accustomed to do, she will spot the lure – and, supposing she has absorbed her training, plummet on to your fist.

A falcon answering to the lure is a thrill almost beyond measure – one born in the bond between man and the wildest of all wild birds. It is a thrill greater than the sound made by a grouse when its dead body hits the heather and bounces two feet into the air, or the sight of a peregrine delivering, as it were, a left and a right and sending a brace crashing earthwards; it is greater than the long battle between gull and falcon or peregrine and rook, with the birds brawling across miles of sky, each spiralling climb followed by stoop and shift, until the rook escapes into a tree to caw at its enemy in the terms of a fishwife or the falcon knocks it to death with one ripping blow of the toe-talon.

It is not the kill that counts. An old rook is a match for the peregrine. I have seen a hare leave a gos panting from a kick in the ribs. The contest 'twixt merlin and lark may last ten minutes or more, with the lark trilling as it climbs and then dropping like a stone into the safety of the tussocks.

The greatest thrill in falconry arises from the training of a falcon, and from the individual hawk's powers of flight and its "generalship" in battle – the way in which, like a sheep-dog shepherding sheep into a fold, it manoeuvres its quarry into a position from which there can be no escape. And, above all, there is a glow in the knowledge that one has trained to one's bidding a wild and lawless bird.

F.I.

THE WEEK-ENDER

SOMETHING FOR NOTHING

"Every blackberry on a hedge was an agony to her until she had bottled it." The words are not kindly meant. They are a jibe at the hoarding, planning, niggling sort of housewife who has eyes for the utility of nature but none for its poetry. But I know so well how that woman felt. I, too, am sensitive to the thrill of getting something for nothing. I find the juicy blackberry, the bursting bilberry, the tender mushroom, doubly attractive because they are *absolutely free*. I have not dug, delved, manured, pruned or sprayed, but here they are just the same, all ripe for my greedy fingers. Nature is generous in September.

Many forms of home pickling and preserving are not worth the candle. The labour is infinite, the results are better at the grocer's – not to mention the fact that the smell of hot vinegar is worse than a gas bomb. But one of the life-preserving acts that really does pay off is drying mushrooms. We do it every year, and congratulate ourselves in the winter each time we dip into our store.

First step is picking the mushrooms, which requires strong nerves and knee muscles: never to ignore the hostile stare of your next-door neighbour who arrives in the best field just as you have cleared it of every snowy white button and are starting for home with your baskets full; knee muscles to endure the constant bobbing and stretching which mushrooming entails.

But after the picking the rest is easy. We pile the mushrooms on the table and all sit round with knives to peel them, throwing out any with a trace of mushiness or maggots. Then we thread darning needles with fine string or three or four thicknesses of sewing cotton, and thread the mushrooms; a good job for the children, who can't do much damage beyond breaking a few mushrooms and losing the needles. Then I hang the strings of mushrooms over the stove for several days until they are dry and leathery (or put them in the airing cupboard if you prefer!), then pack them into a biscuit tin. Soak them well before you use them, and the desiccated bits of leather will expand and grow juicy again, not good for frying but perfect for soups and stews.

Blackberries, of course, are irresistible to the miser instincts which come over me in autumn. We bottle them with apples (they seem a bit pippy on their own), and make the rest into jelly. I find the classic recipe works best: simmer the fruit until it's tender, then strain it through muslin, leaving it overnight to drip. Next day, put a pound of sugar to a pint of juice and boil fast until it's ready to set. Skim thoroughly, and pour into *heated* jars (oh, the misery of cracking a jar and helplessly watching the luscious juice pouring over the floor!), then seal them at once.

We have plenty of apple trees in our garden, both cookers and eaters, from the early Devonshire Quarenden to the late Cox's Orange. But none of them gives me half the kick I get from a basketful of crab apples, because the crabs are pure gain. You feel like a careful squirrel as you range the woods collecting for your winter store.

Crabbing is one of the few occupations where children are a positive advantage. I like to think I could still shin up an old crab apple tree if I had to, but I'd much rather not be put to the test. So I collect a few fairly manageable children between about six and sixteen and we wander through the woods with baskets collecting what we can. It's difficult to spot crab apple trees when they're fruiting – they get lost among the other foliage – but we mark them down in spring in the full flush of their rosy flowers and try to remember exactly where they are.

Wild nuts give the same sensation. Every hedge within miles of our cottage is loaded with hazel nuts. It's true they have ridiculously small kernels compared with cob nuts or filberts, and that you put a lot of labour into cracking them in proportion to what comes out. But they're a present. A present from the woods. And they are as superior to a bag of nuts from the shops as a small bunch of violets sent as a tribute is superior to a handsome bouquet of roses you've bought yourself.

During the war this hoarding of natural foods was carried to extreme lengths, and I remember tasting some pretty peculiar dishes. Rose hip purée was one of them, much vaunted by the Ministry of Food as a substitute for orange juice. (They thought that one up at about the same time as the theory that carrots give you a keen, catlike vision at night.) A still stranger dish was nettle purée on croutons of fried bread, the nettles cooked and sieved like spinach, except that you had to prepare the horrible things in gloves. And I once had a wild salad made with sorrel, dandelion leaves and other weeds and herbs, but it tasted rather bitter, for dandelions need blanching to be tasty. Most of these outlandish dishes I thought merely cranky, a sort of impractical, back-to-nature fad. But the well-tried wild foods are delicious, and this is their season. The blackberries. The mushrooms. The nuts. The bilberries in the hill country. The wild raspberries in the late-ripening North. The crabs for jelly. The sloes for gin. The elderberries for wine.

If you want to fill up your store cupboard cheaply, now is the time to do it. For you have only to take your basket, and you can leave your purse behind.

A.S.J.

THE BIRD WATCHER

STUDYING THE AUTUMN MIGRANTS

A little stream rises from a bog on the side of the high Ward Hill of the Fair Isle, and creeps down to its east coast through some fields. When swollen with the sudden rains of Shetland, it gathers volume and power, and in one place near the coast it has cut down to hard bedrock, forming a narrow gully with small precipitous cliffs on either side.

I remember one autumn, fourteen years ago, watching the seasonal passage of migrants through this astonishing island with L. S. V. Venables, and always finding a few small birds sheltering in this gully. I remember Venables then suggesting that all that was necessary to make a perfect trap was to roof it over.

It is good to see old ideas come true. The whole Fair Isle now belongs to George Waterston, secretary of the Scottish Ornithologists' Club, and is manned in spring, summer and autumn by a field station under the direction of another well-known ornithologist, Kenneth Williamson. Bird traps have been put up in many strategic places, including our old friend the gully.

These traps are Heligoland traps, based on the German invention first tried out over fifty years ago on the equally remarkable migration island of Heligoland, off the German coast. In essence, a Heligoland trap consists of an immense funnel of wire netting, gradually tapering to an apex, ending in a small, detachable handling box. The wide end of the funnel is built over cover, bushes and shelter, into which the migrant birds, some of which are tired after their flights, are driven.

Every now and then a party of bird watchers simply walks up the cover and drives the birds quietly towards and into the funnel. They eventually fly up to its apex and into the catching box, from which they are gently extracted, observed, marked and, if necessary, weighed and measured. Many thousands of passerines are now marked in this way in Europe, and it even happens that individual birds are now caught at more than one coastal station on the same passage.

It is interesting to consider what serves for cover for a tired migrant. A stone wall will do; there is one small Heligoland trap on the Fair Isle which is simply built across such a wall; and the observers have to do no more than gently edge the small birds along the wall (which they are disposed to hug naturally) until the birds find themselves in the funnel.

Another trap high up on the bleak side of the Ward Hill is built not over bushes or other vegetation but over a large number of rolls of barbed wire left over from the days when much of the Fair Isle was a military installation. To a tired migrant on a windy day a roll of wire netting is a haven of refuge; and quite a number of birds, including snow-buntings, have been trapped on this hill-side station, perched more than 500 feet above the place where the Atlantic Ocean meets the North Sea.

Many observers are attracted to these coastal migration stations because of the chance of seeing great rarities – birds they have never seen before. I have certainly added more birds to my British life tally on the Fair Isle than anywhere else. Such creatures as the barred warbler, the scarlet grosbeak, the ortolan and the great grey shrike – anything may turn up. There is always the chance of finding a booted warbler, a red-flanked bluetail, a red-headed bunting, a meadow-bunting, a brown fly-catcher, or another of the couple of dozen species which have so far only once been seen in the British Isles – strays, usually on autumn passage from Eastern Europe or even Asia and North America.

The coastal field stations are beginning to tell us, it is true, that some of these rarities – the scarlet grosbeak, for instance – are not as rare as was thought, and even, perhaps, quite regular on passage in very small numbers. But in the long run their greatest contribution to science will be the discovery of the details of the migration of the common birds, and from this we will learn much more about the nature of migration itself.

Throughout the whole of Western Europe – from the U.S.S.R. through Scandinavia, the Low Countries and France to Britain – there is a tremendous revival of interest in bird migration. On all coasts from the Baltic to the Bay of Biscay many stations are now manned by experienced observers. No longer is there great excitement when the observers catch each other's birds. From this collective effort, in which there is at the same time full scope for local enterprise, we are making entirely new maps and gaining entirely new ideas about the movements of birds. And as we learn more about what exactly happens on migration we are beginning to learn much more about how it works.

J.F.

OCTOBER

MY FAVOURITE MONTH

O ctober last, when I wrote in praise of this mellow, yellow month, to my taste easily the most glorious month of the year, a reader surprised me by asking if I was born in October. In the August of my life, I prefer to forget such matters as birthdays. But I was, indeed, an October baby.

That's the way it always is, said Mrs. Vera Downey, our correspondent: people give their deepest affection to the month in which they were born. It works in my case. It works in my wife's case, who was born in April. And it certainly works in the case of my son who, with shrewd calculation, arrived in the world at Christmas-time.

But what about the people with February birthdays? Surely there's nobody so star-struck, or moon-struck, that they can think February is other than the worst month of the year. I wonder?

M.H.

WILD LIFE

Sunny days in October still find many butterflies on the wing – brimstone, comma, the migrant painted ladies, peacock, the fresh butterflies of the autumn brood of the red admiral; autumn brood, also, of small tortoiseshells, and, if warm season, another of small coppers.

Tremendous movements, dispersals, migrations among the birds. More bird-song than popularly supposed; still frequent snatches from resident song-thrush, dunnock, wren, goldfinch, linnet, chaffinch. Most kinds of tits still have something to say, and in full song are found robin, dipper, skylark.

Many summer visitors stay till October, then depart; these include stone-curlew, most kinds of warblers. Only stragglers from the sand-martins are left behind, but there will be a few late house-martins, and many swallows until well through the month.

October is month of greatest migration activity on east coast: most passage here of waders over, though snipe still come through. But peak movements of the small birds noticeable everywhere; vast numbers of finches, buntings, warblers, larks, and pipits, and some late chats. Observers at migration stations daily cope with "rushes" of lesser redpolls, twites, linnets, chaffinches, bramblings, yellowhammers and reed-buntings.

Now is the time to find flocks, haunting the shoreline, of the rare arctic and sub-arctic Lapland buntings, snow-buntings, shore-larks. Quite a number of sparrows, both house- and tee-, pass from Scandinavia at this time, and there is an influx of wood-larks in Scotland and of really very large numbers of skylarks along the whole east coast of England. Many meadow-pipits, rock-pipits pass, and many warblers. There is a large passage of foreign chiffchaffs.

Most familiar arrivals (winter guests) at this time brambling, fieldfare and redwing (and in some years, also, unfamiliar firecrest and waxwing). But, perhaps most dramatic, the arrival of the great waterfowl from the north; whooper swans, some early Bewick swans, and the wild geese – grey-lag, white-front, beau, pink-foot, barnacle, brent. And the shelduck, which have been off to the Heligoland Bight to moult, gradually return to our coasts.

The ornithologist, despite these distractions, tries to make up his bird-watching note-books for the year, and fills in his ringing schedules.

J.F.

⸺•⸺

One of the most popular, sometimes most busy, months at bird migration stations. "Rushes" of small passerines in suitable weather may keep Heligoland traps busy. Sometimes spectacular influxes (as last year) of Continental robins. An influx from Lincolnshire, southwards, of foreign rooks on our east coast this month. Much woodcock movement on the October moon, though perhaps not quite up to November intensity. But the nightingales, swifts and cuckoos have all gone.

The seabirds only really free month in the North Atlantic, and only month in which the adults have shed all connection with the land; have no urge even to visit it.

The October tours of these birds are their last beats of the northern waters before they return to their nests. Some Tristan great shearwaters even seen at this time in North Sea. Sooty shearwaters and Wilson's petrels not so far north of Bay of Biscay and are joined in or near the Channel by another October visitor, the Balearic shearwater. This is a rare dusky race of Manx shearwater which nests only in the Mediterranean – but not so rare as our published records would indicate. I have seen it myself several times on an autumn voyage from Alderney across the Hurd Deep, and thence across Channel to the Isle of Wight.

In mammal world, young badgers leave their parents in October, move off to form setts of their own. Both these and their parents fuss much, preparing sett for winter, bringing in new bedding, etc. Nearly all British bats (and, incidentally, all British reptiles and amphibians) go into hibernation some time during October. Both red dormouse and the newly established, introduced, fat dormouse also go into hibernation in this month, and are only British rodents to do so; contrary to many statements, neither red nor grey squirrel indulges in anything resembling true hibernation. Neither does badger in Britain. Hedgehogs, which do hibernate, do not usually start until November or December.

This month's quotation from Gilbert White's *Journals* was written on October 2, 1792: "Flying ants, male and female, usually swarm and migrate on hot sunny days in August and September; but this day a vast emigration took place in my garden, and myriads came forth in appearance, from the drain which goes under the fruit-wall; filling the air and the adjoining trees and shrubs with their numbers. The females were full of eggs. This late swarming is probably owing to the backward, wet season. The day following, not one flying ant was to be seen. The males, it is supposed, all perish; the females wander away; and such as escape from Hirundines get into the grass, under stones, and tiles, and lay the foundation of future colonies."

J.F.

Hedgehogs Like Humans

My first experience of a tame hedgehog was when we were living in a stone-flagged cottage in Lancashire. It was overrun with black beetles and, in desperation, I asked the keeper to find me a hedgehog. He turned up one evening with a dilapidated, elderly-looking female – covered with ticks.

Ticks or beetles? Well, ticks don't move so fast. I emptied a tin of Keatings powder over her and let her go in the hall.

We set a saucer of bread-and-milk by the umbrella stand and went up to bed, discussing what we would do with her in the daytime.

Next morning there were no signs of a hedgehog, but the saucer was empty. We thought she must have escaped, and decided to buy some beetle poison. Then, talking of beetles, we realised there were none to be seen.

It was impossible that one hedgehog should have eaten all the beetles in a night, but she had certainly thinned them out. We regretted her departure.

That evening the weather turned chilly and we were sitting by a log fire having tea, two Airedales and a tom cat asleep on the hearth rug. Suddenly one of the dogs growled and all three animals got up and backed away from the rug.

We were amused to see the hedgehog take their place. She stood and blinked at us and snuffled up at the tea-table. I took the hint and put down another saucer of bread and milk, which she guzzled up immediately. When she had finished she turned her back on us and trotted out of the room, and the dogs lay down again looking sheepish.

The cat was a notable ratter and both dogs would tackle rats, cats and other dogs unless they were kept to heel. They seemed to think the scraggy old hedgehog had to be accepted because she was in the house. She appeared regularly at tea-time for her food, trotting off as soon as she had had it. The dogs sniffed at her after a time, at first she would quickly curl up, but when she found they did not try to attack her she ignored them.

When Spring-cleaning began we found the hedgehog in our fur foot-muff, which was kept in the umbrella stand. There she slept all day. I used to tickle her tummy and talk to her occasionally and after a while she would lie on the hearth-rug after her feed and let us play with her.

We saw no more beetles and by the following spring our

hedgehog was plump and well-liking. When the outer doors were left open in summer she disappeared.

Our second hedgehog was found by the roadside in Hampshire. He was fat and only half-grown, but he too was smothered in ticks. The three children were enchanted with him and begged to be allowed to take him home. He was put into a bicycle basket and taken with us.

At that time we had a family of Siamese cats living in the kitchen. The second hedgehog was also quite fearless. He sat in the middle of his bread and milk and ate all round himself. He was duly dusted with Keatings and christened Piggy because of his continuous, *sotto voce* snufflings and gruntings.

I thought I knew what a fuss dogs and cats could make over an intruder, but I had not reckoned with the airs and graces of Siamese cats. We had a Queen and her six kittens. They spat and retreated under the furniture while the mother cat growled and patted him with her paw. She pricked herself on his spines and came to me for help. When I laughed she took her kittens away in disgust.

The kittens soon got used to Piggy. By the following evening you had to dig under a warm pile of kittens to find him. I can only imagine his spines must have relaxed when he felt safe and happy. The Queen spent two days shrieking and swearing round the house, but she couldn't resist the warmth of the Aga and had to give in and join the others.

Piggy shared the cat's food – and their ash-tray in the back kitchen! He was very curious and snuffled in and out of every cupboard and box he could find.

We never tried to keep him in. The back door was nearly always open and he ran in and out at will. If he happened to find it shut he bumped himself against it until it was opened for him. Judging by the noise he made he might have been a St. Bernard. Unfortunately we never managed to catch him at it to see what he did.

Piggy stayed with us until he was fully grown. He spent the first winter in a clump of Pampas grass in the garden. The next summer he was just as tame, but he never spent a night in the house, he would appear punctually at all meals and patter about in the kitchen before going off to the garden again.

He spent a second winter in the garden and we saw him twice in the following spring. After that he went about his own affairs.

There was no question of "taming" either of these hedgehogs. For two or three days both appeared to be nervous, but they both settled down more quickly than many a puppy or kitten.

H.E.

THE FRUIT GARDEN

SIMPLE CUTTINGS: There are few fruit plots where the addition of new stocks is not warranted and so last month we discussed the taking of blackcurrant cuttings. Those of redcurrant and goose-berry are almost as simple. The main difference is that only the top three or four buds of each cutting are retained as these fruits are normally grown as bushes on a leg; opposed to this, blackcurrants are grown on the stool system. Well-ripened wood of the current season's growth is the ideal cutting material for redcurrants and gooseberries. Cuttings ought to be at least twelve inches in length, and trimmed with a sharp knife or secateurs. The tip of each cutting should end in a clean cut just above a bud.

Although both kinds root easily it is worth while to assist rooting by putting a thin layer of sand in the bottom of the cutting "trench." The correct method of inserting these cuttings – like all hardwood cuttings – is to put down a line and cut along it with a spade. The spade is inserted about five inches deep, with its back against the line. The soil is then pulled forward leaving a straight-backed, shallow trench. It is then an easy matter to place the cuttings about six inches apart against the back of the trench. This practice ensures that the cutting remains uninjured; if pushed into the soil the base is damaged and it often fails to root. Cuttings are inserted with just over half their length below soil level. Firming is most important while planting, and should be done two and three times as the trench is filled in; on no account let it be left as the last job to be done.

As with all cuttings, more than the required number should be taken, thereby allowing for casualties and the needs of gardening friends. Any surplus young plants may be trained as cordons, espaliers, fans and in various other forms. Besides being interesting to do this is good practice for the cultivator as the basic principles are the same as those used for the build-up of any specific form of top fruit.

PRUNING OF RUBUS FRUITS: As blackberries finish fruiting so the old fruiting growth should be cut out. Healthy young shoots can then be tied in about nine inches apart ready for next season.

The same method is used for pruning loganberries and other

hybrid berries. If raspberries have not already been pruned this should be done without delay. The old canes are removed at ground level and the young canes tied in four inches apart. In every case weak or damaged canes should be removed.

G.R.W.

—·◆·—

NEW VARIETIES AND OLD ONES. Whatever our efforts, some of us can say our fruit garden is a success and some say it is a great success. The reason for the variation in reward is not usually hard to find for in no small measure it is often due to the selection of varieties. In the first case, for instance, it is comparatively easy to have apples when everybody else has them; in the second, the really good cultivator has apples when apples are both scarce and dear to buy.

For the small garden where space is limited, varieties giving the maximum value and the highest quality should be sought. In addition, when planning a little scheme it must be remembered that the best crops of apples, pears and plums can only be obtained when the tree is cross-pollinated, that is, for example, when pollen from one pear tree fertilises the flowers of another different variety of pear tree. This whole question is a complex one and is often – but not always – the reason for the healthy tree being unfruitful.

With all these points in mind a plan can be considered. For apples, two good dessert varieties are "Duke of Devonshire" (February-March) and "Winston," an apple of recent introduction which is in season from February to April. If an early variety is wanted for this pair, then there is no better choice than the sweetly-flavoured "Ellison's Orange." For cookers that can be kept until March, a good combination is "Crawley Beauty" with "Edward VII." The latter is not a heavy cropper but it stores well and as it flowers late in the season – thereby often escaping frost damage – it will pollinate the other variety. From the list, "Bramley's Seedling" and that crisp-fleshed, well-flavoured variety "Ribston Pippin" have purposely been left out. Neither of these will pollinate themselves or other varieties. Therefore they cannot be considered in the small garden for this reason alone although more might be said about "Bramley's" on other scores.

Pears are not so popular as apples but no fruit garden is cornplete in their absence. Here old varieties are unsurpassed and not many excel "Conference" and the deliciously succulent, musky-flavoured "Williams" Bon Chretien often known simply as "Williams"! These two will give a limited succession of fruit and each will pollinate the other.

Some varieties of fruit, and "Conference" is one, will set a good crop without a nearby pollinator. Many plums are in this category but the performance of all fruits is improved by cross-pollination.

G.R.W.

THE VEGETABLE GARDEN

October is the month which can be described as the true "back end" of the gardener's year. Growth is finished and cleaning up and preparations for next year must be begun. If grassland is to be brought into cultivation, now is the time for it to be done. Bastard trenching is the best method and, if the turf is well buried, no manure is necessary. This is a somewhat complicated job for the beginner and the best way is to seek the help of an experienced gardener to set out the work. It must be done properly or else the turf will fail to rot and a lot of valuable fertility will be lost. It is wise to finish all general digging by Christmas, but do not be in too much of a hurry as in mild weather weeds will appear.

Old cabbage stumps should be pulled up and burnt to reduce the danger of cabbage root gall, but leaves and weeds can be dug in to conserve humus. Land which is showing signs of poverty should be marked down for a thorough manuring. One-third of the garden should receive this treatment each year.

The final bed of spring cabbage must be in by the third week. Some of the August sown winter lettuce may be transplanted into well-drained soil. These should head slightly earlier than the non-transplanted ones, but there is more risk of casualties. Shallow planting is essential to avoid crown rot. The last patch of leeks should be earthed up and the first planting of spring cabbage will benefit by a final hoeing. On no account apply a fertiliser at this time.

The final batch of endive should be brought in for blanching by the end of the third week. This can only be done when the leaves are completely dry, otherwise rotting will occur. If there is danger of frost, pull up headed cauliflowers by the roots and store in a shed. They will keep for at least a fortnight if the floor is kept damp.

Cut down the foliage on the asparagus beds when it has turned yellow. Clean off the weeds and give a good top dressing of decayed manure. Those who have fought shy of this crop should study Mr. Kidner's book on the subject and have a try. The difficulties are not nearly as great as imagined and surely this prince of vegetables is worth a little trouble. Seek all the knowledge you can during the winter months. There are several methods and the simplest is probably the single-row system.

Store bean rods in the dry after dipping the butts in creosote to prevent rotting.

E.B.

THE FLOWER GARDEN

The popularity of the rose seems to increase each year, and the many fine varieties, particularly in the hybrid polyantha section, ensure that there will be many new plantings this autumn. The ground should be prepared as soon as possible, so that it has time to settle before planting takes place next month. In small gardens double trenching should be resorted to, thus allowing the sub-soil to be broken up and the placing at the bottom of the trench of a quantity of well-rotted compost or farmyard manure. A liberal dressing of bonemeal should be worked into the topsoil, which by this method of cultivation remains on the surface. The selection of the best varieties calls for a knowledge of the district and it is a good idea to try a few of the newer varieties each year before contemplating large groups of one variety.

Danger of night frost is with us again, and all half-hardy summer bedding plants will need to be housed. New stocks of many will have been propagated from cuttings, but others such as fuchsias, heliotropes, calceolarias, etc., will need potting up and placing in a cool greenhouse. Dahlias are best left until the first frost blackens their foliage, when they should be cut down and the tubers stored in a frost-proof shed. The tuberous-rooted begonias need rather similar treatment, and as soon as the tops have died the tubers are placed in boxes of dry soil. Gladioli can be hung by their foliage from the roof of a shed and the corms cleaned at a convenient later date.

Summer bedding gives place to plants for the spring, the most popular being wallflowers, violas, polyanthus and pansies. The earlier these are planted the better. The beds should be carefully dug over and manured if necessary. Bulbs such as tulips and hyacinths can be added later to make a really bright display as soon as the winter is gone.

Providing the weather is suitable there is no reason why the herbaceous border should not be transplanted this month. Many of the herbaceous plants prefer to be moved in the autumn. The growths can be retained and give a good guide to the height, thus making it easier to ensure that the border has a good contour.

C.P.

Though it is possible to plant semi-permanent borders with herbaceous perennials like echinops, gypsophila, and peonies which can remain undisturbed for twelve or more years, such a scheme involves omitting many highly desirable plants. To anyone with even an elementary knowledge of gardening the foregoing will be obvious. But it seems to need re-emphasising, as a school of gardeners has come into existence since the war which advocates scrapping all or virtually all those flowers and shrubs which demand more than the minimum of attention.

How much easier, we are told, to concentrate on those plants which carry on happily without human intervention in the way of staking, feeding, periodical division, measures to repel pest or disease attack, and so on. I am not, of course, suggesting that one should grow only the really difficult and tricky subjects, but I do maintain that if you limit yourself to the easy, more or less foolproof flowers, you are losing a great deal in the way of beauty, as well as missing half the joys of real gardening.

There are always arguments regarding the correct occupants of herbaceous borders. Should one admit annuals such as clarkia, eschscholtzia, and godetia to the front of the border to create a succession of colour? While it is probably true that annuals and beddings plants are out of place on a rockery, to me they set off admirably the erect, stately habit of many perennials. Clumps of daffodils and tulips are also pleasing. The purist, however, would doubtless exclude them, confining his choice to perennials which are strictly herbaceous, i.e., plants whose leaves, stems, and so on die away annually.

While the attempt to maintain, as far as possible, a continuous pageant of colour from late spring to early autumn can be very fascinating, it is, I think, often overdone. Do you want to study the characteristics of individual plants, or do you prefer to enjoy a mass of colour? If the latter, then the borders in our public parks will satisfy you.

Some writers on gardening insist on group planting. In *The Herbaceous Border* – incidentally, a really practical and up-to-date book on the subject – Frances Perry refers quite casually to ten or even twelve erigerons as making a bold display where two or three might be overlooked. But surely erigerons will be overlooked only where they are planted too closely. Where space permits, several group plantings of three or more of one variety are certainly more satisfactory than single specimens in isolated positions, but in my view every plant should still be given ample room. For example, delphiniums ought always to be planted two feet apart.

For a mixed herbaceous border, an open, sunny situation is essential, and drainage must be perfect, otherwise there will be winter losses. A border facing south is excellent as it means early flowers. The type of soil is not important provided it allows a deep root run. Thorough digging to a depth of two spits is necessary, and plenty of compost, hop manure, farmyard manure or similar organic material should be worked in. Remember that you will be unable to dig over the entire area again for some years.

Though heavy clay soils are often improved and made easier to work by liming, don't automatically assume that your land needs lime, as many gardeners do. It is definitely worth buying a soil-testing outfit, such as the B.D.H. Soil Indicator, which will indicate the presence or otherwise of lime. Most herbaceous plants appreciate a reasonable degree of lime in the soil, notably gypsophila and scabious. A few such as anchusa and kniphofia often give only mediocre results where there is an excess of lime. Lupins do quite well on soils with a moderate lime content but are a failure on chalk.

Soil preparation ought to be completed a month before planting, to allow the land time to settle before planting. This is, I fear, contrary to the advice of some authorities, who advise early autumn preparation followed by spring planting. In my view this is unnecessary, except where spring planting is desirable for some other reason.

For example, on heavy ground autumn planting is often unsatisfactory, as certain perennials, notably Michaelmas daises of the Amellus group, tend to rot during continuous wet weather. Planting during the winter months when most plants are dormant is best avoided, whether the soil is light or heavy. On light, sandy soils early autumn planting – up to, say, mid-November – is feasible, but the earlier the better, as the land will still be fairly warm, enabling the plants to make fresh roots and establish themselves before growth proper starts in spring.

As regards choice of plants, here are a few of my favourites among the more recent introductions. In delphiniums, the electric blue William Richards, though not a variety for the exhibitor, is excellent for garden decoration and cutting. It is one of the first delphiniums to flower, and lasts extraordinarily well when cut. Mrs. Frank Bishop is a gentian blue self, still very new and fairly expensive, but undoubtedly far ahead of previous blues.

Among the newer Russell lupins there are several outstanding yellows – yellow seems to blend with most colours in a herbaceous border except, perhaps, white. The best is Tom Reeves; but in my experience Kingcup is not far behind, as the flowers remain in good condition for a long while and have a pleasing scent. The cream-coloured My Love provides a restful contrast to the more richly coloured kinds like the wine-coloured Heather Glow and the deep-red Beryl Viscountess Cowdray. Gaillardia Wirral Flame is different in colour from all other gaillardias, being a rich red, with gold on the edges of the petals. It is a strong grower and excellent for cutting.

In Michaelmas daisies there is still room for the old Beechwood Challenger in the reds, notwithstanding its rather small blooms; the new reds and deep pinks raised by Ernest Ballard may supersede many older kinds. I recommend Red Sunset, The Dean, and The Cardinal.

N.P.H.

———·—·———

The danger of frost is with us again and the time has come when we must lift the summer bedding plants and place them in winter quarters. Fuchsias, pelargoniums and other tender plants must be potted and placed in the greenhouse. Tuberous begonias should be lifted with the growths intact and placed in boxes, under cover, until the upper growths part naturally from the tubers. These should then be cleaned and stored in boxes of dry sand or soil in a frost-proof place until the spring. Shorten the growths of cannas so that the roots may be stored under the greenhouse stages as the rhizomes should not be allowed to become excessively dry.

Large-flowering gladioli rarely pass safely through the winter if left in the ground. As the foliage turns yellow they should be lifted and hung in bundles, in a frost-proof shed, until the stems are dry. The corms may then be cleaned, discarding the old withered ones, and storing the plump new ones in a frost-proof room. There are usually a number of tiny corms clustered round the large ones and these should be preserved and, planted out separately, they generally flower in about two years.

Late-flowering chrysanthemums should be placed in the greenhouse as it is unwise to leave them outdoors after the first week in October unless provision is made for their protection. It is a wise precaution to lay the plants on their sides and spray them with a good fungicide, such as "Tulisan," before taking them indoors, as mildew is very liable to make its appearance at this season.

Hyacinths, tulips and other bulbs intended for forcing should be potted as soon as possible. The pots or pans containing the bulbs should be plunged in a bed of sand or weathered ashes, allowing a covering of about two inches above the pots. As soon as the growths show above the covering the pots should be removed to a frame or light room.

Spring-flowering bulbs should also be planted in the open ground during the present month. If it is desired to plant bulbs in the grass, care should be taken to select a site where it will be unnecessary to cut the grass before the end of June so that the foliage of the bulbs can die down naturally before being removed. Narcissi should be planted in open spaces as they do not usually flower satisfactorily, after the first year, when grown in shade. In the light shade of trees where the grass is usually sparse, crocuses, snowdrops, scillas and chionodoxas will brighten the early spring days.

C.P.

FISHING

The trout fly rods hang from the wall by the canvas loop at the top of their cases (or should) and unless the fisherman takes them down again for the grayling or repairs, there they remain till next year, reminders of the season that finished at the end of September. This year I fished the Kennet, the Test, the Loddon and the upper waters of the Frome. The stretches of the first two had improved. Weed-cutting had been done wisely in the Kennet, unlike the previous year when great piles of up-rooted weed showed the evils of the chain scythe. How much better to cut too little than too much! The food of trout is largely dependent on the weed. Wholesale removal destroys this food and also deprives the fish of shelter. Besides it makes the angler's task more difficult; for his quarry is much more easily put down. The upper Test had greatly benefited from wise river management but there were too many fish of just under a pound and too many black fellows, too many grayling, but the mud had gone and, wisely, areas of weed had been left uncut.

Trout will not thrive in weedless water and I recommend all owners to bear this in mind. It is far more important to have plenty of trout and risk losing a number in the weeds than to have poor, lanky brutes. This stocking with big fish is another evil. They soon "go back" and seldom spawn. The old system of fry in the feeders and a few yearlings is much better because they will grow to fend for themselves and be wild fish. The upper Frome, a delightful, sparkling stream was full of splendid, small trout. There was plenty of weed, plenty of food and plenty of sport. Not so the Loddon which appeared to suffer from some form of pollution (so a local keeper informed me) but there were any number of quarter pounders, though few good trout. There was abundant weed but no hatch of fly. The fish were there but not the food. This water had been dredged, dredged too deep and the bottom had never regained its pristine fertility. Water, like land, must be fertile.

Stretches of river that have no deep holes seldom hold big fish. It is worth building small "kiers" at an angle upstream. These can be made of corrugated iron (unsightly), wire netting (fairly efficient) or of oak or larch (most efficient, most attractive and most expensive). The V soon fills up and a hole is made below. The unwise make their "kiers" (Norwegian word) at an angle downstream. This is wrong. A keir is a small dam six or eight feet long which only juts out a short way from the bank. Trout enjoy their shelter and the deep water. So much for retrospect. Now get down the fly rod again and "have a go" at the grayling. The dry fly, I suggest a Rough Olive, will beat the wet fly. The "hopper" may beat both and an expert with a float all three, but give me the dry fly.

R.B.

———•+•———

What a lot is missed by the anglers who put away their rods once trouting ends, or as the colder weather sets in. October is a blissful month in which to fish. The campers and boating parties have gone; the light is pale and golden; the swans have passed the peak of their summer beastliness, and the riverside has returned quite properly to the custody of the heron and the all-round angler.

October belongs pre-eminently to the perch. I would swap all the sea-trout or giant tench that ever swam for just one four-pound perch. A big perch is something like a fish. He bristles with fight as he jag-jags at your line; he veers and flashes until that last second when he lies in the net looking like an infuriated Chinese dragon.

I confess that I have never yet caught a perch of more than two and a half pounds, but this winter I mean to improve on that. Perhaps I have done badly to date because I stick too closely to rivers. In moving water, fast living prevents the perch from growing to a great size.

The trouble is that autumn perching by the riverside is such charming angling that it is hard to resist. Provided the leaf sickness has not over-taken the river, the fish respond readily to live minnows floated down to their recognised haunts on light float tackle. From now on, also, the spinning rod comes into its own, and for river work I recommend a 1½ in. copper Vibro as lure.

But the really big perch are to be found in deep, still waters such as disused gravel and claypits. If the weather has been cold, look for them in the deeps, and by this I mean at anything from fifteen to forty feet down. The reason is this. Once autumn winds have chilled the lake to a uniform 39 degrees, thermal circulation practically stops. Water is at its heaviest at about this temperature. Further cooling simply leaves the cold, unfriendly water on top.

The perch, of course, congregate and feed in the warm, murky depths. Unlike the pike, the perch hunts small fish largely by sight and at these badly lit levels is plainly at a disadvantage. For this reason, deep water perch would much rather forage along the bottom.

The lesson for the angler is obvious. Do not bother with live-bait. Change of water pressure will probably kill it anyway. Put on a large lob worm, cast out your ledger into the deepest water you can find, and await results. If the perch are on, you will not have to wait very long and the fish you catch by this method are unlikely to be small ones.

C.W.

IN PRAISE OF ELDER

The elder is a far more useful tree than is generally realised. When it first comes into flower we pick a large "head" to drop into the pan with the gooseberries just gathered, much the same way as a sprig of mint is added to a boiling of garden peas, and with equally delicious results.

With sugar off the ration, perhaps people will start making country wines again, and elderflower and elderberry are amongst the foremost of these. I have never made any wines myself, but each year we have made some of the very refreshing Elderflower Champagne.

This is so simply made: two sliced lemons, 2 lb. of sugar, 4 tablespoonfuls of white wine vinegar and 8 large heads of elderflower are put into an earthenware crock, together with one and a half gallons of cold water, and left for thirty-six hours, stirring occasionally. The "champagne" is then carefully strained and bottled and is ready for drinking within a week, and a wonderful thirst-quencher it is after an hour or two's hard work in the garden.

The flowers are put to several other uses: our grandmothers made a cream by pressing as many as they could into a pound of pure lard, then simmering the mixture for about an hour. This was very good for all roughness of the skin as well as being a soothing and healing ointment for bruises and bites.

When distilled, the flowers yield a drug valuable for the cure of colds and bronchial troubles, and of course, the fragrant elderflower toilet water is still a favourite in many districts.

But the tree has not outlived its usefulness when its flowers fade, for the berries, as well as making an excellent wine, are used in jams and jellies – particularly in conjunction with apples – and, after drying, have often been sold as a substitute for currants.

We are especially fond of a Summer Pudding made with stewed elderberries in place of the more usual blackberries, and we always keep by a supply of the Elderberry Syrup that is so good for colds and sore throats. Even the leaves of this wonderful tree were until recently dried and ground to be used as an insecticide – no doubt our forefathers knew of this property of the elder too – I well remember the sprays of its leaves that were hung in the house all summer to help keep away the flies. The pith in the stem is still used by botanists in the preparing of their specimens, and the hard wood of the tree is very suitable for a number of things, including butchers' skewers, shoemakers' pegs, and in the making of some mathematical instruments. Nor have we finished yet, for which small boy (or girl) would not delight in pulling a stem and scraping out the pith to make a whistle or a pop-gun!

N.A.B.

LOVELY LOGS

As to the choice of wood to burn ... there are no really bad timbers in Britain, but some are so much better than others that the wise woodman will soon become very fussy over what he puts on his fire! Here they are, very roughly in order of excellence:

ASH is, without doubt, the finest burning wood of all. Well seasoned, it will give a hot smokeless fire, and the glowing embers will last a long time. It will give a good fire when green, and will burn well on the same day that the tree is felled. It is not too common in some areas, and the foresters often prefer to keep it for their own use rather than sell it.

HOLLY is almost as good as ash, and will burn well green or dry, but as there is little demand for holly wood in the timber yard it may come in very large logs that are too big to handle. Holly is also a comparatively scarce timber, so when you are lucky enough to get some ... keep it for Christmas and special occasions.

APPLE and **PEAR** (and this includes other fruit trees such as plum, whitebeam, cherry, mountain ash, and hawthorn etc.) are not normally found in cordwood in any quantity, but all make excellent fires when dry. The wood is hard and close grained, and during the burning the house will be filled with a delightful perfume of scented wood smoke especially from apple and cherry. Fruit wood is sometimes available in large quantities when an old orchard is cleared, and may often be had for the asking. Perhaps that old apple-tree would be better on the fire and make room for some more fruitful cordons? The above timbers are for the real lovers of wood and wood fires, but perhaps the best all round and commonest wood fuel is ...

OAK. A single large oak tree will yield several tons of cordwood in the lop and top, and an old parkland tree may give more firewood than useful timber. Green oak saws very easily considering that the wood is so hard when dry, but the big knots and forks can be difficult. Oak should be kept at least six months, and then becomes a fine and lasting fuel. It is probable that more oak is burnt than all the other woods put together.

BEECH is another excellent firewood that gives a clear lasting fire when seasoned. It is as common as oak in some areas, especially on the chalk, but may be rare in the north.

BIRCH is another fine firewood. It burns rather quickly, and contains natural waxes that give a hot smokeless flame. Green birch is crisp and very easy on the saw, and has the advantage that it cleaves perfectly for excellent kindling wood. Large birch trees are in demand for plywood, but scrub birch is almost a woodland weed in some places with no value apart from firewood. Birch should be kept in the dry for six months before burning, but it will rot in a year if stored in the open. Old rotten birch can be broken with the fingers and is about as good on the fire as wet blotting paper, so be wary about the purchase of an old cord from the woodland.

ELM is often available in quantities now that many trees are doomed with Dutch disease, but it is *not* my favourite fuel. It is difficult to saw and cleave and diseased elm gives out a vile smell in the cutting. Well seasoned elm, say two years under cover, burns well, but the green wood is poor stuff on the fire.

Now for the commoner softwoods:

SCOTS PINE, the FIRS, and LARCH contain much water, but give good noisy, but smoky, fires when well seasoned. The knotty side branches burn beautifully, but are dangerous to carpets without a spark guard.... Larch is a very bad offender in this respect. The softwoods all contain pockets of sticky resin that stains the hands and makes sawing hard work.

YEW is a scarce wood except on the chalk, but it makes a magnificent firewood that lasts almost as long as a similar piece of coal. It is however, most intractable stuff to handle and will take the edge off the finest tools. The writer was once presented free with 5 tons of yew that was too tough for a 3 h.p. circular saw, and he wore out three saw blades in cutting up this "windfall." The beginner would be well advised to start on HAZEL, and leave yew alone. Hazel always comes in light thin pieces that are easy to saw and seldom need splitting. It burns quickly and well and is excellent to warm quickly a cold room.

Where there is a large flat hearth, there is no need to clear the ash more often than once a month. The hot ashes, with perhaps a green log or two, will radiate heat all night, and in the morning a handful of dry twigs or a few pine cones will start a blaze at once. With a small grate, weekly cleaning is enough if wood alone is used. The modern "stay alight all night" fire will behave equally well with timber fuel if a shovelful of ashes is used to cover a couple of green logs overnight.

Logs for burning are best kept under some sort of cover – a porch is a handy and ideal place – but once they have been properly seasoned a shower or two of rain will not impair their burning qualities.

For a quick fire to warm a cold room – use no paper just two handfuls of dry pine cones, some birch sticks or chopped kindling, and half a dozen small split logs, and there will be a warm blaze in two minutes. (It is a strange fact that cleft logs burn better than sawn ones – slabwood from the timber yard that has been sawn down the grain is poor fuel compared with the split cordwood from the same tree!) Now a recipe for a special occasion. Make a faggot of hazel sticks, or better still, apple prunings, large enough to fill your fireplace and bind it lightly with wire and keep it under cover for a year. Place on the fire and stand well back … it is guaranteed to scorch the seat from a pair of asbestos pants!

Wood burns most satisfactorily with a good draught. A log fire must obtain oxygen from somewhere, and will soon show where the draughts come from – if from under the door your feet will be advised! If a room has all cracks hermetically scaled – then the fire will go out! A good fire with complete absence of chilling draughts can be arranged by drilling two or three half-inch holes through the floor boards in front of the fire. Fresh air will then be drawn through the holes from outside and directed straight on to the fire where it will do most good without chilling the occupants of the room. These holes will be concealed by the hearth rug for most of the time but the draught can easily be increased by inserting a small stick under the rug.

L.R.J.

THE BIRD WATCHER

NEST BOXES

If you go to the lonely island of Mousa, off the east coast of Shetland's mainland, you can see the finest surviving specimen of the architecture of the ancient Picts, a magnificent broch, a tall round fort of drystone. In the crevices of the large stones of this prehistoric building nest a certain number of black guillemots, with their white wing-patches and their red legs and feet, and some rock-doves; and I see no reason why the pigeons, and perhaps both birds, could not have nested there ever since the broch was built. It seems pretty certain that the way in which the rock-dove became domesticated unknown centuries ago was because of its propensity to rear its couple of extremely edible young in cracks or ledges in dark sea-caves. The inside of the Mousa broch is as good a "sea-cave" as any rock-dove could desire. It cannot have been long before the human inhabitants of rocky coasts found that they could attract this valuable food by building a few artificial rock-dove crevices in their houses and forts; and the pigeon-cote was invented.

The dove-cote was probably invented separately and independently many times, for there is evidence from wall-paintings of its use by the earliest Egyptian civilisation and by all the early Mediterranean civilisations. In all these places the pigeons were descendants of the hole-nesting wild rock-dove.

Prefabricated nest-places were certainly known and used quite early in the thousand years of Iceland's history. At the famous duck-lake at Mývatn the farmers traditionally "improve" the crevices in the vegetation-covered lava which house so many ducks' nests belonging to a dozen different species.

An interesting early nest-box was the sparrow-pot – an earthenware "bottle" whose base was applied to a wall so that it projected horizontally. House-sparrows built readily in these, and the farmers simply lifted the bottles down to destroy the young or put them in a pie, for these pots were devices to suppress, rather than encourage, the population of sparrows. It seems that they originated in Holland in the sixteenth century, and my friend John Buxton thinks that they were probably introduced into Britain from Delft by the Dutch engineers who were draining the Fens in the 1630s; they are mentioned in a poem of Thomas Randolph published in 1640. With the repeal of the Corn Laws, and the consequent drop in the price of grain, they fell into disuse, and unbroken specimens are rare outside museums.

But it was not until late in the last century that man began to provide birds with artificial nesting-places for his own amusement and not to increase his food or wealth, and it is only in the last twenty years or so that ornithologists have used nest-boxes to provide them with special material for their scientific study of bird life-histories.

Much of the early pioneering of the "aesthetic bird-box" in Europe was done in the last century by the Baron von Berlepsch in Germany. He managed to increase the bird population of his estate very effectively by plastering it with boxes. His designs were derived very much from Nature; he used, most of all, drilled-out sections of branches with fixed bottoms and removable caps. Entrance holes were bored in the side and often little perches stuck an inch or so below and to the side of these holes. These continued to be part of the standard design of bird-boxes for many years, until someone discovered that the birds hardly ever used them, preferring to land on the bark of these "rustic type" boxes or on the lip of the entrance hole.

At one time or another all sorts of materials and objects have been used successfully as nest-boxes, or at least "pre-suggested" as homes by students of bird psychology. Many garden bird-watchers I know plant old kettles and tin cans where they are likely to be used by robins. Boxes have been made out of natural branch sections, out of deal boards, out of flower-pots, specially designed baskets and baked earthenware. Effective prefabs have been designed for, and used by, storks (usually cart-wheels on top of poles), brown owls (invented by Mr. H. N. Southern with thirty-inch lengths of eight-inch planking), barn owls (wooden trays under an entrance in the gable end of a farm building), swallows (wooden trays), house-martins (baked earthenware cups), swifts (long boxes to fit under eaves with an entrance at one end), and tree-creepers (strips of bark carefully arranged to provide them with a crevice rather than a hole).

Of course the post-box kind of nest-box with a hinged roof has been most widely in use. Tits still sometimes seem to prefer real post-boxes to the ordinary round-holed deal tree-boxes. May never goes past without scores of village postmen making special arrangements for the safe progress of broods of blue or great tits in mail-boxes.

In America the bird-box movement has taken a firm hold, and in particular the beautiful and widespread purple martins are offered accommodation on the strict apartment-house system, in little wooden structures on poles which resemble small dove-cotes. There is even one enterprising beauty-spot promoter who distributes these as his advertisements. In Mexico the purple martin houses are often made of basket-work. Henry Ford had five hundred bird houses on his farm, and one of his purple martin houses had no less than seventy-six apartments!

Most people who want to increase the number and variety of

birds in their garden, or who want to make scientific observations on life-histories, put up their boxes in October, so that the birds may get used to them in the course of the winter. It's always a good idea to do this, as quite a number of species will use them to roost in. But I've known a nest-box to be taken over by a pair of tits within a week of its having been put up in early May.

Since the most determined enemy of box-nesting birds is *Homo sapiens* (particularly young specimens) most people find it best to put their boxes at more than twice a man's height on a bare trunk. On the north or east side of trees, boxes get most protection from sun or driving rain.

It is impossible in a short article to give specifications for the perfect boxes for our British breeding birds. There must be thirty or more species of our native nesters which will use boxes, and each has a somewhat different preference, though a standard box, with floor four inches square, and height five inches, and a one-and-a-quarter hole, will take any of our native titmice and the tree-sparrow, pied flycatcher and redstart. It should keep out house-sparrows, though Dr. Bruce Campbell thinks it would be safer to go down to a one-and-an-eighth entrance hole to be sure of this. Last year, with Mr. Edwin Cohen, Honorary Secretary of the British Trust for Ornithology, Dr. Campbell, the Trust's Secretary, brought out a most excellent and useful pamphlet on nest-boxes as the third Field Guide of the B.T.O. It can be obtained from them for 2s. 7½d., post free, at 2 King Edward Street, Oxford. This pamphlet gives the simplest and clearest possible illustrations, dimensions and instructions for those who would cater for various birds, and it goes into most helpful detail about siting, about the weather-proofing of materials, and about the density at which nest-boxes should be placed. The pamphlet also puts an end to some very old misapprehensions. (Birds do not object in the least, for instance, to creosote.) The authors recommend that all nest material should be removed as soon as a brood fledges.

To those about to start the most rewarding and fascinating adventure of bird-boxing their gardens, I would suggest plain deal boxes of the simplest type of three-quarter-inch board, four inches by four inches inside dimension, about six inches high with sloping tops. These can be cheaply made at home. Some people remember the sizes of the holes by coinage: a halfpenny (inch) for blue tits and wrens, a florin for other tits and nuthatches, a half-crown for wrynecks, starlings, etc. Particularly rewarding also are the open-type boxes resembling sheltered balconies which can be placed in creepers up walls as well as on trees, and are very much liked by spotted flycatchers.

Many people have persuaded the wren to nest in the potting shed or some other half-open building by fixing a wooden cover on to an ordinary flower-pot, boring an inch hole in the wooden cover and fixing the pot firmly on its side.

It is quite possible that the bird-box movement may one day materially increase the numbers of our garden birds. Certainly birds that nest in boxes are safer from predators than those which do not, though cats and weasels have learned to open them or can get in through the entrance holes. One ingenious cat-proof nest-box has a double lid, the upper part of which tilts down under the weight of an animal and closes the entrance hole to the nest.

J.F.

—·—

"Telling the Rooks"

A curious custom was associated with a large farm near my boyhood home in North Lincolnshire. The Grange had been occupied by the same family for many years, son following father with unbroken success. Good crops and good harvests were a tradition, the local grey-beards asserting that the continuing prosperity was convincing proof that the old ways were best. Any departure from the usages of the past was considered risky, and for that reason the ceremony of "telling the rooks" whenever a birth or death occurred in the family was maintained.

A noisy colony of rooks occupied a plantation near the house, and tradition demanded that on the first dawn after a birth or death it was the duty of the head of the house, or the eldest member of the family present, to announce the fact beneath the trees before the birds had left on their foraging for food.

In a small recess just inside the hall door was kept the "rook bell," similar to a sheep bell but with a short handle instead of a leather thong. The bell had to be rung vigorously before any announcement was made.

I was present at the ceremony of "telling the rooks" after the old lady died, and I have a vivid recollection of tramping through the dew-wet orchard in the little procession from the house headed by the bereaved owner of The Grange. At three points beneath the trees the bell was rung. "The mistress is dead," announced the old man.

I felt disappointed that except for a momentary cessation of the cawing above our heads nothing happened, though everyone seemed gratified that the old ceremony had been carried out and that the prosperity of the Grange had been made safe for the future.

In due time the old gentleman passed away, and for the first time in living memory the heir omitted to announce the death. His disregard of the ceremony caused much head-shaking among the ancients. Such a thing was asking for trouble they said. "Young Dick may be smartish but he can't go agen Natur," summed up local opinion. My own father considered that the young master had committed a tactical error in flouting a custom that had been carried on for many generations.

When the family returned from the funeral the rookery was deserted. Not a solitary bird was to be seen. "They'll be 'ome at nest," one of the old labourers said, but he was wrong. For the first time that anyone could remember the Grange plantation had no tenants. Where the noisy crew had gone nobody knew, or ever did know. The new owner tried to laugh the matter off, but the old men remained anxious. No one was surprised when affairs at the Grange took an ominous turn. Family troubles seemed to go hand in hand with a succession of bad harvests, and everything that could go wrong on a farm haunted the Grange. A disastrous stack fire at the end of one harvest (the very last load had just been carried), gave the knockout to what had been a prosperous family farm.

Whatever the explanation may be, the bad luck certainly started from the day when a stubborn young man refused to ring the rook bell and make the formal announcement, "*The master is dead.*"

W.H.

THE NATURALIST

BARKING DEER

One of the smallest and in many ways most curious of its tribe, the barking deer or muntjac of South-East Asia has lately taken on a new lease of life as an immigrant to Britain. It has established itself in a wild state in a number of Midland counties, and seems likely to become a permanent member of our fauna.

Although seldom more than twenty-two inches high at the shoulder, and not very formidably armed with miniature horns and movable tushes, the original Indian muntjac imported to Woburn by the Eleventh Duke of Bedford proved surprisingly vicious – so much so that on several occasions dogs which pursued and worried the bucks were maimed and had to be destroyed.

Eventually it was decided to introduce the smaller and more tractable Reeves' muntjac, a native of China. Before these were enlarged steps were taken to exterminate the Indian variety, to prevent cross-breeding. Some Indians, however, had already strayed beyond the bounds of the Duke of Bedford's estate. The sentence of death was not, therefore, entirely carried out; yet hybrids are rare.

Woburn Park and woods today contain large numbers of Chinese muntjacs, many of them quite wild and free to roam entirely at will. They travel about in ones and twos, and never consort in herds like other deer. Both inside and out of the Park they show a liking for very thick cover. I have watched one grazing at dusk in a secluded open meadow, but have never seen one in daytime away from the woods.

One's first view of a muntjac, more often than not, is of a retreating snow-white stern and upturned tail. The length of tail is rather out of proportion to the size of the body, and the hind parts, at close quarters, are seen to stand higher than the fore. A fox-red coat, a quaint ribbed face and a back decidedly hunched complete an appearance which one can scarcely describe as characteristically deer-like.

It is hardly to be wondered at that harriers and foxhounds readily riot on these aliens, which consequently are not precisely popular with Masters of Hounds. A certain amount of mischief is also caused among young plantations, where barking deer are apt to give their name a second meaning. Ordinary rabbit-fencing has, however, proved quite adequate to restrain these deer from young trees and growing crops. The venison is good to eat, and the shotgun is a legitimate and simple means of obtaining it and of preventing the deer from increasing out of hand.

Although killed on sight by many landowners, muntjac have undoubtedly increased in the last few years, and are spreading well out from their original point of enlargement. They occur west through the Vale of Aylesbury to Waddesdon and beyond, and range north-west at least as far as the forests of Whittlewood and Salcey. I have seen them well into Hertfordshire, and I know they have crossed into Essex and parts of Suffolk.

P.H.C.

THE WAYS OF A HARE

The resemblance between the brown hare and the rabbit indicates relationship, though the two animals have very little in common. For, quite apart from their distinctive characteristics in appearance, they differ widely in their behaviour, the hare at all times being a creature of the open, never burrows like the rabbit.

Even when it comes to the intimacies of bringing forth a family the doe disdains all but the slightest shelter. No holes are dug lined with fur for her little ones and in keeping with the scanty preparation made for them, baby hares (or leverets as they are called) come into the world warmly clad in coats of thick fur with their eyes open. They will certainly need their fur coats, for to protect them from wind and rain they have only a thin canopy of over-arching grasses or weed-stalks, and although those youngsters born in the warmer months manage reasonably well, I have known baby hares born in the autumn when life out of doors is not quite so pleasant.

Although four and five leverets have been recorded in a litter it is more customary for each family to consist of two or three. The mother never remains with them in their "form" and visits them only to suckle them. Within three or four days, however, they are able to run about and make little forms of their own. These consist of nothing more than a flattened-out chamber in the growing herbage and although occasionally two of them may settle down together for a while, it is rare to find more than two once they have left the form of their birth. More often each has its own abode.

Hares have a more extensive vocabulary than rabbits and although the doe could probably find her scattered family by scent, I have heard her announce her arrival by a low snorting call, the leverets responding with a shrill squeak. When about six weeks old the young are able to fend for themselves and family ties are severed. Two or three litters are raised annually, the gestation period being about four weeks.

The raising of the families is solely the responsibility of the female, for although the hare's mate-choosing and love-making are accompanied with such elaborate displays the sexual attachment is but a fleeting association, then the couple dissolve partnership. Like rabbits, hares are promiscuous in their marital relationship and once a mated pair have parted company they may never meet again except by some casual encounter during the course of their nocturnal activities.

I have used the word "nocturnal" advisedly, for the hare's movements are confined mainly to the dusk and the darkness, and except during the rutting season it is normally a solitary creature.

Although hares have no substantial residence in the sense that a fox has its earth and the badger its sett, it would be a mistake to regard them as nomadic, for great travellers though they are, each hare returns at dawn to its own form and shallow though it is, to the hare it is as much the perfect home as the burrow to the rabbit.

The general colouring of hares, both juveniles and adults, affords them a measure of concealment when at rest, and seemingly conscious of this, they "stay put" until almost stepped on. They are, however, quick to detect the approach of intruders and in addition to their keen senses of sight and hearing, have a highly sensitive body which records the slightest tremor of the ground. Watching from their forms, they give particular attention to the eyes of intruders and bolt the moment one's eyes spot them. It is possible to get quite close to them by not looking directly at them and I once knew a mole-trapper – wise in the ways of poaching – who could get near enough to hares by this method to suddenly grab them by his hand.

Apart from man, adult hares have few enemies, for they are ever on the alert and capable of amazing speed if under pressure. Foxes sometimes stalk them unawares, but the badger's main opportunity of having hare for supper is when he comes across one in a snare or net, and because hares have a tendency to follow well-worn routes to their feeding-grounds a snare or net set across the course often gets its intended victim. Only twice have I known stoats kill hares, and on one occasion I saw the tables turned so completely that the would-be killer became the victim. A stoat having fixed its grip on the back of a hare's neck could not hold it down, so away the hare galloped with the stoat hanging on. How far they had come before I saw them I have no idea, but I was just in time to watch the hare – obviously an old buck – leap between the bars of a field gate and continue its way. The stoat was knocked clean off the hare's back and never moved again. So far as leverets in their forms are concerned however, stoats take a heavy toll, while most other predatory creatures also claim their share, including buzzards. Some of the most heart-rending cries I have ever heard have come from hares as their pursuers have closed in upon them – it always reminds me of a crying child in pain.

When running from danger hares quickly panic and become so oblivious to all else but their pursuers, that I have known them barge into grazing cattle, even though their eyes are so positioned that they can see backwards as well as forwards. An elderly doe which escaped the hounds by entering a chicken-house died a few minutes later from exhaustion, her limbs being absolutely rigid at the time of death.

In weight a normal brown hare is about eight or nine pounds (heavier specimens have, of course, been recorded) and a bigger animal than the blue or mountain hare found in Scotland and some of our extreme northern areas, but although reports have been circulated of these two species interbreeding I have never come across any authentic evidence.

The Irish hare, which has also been introduced into Britain, comes about midway in size between the other two species and all of them behave similarly in their respective habitats. Their food is entirely vegetarian and where they are numerous they often play havoc with turnips, mangolds, sugar beet and cereals, and at times cause considerable damaged by "barking" fruit trees.

B.M.N.

THE NATURALIST

FAST ASLEEP FOR THE WINTER

A cold autumn day was fading into twilight and a keen easterly wind whipped the tears from my eyes as I took my usual stroll through the meadow. Here and there pheasants scratched vigorously among the fallen leaves; in a nearby shallow stream a tall grey heron stood patiently waiting to thrust its sword-like beak into any unsuspecting fish.

But what was that? A movement near my feet attracted my attention as a hedgehog emerged from beneath some gorse with its little mouth crammed full of leaves. It hurriedly toddled along the hedgerow to an old ash stump, beneath the roots of which it disappeared. After a brief pause I followed it, and there, tucked away in a hollow, was an enormous accumulation of mosses, leaves, and grasses with the hedgehog trying to adjust them to its liking. It was a very sheltered situation where neither frost nor snow could penetrate.

The little animal had certainly worked hard to collect such a lot of materials, and as I quickly left the spot I recalled to mind the many strange and untrue tales I had heard about hedgehogs. One was that they would climb fruit trees, knocking off the cherries, pears, and plums, then roll over on the fruit until it became impaled upon their spines. Of course, such stories are absolutely false. There are many people who also believe that hedgehogs collect their bedding in a similar way; but in this respect, also, the idea is based on fancy rather than fact.

Hedgehogs, however, are not good architects, and when I next visited the little chap about which I am writing its winter dormitory was complete; more materials had been collected, particularly leaves, but their arrangement gave no evidence of pattern or design. Comfort rather than skill characterised its accommodation, and the little occupier was so soundly asleep that although I lifted it from its bed and photographed it, it did not even blink an eyelid.

But it was covered with parasites! The nest, too, was literally alive with them – small greyish-black fleas – and much to my dismay I soon discovered that they had found their way up the sleeve of my coat. So with all possible speed I replaced the hedgehog to continue its sleep.

I noticed that its heart-beats were reduced to the merest flutter, and that it was stone cold to the touch, but in a very plump condition. It had probably been feeding well before "turning in," and would now find those stores of fat a useful reserve upon which to draw during its period of winter inactivity.

A hedgehog's normal dietary consists of insects, worms, slugs, mice, and reptiles – including the poisonous adder – and although it was once thought to be destructive to growing crops, it is now known to have no vegetarian tastes.

In the course of a year it destroys hundreds of field-mice, mainly by digging up the helpless babes in their nurseries. Baby voles are also eaten, and thousands of slugs accounted for. An adder is seized savagely, and although the injured reptile strikes back with all its power, the hedgehog's spiky armour proves an effective shield. Eventually, the infuriated adder beats itself to the point of exhaustion, when the hedgehog knows the battle has been won and begins to enjoy the feast, invariably starting from the tail-end.

The hedgehog's ability suddenly to roll itself up into a prickly ball is its main means of defence, and although the majority of dogs have to withdraw in disgust from such a formidable object, now and again I have known determined terriers overcome its passive resistance. The animal's power instantaneously to pull its prickly coat around itself is unique among wild animals, and accomplished by the contraction of certain muscles which control the spine.

It is surprising, however, how quickly it learns to distinguish rabbits and other harmless creatures from such natural enemies as foxes and badgers, both of which have the reputation of being able to claw open the hedgehog even when tightly rolled up, while the cunning fox is said to have the wisdom to push hedgehogs into water to make them straighten out. Certain it is that water has that effect upon the hedgehog, but to credit the fox with such a knowledge would be, I think, to place it on a plane of almost human intelligence.

In game preserves the hedgehog is most unpopular, and keepers take toll of hundreds of them annually in the belief that they are the enemies of young game. My own experience of hedgehogs, however, both wild and tame, does not substantially support such a charge, and although in a few cases I have known them steal eggs from ground-nesting birds the species concerned have generally been larks or pipits.

I have often kept hedgehogs in a large, wire-netting enclosure where bantams hatched their eggs in the open, but neither the eggs nor chicks suffered, and for two years pheasants were reared there without any interference from the hedgehogs.

By keeping hedgehogs in captivity I discovered that they were good climbers, and one afternoon Peter (of blessed memory) escaped from his enclosure by climbing up an apple tree and then walking along a branch which took him beyond the range of the enclosure. I happened to be near enough to watch his descent, and instead of jumping down, he lingered for a few seconds looking to the left and right, then rolled himself into a ball and let himself go. When he reached the ground, a drop of nearly twelve feet, he was none the worse for his adventure, for his resilient coat of spines took the shock.

Except for a low grunting voice – by which it seems to express both satisfaction and annoyance – the hedgehog is a silent animal, but when caught, as is often the case, in a steel-toothed rabbit trap it utters very shrill screams, and will also cry bitterly when attacked by a badger. There was, for example, a certain night when a friend and I were homeward bound from a village club and heard most piteous cries coming from a short distance ahead. Our first interpretation was that a rabbit was in the grip of a stoat.

A thick fog added to the difficulties, but we had a torch, and as we crept onwards discovered that the scene of the tragedy was a narrow lane where we saw the white-striped face of a badger vanish over the hedge into an adjoining field to go rushing away through the tall wheat. Searching among the herbage we later discovered a hedgehog still tightly rolled up into its defensive posture. The moment I touched it, it squealed bitterly – similar cries to those we had heard a few minutes earlier. I took it home, and next morning examined it carefully, but saw no marks of violence.

So far as the hedgehog's hibernation is concerned, it sleeps throughout practically the whole of the winter, but a settled spell of sunny weather may temporarily revive it. Its normal food supply, however, is no longer available, and the drowsy little animal soon realises that it had better return to its bed.

B.M.N.

HOW TO CLEAN A SHOTGUN

1 Few shooting men take the trouble to clean their guns properly. The cleaning gear supplied in gun cases, even by the best makers, is inadequate for the proper care of a weapon. Contrary to general practice, an old gun, or a cheap gun, needs more care than a new gun, or a best gun. One round makes a barrel just as dirty as a hundred rounds.

2 Barrels which suffer the indignity of being left dirty overnight should be scoured, before subsequent cleaning is attempted, by firing a cartridge through each tube, or by cleansing

with boiling water from a kettle. In carrying out the latter operation, hold the barrels well wrapped up in a dish cloth, because the metal becomes uncomfortably hot.

3 After a wet day's shooting, dismount the gun and wipe it over with a dry cloth. It is advisable, on breaking up the gun, to grip the small of the stock and shake it thoroughly. It is surprising how much water can be cleared from the action by this process. *Don't* dry a wet gun in a linen cupboard or in front of a fire. Gun should be dried like boots, slowly and in an even temperature.

4 When the gun is dry, scour out the worst of the fouling from the barrels by pushing through a piece of newspaper screwed in an appropriately-sized ball. Don't force the paper through. You can bulge a barrel if you're careless.

5 When the barrels are reasonably clean, soak a wire brush in one of the many excellent proprietary gun oils. Scrub out the barrels thoroughly, inch by inch, with especial attention to the area immediately above the chambers and below the choke.

6 Dry out barrels with a dry flannel patch – old pyjama material is excellent – and then, holding tubes to the light, examine the surface carefully for signs of leading. Leading shows as a dull streak, or streaks, on the polished surface. If present, treatment with wire brush soaked in oil should be repeated on tarnished places.

7 If barrels have an even glitter, studied from both ends, wipe out with another oily rag, or use a wool mop for the purpose.

8 When inside of barrels is clean, put a drop of oil down each side of the top rib, and wipe over. Another touch of oil in the ejectors. If you wish to be very careful, chamber cones can be cleaned out with a special brush.

9 The metal parts of the stock should be wiped with an oily rag, and a trace of oil put into all working parts, including trigger bases, action lever, pin-holes and safety catch. Beware of over-oiling. A gun leaking with oil is no pleasure to you, it, or to your clothes. A fine film of oil on all metal parts is the ideal.

10 A high-quality wax polish should be used on the stock. It improves the appearance of cheap guns, brings out beautifully the figuring of the walnut on good guns, waterproofs and hardens the wood.

11 Before the gun is put away, the barrels should be carefully studied for dents, which usually show as unimportant scratches on the blueing. If the inside of the barrel under these scratches is examined, a shadow in the surface will reveal a dent. It is essential that the gun should be sent to a reputable maker to have dents tapped out the moment they show. If this is done, no harm results. If not, the damage from shot charges rubbing against the bulge may ultimately be considerable. More guns are ruined by indifference to dents – which can be caused by a fall or even a tap from a shooting stick – than any other cause.

12 Ruts in the stock, mostly caused by the brass buckles on cartridge bags, are in themselves harmless, but they spoil a gun's appearance. Gunmakers can raise ruts, if requested,

to a quite remarkable degree. Anyhow, any man who owns a decent shotgun is prodigal of his property, and the money a gun costs, if he fails to send it back to a first-class gunmaker for cleaning, regulating, and minor repairs at least once every two seasons. The cost, by comparison with the price of a gun these days, is trifling. And, however careful you are, it is essential that the locks should be dismounted for cleaning at regular intervals. If you want to experiment with the job of removing lock plates yourself, try it on somebody else's gun.

13 Finally, people who appreciate and value their guns don't allow other people to clean them for them. Get the proper cleaning gadgets – they're cheap enough – keep them nicely, and then messing about in the gun-room can be a pleasure in itself.

14 Useful cleaning gear is as follows: three rods (one is not enough, because you have to keep on screwing and unscrewing different gadgets); a horn-covered jag with flannel cleaning patches cut to size; spiral wire or brass brushes; several wool mops; a chamber-brush; two old tooth brushes, one for metal-work, one for removing mud from chequering on stock; a tin of wax polish; a small oil-can; a collection of dry and oily rags.

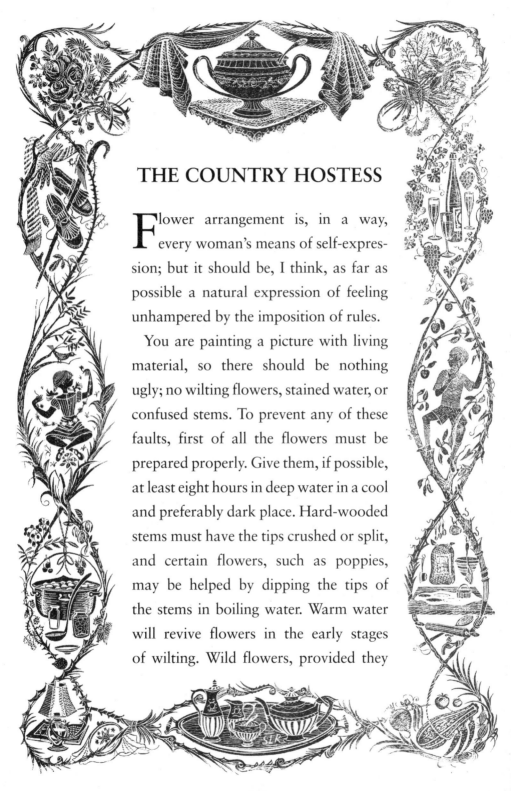

THE COUNTRY HOSTESS

Flower arrangement is, in a way, every woman's means of self-expression; but it should be, I think, as far as possible a natural expression of feeling unhampered by the imposition of rules.

You are painting a picture with living material, so there should be nothing ugly; no wilting flowers, stained water, or confused stems. To prevent any of these faults, first of all the flowers must be prepared properly. Give them, if possible, at least eight hours in deep water in a cool and preferably dark place. Hard-wooded stems must have the tips crushed or split, and certain flowers, such as poppies, may be helped by dipping the tips of the stems in boiling water. Warm water will revive flowers in the early stages of wilting. Wild flowers, provided they have not been exposed to sun and wind, will respond particularly to hot water.

If a flower arrangement is designed to enhance some other quality of colour or line in the room, to pick up, perhaps, the tones of a picture or be associated with a piece of decorative china, the general effect is enhanced. When choosing flowers for a one-colour group it is good to keep an open mind in the choice of material, taking whatever of colour or shape may seem good and disregarding labels. If a spray of redcurrants or a bright scarlet beetroot leaf suits the purpose, these need not be discarded because they come from the kitchen garden.

It is possible to mix together tones and shades of colour with flowers that might not look so well in less translucent material. The interplay of light through the petals is probably the reason for this, so apparently clashing colours may on occasion be used to give exceptionally brilliant and not discordant effects. It is also well to bear in mind that the strength of any colour group is diluted by the incidence of green, so that if green is introduced, or green leaves allowed to remain on the stems a less-brilliant colour effect is achieved.

In dealing with mixed flowers, either of one kind or of many kinds, unnecessary fussiness may be avoided by arranging the flowers, not in units but in groups of one colour or of one kind of flower, and in all groups of mixed flowers it is advisable to have one restful, focal point in the picture, achieved either by the use of large, bold leaves or of flowers of well-defined shape, a lily, perhaps, or an arum, a peony or a sunflower. It is very necessary in mixed groups of flowers to remove as many basal leaves as possible so that there is not a crammed look at the point where the stems meet the vase.

It is difficult to achieve one's vision of an arrangement unless one can be sure that even the heaviest stems will remain in the position required. This is best assured by using as a holder firmly secured wire netting of large mesh and of thin wire. This is easily crumpled up and pressed into a vase. For shallow bowls it is necessary to secure a crumpled dome of wire netting in place by tying over vase and netting with a piece of string, just as one ties up a parcel. When the arrangement of flowers is finished, the string may, if necessary, be cut away, for the interlocked stems will hold the whole group in place. For glass vases a ball of netting may be kept near the surface by hooking an "ear" of it over the rim. An overhanging flower or leaf will provide cover.

However beautiful the decoration may be of the room one lives in, after a while the eyes become accustomed to it; it is possible to pass by even the most beautiful picture almost without noticing it after one has lived with it for a long time. To a lesser degree, perhaps, as they vary with the seasons, the same applies to flower arrangements. If these are always in the same place and in the same range of containers one loses the value of change.

It is a good plan, therefore, to have a supply of different containers suited to certain flowers, and to set them aside, using them at intervals only. Clear glass for beautiful stems, such as a stem of a rose with handsome thorns, simple garden baskets, with linings, for garden bunches, decorative china for pinks and old-fashioned roses, silver or pewter for pastel-coloured flowers, and wooden containers, such as old work-boxes, milk bowls or knife-boxes (supplied with metal linings) are effective containers for such flowers as polyanthuses, wallflowers, outdoor chrysanthemums, and so forth.

Some flowers look best when the light shines on them, a few look well set against the light. Mixed flowers nearly always look best with the light shining on to them, and a few translucent petalled flowers, such as willowherb, mallow, poppies, look very good with the light shining through them. Where a spotlight can be contrived to light up a group of flowers, dramatic effects become possible and exciting.

Flowers are really very like children and need, each one of them, individual consideration and appreciation. Given this, they repay by providing the widest possible range of living material with which an amateur may paint pictures.

C.S.

IN PRAISE OF MUTTON

Some time between Midsummer and Michaelmas, when buck venison is in season, a keeper used to bring a present of it, calling at the kitchen door of our old-fashioned farm and handing it in with the squire's compliments, when the master would descend to the cellar and draw the man a mug of home-brewed.

Often the present was a good cut of shoulder meat which, after hanging, was boned and trimmed, cut up into small pieces, stewed gently with seasoned stock until tender and made into a venison pasty. But occasionally the gift was, to the master's modest satisfaction, a sizeable piece of the haunch.

He knew all about haunch of venison and remembered the days of past plenty and lavish cooking at the farm, when a whole haunch might be roasted in our kitchen, not in an electric oven or a solid fuel cooker, but in front of an open fire, hung on a spit which was turned by a jack.

The fat on the haunch was carefully preserved from wastage by protecting it with a flour and water paste, but just before the cooking was finished, the fat was uncovered and the whole joint thickly spread with farm butter and dredged with flour before putting it back in front of the fire until a golden brown froth rose on it.

At the master's table it was served with its own gravy and red currant jelly, but at the manor the squire's cook made venison cream sauce to accompany it, and this required, among other ingredients, a pint of cream, the yolks of two eggs and a thick slice of butter. The cream was run over the haunch, just before it was taken up, and was caught in a vessel held beneath by an assistant cook, then poured into a saucepan and simmered with the well-beaten egg yolks and the butter rolled in seasoned flour.

But even if venison cream sauce had appeared at the master's table he would not have admitted that haunch of venison from the squire's park was the equal of leg of mutton from a sheep of his own breeding, fed on the rich pastures of his own farm.

Years ago, on the last market day in October, he used to choose a young, plump sheep from his flock and take it to the butcher in the morning, returning later in the day, after his business at the market and his pleasure at *The King's Head* were both finished, to view the carcases and order a leg and a shoulder to be sent to the farm the next day.

Then he would hang the two joints in a current of air in our big, cool larder. The shoulder, not requiring so long a hanging as the leg, would be cooked first, after only a week's hanging. Often it was boned and stuffed with an onion force-meat, roasted, served with onion sauce and accompanied by turnips mashed with cream and well seasoned with pepper, and with potatoes mashed with butter.

But the leg was the master's favourite and he hung it for as long as fourteen days when there was no humidity in the air. He tells us that during the last three days of the hanging he fed the leg with port wine, making incisions in the thick part of the meat for the purpose, but it must be confessed that nobody else remembers this operation, while home-brewed or brandy was his favourite drink and port wine not normally available.

He also liked the leg roasted in front of an open fire in the same way as venison, but oven roasting was good enough for us, and when the well-basted joint came to the table, the flesh was not only as tender as lamb, but richer, succulent and delicious.

The master carved it in thick, juicy slices, while the red gravy which spurted out immediately the long, sharp carver was inserted, ran into the deep *gravy well* at the end of the carving dish and was liberally helped with the meat, poured over the boiled batter pudding which usually accompanied it. No sauce was ever served with it, the potatoes were roast and the only green vegetable Brussels sprouts.

R.W.H.

READER'S LETTER

A WALK WITH THE PIG: Your article by J. Kenneth Habgood, "Taking the Pig for a Walk" (July), reminded me of my father who really did take the pig for a walk.

Our home was a rather remote village not so very far from Oxford and in his later years, until he was too old, Father always kept a breeding sow. The one I remember in particular we called Betty, a big "Berkshire." She was housed in a sty in one corner of a grass area we called the paddock which opened by a gate on to a lane having a wide rough grass verge and a hedge on either side. Occasionally, on a fine afternoon, Father would open the sty and paddock gates when Betty would quietly walk out and down the lane with father in control using nothing more than a little twig of a stick, pressing it gently to one side or the other of her nose, steering her, so to speak. And so she would proceed for an hour or so, down the lane and back, grubbing along in the rough herbage. But Father would never allow anyone to go near her because, he would say, "She'll lean against you and break a leg before you know it."

R. PAINTON, Kildonan, by Campbeltown, Argyll.

WHAT EVERY COOK
SHOULD KNOW ABOUT

PRESSURE COOKING

There is much that is magical in pressure cooking, especially when it is done for the first time, and it is certainly apt to lure husbands into the kitchen to take complete charge of the process of getting dinner cooked. I will assume that you have your pressure cooker, with the little book of instructions that always goes with it, and that you would like some hints on how best to use it. May I begin by telling you what I cook in my own pressure cooker, and why?

I use it for all stocks, to begin with, for two reasons. First, to save time. Stock-making in a pressure cooker takes twenty minutes, instead of 2½-3 hours. The stock is excellent, small in quantity, but all that can be made from the present meat ration, or the remains of it. Second, it does not make the kitchen smell of stock.

Then for nearly all vegetables, and all fruits. Again to save time and for fine flavour. Be careful not to over-season; a small flat teaspoon of salt and a quarter-pint of water is enough for all vegetables. Fruits can be cooked in a light syrup: quarter pint of water and 4-6 ounces of sugar for tart fruits, less sugar for sweeter berries. "Perfume" your syrup as you wish – a vanilla pod is good with pears and delicately flavoured apples, or with peaches, and can go in with the syrup.

Most instruction books give a timetable for cooking vegetables, and a little experience is needed to tell you how far to go by this. Tastes vary; some like their cauliflower soft, some prefer it crisp. What is always necessary, however much time you allow, is to watch the clock closely. One or two minutes of pressure cooking does more than a quarter-of-an-hour's ordinary cooking to soften vegetables and make them mushy, so watch your pot carefully.

Then for all vegetable soups the pressure cooker is invaluable. Time-saving and good flavour may be taken for granted, but do not try to make pea soup. I have quite given up this excellent soup, so far as pressure cooking is concerned. Peas make a thick, floury liquid while they cook, and this is apt to boil up into the safety device that keeps the cooker safe to use, and may choke it altogether and give you a nasty mess to clear up.

If you badly want to cook either of these – and there are good reasons for doing so; they cook in less than a third of the usual time, and taste very good – watch your cooker carefully all the time. So long as a thread of steam puffs out of the escape valve, all is well. If it stops, and the cooker feels very hot, take it off the heat at once and plunge it into a basin of cold water to reduce pressure. Let hot water from the tap run through the escape valve, and make sure that it is clear before you put the cooker back on the heat.

Remember your pressure cooker when you have tough meat or an old bird to cook. Now it is rightly called a witches' cauldron, for anything that comes handy can go in with the meat – a sprig of rosemary, a *bouquet garni*, garlic, vegetables of all kinds, an onion stuck with cloves, and a dash of wine or cider. The toughest old rooster takes only forty minutes to cook, and produces an excellent savoury stock from the water it cooks in.

One of the best features of pressure cooking is the excellence of the stock produced by cooking not only meat, but vegetables, especially green vegetables. Spinach gives so delicious a stock that the temptation to drink it off at once is always too much for me. Cabbage and Brussels sprouts, even cauliflower, give stock almost equally good, invaluable for making gravy or for adding to a soup or for making or mixing with a sauce to go with themselves.

Be careful, all the same, not to boil cabbage or cauliflower water too long; like all greens they are apt to ferment when overcooked, and their flavour suffers. Either cold or boiling water may be used for cooking all vegetables; the temperature makes very little difference to cooking time. To a very acute palate, cold water gives a slightly better-flavoured stock.

Now a word or two about the care of the cooker. Much the best way is to wash it out, yourself, with hot soapy water as soon as cooking is over. Cooks, however conscientious, are not so light-handed as they ought to be to deal with the somewhat intricate machinery of a pressure cooker – I mean the safety valve and the escape valve, and the lid, which is the most important part of the pressure cooker.

All these should be carefully washed after every use; then the inside of the cooker wants washing in hot soapy water. If any stains appear they may be scoured off with fine wire wool and soap. You won't, of course, use soda; it turns aluminium black. A very good way to get rid of stains is to cook apples, rhubarb or any acid fruit in the cooker. Weak acid keeps it clean. If you use your cooker for a steamed pudding, which takes longer cooking and may produce stains, put the squeezed half of a lemon in to cook with the pudding.

I have said nothing here of recipes: they take up too much room. It is worth remembering, however, that any recipe can be used in pressure cooking provided it allows for stewing or simmering or steaming. Cut down the time by two-thirds and be very sparing in the use of liquid and all should be well.

M.B.R.

HOME HINTS

This month of the Hunting Moon means to many country-dwellers pickling, preserving, bottling and wine-making.

Here is a particularly good sweet chutney; it tastes so much better after six months' storing that it is well worth while to wait that long.

SWEET APPLE CHUTNEY

3 lb. apples

4 oz. walnuts, weighed after shelling and peeling

1 teaspoonful salt

½ lb. sultanas

1½ lb. sugar

1½ pints malt vinegar

Rind and juice of one sweet orange, or two tangerines

This is a particularly good chutney for those who have a walnut tree. Peel the nuts carefully; the result is well worth the extra trouble. Peel the apples thinly, quarter and core them and cut them in rough pieces. Put them in a pan with the sultanas, peeled and broken nuts, chopped thinly pared rind and strained juice of the orange or tangerines, salt, vinegar and sugar. Cook gently until the apples are quite soft. I make this chutney in a pressure cooker, cooking all together under pressure for ten minutes. Then, if the chutney looks too liquid, cook rapidly with the lid off the cooker for another five minutes. The chutney thickens with keeping, so don't reduce too much. Pot and tie down, and keep for three to six months.

This next pickle is not quite so sweet. On the other hand, it does not need keeping quite so long.

SPICED CUCUMBER PICKLE

4 large cucumbers – ridge cucumbers are very good for this pickle

1 green pepper

1 lb. brown sugar

1 small flat teaspoonful allspice

½ stick cinnamon

2 large Spanish onions or 12 small picking onions

4 tablespoons rough cooking salt

1 tablespoon mustard seed

1 small flat teaspoonful celery salt

1¼ pints mild vinegar

Scrub the cucumbers and cut them unpeeled in thin slices. Slice the onions thinly, seed and shred the green pepper and spread all together on a large dish. Scatter rough salt all over them and leave them for an hour or so. Then put them on a colander or on a sieve and wash them well with cold water. In the meantime, put sugar, vinegar, mustard seed, celery salt, allspice and cinnamon into a pan and bring slowly to the boil. Boil for 5 minutes, then add the vegetables and heat very slowly. When just below boiling point take off and pot while still warm. This pickle can be eaten after three weeks.

M.B.R.

NOVEMBER

WILD LIFE

It is interesting to note how long it is before our winter visitors really sort themselves out and settle in their permanent feeding-grounds. Hardly ever is this process complete by November. Two years ago, for instance, at the Severn Grounds, observers in the hides of the Severn Wildfowl Trust found the whitefronts almost steady at about 470 or 480 for the whole of the month until the 27th. If they had left off their counting on that day, they might have got the impression that such was the winter population. But on the 28th about 300 came in, on the 29th another 300; by mid-December the numbers had risen from a thousand to over two thousand, by the New Year to over three thousand, and the peak was not reached till January 27th with about 3,700. So do not trust November to show the winter permanence of wildfowl. Whooper swans are still arriving from the north in November, won't be resident in winter quarters sometimes till Christmas. Much the same goes for Bewick's swans, main arrivals not settling in November. Greylags from Iceland will still be shifting, moving about. The bean-geese may still be coming in from north-west Russia.

Among duck still arriving are those winter mallard that visit us from abroad, and teal, wigeon, shoveler, pochard, tufted, scaup, goldeneye. Those more likely to be settled this month are gadwall, pintail, and the sea-ducks (long-tails, eiders, scoters, goosander, red-breasted merganser, and, in the second half, smew).

This month's quotation from Gilbert White:

"November 24, 1770. The wild wood-pigeon, or stock-dove begins to appear. They leave us all to a bird in the spring, and do not breed in these parts; perhaps not in this island. If they are birds of passage, they are the last winter bird of passage that appears. The numbers that come to these parts are strangely diminished within these twenty years. For about that distance of time such multitudes used to be observed, as they went to and from roost, that they filled the air for a mile together: but now seldom more than 40 or 50 are to be anywhere seen.... They are much smaller than the ring-dove, which stays with us all the year."

White was, of course, alluding to the wood-pigeon or ring-dove, and not the bird most of us now refer to as the stock-dove. And (as recent correspondence in COUNTRY FAIR has illuminated) it seems to be the case that the visitors, or some of them, are "much smaller" than the ring-dove. Such as are smaller are the young of the year, and the evidence remains powerful that most, if not all of the wood-pigeon invaders of England come from Scotland.

J.F.

THE FLOWER GARDEN

Roses have never been more beautiful than in the past season, and the influx of new varieties during recent years has provided plenty of interest for the grower. There have been some notable advances especially in the Floribunda section and the only disturbing factor is the decline in scent. The Hybrid Teas are still the favourites and new varieties which appear to have established themselves as good garden value are Karl Herbst, Sutters Gold, Show Girl, Symphonic, Eden Rose, Virgo, Speks Yellow, Marcelle Gret, Opera, Independence, Ena Harkness, Grandmere Jenny, and, of course, Peace. The growing popularity of the Floribunda section is much in evidence and here Frensham, Fashion, Cocorico, Siren, Goldilocks, Alain, Masquerade, Irene of Denmark, and Concerto are all excellent., There are many more to choose from, and it is a matter of personal taste and also which varieties succeed best in your area.

Thorough preparation of rose beds before planting cannot be

overstressed. A liberal supply of good rotted compost or farmyard manure incorporated in the ground when trenching and a top-dressing of bonemeal worked into the soil during planting should give good results; Planting is only possible when the ground is in good condition, and plants arriving at other times should be heeled in temporarily or if frosty placed in a good shed and the roots covered with damp sacks. When planting, the hole should be large enough for the roots to be spread out and the rose should be about an inch deeper than previously so as to encourage the production of its own roots. It may be just a case of filling in beds where odd plants have died and then it is advisable to renew the soil before replanting. Roses must be planted firmly and a careful check should be made during frosty periods or after strong winds.

In the rock garden some of the greatest treasures may need protection from excessive damp by a sheet of glass or windowlite firmly held at an angle. The addition of coarse chippings or similar material to sharpen the drainage is also most beneficial. Fallen leaves always accumulate between the rocks and should be cleared away but dying growths are best retained as they often afford some protection from the excessive cold. The Asiatic Gentians are an exception however and decaying shoots soon rot the crowns if left.

C.P.

———————

The maintenance of an adequate supply of organic material in the soil is of great importance to all gardens. Shortage of farmyard manure has led to the systematic composting of all available material in the garden. The tops of herbaceous plants, grass mowings and vegetable waste can all be rapidly decomposed to form excellent compost. Fallen leaves are of course one of the main natural methods of maintaining humus and these can be swept up and added to the heap. Oak and beech leaves however make good leaf-soil for potting composts and should be placed in a separate area. Although peat is now extensively used in the general potting soils, leaf-soil still has many uses and is home produced. Shrubberies are often neglected and here the fresh leaves may be forked into the soil and left to rot down, especially Rhododendrons, providing the roots are not disturbed.

Although November is perhaps rather depressing after the bright summer flowers and the autumn colour, it is the month when the garden lover can gain much pleasure from the planting of new deciduous shrubs to increase the colour and interest of the garden next year. Providing the weather is good this task should be completed as far as possible, digging a good hole for each plant, spreading out the roots and making sure they are firmly planted and adequately staked.

It is also the best time for rose planting, and no doubt those ordered during the summer will be arriving from the nurseries. If the soil is too wet for permanent planting, heel them in a spare plot, or if frost is about they will come to no harm in a frost-proof shed providing the roots are wet and covered with damp sacking. Roses are planted about an inch below the soil mark left when lifted previously, for it is an advantage for the union of the stock and scion to be below soil level, so as to encourage the rose to make its own roots. If odd spaces are replanted in existing beds it is advisable to renew the soil, as plants seldom do well if planted in the same soil as one that has died. Make sure that any standards are well anchored and all roses are firm for they suffer greatly if they are loosened by wind.

A start can be made on the winter pruning of trees and shrubs. Those requiring most attention at the moment are the late summer and autumn flowering group and those grown for their ornamental value. The removal of dead or weak growths and suckers should be a matter of course, whilst the centre of the plant must always be kept open otherwise the lack of light causes much dead wood.

C.P.

THE VEGETABLE GARDEN

Now we have the winter before us. In spite of that, seed-sowing time will still catch us unprepared unless we get forward with cultivation while the ground is still workable. It is a great help, later, to have a good idea now of what is to be grown next season, because the position of different crops will decide just what preparation the ground requires and will prevent wasted labour. For instance, the ground should be thoroughly turned and well manured where there is to be a permanent bed for asparagus, onions, or seakale.

Celery or celeriac need similar treatment, with the earth left rough, but root crops on the whole do not want freshly manured soil. Beans – all kinds – do not need so much preparation, and if any part of the plot *has* to be left, let it be the bean section (unless exhibition standard is aimed at). The ground where brassicas are to go should be limed as it is dug, except where the soil is so open in texture that liming has to be done nearer planting time. Salads need a fine, firm surface, absolutely free of weeds, so here again preparation must be thorough. One of the measures that can be taken against scabby potatoes is to leave the proposed site in ridges and dress with soot, but this must be put down soon to give it a chance to weather. If no-digging is being practised, the idea is to keep the soil warm and undisturbed, so remove any perennial weeds, then cover the surface with deep leaves or compost.

It is a good idea to put down straw where there are leeks, parsnips, turnips or similar crops; not because they need protection, but to make it possible to get them out during hard frost. Kohlrabi is also hardy enough to leave out until it is wanted; try peeling off the outer skin and eating it raw; it has the taste of very young leaves from the heart of a cabbage.

Broad beans can still be sown if this was not done last month. Peas, too, of a hardy, round-seeded variety, will come through the winter and be ahead of the spring ones if they are sown now in a sheltered place. The crowns of globe artichokes will need some protection, if only earth drawn round them. Jerusalem artichokes must be kept in hand; it is difficult to clear the ground entirely of them once they have got established, and it is really better to give them a permanent site where they will be useful as windbreak or shelter for smaller plants.

Make sure of some really early rhubarb by packing straw or other clean litter round the crowns, then covering with boxes or tubs. The only worthwhile way to eat rhubarb is to take it young.

C.M.

⎯•⎯

VEGETABLES: Finish celery earthing if not already done and draw up earth on each side of the spring cabbage. Collect sound tomato stakes and bean rods and store under cover. If possible dip the butts in a mixture of tar and creosote.

November is the month of planning and preparing for the spring sowing. If manure and compost is scarce concentrate on the plots intended for Brussels sprouts and cauliflowers. All the brassicas are heavy feeders. Take every opportunity to dig, once the ground gets wet and soggy the job is much harder. Take out a deep trench to begin with, keep the spade upright and be certain to bury weeds deep. Turn the spit completely over and do not break down too much. The rougher the soil is, the more chance frost has of getting in and doing far more good than you can. When faced with heavy clay soil – ridging can give excellent results, more of the surface being exposed to the weather. Dig in all the weeds and decaying vegetables.

November is also the month for liming, if necessary, but it is advisable to have the soil tested. Light and frequent applications are more successful than heavy ones at longer intervals. Basic slag – being slow acting – can also be applied. Lift seakale and rhubarb for forcing. The latter should be left lying on top of the ground where it will remain dormant and consequently sprout with great rapidity when brought into a warm greenhouse in the spring for very early pulling.

If frost threatens, pull up remaining cauliflowers with root complete and place in a shed. They will often last three weeks by this method.

FRUIT: Early November is the time for planting new trees and bushes provided the soil is in a friable condition. Planting in wet, soggy soil is madness. Remember to plant at the same depth as already grown in the nursery. Firm well and stake immediately. Care must be taken to wrap the tree with felt or sacking to prevent chafing.

Cutting of black- and red-currants and gooseberries should be taken this month, but only from clean, healthy stock. Take about ten inches of the current year's growth and in the case of red- and white-currants and gooseberries rub off all buds except top four or five to enable a clean stem to develop. Black currants should have all buds left to encourage growth from below ground. Plant cuttings in well firmed ground about a foot apart. They will be ready for planting in permanent positions the following year.

E.B.

THE FRUIT GARDEN

For gardeners with new gardens and those with space to spare a small plot of fruit is a good investment. Cultivation is comparatively straightforward providing always the grower is not tempted to commit the sin of intercropping with flowers and vegetables. Such a plot can give a supply of fruit for most months of the year and a profitable return for the time spent on it.

In the majority of gardens fruit is sadly neglected, not least in the initial planning of the layout. As much care should be taken with this as in the actual preparation of the ground. Plums are best grown as half-standards and as such become the tallest inhabitants of the plot. Therefore they must be kept to the north to avoid shading the other fruit. Unless there is some specific reason, full standards should not be used for any fruit; they complicate picking, pruning and spraying – the latter two usually being neglected as a result. Half-standards and various restricted forms are available from most nurserymen.

With apples and pears there is greater scope for planning as both of these can be grown in so many different forms. The most straightforward method for apples is the dwarf bush. This is grown on a dwarfing rootstock which influences the tree to fruit early – say in its third or fourth year. Ask for trees on Type VII or IX for good soils, Type II for poor soils. Alternatively the dwarf pyramid form can be used although this is best reserved for pears as with their upright growth they are much more suited to it. Oblique cordons are ideal for both apples and pears particularly where space is restricted. In the layout apples and pears should be grouped together on one side of the plot leaving the other entirely free for soft fruits. If, however, tall growing forms of apples and pears are preferred then the soft fruit must again be to the south of these rather than to one side.

If only for its quick return soft fruit is the most important section. To obtain the best results advantage should be taken of the varieties available by choosing those which will give a succession of fruit. As an example a bush each of "Boskoop Giant," "Blacksmith" and "September Black," will give blackcurrants over a period of 6-8 weeks. This avoids a glut and is surely better for both gardener and housewife. Such applies to all fruits although for apples and pears emphasis should be on late-keeping varieties.

For planning even a small fruit garden a visit to (or literature on) the excellent model gardens at East Malling or the R.H.S. Gardens, Wisley, is well worth while.

G.R.W.

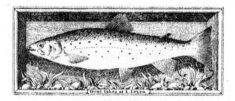

FISHING

I used to think that I was in a minority of one when I held that the best fishing of all came with the onset of winter. Recent seasons have made me change my mind, for I see more and more anglers on the bank once the leaf has fallen. There is a very powerful case to be made out for winter fishing, With the exception of carp, tench and perhaps bream, coarse fish are in top form both as to fighting and to feeding.

That is purely a practical consideration and it by no means exhausts the attractions of winter fishing. For me, at least, the countryside has a beauty that equals that of high summer. There are no trippers, no pleasure boats, no waste-paper, no flies, no long blank periods at midday when the sun shines and few fish will bite. Most important, there are no arrogant parental swans with impudent broods of cygnets. There are, moreover, fewer anglers and this – brothers of the angle that we undoubtedly are as long as we don't occupy each other's swims – is no small consideration.

At the risk of increasing the number fishing, may I suggest that more would risk the rigours of the winter waterside if they (a) had better circulation, (b) made better use of what they've got.

Enjoyment of winter angling hinges upon what you wear. I myself favour a waterproof windproof zipper jacket rather than coat or mac. Under this I wear a varying number of sweaters. When it's really cold I even put on a string vest (Government surplus).

For the legs I incline to two pairs of trousers, since the vital thing is to insulate the body with pockets of warm air. Pyjamas worn under flannels are excellent, with waterproofs on top if necessary. Ideally, the feet should be encased in oiled wool socks and these surrounded by fleecy flying boots. Gumboots are cold and should only be adopted if one actually expects to stand in water. With waders two pairs of socks are advisable and a layer or two of paper beneath the foot helps. Brown paper is, incidentally, an excellent protection and I know one angler who always slips a piece under the back of his jacket to protect the kidneys. On the head, a woolly cap, or sou'-wester if wet; on the hands, the only possible wear is mittens.

You say that I shall look odd. Very well, and so I do. You will, too. But you will find sport and exhilaration beyond your fondest expectations.

C.W.

———

"More lies – to put it in very plain language – have been told about the pike than any other fish in the world; and the greater the improbability of the story, the more particularly is it sure to be quoted." So wrote Frank Buckland in 1881, and he had very good reason to label many of these stories as lies.

With the exception of the Wels (*Silurus glanis*), the pike is the largest freshwater fish to be found in Europe, and this, coupled with an appearance of extreme rapacity, has earned it a most unenviable reputation. Like most fish stories, they mainly centre around the great size and age attained by this fish; the secondary theme is its strength and belligerence.

One of the earliest references is found in the *Historiae Naturalis* of *Plinius Secundus* (A.D. 23-79), in which he refers to a fish found in the Rhine which rivalled the tunny in size. The name he gave this fish, *Esox*, was later adopted by Linnaeus and is still in use today as the generic name of the pikes. Strangely enough, the word that Linnaeus used for the specific name of the European pike, *lucius*, was in use centuries before in this country, in its Anglo-Saxon form of *luce*. Thus Chaucer, in the *Prologue* to the *Canterbury Tales*, when introducing the Franklin, used the following couplet;

"Full many a fatte partricke hadde he in mewe,
And many a Breme and many a Luce in stewe."

One of the most persistent of pike stories is that of the German fish reputed to have been at least 267 years old. Like all old records, however, the accounts differ in some details. In 1497 an enormous pike was caught in the Kaiserslautern lake in the Palatine, and fastened through its gills was found a gilt brazen collar, engraved with the legend that it had been put there by the Emperor Frederick II, "Governor of the World," on the fifth day of October, 1230. The fish was taken to Heidelberg Palace where a line drawn along its length measured 17 ft., and here its portrait was painted. This was hung in the Château de Lantern, but one hundred years later a portrait of the same fish was reported to be in a castle between Heilbronn and Spires, together with the ring, although it was not stated that it was the original painting.

A painting of the same monster, unfortunately of uncertain origin, was to be seen in one of the galleries of the Natural History Museum in Kensington, before the last war. The legend, in English, read, "This is the biggest of the pike which the Emperor Frederick II with his owne hand hath put the first time into a poole at Lawtern and hath marked him with this ring in the yeare 1230. Afterwards hee brought him to Heydelberg, the sixth of November 1497, when hee had beene in the poole 267 yeares." The skeleton of this fish was preserved in the Cathedral at Mannheim, but alas for this record pike, when examined by a German anatomist it proved to be the remains of several fish, not one!

More recently, a fish that attracted a great deal of attention from both popular writers and scientists was the famous Kenmure pike. I believe that the first notice of this fish in print is in the second volume of *Rural Sports* (1801-1813), by the Rev. W. B. Daniel, who suggested that it was the "biggest taken by a line, or perhaps ever known in this country, and which was caught in Loch Ken, near New Galloway, in Scotland, with a common fly, made of the Peacock's feather; it weighed *seventy-two pounds*; the skeleton of the head is at Kenmore Castle." Most later writers agree with Daniel on the weight of this fish, except for a Dr. Grierson, who in 1814 published some Mineralogical Observations in Galloway, where he stated that it "was caught about forty years ago in this lake (Loch Ken), by John Murray, gamekeeper to the Hon. John Gordon of Kenmore," and that it weighed sixty-one pounds. That eminent ichthyologist, the late Dr. C. Tate Regan, examined this skull in Kenmore Castle, and by comparison with the heads of pike of known weight came to the conclusion that the fish could possibly have weighed 72 pounds if it were in good condition, and in all probability weighed 61 pounds or more.

Probably the most intriguing of all pike stories are those related by Llewellyn Lloyd in his *Scandinavian Adventures*, published in London in 1854. Quoting from the letter of a friend, he writes: "My brother, Captain Axel Westfeldt, Lieutenant J. Lekander and the fisherman Modin, were one day fishing ... in a large lake in Fryksdal, in Wermeland, (Southern Sweden). When they had proceeded a considerable distance from the land, Modin suddenly pulled the boat right round, and in evident alarm commenced rowing with all his might towards the shore. One of the party asked the man what he meant by this strange conduct. "The *Sjo-troll*, or water sprite, is here again," replied he, at the same time pointing with his finger far to seaward. Everyone in the boat then saw in the distance something greatly resembling the horns of an elk, or reindeer, progressing rapidly on the surface of the water. "Row towards it," exclaimed Lekander, "the deuce take me if I don't give the *Sjo-troll* a shot, I am not afraid of it."

"It was with great difficulty, however, that Modin could be prevailed upon once more to alter the course of the boat, and to make for the apparition. But at length the man's fears were partially allayed, and the chase commenced in good earnest. When they had neared the object sufficiently, Lekander, who was standing, gun in hand, in the bow of the boat, fired, and fortunately with deadly effect. On taking possession of the prize, it was found to be a huge pike, to whose back the skeleton of an eagle was attached. This fish, or rather the bones of the bird, had been seen by numbers for several years together and universally went under the above designation of *Sjo-troll*."

The Rev. Charles Badham in his *Ancient and Modern Fish Tattle* (London, 1854), alludes to the voracity and omnivorous diet of the pike in the following list, "— a swan's head and neck, a mule's nether lip, a Polish damsel's foot, a gentleman's (probably, however, no objection would be made to a lady's) hand; plump puppies just opening their eyes, and tender kittens of an age to pay the penalty attaching to a mother's indiscretion...." Although the author warns us in the introduction that his purpose is to give not fish science but fish tattle, the seemingly unlikely attacks on human beings by pike are in fact likely to be true. There are at least two instances which have the ring of truth about them, one when a boy was mauled on the hand by a large pike in a receding pool of flood water, and the other a man trying to capture a pike stranded in shallow water. It should be noted, however, that both these incidents occurred when the fish were in a condition where escape was impossible; it remains extremely doubtful that they would actually attack a man without provocation of some sort.

That their food is varied cannot be doubted. There are well testified accounts of weasel, fox, ducks, goslings, coots and even a swallow being among the more surprising items.

A.C.W.

This is the time of year that "sorts out" the members of our fishing club. The "have-a-good-timers," "much-of-the-day-in-the-pubbers" and those who bring their families to enjoy a holiday by the river fade out; in their place the earnest fishermen, who think nothing of rising at 3 a.m. for an early assault on the bream and to whom rain, wind, snow or frost are no deterrent, remain. At dawn they congregate at corners of the town to catch the bus and at night, tired but content, they return often with empty bags but ready for the next time.

It is strange that twenty-five stalwart men and one brave woman will sit all day on their camp-stools in combat with some other team. Sometimes there is only ten ounces two drams to show for all their preparations, all their patience; yet that tiny weight may win a trophy. However unsuccessful their endeavours, the keener they seem to be for more of the sport that grips them.

The care which the float man bestows upon his tackle is worth the attention of many trout and salmon anglers. The match-fisherman especially is most diligent. The roach seeker with extra-fine gear is an artist worthy of the name.

November's falling leaves can be a nuisance, but to the chub enthusiast they can prove a blessing; for on a warm day a bumble fly falling upon the nose of some great chavender will not frighten him as he waits beneath a bush or branch. Inquisitive and expectant he will accept the offering when at other times he would be more suspicious. Chub like berries. If the fly does not tempt him, an elderberry may be more successful, or any other berry that his assailant may try. Recently there was correspondence concerning the eating qualities of the fish termed coarse. Chub is undoubtedly made of cotton wool, yet the Midlander will eat him and proclaim him ambrosial. Winters are hard in the Midlands so that wool inside and out may be beneficial. Of the others the perch is much the best. A good perch has the taste of sole, being firm and clean tasting. Pike, baked and stuffed, are relished but I need a good smothering of white wine (over the fish) to gulp him down. I can find no satisfaction in a roach.

Most worthily the members of our club return every fish to the water after the weigh-in but, splendidly humane, they are also wise not to bring most of them to the kitchen. A brace of trout, a pike or a couple of perch will cause an irate wife to forgive so late a return but a chub, a roach or a mighty barbel is not likely to soothe a ruffled spouse.

R.B.

SHOOTING

S HOT SIZES: The problem of what size of shot to use is permanently with us. It can be argued, rather plausibly on the theory of killing chances, that the smaller the shot the greater number of chances and, equally plausibly, that larger shot penetrate better and have more shock effect than small ones. Number six shot is probably used by most sportsmen, although twenty years ago an appreciable minority who were all excellent shots would have nothing larger than number seven. The farmer whose aged gun probably throws a rather individualistic pattern remains faithful to number five. The ballistic arguments are of little value, for driven birds coming with a strong following wind can probably add almost ten per cent to cartridge catalogue velocities, and as anyone who has been hit by a falling bird can say, they possess considerable momentum.

The farmer usually shoots ground game moving away from the gun and the probable answer to his preference for the larger size of shot lies in the difference of range and quarry. There is one other conservative class devoted to the number five. Towards the end of the season old grouse on the moors may have to be reduced. The late autumn grouse is a hard fellow to stop and he has a very good idea of keeping the range long. Here again the majority of keepers prefer the larger shot. Even smaller shot have their uses in snipe shooting and incidentally for war against jays, but there is seemingly no demand for number four, although formerly used by wild-fowlers. I think the reason is that number four, for some obscure reason, tends to give poor patterns in game guns, but so far all we know about pattern is empirical, no scientific theory exists.

THE AGE OF GAME BIRDS: One of the results of ringing wild birds has been some information on the period of their lives. We have very little exact knowledge of how long game birds can live although occasionally an oddly marked or recognisable bird is alleged to have been about "all of ten to fifteen years." Old cock pheasants with prodigious spurs may be six or even seven years old and oddly enough I know of no really authentic and precise records.

The ringing of game birds might yield knowledge, but it might also lead to some heart burning if one received from a shoot too many mortuary rings of birds expansively raised and tenderly nourished on one's own ground! Still I do not know what might be the life span of a veteran or for that a great-grandmother of any of one's game birds. There are, I believe, some aviary records but so far as I know nothing unshakably reliable about wild game birds.

H.B.C.P.

<hr />

PIGEONS: November is one of the best months for pigeon, and full advantage must be taken of the weather. The foreign flocks are beginning to come in, though the main lots will not be here in force until the end of the winter. But our home birds will be flocking and they are much better birds than the skinny, drab foreigners, which are very much smaller. The foreigner is of a more sober plumage, its greys are browner and the ring less conspicuous.

Foggy days are deadly for pigeon. Like most birds, geese included, they are quite lost in fog, and will sit in the tree tops for hours together hunched and motionless. This is the only time they may be stalked and in thick weather it is possible to get within easy range of the big lots. Moreover, when you have fired they will mill around and frequently come back to the same tree. Pigeon are one of the most harmful of all pests; they can stow an amazing amount into their capacious crops, which are like miniature handbags: 198 beans and a dozen small snails have been found in a single crop. Pigeons eat a great many snails, and I am inclined to think they do so chiefly for the shells.

MALLARD: This is a good month for duck, and they will continue to frequent barley stubbles until the plough comes. They like a field on a hill, and they may be gleaning at night without you knowing it. Walk over your barley stubbles in the day and note if there are any duck droppings.

PARTRIDGES: These are becoming wild, and walking will soon be a thing of the past. Partridges usually have their favourite route for leaving a field and this should be noted carefully and the guns posted accordingly. A hedge corner is a favourite escape route, and guns should always watch the corners.

WILDFOWL: This, of all the months in the year, is best for geese. The big skeins are just in and have not split up and scattered. More wild geese are shot in November than in any other month of the season, though, for my part, I would rather shoot a single goose in a fortnight's fowling in "rough winter weather" than a dozen during these humid foggy days.

PHEASANTS: This is perhaps the keeper's busiest month. It is his "harvest" time and now he knows the success or failure of months of summer work in the rearing field. So when inviting friends to shoot remember your keeper and his work. Bungled shots and bad shooting undo all his labours.

B.B.

How to Shoot Straight

The townsman whose guns have been put away from the close of last shooting season often feels some doubt of what showing he will make in the first days of the new one. The best advice is to spend a few hours at the shooting grounds on clay birds, but not everyone can afford the necessary time for this.

Actually, shooting involves little muscular effort, but it does involve the use of muscles in positions and under tensions which are not met with in daily life. Young men are not as a rule bothered by this disuse of shooting muscles, but middle-aged men become increasingly aware of it. I am wholly in favour of a little "dry practice."

That is simply a daily few minutes' practice in mounting the gun to the shoulder, swinging and snapping practice with "snap-caps" in place of cartridges in the chambers. It can be achieved in the privacy of one's room, or, even better, on the lawn if someone else will obligingly throw tennis balls for you.

In all shot-gun shooting one should wholly forget about the gun, never "see" it, and be wholly concentrated on the bird. This practice of "dry snapping" not only loosens up the muscles but refamiliarises one with the gun, so that it loses its identity as an external object and once again becomes part of oneself.

Probably nine-tenths of the art of shooting straight with a shot-gun is comprised in the action of gun-mounting, and in this "dry practice" drill we have to remember the basic essentials. First, the foot position. This is not the position one instinctively tends to take with the left foot slightly advanced, but simply the "stand at ease" position, but with the heels only a few inches apart; this allows a wider angle of pivoting on ball and heel. It has, however, to be remembered at first, but soon becomes the "natural" stance.

Next is the right-hand grip. A rather natural tendency to have one's thumb close to the safety is prone to make us forget that the right hand should be well round underneath the grip of the stock. This gives a vertical lift without that disconcerting elbow movement which is the source of so many misses.

The left hand no less than the right also needs a little schooling. The grip of the fore-end should be forward; this depends on the length of one's arms. But, in general, only about half-an-inch of the fore-end and take-down button should project over the left forefinger.

The grip of the left hand, while mounting the gun, should be as light as possible, but at the moment of butting it to the shoulder the trigger-pressure should be increased. The left thumb should not be curled over the barrel but left approximately erect. This prevents tilting the barrels, and also, to some extent, it masks the vision of the left eye.

Now, having remembered about one's foot position and the correct grips, comes the matter of the "ready" position. One's natural tendency is to hold the gun with the muzzles pointing rather upward. It should be almost level, and at a convenient mid-breast height, say "third button of the waistcoat." Held thus, there is no waste of time dropping the muzzles for a straight-away bird, and a slight bend back brings one with equal economy of movement on to an overhead one.

In mounting the gun to the shoulder, *one keeps one's left hand on the bird*, at the same time pushing the left hand forward while the right hand pulls the butt into the shoulder. It is best, perhaps, to imagine that the gun is elastic, and can be strained or pulled out between the hands. Lastly, exactly as the butt comes firmly home on the shoulder, the trigger should be pressed.

Keep your gun ready assembled, and "snap practice" at intervals, but never long enough to get really fatigued. If you find that, despite practice, you are not consistently "on" your target, particularly low ones, it is a possible indication that age is stiffening your neck muscles, and you are not unconsciously dropping your head down to the stock as you did when younger. The cure is a slight attention to your gun stock. It should be dropped a quarter of an inch or so lower at the heel of the butt.

Youth can shoot with almost any approximately standard gun, but middle age needs a gun which fits perfectly, and in later middle age this original fit may need a little amendment to compensate for changes in its owner's sight or physique.

All good shooting is performed in one unbroken movement or swing, and the aim of one's practice is to get into the swing and subconsciously to press the trigger without checking the swing. Moving targets can be improvised, or one can discreetly use passing motor traffic from suitable seclusion. In the field you may find you are shooting quite well, and there is no finer tonic than success. But if you are missing, it is fifty to one that you are behind and below your birds. There are various palliatives.

One of the best of these is to fold a glove, a handkerchief, or even place a lightly filled tobacco pouch in your left hand under the fore-end of the gun. This will give you more lift, and if the device works well, it shows your error is "below." You can probably counter this by giving a little more upward chuck to your left arm. As a cure for shooting "behind" birds, no mechanical device can serve, but there is a very serviceable psychological one.

You have to imagine each bird has in his beak a yard-long walking stick with an orange stuck on the projecting end. Having mentally adorned your birds in this way, point your left hand at this imaginary orange. If you still do not kill, lengthen the stick to an imaginary six feet, and, to your surprise, the bird will obligingly fly into your shot and be killed, although you thought you fired yards ahead of him.

As for the head-on or quartering driven partridge, or grouse late in season, it is almost impossible to take your first shot too early, and a great many birds are missed simply because the range is too short and the spread of shot inadequate. In many cases keepers put mark sticks too near hedges, when it would be far wiser to place the guns a great deal farther back.

Whatever the conditions of the cover, make a point of taking your first bird as far away as you can, which gives you time to take a second and possibly a third without undue hurry. As birds always rise as they approach a fence or any obstacle, that little extra up-chuck to the left hand is invaluable. The shot which is nearly vertical and involves a bent back is seldom successful. It is far better to pivot and take it conveniently from behind.

Lastly, how long is it since your guns were overhauled? A very little wear will tend to increase trigger pull, and old clogged oil will give the same effect. Very slight differences in the crispness of trigger pull have a marked effect in slowing discharge and interrupting the smoothness of one's swing. If, despite practice, you make a consistently bad showing, seek out your gun-maker and see if you are not overdue for that attention to the fit of your stocks which is as inescapable as the occasional visit to one's occulist for a change of glasses. No man can shoot well with a gun to which he cannot adapt himself, and correct gun-fitting is more and more important as one's burden of years increases. A very slight alteration to the guns you have used all your life may make all the difference to your performance and your satisfaction.

H.B.C.P.

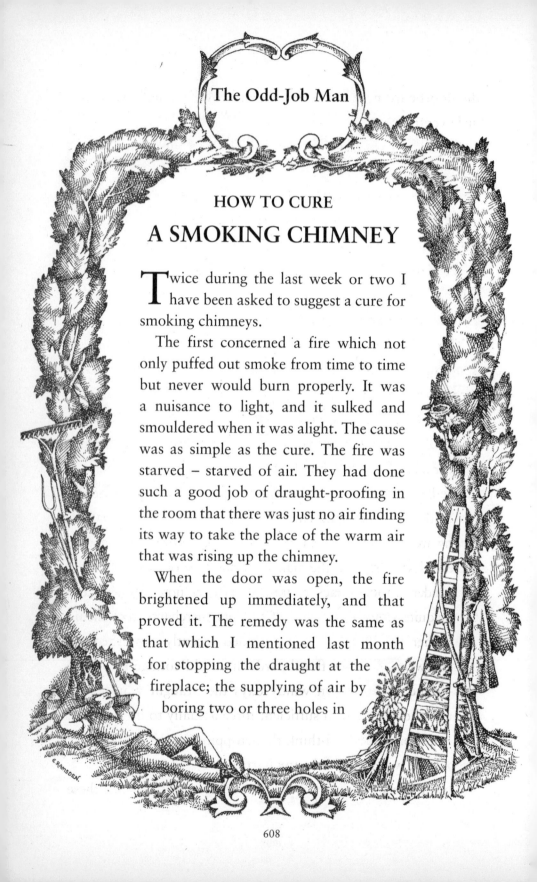

HOW TO CURE

A SMOKING CHIMNEY

Twice during the last week or two I have been asked to suggest a cure for smoking chimneys.

The first concerned a fire which not only puffed out smoke from time to time but never would burn properly. It was a nuisance to light, and it sulked and smouldered when it was alight. The cause was as simple as the cure. The fire was starved – starved of air. They had done such a good job of draught-proofing in the room that there was just no air finding its way to take the place of the warm air that was rising up the chimney.

When the door was open, the fire brightened up immediately, and that proved it. The remedy was the same as that which I mentioned last month for stopping the draught at the fireplace; the supplying of air by boring two or three holes in the floorboard next to the hearth, and covering the holes with a little ventilator grid.

The other case wasn't so simple. The fire burned well unless the wind was in a certain direction – but if a fire was lit at this time the room filled with smoke in five minutes. It turned out to be a case of down-draught by deflection. In plain English, that means that the chimney pot is below the level of something else in the vicinity. The result is that the wind comes along, hits this other object, is knocked sideways down the chimney and blows a cloud of smoke out into the room.

This object may be a taller building, a tree, or even the side of a hill; or it can be caused by the roof itself, if the chimney stack comes out at the eaves and the top of it isn't a good bit higher than the rider. In this last case you can cure the trouble by adding to the height of the chimney, but you can't put up a twenty-foot chimney to clear a tree, or a two hundred-foot chimney to clear a hill.

The best way is to fit a chimney pot or cowl specially made to deal with down-draught. These are made in such a way that the downward current of air is turned into an upward current, and so successful are they that the makers of one type of cowl promise a cure under a money-back guarantee. They're not very dear, and they're quite simple to fix, and all builders' merchants stock them.

Another job that had to be tackled recently concerned the gaps between the wide floorboards in an old cottage belonging to a friend of mine. On windy days the draught whistled up through these gaps with sufficient force actually to lift the rugs. The question was: did I think that stopping up the air bricks in the outside walls would do any harm?

Now I think that's always a bad thing to do. In fact, these

air bricks should be kept quite clear. They're the best insurance against dry rot, because this pest just won't develop where there is a through current of air.

As far as the gaps are concerned, they are best filled up. As these boards were of oak I had some thin strips of oak ripped at the timber yard and planed them to fit the gaps. I made them a little thinner at the lower edge so that they wedged tightly as they were driven home with a touch of glue.

W.P.M.

WHAT EVERY COOK
SHOULD KNOW ABOUT

SNIPE AND WOODCOCK

The trouble about woodcock is the difficulty of getting quite enough of them at one time except in Southern Ireland. It follows from this that the bulk of receipts for woodcock incorporate a good deal of extraneous matter in order to "stretch" the bird to an adequate dish for a good appetite. As for snipe, the same argument applies, and the odd snipe or brace of snipe are an entrée of merit but no complete meal for a sportsman.

Both birds are the better for a little hanging, but do not hang as long as other game as they are cooked with their insides in, and these ripen moderately rapidly. The French hang a woodcock by his neck over a clean white plate. The moment a single drop of blood appears on the plate, the bird is raced to the kitchen. If they are hung too long, plucking without tearing the skin is not an easy operation.

Roast woodcock is the simplest and, I think, the best receipt. Pluck carefully, including the head and neck, remove only eyes and crop (this is just opened). Cook in butter with lavish basting. A moderate oven is best as the bird needs cooking all through, and a high oven will tend to overcook the outside before the inside is done. Almost continuous basting is necessary for perfection.

Prepare two deep rounds of toast and cut off the crusts. These must be big enough to serve as a mattress for the bird. When done, pour the butter and juice of the bird on to these, place the bird on them, and serve the toast on to which you spoon the insides of trail with each half of the bird. Technically, one should have a rum butter sauce sharpened with a little lemon juice and cayenne, but many people will prefer a little clear gravy with the lemon and cayenne.

The traditional woodcock pie is a matter of a brace of cock blanketed in fillet steak, chopped bacon and onion rings, and covered with a light piecrust. It is doubtful if it is practical in this country under "Planned Economy" of rations, but a woodcock, oyster and mushroom pie may be practical. The birds are quartered and the trail chopped and mixed with bacon dice, a cupful or so of stock, the oysters in halves and the mushrooms in quarters, is added. A little wine and lemon juice will adjust the sharpness and a little onion might be advisable. The piecrust takes the place of the traditional toast.

The problem of the single snipe admits only one solution. Like the woodcock, he is not drawn and customarily has the head and neck left on. I think it best to remove these and the legs, and, choosing a large and shapely potato, scoop out both sides to form a suitable box or coffin for the bird and some extra butter. If the potato is halved across its diameter much will leak, but it is possible to find one of more convertible shape which is preferable. Bake your buttered snipe in the potato.

With adequate snipe, roasting is best, and four birds can be threaded on two long skewers with a roll of bacon between each. In this way the whole array can be turned and both sides well basted. They will take about a quarter of an hour, and should be served on toast with the basting butter as with woodcock. Lemon slices and a bedding of watercress are traditional.

Snipe au choux is basically the same as *Partridge* and *Pheasant au choux*, but as the cabbage takes longer to cook than these little birds the cabbage should be cooked in stock first, and it is better that this should be a stock flavoured with game to which the chopped trails of the snipe are added when the birds are put in.

They will take about a quarter of an hour, when the dish should be drawn aside and a little lemon juice and white wine added.

Actually, white wine and snipe agree very well indeed, and a quick and excellent way of cooking snipe is to fry up four chopped shallots and a small fragment of garlic in butter in the bottom of a stew pan. When these turn brownish (but not burnt) add your snipe and turn them to brown slightly so as to seal in the juices. Then add a breakfastcup of white wine and about a tablespoonful of dried breadcrumbs. Stir up and simmer with the lid on for five minutes. Move to the side and, if necessary, spoon out the trails into the sauce. Cook for a further five minutes or less. Add to taste a very little lemon juice and a trace of cayenne and serve on rounds of fried bread or plain toast.

In general, the flavour of both woodcock and snipe is individual and pronounced, and if it is necessary to "stretch" a dish for family use, either diced chicken or even diced rabbit added to any four of the above braises or stews produces a very good dish.

The old mixture of snipe fried in bacon fat with cakes of fried mashed potato done at the same time in the same fat is still a good country favourite. A rather unusual version is snipe and parsnips. The latter are cut in thin fingers, like fried potatoes, after boiling, and fried with the snipe in bacon fat. It is voted particularly good even by those who shudder at the word parsnip.

H.B.C.P.

IN PRAISE OF CIDER

In the West Country in this month of November the last harvesting is under way. Many of the farms around our house in Devon still have their traditional orchards of cider apple trees, and at this time of the year the fruit is being gathered in for the presses.

Wind is the enemy of the grain crops, but apple-gathering is helped by the boisterous autumn gales, which do the work of stripping the trees. Most of the orchards I know are gnarled and ancient, the trees bearded with grey lichen, their branches unpruned and unkempt like an old tramp's hair. The ground is carpeted with the small apples, some of which have been lying for many weeks. The whole orchard scene is derelict, and it is difficult to believe that both profit and pleasure lie in the bruised fruit under the twisted trees.

In our house we have only taken to keeping barrelled farm cider within the last two years, after we had been offered some to taste in a local inn. We accepted a glass only because it would have given offence to refuse, for we had never much cared for the sweet bottled cider nor the draught cider of the factories. This farm product, however, was a different drink. It was a turgid, honey-coloured liquid, rich in body, which could no more be swallowed in haste than could a full-bodied wine. It tasted smooth, yet with an underlying tang which robbed it of sickliness. It was as near an apple liqueur as we could imagine.

After our first sample drink we came to buy for ourselves, and found that the price was as low as tenpence a pint, where a decent beer was, perhaps, one and sixpence. I apologised one day to my friend the landlord for spending so little money, but he assured me that he made as much profit out of the cider as he did out of the beer, for, remarkable in these days to relate, there was no duty on it.

We did not for some time buy a barrel to take home with us, for we had been told that cider did not keep. A neighbouring farmer pooh-poohed this tale, and said that the drink would keep as long as it was likely to be required to do so – here he gave a heavy wink – provided we obeyed two rules: we must keep the barrel cool, and, most important, we must exclude air from its interior as much as possible. Boldly, we carted back one day a nine-gallon keg from the cellar of my friend the innkeeper.

I will not say how long the keg lasted us, but I had no trouble with it. I drilled a vent in the top, plugged it with a wooden peg, and then banged the wooden tap, bought from the ironmongers, in the end bung. I cut a felt pad, with a hole left for the vent-plug, and laid it over the barrel, like a saddlecloth. I kept the pad moist, and, on the principle of the felt-covered army water-bottle, the evaporation cooled the cider. It was not possible, of course, entirely to exclude air from the barrel, but I cased the vent-plug only just enough to allow the tap to run, and rammed it tight home when my jug was nearly filled, so that the last trickle induced a partial vacuum.

Many a barrel has followed that first one into a cool corner of our dining-room, and none has ever gone off condition.

We and our friends were used to beer as a long drink, and the cider caused us to revise our habits. We became accustomed to its effects, but it plays tricks with the novice. He may be a seasoned ale-drinker, but two pints of farmhouse cider is usually enough for him. The trouble is that he does not find out that he has treated the brew too lightly until he attempts to rise on leaving. His head has remained perfectly clear, but his legs take no notice of any orders from his brain. The result is diverting to the onlookers, but humiliating to the novice.

However, if a man is working hard in the sun, he may quench his thirst with copious draughts of cider, quart upon quart if he wishes, and take no harm. Hereabouts at harvesting, a keg always lies in the shade of the hedge, and its contents never survive the day. Yet the harvesters do not become slap-happy with pitchforks, nor do they fall asleep in the rick-yard, as they might after access to free beer.

I now buy my cider direct from a farm. Unfortunately, as with the practice of so many of the old crafts, home cider-making is on the decrease. Most farmers now sell a large proportion of their apples to the factories and do not make much more of the drink than they need for their own use. Gathering, pressing and barrelling take a good deal of labour at a time when the winter ploughing is on hand, and few farmers at this time of high wages keep any surplus hands for such semi-luxuries. However, most of them will make some extra if a private buyer has a word with them in good time during the summer. They will store the new liquor through the winter, and have it ready matured for collection by the next spring. At present the price is something less than four shillings a gallon.

I have found that cider improves up to an age limit of three years, becoming smoother and stronger, but it must be well made and well kept if it is not to be vinegary at that age. It is perhaps safer to broach it at twelve months.

T.F.

PUTTING THE GARDEN TO BED

I have always regarded November as one of the most important months of the gardening year. For the rose and shrub enthusiasts it often involves considerable hard work. Deciduous and evergreen shrubs, ornamental trees, top and bush fruits, and roses, all have a decidedly better chance to establish themselves if planted by the end of November. Should this be impossible, it is usually better to postpone the balance of work until late February. December and January may well be cold, wet months and root action consequently slow.

It is often claimed that the best time for transplanting shrubs is in the spring. Surely, to make a start when faced with the cold, drying winds associated with late March and April, is a far more tricky business than in early autumn, when weather and soil conditions are often just right? If, however, you garden on cold, wet land (not to mention very heavy ground), it is advisable to defer planting until spring, or rather, any time from late February onwards.

Text-books are frequently chary about recommending November planting for herbaceous perennials. In my experience you are perfectly safe in planting up to mid-November on light land. There are, however, certain herbaceous plants which resent autumn moving, irrespective of soil and locality. They include achillea, anthemis, Michaelmas daisies of the Amellus group such as King George and Moerheim Gem, chrysanthemum maximum (the white Ox-Eye or Shasta daisy), pyrethrums and scabious.

If you are in a cold district, nepeta or catmint, though seemingly indestructible, is best shifted in spring. Gaillardias have a knack of disappearing in winter, though if planted early this month and protected from slugs by a mound of ashes and if necessary a proprietary slug bait, they will often survive with no apparent discomfort. If you like gaillardias (and they are among the finest of all herbaceous perennials for cutting), try the new Wirral Flame, which is a real colour break. The catalogue description "rich ox-blood red, tipped with gold on edge of petals" is no exaggeration.

Apart from the planting question, there isn't really much to do in a herbaceous border at this time. Thinning the shoots of plants such as Michaelmas daisies is left until early spring. Faded blooms and stems are, of course, always cut off, but foliage should not be removed until it has ceased to function. Plants like irises and Kniphofias which are virtually evergreen, must be left alone.

Don't choke your plants with farmyard manure in autumn. Far better to mulch them with this material in spring or early summer, when prolonged dry weather often sets in. The same applies to rose beds, which used to be covered with layers of farmyard manure spread thickly on the surface in late autumn, on the assumption that the trees liked to be warm and cosy during the winter months. This was, I am sure, quite unnecessary. Most plants are a good deal hardier than is commonly supposed. They dislike cold winds, drought, poor drainage, excessive wet, far more than sharp frosts. Bonemeal is relatively slow acting and established borders may be top-dressed now at the rate of 4-6 oz. per sq. yd. If your soil needs lime, November is a good month for application, though on light land where ground chalk is sometimes more effective, it is probably better to wait until early spring.

Top and bush fruits (mulberries excepted) are best planted in November. They are, however, more accommodating than herbaceous plants and can be moved throughout autumn and winter, provided the soil is neither frozen nor sticky. Have you ever tried to grow the mulberry?

Once established, mulberries are seldom attacked by insect pests or fungus diseases, require very little pruning and no feeding save a mulch of farmyard manure in dry summers. We now come to the drawbacks! The long, fleshy roots dislike transplanting and must not be cut back or they may bleed and cause the tree to collapse. If planting is undertaken in late October or the first half of November and a warm well-drained soil with a good water-holding capacity is chosen, success is possible. If early autumn planting is impracticable, wait until February.

If you are thinking of putting in some raspberries I strongly recommend Malling Promise. It is an exceptionally vigorous grower and a very heavy cropper, even on light, dry land. Plant this variety a good 3 ft. apart and allow 6 ft. between rows. I used to regard Malling Promise as inferior in flavour to some of the older varieties, but I must have forgotten that plenty of sunlight improves the flavour of all fruits. Last summer was very dry and sunny compared with the continuous rains in 1951, when the berries tasted slightly acid. The same fruits in 1952 were quite sweet. Malling Promise makes about the best raspberry jam I have yet tasted. Pyne's Imperial is another good variety for jam, though in my experience the flavour when gathered for dessert is inferior to Malling Promise.

N.P.H.

Dung at the Door

As the garden settled for its winter rest, we reviewed the year gone by with quiet pleasure. The rich, workable earth of the borders and beds, so little resembling the clay from which it originated, had given us a happy and satisfying season all round, on a diet of compost.

In a garden such as ours, a colourful homely garden for our personal enjoyment, rather than one for a specialist or connoisseur, we find that a good helping of compost usually suffices as food and humus for two out of every three years. The compost we make contains no chemicals or artificial stimulants, but, rotting entirely through the progress of time, it includes all the goodness that oak roots can draw from the depths of the earth and deposit in their prolific leaves on our garden.

But if the soil is to keep giving of its best it must be fed in rotation with animal and vegetable fertilisers, which meant a load of farmyard manure for us this year. Almost as if thought were father to the act, a lorry drove up to the door.

It was a large lorry, containing, we were told, six cartloads of bullock manure which, for a general purpose, is little inferior to cow dung, and was about the right amount for our size of garden.

Farmyard dung can be used as fresh as it comes and do nothing but good, which cannot be said for any other kind of manure. But speaking personally, I would not want my garden to be littered with undecayed straw, and I would always wait to use it at least until the straw was well rotted in, unless, of course, the ground was unusually deficient in humus. During the decaying process the pile will be steaming, and when it no longer steams it will have finished "working." That is when it is at its best. Like brandy in bottles it will not go on improving with age, but (unlike the brandy) will very gradually lose something as it becomes more dry.

Our lorry load was not at the peak of freshness most desired, but unmistakably it *was* well rotted manure, and as it was shovelled out, we could see that it really was quite moist enough. An inspection first thing the next morning, when any dung will greet the dawn most pungently, revealed that it also had the right kind of smell.

The pile was quickly spread. There was no part of the garden that did not receive its share, whether lying vacant, rough dug for the spring, or with crops already growing; nowhere was any harm done.

Had the load been of pig dung, which contains a rich amount of ammonia, any growing plant would probably have been scorched by this treatment. Pig is a manure that is particularly good for building up a light soil and is perfectly all right used in preparing vacant land for future planting, just so long as it is left long enough to lose its heat.

There would be no mistaking a load of pig dung at the door. It is the most powerfully and unpleasantly scented dung of all.

Horse manure is similar to pig in that it contains a good deal of ammonia and is dangerous to use fresh because of its burning qualities. But when well rotted it is the next best thing to cow dung, and half rotted it will lighten heavy soils. There is no mistaking horse manure; it smells exactly like the stables.

Chicken droppings, as such, are unlikely to appear in a lorry for sale at your door, and would be recognised if they were, but, because they are so rich in nitrogen, they are worth mentioning. Used as a top dressing they are wonderful, if you can bear the smell, but they are definitely dangerous to dig into the ground.

Perhaps their greatest value lies in putting them on the compost heap. There their heat helps quick decomposition ... and kills seeds ... weed seeds.

M.H.

A FRIENDLY SLUG

If, during the winter digging, or moving some stones, you come across a pale putty-coloured slug two or three inches long, have a good look at it before you take its life. This may be one of the *Testacellidae* (or shelled slugs) and if so it never touches vegetation, but preys on other insects, including snails and smaller slugs. These shelled slugs are not often seen, because their carnivorous habits take them a long way underground, hunting insects in their own burrows, and during the winter they bury themselves deeply in earth or go into hibernation beneath stones.

Probably the most common of this species is *Testacella haliotidea*, which, when fairly closely examined, will be seen to have a small, light-coloured shell covering its "tail." This is its chief distinguishing mark from slugs which eat the greenstuff, though it is rather different in shape also. Instead of having the powerful shoulders and slim rear of our familiar salad eaters, *Testacella* has a tapering neckline and becomes "broad in the beam" at the shell end of its body. (Actually this is a protection for its breathing apparatus.) It is, however, probably the colour which first attracts the attention, for there is something about the pale buff colour, with its clearly defined pattern, which makes it look a little different from other slugs.

There is also another species of shelled slug in this light colour, though being more speckled than *T. haliotidea*. A third species is dark brown. But all *Testacella* slugs have this in common: they carry a shell on their rear as a signal to gardeners to leave them alone.

C.M.

HOME HINTS

HOME-MADE WINE: "Home-made wines," says an old cookery book of the last century, "would be found particularly useful, now that the foreign wines are so high-priced, and they may be made at a quarter the expense," The author goes on to say that "they should be kept for six to seven years ... and would cause a very considerable reduction in the expenditure."

Today, recipes do not call for quite so long a time in storing, but the reduction in "the expenditure" is still considerable.

The necessary equipment is: a wooden cask for storing. (If this cannot be had, a stone ginger-beer bar, with a tap, is the next-best thing.) A wooden tub, for the mixture to ferment in, or a large china basin. Do not use glazed earthenware, or metal or enamelled pans. All are unsuitable for wine making. Have a large wooden spoon, or a rolling pin, for mashing the material, a clean cloth for filtering, and a funnel for use in bottling the finished wine.

If root vegetables are used, parsnips for example, they should be cooked first until soft. Fruit should be sliced, uncooked, and left to soak. Any material, after these preliminaries, is put to soak in water, a gallon to every 7 lb. of fruit or vegetables, and left for three days or more, with an occasional stir.

When fermentation starts, leave undisturbed, until a crust has formed all over the top, and keep covered with a cloth or a loosely fitting lid. This process should go on as a rule for ten to fourteen days. Now skim, strain through a clean cloth, and measure. Add sugar – 3 lb. to every gallon – and dissolve. Strain again into a wooden cask or stone jar and leave to work for another fortnight. While the working goes on the wine will overflow from time to time, so keep back a little extra wine to make up the overflow. When the working is over, the wine may be bottled, corked, and laid away to rest for at least a year – more if you can bear it. Generally speaking, a year or eighteen months is enough. Often a small piece of yeast, spread on a scrap of bread, is added to help the wine to work.

Here is a recipe for crab apple wine:

7 lb. crab apples
3 lb. sugar
I gallon water
6 cloves

Slice the apples, unpeeled and uncored, and lay them in water. Let them soak for a fortnight, stirring well until they begin to ferment. Then leave for three days undisturbed. Strain, add sugar and cloves and allow the sugar to dissolve. Strain into a cask or jar, add the cloves, and leave to work for a fortnight, with a cloth laid over the top. Pour off, strain into a stone jar with a tap and cork the jar tightly. After three months, strain into bottles, cork, and keep for at least a year.

M.B.R.

WHAT EVERY COOK
SHOULD KNOW ABOUT

A CUT OF VENISON

In these days a substantial joint of venison is rather an "occasion" and if it runs to a haunch it may involve a visit to one's bank to dig out the appropriate plate on which to serve it, for it is long since small families have seen such a massive joint of real meat!

Actually "venison" may be red deer, stag or hind or it may be fallow deer or doe or even roe. From a culinary point of view these are all slightly different but the general treatment is much the same. As a rule the gift arrives in a hamper or in sacking and presents a somewhat barbaric appearance when unpacked. The keeper who performs the dissection is not always as neat an artist as a professional butcher and the joint may look a bit unfamiliar and be in need of trimming up.

The first question is, when will it be ready to eat? This is a variable factor and if you do not hang the meat long enough it will be tough and tasteless, if you retain it too long it will develop rather more "bouquet" than most palates appreciate. If inexperienced, the best thing to do is to ask your butcher to keep the joint for you in his cold room and to give you his opinion when it is likely to be at its best.

Now most venison, and particularly stag venison, has a perceptible smell. Travel in hot weather accentuates it and many a good joint has been wrongly condemned as being "too high" for consumption, or tainted. The proper treatment is to sponge the joint over with a little Milton and water, dry off and hang it in loose muslin where there is free circulation of air.

The saddle is a rather more manageable joint than a full-sized haunch, for the latter will not go into the average gas oven without being cut down to several smaller joints. Years ago I brought down a haunch from Scotland for a club dinner and it was too big for the club oven. Rather than reduce its magnificence, the steward arranged for it to be cooked in a neighbouring baker's. This was convenient as the haunch had to be cooked in a covering of flour-and-water dough. It was an enormous success – and there was enough of it!

A haunch needs at least three hours in a good oven as the paste coating adds to the cooking time. With the possible exception of a "yeld hind" venison is not as a rule fat and small joints are all the better for being larded frequently with pork fat or the fat of a mild bacon. The sauce or gravy to go with venison is a well-reduced stock made for preference out of venison trimmings and reinforced with a spoonful of redcurrant jelly and a good glass of port. Currant jelly or apple sauce with a few cranberries added are excellent accompaniments. For smaller portions of venison, rather the classic banqueting joints, I think that a pot roast or braise is more suited to present times. Very often these portions consist of a good deal of bone and trimmings. Inspection may show that the best of the meat can be artfully cut away from the bone and then treated either as a fillet or in smaller portions as "tournedos" or small steaks. I think this is also the best way with portions of shoulder, for venison needs to be eaten hot and is not very attractive as cold joint; so either a stew or braise which can be re-warmed, or manageable portions like small steaks or fillets, represent the best investment.

The general treatment is much the same as for equivalent portions of beef, but accompanied by higher-flavoured gravies or sauces and "sweet-sour" effects. For a sound venison dish cut the meat off the bone in substantial pieces. Colour these in hot fat or oil to seal and brown them. In the same fat cook two large sliced onions to a very light brown, remove and drain carefully. Three sliced carrots are cooked a little further. Chop two cupfuls of celery and place all these vegetables in a casserole. Add two bay leaves, peppercorns, three cloves, thyme and parsley. On this place the venison. Add stock, which is best made out of the bones and trimmings of the venison, and half a bottle of claret or a quarter bottle of port. Seal down the lid of the casserole and first let it cook very slowly for three hours. Before serving pour off the gravy in the casserole, de-grease it and judiciously taste, adding redcurrant jelly and possibly a little more port.

Both celery and chestnuts are good seasonable accompaniments to any form of venison but a good dish of grilled, stuffed tomatoes can be well accompanied by venison steaks "minute." A very little olive oil is put in a thick frying pan and heated till it just smokes. The venison steaks which should not be more than three-quarters of an inch thick are dropped into the pan, turned quickly to prevent sticking and to seal the other side and kept in motion for one minute, no more. The process creates some smoke in the kitchen but it should produce a perfectly cooked steak, brown outside and underdone but not raw within. It is, I think, wise to let the steaks get warmed through – but not to cooking point – before they are dropped in the pan.

In addition to the conventional wine sauce for venison, any of the sharp sauces go well. A tartare made with chopped pickled shallots is excellent and any form of piquante sauce can be improvised from what is to hand.

Offals such as kidney and liver are the perquisite of the ghillie – but if you do chance on them they are most excellent eating; for as worthy Dr. Fuller observes: "Deer when living, arise the stomachs of the gentleman with their sport; and when dead, allay them again with their flesh."

H.B.C.P.

THE NATURALIST

SEALS

If seals had legs instead of flippers there would be no dogs. Seals are very affectionate and intelligent, and completely charming; if only they lived on land we could get to know them properly, and then the dogs would be eclipsed. But recent work has added much to our knowledge of them.

Two sorts of seals live on the British coasts, the Common Seal that is uncommon in most places, and the allegedly rare Atlantic or Grey Seal that is common in many. The Wash is the headquarters of the Common Seal on the coasts of England and Wales, and there the herd numbers some thousand to fifteen hundred; the Grey Seal abounds on the coasts of Pembrokeshire and its islands, of north Devon and Cornwall, the Scillies, and the Farne Islands.

Although seals spend most of their lives at sea they have to come ashore for breeding; the young must be born on land. The Common Seal likes a low shore with plenty of dry sandbanks at low tide; and on the sandbanks the females bring forth their young. The pups are precocious; they must be, for within twelve hours of their birth, at most, the tide returns and they have to swim off and follow their mothers in the water. It is unlikely that lactation lasts less than several weeks.

The Grey Seal is different, for the pups spend two or three weeks on land before they are weaned. The Greys like a rocky shore where towering cliffs make the pebbly beaches and deep sea-caves inaccessible to man. There, in the autumn, the cows haul out to give birth to their pups, and shortly afterwards the bulls join them to start the next generation for the following season – gestation takes nearly a year.

Grey Seal pups grow at a surprising rate; they weigh about thirty pounds when they are born and three weeks later, when nursing is over, they weigh about ninety pounds, a gain in weight of about three pounds daily. No wonder. Seal milk is thick and viscous, and analysis shows that it contains over *70 per cent. of solids and over 50 per cent. of fats*; ordinary cow's milk averages about 3 per cent. of fats, and the richest samples do not exceed 10. And the cow seal manages this while she is fasting, for she herself does not feed, even if she goes to sea, between the feeding times for her baby.

A team of naturalists spent the last two seasons studying the Grey Seal at its breeding beaches; we captured a female and her pup and kept them under daily observation. We were at once surprised by the docility with which the female accepted captivity and the presence of man. She was either very stupid, or else very intelligent and felt that we meant her no harm. Within a day we could pat her head and pull her whiskers and take all sorts of liberties with her.

We weighed her and her pup daily and found that the pup gained about three pounds while she lost about four and a half pounds a day, a daily net loss to the whole system of about a pound and a half. This extraordinary transfer of material from mother to pup was made from the thick layer of blubber under her skin; the blubber was made into milk and transferred to the baby, who turned it back into blubber again and built up a thick layer under its own skin. The cow weighed about four hundred pounds when her pup was born, and about ninety pounds less at the end of three weeks.

It was easy to get samples of milk for analysis; the cow has two teats and when the pup was suckling at one a breast-pump drew off as much as was required from the other. The milk looks like cod liver oil emulsion – and tastes like it too, having a sickly fishy flavour.

The new-born pups are clothed in a thick coat of white fluffy fur, very soft and silky. This baby-coat is moulted by the end of three weeks to disclose the first coat of steel-grey hair. The fluff flies out like thistle-down if you touch it. The moult may start even before birth, so that the new-born pup may have some grey patches on its face, or it may not start for a week or more. When the pup is weaned the hitherto devoted mother suddenly deserts it, and leaves it to finish its moult alone on the beach. The pup does not at once go to sea to find its own food, but stays on land for a week or two.

Although the pup can swim quite well at birth it does not venture to sea, for it cannot cope with the roaring Atlantic surf. Whenever a gale sends the swell raging up the beach the pups that are not safely high and dry are drowned or pounded to death on the pebbles.

When the pups are moulted and weaned they go to sea after a period of several weeks fasting on the beach. Last autumn Miss Grace Watt marked a number of young seals on the Farne Islands with metal tags, much like the rings used for marking birds. She expected to find that any of these seals that might be seen again would be reported from somewhere nearby. But to everyone's surprise one of these youngsters, not much over a month old, was found within a fortnight near Bergen on the coast of Norway.

This discovery raises a host of new questions about the Grey Seal, which was thought to be a rather sedentary animal of the coasts. If a youngster can travel so far, who knows where the adults may go? The more we study these fascinating creatures the more we realise how little we know about them.

L.H.M.

LETTER TO THE EDITOR

THE ANGRY JACKDAW: As I was looking out of my bedroom window one evening, I saw a little boy come along and pick up out of a ditch baby jackdaw. He took it out into the open to have a look at it more carefully, when one of its parents came hurtling out of a nearby tree, and landed on his shoulder. It then proceeded to peck him savagely on the top of the head, and consequently drew quite a lot of blood. Could James Fisher tell me if it is a usual thing or not for birds to guard their young in that manner?

IAN FINCH, Tokat House, Sible Hedingham
near Halstead, Essex

James Fisher writes: Mr. Finch should read the chapter on jackdaws in the remarkable book, "King Solomon's Ring," by Dr. Konrad Lorenz, recently published by Methuen's. This master of animal behaviour shows that the jackdaw has an innate disposition to recognise as an enemy any living creature carrying something black dangling or fluttering. This, in his words, "becomes the object of a furious onslaught; this is accompanied by a grating cry of warning whose sharp metallic echoing sound expresses, even to the human ear, the emotion of embittered rage." Dr. Lorenz describes an incident experienced by him very like that of Mr. Finch's little boy.

DECEMBER

WILD LIFE

Garden sounds this month. Winter song of the robin, hedge-sparrow, and now also the wren. From under the old bridge over the rocky stream comes the sweet warbling song of the dippers, both male and female alike, jerking, bowing, trembling and posturing like great wrens as they display to each other.

There are twenty-six regular winter bird visitors to Britain, all here in December, most of them waders and water-birds. Besides the glaucous and Iceland gulls, which come to us from the north, we get regular, if small, invasions of little gulls from Eastern Europe.

Our five winter Arctic waders – jack-snipe, turnstone, knot, purple sandpiper and grey plover – are in their expected haunts. Any big movements of these birds are due to the weather and are not truly migratory.

From the New World and Iceland comes a regular invasion

of great northern divers, mostly in evidence offshore along our coasts, feeding in shallowish water; occasionally examples are blown to inland waters. Expect also a few red-necked grebes from Northern Europe.

The ducks, which are primarily winter visitors, are two which nest in holes in trees in Lapland and other parts of the conifer-growing Arctic, and two sea-ducks. The tree-ducks, which are also to a great extent sea-ducks, are the goldeneye and smew, the former being much the commoner.

The sea-ducks are long-tailed duck and velvet scoter. Both have been suspected of breeding in northern isles of Britain, the former probably truly; but they are normally offshore wild-fowl of winter, diving for molluscs along many parts of the coast.

List of winter wildfowl is completed by geese and swans, which come mostly from north of the Arctic Circle, or the upland wildfowl grounds of Iceland and Northern Europe. Among these are the black geese, brent and barnacle, the latter breeding only in the high Arctic, the bean-geese and pink-feet, which are supposed to be of the same species, the white-fronts from Northern Russia and Greenland, Bewick's swan from Russia and the whoopers from Iceland.

Our list of pure winter visitors is closed by one bird of prey, the rough-legged buzzard, and the half-dozen passerines I mentioned in my notes last month. But undoubtedly the chief attraction of the month is winter herds of wild geese; though these make more substantial weather movements from one great estuary to another than has been supposed, December catches them most stable in their habits and at their highest numbers.

J.F.

For some months now those lovely Scandinavian thrushes, the fieldfares and redwings, have been with us, but it is on our Christmas walks, I find, that we best become familiar with them. Though on the hedges, naked except for their berries, the birds are easy to see, it is often their note that draws attention to them. The harsh chattering and scolding turns your head, and then you see the big fieldfares with their grey heads and rumps and their chestnut backs. Almost any berries will do for fieldfares – hips, haws, holly, rowan. They will even eat yew berries, which are poisonous to some animals. Redwings eat berries, too, though it takes hard cold weather to make them eat as many kinds as the fieldfare does. Very often the first encounter of redwings is the quiet rush of a flock's wings as it drifts from hedge to thicket, and with it we hear a gentle, almost whispering, *see-you see-you*.

A waxwing warning is worth while this month, as invasions of this agreeable bird from Scandinavia certainly appear to be getting more frequent, and one is due any winter now; although they're irregular and follow no cyclical rule. When waxwings do come, they often arrive as early as October, but if they've not come by Christmas it doesn't mean the invasion is off. The great arrival of '46-47 didn't warm up till December, that of '48-49 not till January. The Bohemian chatterer (the old books called it that) is another berry-eater. Crested, a subtle brown, not quite as large as a thrush; the tail has a yellow tip, its wings have white, yellow and red markings – these last, tips to inner flight feathers which make them look as if they'd been dipped in wax. When they work the hedges they wheeze, click, crackle and stutter.

Last important invasion was in winter of '49-50, so accurately reported by John and Christina Gibb. The first bird arrived on October 28th; a little under 2,000 detectable individuals were eventually recognised, which compares with about 12,500 in the great invasion of '46-47 and about 200 in the little one '48-49.

This month's extract from Gilbert White: "Dec. 1, 1775. Many species of flies come forth. Bats are out, & preying on phalaenae. The berries of Ivy, which blowed in the end of Sep.: now half grown. A noble & providential supply for birds in winter & spring! for the first severe frost freezes, & spoils all the haws, sometimes by the middle of Nov. Ivy-berries do not seem to freeze. *Footnote.* Large, grey, shell-less cellar-snails lay themselves up about the same time with those that live abroad: hence it is plain that a defect of warmth alone is not the only cause that influences their retreat."

J.F.

No sun, no moon, no stars, no noon, no proper time of day. Wild life seems to be in retreat from, or in alliance against, the no-ness of November. Those creatures which are not sleeping or hibernating often move gregariously in mixed flocks and packs for mutual protection, and stimulation in the hunt for food. Golden-crested wrens and the delicate long-tailed tits mingle with other titmice and wrens, tree-creepers and nuthatches in a straggling flock which drifts along hedgerow and wood, feeding on insects and seeds, keeping in touch with a medley of tinkling calls.

Flocks of lesser redpoles, goldfinches and siskins cling acrobatically to the tips of alder and birch, extracting the seeds from the mast. Linnets, chaffinches, greenfinches, bramblings and buntings in vast flights settle to feed in threshing yards and weedy fields, and at night roost in dormitories in evergreens, conifers, old thick hedges and reed-beds. Starlings join with rooks and daws in a noisy combined operation of scouring the grasslands, pitting the surface with stabbing bills and rolling forward in surf-like waves as the rearguard perpetually loops over to assume the advance position.

At sunset the starling flocks return from all points inwards to the roosting centre, and mass determinedly in shrubberies, reeds and city rooftops and façades, ignoring man's efforts to scare them away. Ravens, crows, rooks, jackdaws and magpies seek sleep, often together in large numbers, in the tops of high trees in deep woods.

Partridges are in strong coveys by day in the root-fields; by night they "jug" in the open. But the young pheasants, hitherto ground-roosting, fly heavily to favourite trees at dusk. Grouse form winter packs on the moors; they are fat with berries and the shoots of heather and heath plants. So are the ptarmigan of the high tops, now putting on white winter plumage. The hardy mountain hare has also changed its coat, and with snow and gale descends to less exposed ground; it seldom goes white – its blue winter dress is acquired by a genuine moult, not by a fading of hair-colour. Wood-pigeons are crowding in from the Continent, devouring beechmast, acorns, corn, seeds and brassica leaves.

When snow covers the riverside the otter's trail can be studied. Frequently it hastens by tobogganing along the level or a downward slope. Always it has special places for sliding in and out of the water; often these become play-places for the juveniles or well-fed contented adults, which race in and out of the river, whistling excitedly.

R.M.L.

THE VEGETABLE GARDEN

When the weather is really unspeakable and the fireside is the only possible place, time spent in studying seed catalogues and noting new varieties is never wasted. Do not be carried away by glowing descriptions. Seventy-five per cent. of the garden should grow trusted and well-known types and the other 25 per cent. can be used for experiments. When doing the seed list be quite certain to remember that some varieties are intended for early production and some for late. Avoid the temptation to order just one sort and leave it at that. For example, the short horn carrot is for early sowing and the medium for main crop. Intelligent seed buying makes it so much easier to maintain a good succession of tender vegetables. Plan your plots first, order your seeds after. Bear in mind that, roughly speaking, all brassicas like well-manured ground, and root crops do best in ground manured the previous year.

Continue with digging and manuring, provided the weather is suitable. Snow and frost must never be dug in, otherwise the ground will remain soggy until next spring. Leave the turned-over earth in largish lumps to enable the frost to get at it. Be strong-minded about removing unproductive fruit trees and old bushes which get in the way. These draw the ground over a large area and are quite useless. A dressing of basic slag is a help for ground which has been undisturbed for some years.

Picking vegetables in winter can be an agonising performance and in really hard weather must be done with care. Sprouts should never be touched with the frost on them. The buttons are brittle and break to pieces. Not only do hands freeze but it is bad for the plants. Cabbages may be cut in frost and snow but should be put in a warm shed for at least 12 hours to thaw out gently.

Keep an eye on roots stored in outdoor clamps. A covering of four inches of earth is necessary to keep out a really hard frost. Select some good established rhubarb crowns for forcing. Cover these with a good layer of straw and over this place a box or barrel with holes to provide air. At least three weeks can be gained by this method. Early mint and tarragon can be produced by planting in a box covered with a sheet of glass.

When cutting the endive which are being blanched, do not be put off by the appearance of an apparently rotten lump of leaves. The outside leaves are invariably almost putrid but the heart will be white and firm and excellent in flavour. On fine days – admit air to the frame but not light.

E.B.

THE FLOWER GARDEN

The gardener's year never ends, but the long winter evenings afford a short respite in which to assess the successes and failures of the past season and to plan for next year. The latest catalogues offer many novelties in addition to the older and well-tried favourites, many of which deserve to be more widely planted.

Trees and shrubs enjoy wide popularity due to the vast selection available and to the subsequent low upkeep costs. If they are carefully selected they give an admirable display throughout the year, although there is a tendency for the flower to be concentrated in the spring, leaving a comparatively duller summer period before the lovely autumn foliage and berries once more make the garden a blaze of colour. There are, however, many shrubs which flower in mid-summer, such as hydrangeas, fuchsias, hibiscus, potentillas, buddleias, Spanish brooms, ceanothus and hypericums, whilst much use can be made of the lovely clematis if supports are provided.

In all gardens the choice of shrubs with attractive foliage, whether it be shiny dark green, bronze or variegated, can do much to add colour to the shrub border. Where the soil is lime free, the interplanting of ericas will not only provide flower throughout the year but also keep down the weeds. Many summer flowers lend themselves to planting between the dwarfer shrubs, such as Thalictrum dipteriocarpum, Dierama pulcherrima Galtonia candicans, montbretia, Hosta glauca, peonies and the lovely Liliums, especially the new hybrid races. Interplanting of all kinds of bulbs adds to the spring display and in the winter the beautiful trunks of the white birches, Prunus serrula and Acer griseum always provide interest.

The popular herbaceous plants have almost all been improved in recent years, and Russell lupins and the new strains of delphinium are already well known. The new Symons-Jeune phlox should be in every garden, and three varieties, Magna Carta, Refinement and Cecil Hanbury, are outstanding. The new strains of kniphofias are not only in many shades but hold their flowers without fading until the whole spike is open; Wrexham Wonder and Samuel's Sensation are perhaps the best. The later-flowering Michaelmas daisies and outdoor chrysanthemums improve each year and are most valuable for extending the season and for providing cut flowers for the house. The blending of the colours is of primary importance in the herbaceous border and it is here that the silvery-leaved artemisias and salvias can be of considerable assistance.

C.P.

The pruning of trees and shrubs should begin this month. This operation does call for a knowledge of the character of the plant and its time of flowering, for indiscriminate pruning can only result in the loss of the shrub's full beauty. Established plants often need little attention except for the removal of dead wood and crossed branches, although a little thinning will help where growth has become too thick. Early-flowering shrubs such as Forsythias should not be pruned until after they have flowered, when they should be cut hard back in order to induce long flowering shoots for the following year. Young shrubs need careful training so that they grow into shapely adult plants, but their natural habit should be preserved. The danger of fungoid attack through the open wounds can be lessened by dressing all the larger cuts with coal tar. When pruning has been completed the beds may be carefully forked over, incorporating any rotting leaves or compost that is available, for although trees and shrubs grow with little attention, the addition of extra humus is amply repaid by their increased growth and beauty.

Root cuttings present an easy method of propagation of several popular plants which are otherwise rather difficult to increase. *Papaver orientale, Anchusa italica and Romneya coulteri*, to name just three plants which are in most gardens, are readily multiplied by this method. Select a few of the strongest roots and cut them into pieces about three inches long. Growth takes place from that portion of the root nearest the stem, and to ensure that this is inserted uppermost this end should be cut squarely and the base at an oblique angle. Boxes of well-drained soil should be used, inserting the roots just below the surface of the soil. If placed in a greenhouse they soon grow and can then be planted in cold frame until large enough to go into the garden.

Whenever the weather is suitable, vacant borders should be trenched, so that they have time to settle before they are needed for planting. Rough compost and fallen leaves can be used in the bottom of the trench preserving the more valuable manure for incorporation in the upper soil. New herbaceous borders especially require ample humus, for there is a rapid drain on the food reserves and the opportunity for retrenching only presents itself every three or four years.

Hard frosts usually become more prevalent towards the turn of the year and extra protection should be readily available for any doubtfully hardy plants. Much can be done by the use of straw, hessian sheets or branches of conifers and by the provision of windbreaks.

C.P.

There can be few garden lovers who are sorry to see the end of this disappointing year. The lack of sun and warmth spoilt the summer flowers and many vegetable crops, the fruit was damaged by the gales, and although the shrubs enjoyed the rain the soft growth they have made remains very prone to frost damage if the winter is severe. However we are all optimists in our gardens, and these failures will soon be forgotten and our thoughts full of new ideas for next year's display when we hope the sun will really shine.

It has been a most difficult year for the seedsman and as supplies are short there should be no delay in completing the seed order. Each year brings its crop of novelties and it is as well to experiment with some of these for they add interest to the garden and keep it up to date. For example the new

Excelsior strain of foxgloves is suitable for both the formal or wilder parts of the garden and their culture presents no difficulty to anyone.

Pruning is an art which appears to be largely misunderstood and you either get the enthusiast who cuts all his shrubs hard back regardless of variety or the gardener who leaves them severely alone. Of course the right path lies somewhere between these two, with a heavy leaning towards the natural growth of the plant for it is surprising how many shrubs really need little attention. The removal of dead wood, rubbing branches, and the prevention of a crowded centre is all that is required in most cases. As a general rule shrubs which blossom before June should be left until after flowering but others should be pruned whilst there is less to do elsewhere in the garden. The exact treatment often depends upon the personal taste of the owner; for instance, *Buddleia Davidii* cut to the ground will produce strong growths bearing large trusses of flower, but if treated more moderately a greater profusion of smaller flowers is the result. One thing is important, have a good sharp knife or secateurs, and do clean up any large wounds and paint them with gas tar.

The sharp frosts recorded in February should serve as a reminder that the coldest period of the year is approaching and that some of the doubtfully hardy plants may need extra protection. It is surprising what improved windbreaks can do to save a plant, whether they be of hessian, straw, bracken, conifer branches or any other material. Avoid tying the material tightly around the plant but rather allow an air space between it and the protective covering.

C.P.

SHOOTING

December is perhaps the greatest of all the shooting months: everything in season and, as yet, fair quarry even where the problem of next year's breeding stock must be considered. Admittedly serious summer rains put paid to the partridge season before it started in some parts of the country, but, generally, both partridge and pheasant shooting continues and more besides.

Pigeons fly to feed in vast flocks as fields are drilled or turn to greenstuffs – kale, rape and sprouts – when the land is bound by frost or covered with snow. Excellent shooting for the man with decoys. Shooting expenses may be cut if authority to shoot "harmful birds" is obtained from the farmer and an approach made to the Pest Officer who is entitled to issue cheap cartridges for this purpose. The roosting places of the birds offer fast sport of a different kind as dusk approaches. It is no easy thing to maintain a good average of kills as wary pigeons circle above tall trees; heavier shot sizes should be used, although No. 7 is still useful when you are decoying. A solid artificial decoy or a stuffed pigeon or two will help to bring the birds to roost more confidently. A long light sectional "lofting pole" is required to lift the decoys to the high branches.

Rabbits need to be killed off and there are few more sporting ways than by shooting them in the open after they have been "stunk out." Stinking should be done two days before the shoot and a mixture of paraffin, creosote and one or other of the proprietary repellents smeared on newspaper and pushed down the holes with a stick will ensure that the animals lie out. A spell of fine and frosty weather is ideal for this.

Wild ducks frequent many inland pools but the sporting opportunity they provide is all too often neglected. Normal practice seems to place the guns in cover round the pool so that the birds, once disturbed, fly out through a barrage of shots which rarely produces more than an odd bird in the bag. So much better to encourage the birds to rest by day and to organise occasional "flight shoots" in the early morning.

Flight shooting, at dawn, at dusk or under the moon, must never be overdone. When shooting ducks or geese on their feeding grounds the gunner should make a point of leaving before the last birds come in. In the same way ducks should be spared towards the end of the morning flight while geese should *never* be shot where they go to roost.

Feeding a marsh will enable it to attract far more birds than it would do under natural conditions. Geese and ducks will come to grain, rotting potatoes and paunches. Snipe, too, may be encouraged by vegetable matter left to rot in boggy places.

M.S.

———•·•———

About twenty-five years ago the dark-plumaged pheasant, or melanistic mutant, became common and achieved the rank of a Game Farm variety. This is to say you could put down melanistic eggs or poults; as it happened, I raised a number of them on a farm I owned, and for a year or two they predominated in the bag and spread fairly widely to adjoining shoots.

This year I was shooting as a guest over what was predominantly the same ground, though there have been local agricultural developments and some changes since my day.

Our instructions were to take pheasants early, for postwar experience had shown that the woodland did not seem to hold birds well in winter. Felling, and a rather spendthrift policy of cutting coppice and undergrowth, was thought to have altered the conditions. This may be so, but there was no "feeding" and none of those useful mounds of old chaff and weed seeds from the rick thrashings.

It has always been rather difficult to manage, as the coverts run into adjoining woodland, and some are hilly and have to be beaten downhill, which is contrary to the pheasants' ideas. They like to move uphill when disturbed.

Nevertheless, with the same number of guns and rather fewer beaters, the bag, rather to my surprise, was up to average, although I doubt whether we got more than half the birds up and over the guns.

The black mutant strain still showed but was down to a proportion which probably did not exceed about five per cent., and maybe even less. The inference is that the mutation in that particular area has bred itself out again, by persistent crossing, and that it is not a permanent mutation. A few darkish hens were difficult to judge but were closer to the versicoloured type of pheasant than the melanistic mutant. In general the predominant type was what is called the "Old English," rather than the lighter coloured "Chinese" birds. But it is probably time that there is, ornithologically speaking, only one pheasant and that many of the labels we attach to them are scientifically invalid – though convenient for descriptive uses.

The birds were, despite the year, in very fair condition but on the lightweight side. I have often noticed that pheasants stand a wet year well. Although we think of them as woodland birds, they originally came from the swamps and wet ravines of the Oxus and seem to carry on this convenient gene without mutation.

H.B.C.P.

FISHING

This is the month when our angling club really gets under way. Shorn of the fair weather brigade, the serious members set forth on a Sunday soon after dawn and travelling to distant waters cause havoc amongst the roach, pike and other fish who bear the misnomer "coarse." Since we are situated in a chalk stream area there is little local fishing. Only one pond, whose roach cannot escape, has provided sport in the immediate district. This year two owners of trout water have allowed us to attack the grayling. In return we are helping with the netting. What a splendid idea is this sharing with the less fortunate a river that hitherto has been barred to them.

Our experiment will be controlled. There will be a leader who will be responsible to see that trout are not injured and the parties at first will be small.

The fine-tackle roach man is just as expert as the average dry-fly man. I have tried to catch grayling with a gentle and failed miserably; not so the roach fisher, who, fishing with the finest gut, the smallest quill float and a great length of line, has had big bags even in shallow water. "Fine and far off" is his motto when confronted with a chalk stream. It is worth watching one of these artists at work. I have seen one of them "trot" his float twenty yards below him and catch a grayling under his own bank.

I usually spin for pike on the Sunday outings, because I know my shortcomings (and short patience) with a float or ledger. There is a rule "no spinning before lunch," this it seems I alone am privileged to break. Now that the weed is disappearing I enjoy casting a spoon and varying its speed to conform to the depth of the water and the obstacles it must pass over. I am sure pike prefer a fast travelling bait, though if it travels too fast they will miss it. I prefer a plain silver and brass spoon with a single triangle and no frills. The size can depend on the size of fish in the water. If a fish follows it do not in excitement stop winding in. Pretend nothing is happening, use self-control and only strike when you feel the fish.

Pike are kindly. If they fail to get a hold they will usually have another "go." Don't use a gut trace, but Piano or Alasticum wire.

I catch perch spinning, but the natural minnow fished on a ledger or (better) by "sink and draw" is much more effective. The perch is one of the best freshwater fish to eat. It tastes like sole and the flesh is firm and white. When *they* are on the feed, they commit suicide with such rapidity that I have seen a whole shoal (in one of the Tring reservoirs thirty years ago) surrender itself to a small boy (myself) lowering a hook and worm into the clear water inside a boathouse. On other days they are uncatchable.

R.B.

THE CHATELAINE

TEACHING KIDS TO RIDE

I believe in starting a girl riding a year before I would a boy. A girl's nerve at an early age is much stronger, although later on the situation is very often reversed.

I have a daughter and three sons. Caroline is the eldest – she rode before she walked. She started on a very old pony called Kitty, upon which we all hunted as children. I rode her until I was fourteen, when my legs grew too long.

Kitty was wonderfully wise through teaching so many children to ride. She took charge of the situation and played the part required of her according to the age and the experience of the child. If she was being nurse to a baby, she ambled along, quiet as an old sheep. If the child was older and needed more excitement, Kitty would sneeze and friskily tweak her nose as she tossed her head. She has gently bucked off children who were becoming too cocky; having grounded the child, she always stood still and began grazing in a nonchalant fashion, allowing herself to be caught and remounted. She went nicely in harness, pulling a little round trap, the kind Cornishmen call a jingle.

Our old Nanny liked taking the small children out driving, and learnt, rather inexpertly, to harness Kitty. She used to get into a dreadful muddle over this and very often the bit would be under Kitty's chin, but this made no difference. When it rained Nanny would get out of the jingle and walk beside the pony carrying an umbrella over its head.

Caroline's early riding was done in a wickerwork basket chair, which faced the pony's ears, and not sideways. It had a little platform for her feet, and she could sit up, strapped in, holding the reins as if driving. She started riding very young, but that was because we had Kitty, who was champing at the bit, longing to school a baby of the second generation.

As a general rule, I think that six is the right age for a girl to begin and seven for a boy (unless he shows a particular desire to begin earlier). The pony should be a narrow one. A Welsh pony is preferable to the more tubby Shetland. Ponies so often play up much more than horses do, as I have found out when riding my children's. All seemed so much easier when I was promoted from a pony to an old safety-pin of a hunter – a flea-bitten grey called Grey Dawn. Lord! How proud I was.

I believe in a child being given a pony which has to be pushed along without being a slug. In the first stages of learning to ride, it is best to have only a single rein to bother about, but as soon as possible I like a child to get used to the feel of two reins. If the pony has a light mouth, it is best to keep it in a plain snaffle with double reins to the rings of the bit.

The smartest and the most practical turnout for a boy or a girl is jodhpurs, a tweed coat, a polo-necked sweater, brown jodhpur boots and a hard black velvet hunting cap. The way children grow out of their jodhpurs is a real problem. They look terrible unless they are well fitting, and the discomfort of too tight or too big jodhpurs is horrid. The only solution is to evolve a system whereby one can hand down the outgrown garment to a smaller child and inherit a larger pair from some other source.

Riding manners must be learnt when very young. It is really maddening when children out of control cut in at jumps right under another horse's nose. Children should be taught how to open a gate and that the last one through must shut it. They should be given a well-balanced hunting whip with a horn handle and a screw in the bottom to help hold a gate, and they should be told never to call it a crop. Also impress upon them that they must not ride on when anyone has had a fall or is about to mount.

It is no good imagining that you are going to enjoy a good day's hunting if you are shepherding children. You will have to dedicate yourself to this role and just be a jog-around looker-on, taking cunning short cuts to see the hunt. You must let them go in front of you through gaps, and make room for them in gateways; it really is very nice and soothing for a change.

If children become nervous about riding, let them stop if they want to. Caroline went through a period of lost confidence through a pony who took too much of a hold out hunting. She developed a temporary complex about jumping anything that had a drop to it. At every tiny jump a nervous voice would squeak, "Need I jump it, Mummy? It's downhill."

Here are a few practical hints concerning the children's riding.

Don't let them carry a metal flask or sandwich case in their pockets. If they have a fall, these may break a bone. Send them out with a sandwich case and flask in a leather case, strapped to the saddle.

Have as little stuffing as possible in the saddle flaps. Safety stirrups that come open when the child falls are advisable for a beginner. *Riding*, by Cecil Aldin and Lady Hunloke, is a classic for children. Moss Bros. and New and Lingwood of Eton cut good jodhpurs and corduroy trousers (which can be worn for hacking with knee straps). Huntsman and Thomas both make excellent breeches. Children's jodhpur boots can be got at Moss Bros., Fortnum and Mason, Harrods, and Daniel Neal. Lock supplies the best hunting caps and bowlers, Swaine and Adeney for hunting whips and sandwich cases.

If a child really loves its pony, it will not be necessary to encourage the daily offerings of carrots, apples and the sacrificed lump of sugar. Let the pony run out in a field; the relationship is much better when the child catches up its own mount.

D.B.

I'VE GROWN A TREE FROM A NUT

I have in my garden a walnut tree. At one moment it's just a tree to visitors: a moment later it's an object of admiring curiosity. In between I have casually remarked: "I grew that tree from seed."

Quite a few people don't believe me at first, particularly when I add that it won't be twenty-four years old till November, 1955, for it is very definitely a large and well-built tree. Indeed, it seems such a fine and notable specimen that I have just been checking up on it.

To begin with, though the books say the walnut is rarely productive before twenty years, and the old proverb even has it that "he who plants a walnut tree expects not to eat of the fruits," my tree produced the first nuts in 1942, i.e. when only eleven years old, and has borne with increasing abundance ever since. Why, I could almost have planted it this present autumn and still "eaten of the fruits," even though minus the teeth to crack them. As to size, it measures 3 ft. 2 in. in girth at 3 ft. from the ground and 3 ft. 1 in. at 6 ft. Its spread is 35 ft. and would have been much more if we hadn't had to lop it back from overshadowing flower borders. And its height is now 32 ft. Not bad for a youngster just attaining its majority.

To digress for a moment, do you know how to measure the height of a tree? There are two methods: the geometrical and the domestic. For the former you must have an adjacent flat lawn on which you mark the point at which the shadow of the top of the tree falls at some suitable time of day. Next take a pole of an exactly measured length, say six feet, and, holding it absolutely vertical on the lawn, measure its shadow; then immediately afterwards measure the shadow of the tree from the estimated centre of the bole. The tree's height in feet will then be six times its shadow divided by the pole's shadow.

I personally used the alternative, or domestic, method, which is to send a younger daughter up the tree with a pole and a long string tied to the bottom end of it. She climbs high enough to hold the pole up so that its top is level with the topmost twigs, while the string, weighted, hangs vertically to the ground. Measure, subsequently, from the top of the pole to the point where the string touches the ground. I say subsequently, because at this juncture the younger daughter loses interest in the job in hand, starts pelting you with dead twigs and walnuts, reports excitedly on the coleoptera observable in crevices of the trunk and on the beauties of the view obtainable, considers building a hut up there to sleep in, and wonders how far she can crawl out along a branch without its breaking. At this point she has to be brought firmly down by threat of withholding the shilling which was her rock-bottom price for climbing up in the first place.

If starting off a walnut tree *ab initio* can hardly be called in my case planting for posterity – as every good gardener should – at least I have balanced out in other directions. For in middle age I began to plant a yew hedge from seed – a real gesture of longeval altruism.

To say I planted it is not strictly truthful; it was the birds who did the job in their own intimate fashion, while I collected and transplanted the baby seedlings as soon as they appeared in various corners of the garden. It gave me some idea of the large part birds play in seed dispersal; over a period of twelve years now I not only have my first yew hedge of fifty treelets – nearly three feet high in one or two places – but another even tinier one alongside a ten-foot high wall of macrocarpa – an insurance for my grandchildren against the macrocarpa dying off, as it has an illogical habit of doing. And in this newer hedge there are to date over eighty baby yews: in other words, in our not very big garden birds are responsible for eleven new yew trees every year.

Other trees which appear as seedlings in the garden with such regularity and profusion that we have to wage relentless war if we don't want to find ourselves living in the heart of a wood are ash and holly, though we possess neither of these as grown specimens. Our solitary Tree of Heaven also seems set on turning our small domain into a Forest of Heaven, while our sumach and white poplar, working on a home-based policy, send up positive jungles of youngsters from their spreading roots. There are at the moment some fifty of the latter, this year's crop only, at distances anywhere up to 40 feet from the parent, waiting to be dealt with. (Secateurs are useless; they grow again within a fortnight: the best weapon I've found is an Army entrenching tool.)

Of course, there are two old stand-bys, horse-chestnut and oak. The conker and the acorn are extremely easy to raise, the former being most rewarding because it is fairly swift-growing: the impatient young can see results. Indeed when my children were small we had to be rather firm about the number of trees that were started off every year, because, as other parents will appreciate, they can never, never be destroyed – "but, Daddy, I *grew* it – you just *can't*!" – though with the passage of time we have managed a little thinning out without tearful temperaments. In fact, we have only one horse-chestnut left in a far corner, while elsewhere two sturdy oak trees alone testify to that prolific period of my son's life – eight to eleven – when he was, as we called it, still "sowing his wild oaks."

A.A.

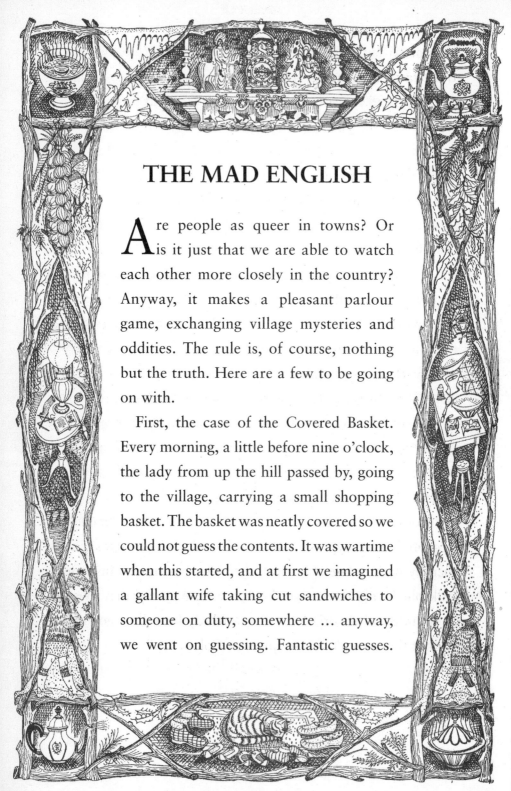

THE MAD ENGLISH

Are people as queer in towns? Or is it just that we are able to watch each other more closely in the country? Anyway, it makes a pleasant parlour game, exchanging village mysteries and oddities. The rule is, of course, nothing but the truth. Here are a few to be going on with.

First, the case of the Covered Basket. Every morning, a little before nine o'clock, the lady from up the hill passed by, going to the village, carrying a small shopping basket. The basket was neatly covered so we could not guess the contents. It was wartime when this started, and at first we imagined a gallant wife taking cut sandwiches to someone on duty, somewhere ... anyway, we went on guessing. Fantastic guesses.

But not so fantastic as the truth. For the lady goes shopping, to the farthest village grocer. There she buys *one* slice of bacon, every day, and returns to cook it for her husband's breakfast. He prefers it fresh. Think of it ... one slice, every day ... for years and years.

Secondly, in another county, there is the retired admiral who sleeps all day and potters about all night. He breakfasts at about five p.m., reads the paper, does his correspondence. Then, by moonlight, he gardens, weeding the paths and busily raking the gravel. His wife is often lonely, but she is a good friend to all the delivery men, the baker, the laundryman and so on, who sit around in her kitchen for nice rests with cups of tea and cigarettes and much merry laughter.

A third specimen is the elderly aristocrat who wears digitated socks. It is always a pleasure to take fresh visitors past his drying ground on washing days, to view the queer little objects hanging on the line. Many people agree that they have heard of socks with a separate place for the big toe, but socks with special divisions for every toe – well, that *is* something.

It would take too long to go into the case of the gentleman who is covered in eucalyptus all the year round, and who dabs himself liberally with iodine ... or the other who has trained his wife to walk obediently three yards behind him. Anyway, they exist, as do countless other originals. Why, already I can hear you saying ... "but those aren't half so queer as Colonel ..."

E.C.

THE NATURALIST

TRACKS

It is more than likely that there are animals living in your district which being nocturnal in their habits quite escape your attention until perhaps one is caught in a trap or found run over by a car. You probably see more dead hedgehogs along the roadside than you see at any time or even imagined existed.

Unless these animals are found in this way or your chickens disappear you need not suspect they are about, but when winter comes you have an opportunity too interesting to be missed if there is a light fall of snow.

Although most animals lie up during snow they cannot do so indefinitely. You are bound to find tracks sooner or later. These you should learn to recognise.

From these tracks you can learn quite a lot. You can see what animals are about, where they come and go and the range of their wanderings. If you care to study the matter a little more closely you can make a sketch of footprints for identification, especially if one print in four is unusual in some way. Animals often have one odd claw growing at a slightly abnormal angle or position, and from this you can pick out one animal from others of its kind and even recognise its tracks perhaps a year or so later.

During the winter months there is often a lot of timber hauling taking place in woods. This generally means muddy tractor marks but also a wide smooth swathe where a trunk has been dragged, often a long way. If you watch these you are certain to find fox marks and possibly those of a badger also. Although I have watched foxes daintily pick their way across wet mud like a cat, they can seldom move about much in a wood where timber hauling is going on without leaving some well-defined marks.

In summer the wet margins of ponds which are drying out will reveal the same tracks. Dew ponds are excellent for this, as their water level is constantly fluctuating and since they are quite shallow this leaves a nice wide margin each time.

Having once seen an animal track and learned something of the animal's movements it is then not difficult to go a stage farther and lie in wait in a suitable hide to watch the animal go to its favourite drinking place.

For real beginners your local rat in the chicken run provides quite an interesting study if the snow lies a long time and is not too deep. You will see the rat moves about quite a bit and tracks extend hundreds of yards or more to other warrens, and that the main source of the rat supply is some way away and that your chicken run is only used for food and cover when danger is imminent.

Don't forget that muddy marks left on clean objects can tell you almost as much as marks in mud or snow. You have no doubt seen cats jump off a high fence. Next time watch a little closer and you will still not see what happens. Although it looks more like a jump than anything else their muddy paw-marks on a suitable fence will show you that they must almost walk down since the marks extend nearly to the ground. A dog will jump clean off after perhaps making a tentative paw-mark with one foot before jumping. A fox on the other hand will leave marks for nearly two feet down the side of the fence.

It is useless, unless you want a marathon, to follow a fox track in winter, but a badger will sometimes go on one of its visits to neighbours in snowy weather and you can follow its path for a mile or more.

The next time it snows watch out for the track of a dog when you are out walking and have a guess at its size and kind. It's more than likely you will catch up with it and then you can see how far out you were. You'll be surprised.

R.F.

DEATH OF A DOG

When I phoned the vet the last time, I said "I'm afraid he's in pain." He was; but a great deal of the pain for which I was summoning release was my own. And I had to help the vet do the releasing. I was watching myself helping a man do what I would later pay him for having done ... kill a dog I had loved for eight years ... and thus kill the dog's pain and some of my own.

It was a muddling business, the more painful intellectually, perhaps, because the dog's personality had changed in the final indignities of illness. There was an exact stage, two days before the end, when the dog ceased being a pathetic form of his own loved self, appealing to us for the thousandth time to get him out of a jam. He became another being, his whole purpose turned inwards to fight the damned disease that was griping his vitals, fouling his breath, dulling his coat, clouding his eyes and, worst indignity of all for him, betraying him into making messes indoors. I knew he had given up the struggle when, on the penultimate day, he was sick near his basket and did not look at me sheepishly afterwards.

Pray for a dignified death. My dog wasn't granted that, and dignity had meant something to him all his life. He was a fool, and a coward, and a sentimentalist; and that was just the way we loved him. But he had dignity and a sense of dignity. He didn't like being laughed at. He didn't like skidding on a slippery floor. If he put on the clowning act himself, he could be a clown. But he didn't like being made to look silly. Ever since he was a puppy, he had liked being picked up off his back and swung – one hand holding his front paws, one hand holding his back paws. That was a clowning moment, and it wouldn't have occurred to him that it was undignified to swing upside down like that. I carried him that way, for the last time, from the draining board of the scullery, where he died ("I must have him up off the floor, please. Let's have him here where I can have the light"), to the grave I had dug for him at the bottom of the garden.

The vet seemed more in need of kindness and sympathy than I, when it was over. I provided him with a serious measure of whisky. He is a kind, shy person, and he appears to think *we* think it is his fault if he "loses" a dog on us. He has "lost" two now, through no fault of his that I know of. Over the whisky, he talked. He said that what he really hated was putting down dogs that were perfectly well. But if people go on very long holidays, or leave the district, it is often the best way. But he hates doing it. He also hates to see that kind of discarded dog given to a "good home," which then decides that the dog is dangerous, or a barker. Barking is generally the trouble. Mrs. A gets Mrs. B to give Fido a good home, and Mrs. A goes off to live somewhere else. Mrs. B decides after a month or so that Fido is costing a lot in Doggio and attention, and he barks. Perhaps Mrs. B hears of a builder who wants a barking dog for his yard, to tie up. The vet thought it would be much the best if Mrs. A had brought Fido to him at the beginning. But he hated having to do it.

But animals don't feel all that. Not physically. Mentally, perhaps; especially dogs. Dogs acquire a sense of companionship and sympathy, living with people who are kind to them. They miss you and pine. But, the vet thought, even dogs aren't hurt by physical pain as much as humans. Take him, himself. He remembered when he had poisoned the top of his little finger, and was in hospital for a whole month, unable to sleep for pain, except when they gave him something. Just the top of his little finger. And he had seen dogs with crushed paws – run over, you know – take a single aspirin and sleep like babies. Chickens, now, He sometimes had to cut open chickens' crops – and turkeys'. It's a disease they get. He used to do it with an anaesthetic, and sew them up afterwards before they came round. Once he had to do it in a hurry to a turkey when he hadn't got the dope. The bird never batted an eyelid. The vet reckoned she never felt it at all.

Pet birds – extraordinary the number of people who brought him canaries and budgerigars, and called him in. He had once been reported to the RSPCA for being cruel to a budgerigar. Silly old fool of a woman! Fact is, he thinks, it's no good looking after a sick pet bird; look after the ones that are not sick yet. Or they soon will be. If a bird is sick, it's much better to b … The whisky was loosening his tongue. He was just going to say "bump it off"; but he felt that would sound flippant. Not that he thought I'd report him to the RSPCA. But he had just put my dog down, at my request.

Now, but a few days after his death, the lawn seems full of hopping squirrels, sneering cats and pompous woodpigeons. The squirrels come in through the fence from the next door woodland, just over where their old enemy lies buried. They stamp o'er his head while he lies fast asleep.

He was a friendly, cheerful, sensible dog, and bossy in a sort of way. We, who have loved all our dogs, loved him. The last words I could think of to cheer the vet up were to say that I'd surely be bringing a new pup along to him one of these days for the puppy "shots," for hard-pad and whatever else vets can inject puppies against, when the time comes.

R.K.

A FOXHUNTER'S TALE

It was a gorgeous autumn morning. The sun made little rainbows on the cobwebs in the hedgerows, and in the lane the dust rose in a tiny cloud above the sterns of the hounds. Already at seven o'clock the sweat showed dark on the neck of my little bay mare.

I had bought her six months before, and now at five years old she stood 15.2 h.h. and had plenty of bone. This was her first day with hounds, and she trotted lazily, forging and shying, having had enough oats to make her opinionated but not enough work to make her realise that the holidays were over. There were several foxes in the thick wood, and the hounds hunted well. The mare enjoyed it. She tensed with pricking ears at the wild melody of their voices and snorted as the undergrowth crashed to give them passage. Soon I felt her sides heaving at the unaccustomed exercise while her neck lathered white where the reins had rubbed.

Without leaving the wood the hounds marked to ground and, thinking that the mare had had enough, I turned for home following a track through a gap into a grass field. When it petered out I was not perturbed for the telegraph posts on the road were near and there was surely some way over or through the fences which lay between. A plain grass bank, broad and gently sloping, faced us bounding the field and as we trotted towards it the mare cocked her ears enthusiastically. At the last moment she dug in her toes, but I rammed my knees into her fat sides and she jumped, landing sideways in the middle of a little furze bush craning her neck down at the ditch.

She tried to pivot on her hocks and jump back, but I held her straight and a clout from my crop made her rocket over the ditch into the field. It wasn't a polished performance, but she was only a beginner. Almost at once I felt she was uneasy. Sweat began to show on her neck and she reached at the bit trying to break into a canter. A low grumbling made me look round. Trotting behind shaking his head was the wickedest Shorthorn bull it has been my misfortune to encounter. His tail was raised and his breath came in angry snorts. He was about twenty yards away and I calculated that if we could keep that distance till we reached the fence that there would be time to jump. At all costs the mare must not be frightened, if she lost her head and bolted there might be a nasty spill.

I patted her neck, gentling and talking to her and we trotted on without increasing speed. Every now and then I glanced back. The bull followed, tossing his head, but the distance between us did not shorten. The fence was nearer and I began to look for a place to jump. Then I saw that it was wired up and there was no gate. A quick glance to right and left showed that the other two sides of the field had been treated in the same way. I was in a trap and the only way out was back across the bank and ditch where I had jumped in. Would the mare face the ditch on the take-off side?

My speculations were cut short by the bull who at that moment put his head down and charged. I tried to pull the mare round on her hocks, but the proximity of the savage beast had maddened her and she sprang forward out of control. Somehow I slewed her round away from the fence and we went back across the field at a speed which would not have shamed a racehorse. Luckily the bull did not follow. He stood still bellowing and tearing up the ground with his horns.

I could feel the mare's sides heaving under the saddle. The fright and the pace she had come had told on her. The sweat ran down her legs and dripped from her belly. I walked her to the edge of the ditch to calm her down hoping to find an easy place to jump, but there was nowhere better than where we had come in.

The bull, who had been observing us, now began to lumber in our direction flicking his tail and giving little angry grunts. The sound terrified the mare who reared up pawing the air with her forefeet. I leaned forward praying that she would not come over.

For a moment she hung poised, then as her legs touched the ground I drove her hard at the ditch. She jumped wildly, landing in a sprawl, half on and half off the bank. I felt one hind leg slip down and I threw my hands forward so that she should have her head. With a heave she recovered and hurtled off the bank with a corkscrew twist to her hindquarters. Perhaps my weight was too far forward, or perhaps her acrobatics on the top of the bank had unbalanced her. Whatever it was, she pecked badly and fell. I was thrown clear, but as she hobbled to her feet I saw that she was lame.

Baulked of his prey, the bull charged. He saw the ditch too late, for the slippery ground gave no grip and with a splash he slithered into the water. I did not go back to see if he was hurt. The water would cool his temper and he could walk along till he found a place to scramble out.

I picked up the reins and started to lead the mare on the long five-mile walk home. My recollection of this is vivid, far clearer than the incident with the bull in the field. But then I was wearing tight-fitting boots.

E.J.T.R.

ON GOING TO CHURCH

We lived in the country when I was a boy, and my mother used to take us to church in a troupe every Sunday morning. The rhythm of Sunday morning soaked itself into my growing bones. The clean shirt and tidy suit. Breakfast half an hour later than usual. The search for prayer books and offertory pennies. Fingernail inspection. My young sister surprisingly wearing a hat. The spaniel being told "Church, church, poor old boy, church," and his depressed acceptance of the fact that he wasn't in on the party. (A nice problem in morals: Was it sinful of us sometimes to say "Church" to him on week-days when we were going out to cinemas or the roller skating rink?) The procession up the road with the tinkly five-minute bell going.

The long pew with our name on it in a small framed card. The comfortable hassocks. The brass lectern, an ugly, leering eagle. The scrubbed choirboys, one of whom had delivered the joint yesterday. The Dean. The bachelor curate, a great friend of ours, who, of long Saturday custom, had come to our house last night for a bath, for supper and a glass of whisky. He digged in a farmhouse that lacked *mod con*, and Saturday was his night out. He could blow smoke rings, and vamp and sing at the piano most of the songs from the Oxford Song Book.

On some Sundays the hymn board in church was heavy with extra numbers. It had been designed for a possible four hymns to be telegraphed. The usual number was three. But at Christmas and Easter the numbers proliferated, and the proliferation had its counterpoint in the shops. Turkeys and geese festooning the butcher's shop, or Easter eggs piled in the sweet-shop windows ... and hymn numbers thick on the tallywag in church. Was I a boy who noticed these things? I didn't think so. But now, twenty-five and thirty years later, my memory sorts out the points and counterpoints. I am going to church in the country again, regularly, and the rhythm returns to me.

It was Sussex when I was a boy. Now it is Surrey. I go with a (smaller) brood of my own young. The rhythm is just as satisfying. Later breakfast on Sundays, though now we wash up and make the beds ourselves. The same search for prayer books and offertory money. My daughter surprisingly hatted, my son with clean shirt and fingernails. The spaniel (his name the same as all the spaniels we had then and have had since) being told "Church, church, poor old boy, church." The five-minute bell tinkles across the common, woods and the fields, telling us when we are running in time. In Sussex the bell rope was in the west porch. Here in Surrey it is behind the lectern, and it has, for some reason, or for no reason at all, a gay, fluffy grip in the Free Foresters' colours. It is a modern-built country church. Such must be rarities. This one is part of a large village built munificently in this century by a London store tycoon as a place of retirement for his aged staff. Though quietly Gothic, the church has sensible modernities. No leering brass eagle, but a double, swivel desk-lectern, with a Bible on each side. The reader takes the First

Lesson, and then swivels the lectern round to the other Bible, which already has the place found for the Second Lesson. The font at the west end has a cover which is lifted by a rope-pulley on a rafter. The church furniture is in unstained oak, and young enough to be still almost white. But the hymn-telegraph board is still not big enough for all the Christmas hymns. A Red Admiral butterfly occasionally gets himself caught in summer on the wrong side of the mullioned window, and the motes still hang in the sunbeams when the sun shines in.

The little boys and girls still scurry, blushing, down the aisle during the penultimate hymn. They are cutting the sermon by right of extreme youth. I suppose they sit in the front pews (as they did when I was a boy) so that they may be under the eye of surpliced authority, to quell them if they giggle or suck sweets. And still they fumble with the great iron latch on the south door. And still, as the door opens with a clack, a draught of air (with leaves in it in autumn) blows in. And still the urchins fail to shut the door properly after them. The verger steps out of his pew and shuts it, singing his hymn meanwhile.

That singing verger, sidesman, vestry-man and offertory collector ... I think it was he who took my memory by storm when I first came to this church. When I was a boy, of pre-prep-school age, my mother hired the village schoolmaster, Mr. Tutt, to come and teach me the elements of school knowledge. He had chalky fingernails and a beautifully executed copperplate handwriting. And no mathematical answer was a proper answer for him till it had the word *Answer* written against it, and the whole twice underlined, preferably by ruler. Mr. Tutt could underline double, by ruler, in ink, and without getting anything blotched. I don't think I liked him. But on Sundays he was a pillar of the church (I have no doubt his obit in the parish magazine said just that). He bawled the hymns, the psalms and the responses, and did not stop bawling, by impressive rote, when he came down the aisle, one arm folded behind his back, the other proffering the collection bag. I imagine that in the vestry after the service he counted up the takings and put the *Answer* in the book with two thick, parallel and unblotched lines underneath it.

In our church in Surrey today the offertory man hooks his left arm behind his back just as Mr. Tutt used to. He sings the hymns from memory as he proceeds down the pews. His voice isn't a patch on Mr. Tutt's, and his fingernails have no chalk in them. But he has the same shape as Mr. Tutt, the shape of a pillar of the church. I don't know who he is.

We have been regulars at the village church only two years, but we already exchange smiles and good mornings with one or two fellow worshippers on the churchyard paths after the service. It may be another five years before we know each others' names. But it is a cosy, friendly anonymity. They are of the village. We are, in the historical sense of the word, pagans from the fields beyond the village gates. But they accept us with kindness. If we are noticeably short of a prayer book in the family, be sure someone will bustle across the aisle with a red leather prayer book from the store, The Property of ———— Church, Not To Be Taken Away. They look a bit askance at us if we arrive late. But I think that they have forgiven us our trespasses by the end of the service.

Our vicar is a master of surplicemanship, and of

spectaclemanship, in the pulpit. I wonder today, as I wondered thirty years ago, what are the pocket arrangements of a cassock. When the vicar suddenly withdraws his hand up the sleeve of his surplice and brings it back with a handkerchief, I am still slightly awed by his prestidigitation. And his skill with spectacles is very fine. He does not read his sermons. But occasionally he likes to "remind" us of a passage from Gibbon or Tertullian (he was a schoolmaster, Crockford's informs me). While fluently talking, like a conjurer he pulls a hand up his surplice sleeve, and into the recesses, perhaps of his cassock, perhaps through his cassock into his Sunday suit. He brings out another pair of spectacles. He opens the case with a flourish, still without having said he is going to read. He removes his current pair of spectacles from his nose, appearing, for the moment, rather oddly naked. He puts his reading spectacles on and his others in the case. And now, with exact timing, he tells us he is going to read some Gibbon to us. When the reading is over he gives us another play of spectaclemanship and surplicemanship. It is good stuff.

I do attend to the sermon, but still sermon time is about the best time of the week for pondering fine, wayward thoughts, too difficult for the fettered workaday mind. I have come to take note of my children's and my wife's first remarks in the car after the service, to see what they have been thinking during the sermon. One late August Sunday I was electrified, during the Old Testament lesson (the strange, lilting Shadrach, Meshach and Abednego story from *Daniel*), to hear, or seem to hear, that the trio went into the burning, fiery furnace wearing their hats. I worried over this all through the sermon. Surely nobody wore a hat in either Testament? I would ask my kids when we emerged. And, in the car, I was just about to break the silence when my daughter, who had been busy with her own good thoughts, said "Do dogs go red in the face when they hold their breath? Or don't they hold their breath?" We discussed that one till we got home, and then I went to a Bible Concordance to look up hats. Nothing in my Concordance. What was I mishearing then? I looked up Daniel 3. By gum, they *were* wearing hats. I *had* heard right, and my Concordance had missed this happy, once-only monosyllable.

But I am not always so quick in checking my facts. The Vicar makes us sing the *Jubilate* on most Sundays. Perhaps fifty times in the last two years I have been reminded by my prayer book that this is the Hundredth Psalm. Fifty times I have remembered from schooltime reading that, after the Battle of Dunbar, Cromwell stopped his victorious troops for the singing of this psalm before the pursuit of the beaten enemy. Fifty times I have determined to look up the facts in the chronicles. I haven't done so yet. How fast did the Roundheads take the psalm? Did they have a band to keep them in tune? Did they give the psalm the full treatment, with the doxology?

I must get to know our vicar, and ask him about hats in the Bible. I like his sermons, his spectaclemanship and his surplicemanship. I am sure his house in the village is well equipped with *mod con*. But he may like supper and a glass of whisky one Saturday evening. Perhaps he will be able to vamp the songs from the Oxford Song Book for my children on our old piano. Yes, I'll introduce myself somehow, one of these Sundays.

R.U.

THE BIRD-WATCHER

THE BEST BIRD-TABLE

It is extraordinary what a well appointed bird - table will attract once the weather becomes hard. In the more southerly parts of England some years may pass without the surface of the ground becoming frozen enough to kill important numbers of our wild birds. But periodically there comes a winter like 1946-47, when the deaths from starvation and exposure amount to a phenomenon.

It seems to be more often starvation than exposure that is the killer. For if the smallest birds are plentifully supplied with food, they can stand temperatures extraordinarily far below those to which they are accustomed.

The trouble is, of course, that in Nature hard weather usually strikes when the supply of natural food is low, and when the hours of daylight available to hunt in are limited. So it is that the numbers of many of our animals are controlled by their fortunes in the hardest weeks of the year, which usually fall between December and March. If a spell of frost catches us this December, the fate of many birds will depend on whether it is accompanied by snow. Snow, even if very deep, is not necessarily harmful to animal life; under its mantle and drifts small mammals and birds carry on their normal occupation of insect-hunting, and still find insects to hunt.

The numbers of our tiniest birds – even wrens – do not necessarily become diminished by thick snow. But if a hard frost strikes without snow and freezes the ground surface or covers it with sheets of ice, things can be much more difficult for wild animals. Thrushes and blackbirds cannot find earthworms. Rooks, for the same reason, are compelled to raid stack-yards. Green woodpeckers, which hunt their food on the ground much more than most people think, may die in numbers simply because even their powerful bills cannot penetrate the frozen crust of anthills to get at the prey inside.

Hence, a bird-table in a garden may make an important difference to the future of the local bird population in a spell of hard frost. Normally the bird-table is resorted to by the familiar gang of starlings, sparrows, robins and tits. But when the weather is hard, many birds turn up which are usually shy and retiring and never seen there as a rule. Blackbirds and song-thrushes may be joined by missel-thrushes and redwings, and even, on occasion, fieldfares. The tits and nuthatches may be joined by tree-creepers, and green and spotted woodpeckers may descend upon the food.

Among notes I have of curious birds seen at tables in really hard conditions are details of rooks, jackdaws, magpies, jays, hawfinches, partridges and moorhens (gathering scraps underneath), and several species of gulls; also many fairly retiring finches which normally tour the hedges in flocks in winter and do not come to bird-tables – chaffinches, greenfinches, linnets, goldfinches; also tree-sparrows and yellowhammers.

It is not a good idea to build an edifice with several storeys of trays and perches, since the droppings of the birds which use the top layers often foul the food on the trays below. Perhaps the best idea is to have a single table on a pedestal for the larger birds such as thrushes, starlings and sparrows. On this table can be placed scraps from meals, grain, bread soaked in water (hot water in winter), bits of suet, heads of sunflowers, and so on. Some way from the table should be a separate pole with several horizontal perches jutting out from it. Various things can be hung from these perches – sprays of millet, inverted coconuts, little cylinders made of large-gauge perforated zinc filled with monkey-nuts, wooden bells with their hollows filled with fat. The hanging coconuts, cylinders and fat-bells can be used only by tits and nuthatches, since other kinds of bird are not able to hang on them with their feet, the only way of getting at the food. Sparrows and starlings will have to go to the table and leave the pole for the tits.

Most people think of bird-baths as a desirable convenience for the summer. They are just as important in the winter. Some bird-baths are made on pedestals. These can be untidy if they are taken possession of by starlings, who can splash and foul the surrounding ground. The best bird-bath is perhaps one let into the ground, some distance away from the feeding table and pole.

Best of all is one made of concrete with an electric circuit let in, so that when the ground is frozen a hundred-watt bulb under the concrete can be switched on to melt the ice. In frost, birds need water to drink even more than in the heat of summer.

J.F.

TREE SURGERY

The admission that one is a "tree surgeon" affords some amusement to many people usually with little knowledge of what the name implies. It is distinct from the "topper" and "lopper," words that describe an operation which usually leaves the tree with an unsatisfactory appearance.

Skilled tree surgery can often save or prolong the life of ornamental trees, many of which have not only aesthetic appeal to the owner but sentimental attraction as well and are the main features of many gardens and parks.

That most people appreciate the beauty of trees is obvious from the protests at their removal, but few take any steps to preserve them during their lifetime. Timely inspection and the various methods of a good surgeon can be of immeasurable benefit.

When inspecting a tree some of the things the tree surgeon looks for are defects in the leaf, namely size, colour and density; discoloration of the bark denotes that all is not well and the bole and root system should be carefully inspected for the presence of fungi and cavities.

Two main items must be considered in the treatment of a tree, namely the arresting of any disease present and the prevention of future attack. This includes the skilful use of ropes and undercutting when removing large or awkward boughs to prevent them ripping down the bole or branch, all cuts being made flush and the wound treated with an anti-fungicide, and cavities being cleared of diseased wood and either filled or drained in order to ensure the exclusion of moisture. Fertiliser can often be applied with excellent results to trees which have been retarded by disease or where the soil is not supplying sufficient nourishment.

The removal of weight and the unobtrusive bracing of large limbs can save the shape of many trees. Cedars especially benefit by these methods, many having been completely ruined by the extra weight imposed by heavy snows piling on their dense foliage causing boughs to break off.

The scope of tree surgery usually covers the removal of dangerous trees, often by the roots, in public thoroughfares, overhanging power lines or buildings, etc., where the tree must be taken down in sections by means of ropes. In this work experience, good equipment and adequate insurance are essential. Many hundreds of pounds' worth of damage has been done by men without these essentials and usually working on a part-time basis, leaving the unfortunate owner with no means of redress.

Much difficult and expensive work would be avoided if more imagination were given to the planting of amenity trees. Poplars which can cause a 4 inch lateral movement of clay by consuming as much as 12,000 gallons of water in a season, are often planted close to walls and houses with eventual cracking by movement of foundations. The size of the mature tree must be considered when planting in confined places, especially near houses where the reduction of light and air will become a nuisance.

The planting of good common trees suited to the neighbourhood will afford better specimens than the more unusual ones that may not flourish.

Thus with skilful treatment, the co-operation of private owners and public authorities, much can be done to extend and preserve the beauty of amenity trees which are a source of increasing pleasure in a Britain rapidly losing its rural character.

W.E.M.

READER'S LETTER

SLOE GIN: Here is an old Bedfordshire/Hertfordshire recipe that I can guarantee is as potent and velvety as any – and no gin is thrown away in the discarded sloes. Take a 2 lb. preserving jar and fill it with alternate layers of sloes (unpricked) and brown sugar. Use "pieces" for the best flavour. While packing the jar put in three or four blanched almonds.

Place the jar in a cool place – do not stand on stone – with the glass lid resting in position. Top up with sugar every two or three weeks as the top layer melts. Altogether about ¾ lb. of sugar will be needed. After Christmas strain off the sloe juice and mix with an equal amount of gin. Bottle and leave corked until next year's sloes are ready for picking.

(Miss) D.M. Cook, 30 Manor Road,
Barton-in-the-Clay, Bedford.

HOW TO MAKE MEAD

Mead is not unlike heather ale, which was a favourite thirst-quencher of the Picts; but the secret of making heather ale died with the Picts, whereas mead is still made in some rural districts, from receipts handed down from one generation to another. Mead (the name comes from madhu, the Sanscrit word for honey) varies according to the season and the quality of the honey; this year should prove a vintage year.

It is not necessarily a strong drink; it is delicious when newly made, while it still has the delicate honey flavour, but the alcoholic content increases the longer it is kept.

The ingredients are:

8 quarts water,
2 pounds honey,
1 lemon,
1 pint pale ale,
¼ teaspoonful yeast,
A few raisins (or sultanas),
A little sugar.

The method is simple:
Boil water in jelly-pan, and dissolve honey in it. Peel lemon

thinly and slice it, removing pith and pips. Put slices and peel in pan, and remove from the fire. When mixture is nearly cold add ale, and yeast dissolved in a little tepid water. Leave standing overnight.

Strain into bottles, putting two washed raisins and a teaspoonful of sugar in each bottle. If possible, use screw-top bottles; but if corks have to be used, tie them down securely or they may "pop." Seal the bottles and leave them for four or five hours in a warm room; then store in a cool, dark place.

The mead is ready to drink in about a week. Handle carefully when you pour it, so that the sediment is not disturbed.

At first it foams in the glasses, and then sparkles with little amber-coloured bubbles, and looks like liquid sunshine.

A.M.A. FRASER

THE CHATELAINE

I have been having a lovely time rummaging in the old library at Longleat, my favourite room in the house. The most incongruous assortment of objects has come to rest in its honey-coloured light: a collection of wax flowers under glass domes is stacked against a book-lined wall; on a shelf in a dark corner ostrich eggs, like anaemic bald heads, glow luminously;

metronomes stand sentinel over cases of stuffed birds; an anti-indigestion rocking-chair commands a regiment of mahogany and sandalwood bidets.

It is said that Bishop Ken returns to read his Bible in this room where he lived the last twenty years of his life. His bedroom used to be next door, but was turned into a china cupboard when terrified housemaids refused to sleep there any longer because of the visitations of the good bishop wrapped in his shroud.

The household account books are preserved here, including the "dispensary books" which contain detailed records of the invalid delicacies and remedies; many of them prepared in the Longleat still-room. I am struck by the imagination and thoughtfulness shown in these books. The food is by no means sick-room food but seems to have been varied according to the individual's needs and taste. It is fascinating to follow the course of an illness through the dispensary book by the list of gifts made to the patient.

Enormous quantities of port wine were given away weekly, and sometimes bottles of gin and whisky. A large amount of beef-tea for the sick and poor must have been made every day at Longleat. I find an entry in 1875: "Feb. – March, Mrs. Miller 5 lb. of Mutton." I imagine that must have been for the use of the whole family during a period of unemployment or sickness of the wage earner.

The third Marchioness of Bath wrote a charming little book on Domestic Economy for Cottager. It starts with detailed instructions on the art of home brewing. She is very strongly critical of tea-drinking as a habit, on the grounds that tea, "besides being good for nothing, has badness in it because it is well known to produce want of sleep in many cases, and in all cases to shake and weaken the nerves."

She works out a sum to prove that tea-drinking would cost a cottage family £10 a year, and do them nothing but harm, whereas home-brewed beer would cost them £7 5s. and benefit them in every way.

The book instructs on bread-making, keeping cows, pigs, bees, fowls, rabbits, goats and ewes; making candles, rush lighters, mustard, dresses, household goods and fuel and the sowing of Swedish turnip seed. It also gives some simple cookery recipes, drinks for fever and illness and gargles made from herbs.

The author writes eloquently on the subject of bread-making and says – "Every woman high or low ought to know how to make bread. If she do not she is unworthy of trust and confidence."

The Longleat library contains the only recorded copy of one of the earliest known cookery books. It was printed by Richard Pynson in 1500. Its title page reads "This is the boke of cookery." Cookery books of this period are extremely rare, because they were naturally in constant use and were literally worn out through daily handling. I do not know how this particular copy escaped the common fate. It belonged to the second Duchess of Portland, whose daughter Elizabeth brought it to Longleat in 1759 on her marriage to the third Viscount Weymouth, who was later created the Marquess of Bath.

I have copied out a few of the recipes in which some of the early English culinary terms must be left to the imagination. They read as though they have been taken down verbatim from the cook.

The gourmets of those days evidently liked everything highly spiced: ginger, saffron and cannell (i.e. cinnamon) are used a great deal. They were also very lavish with their ingredients. To make "Mamone," for example – whatever Mamone may be – you "take Whyte Wyne and plente suger and putte them in a potte than bray the brawne of 8 capons to a galon of oyle do thereto a quarte of hony and a pound of powder ginger, galyngal and canell and cast thereto and sette and serve it."

Here is another recipe which ought to disguise dry cod most efficiently:

SYRUPE FOR STOKFYSSHE FRYED

Take the mylke of raw almonds made with rede wyne and put it in the potage, thanne take onyons perboyled and mynced and put thereto and lette it boyle and thereto a quantyte of malvessye (i.e. malmsey) and oyle and cast in suger and powder of gynger and rasyns and salte and thane take your fryed Stokfysshe and couche it in dysshes and poure on the Syrupe and so serve it.

And lastly, another mystery dish:

FRAUNT HEMELLE

To make fraunt hemelle take and swynge egges and creme togeder put myed brede and powder of peper and saffron, thane mynce swete fiesshe and fylle the bagge and sowe it, fast and roast it on a gredyron and serve it forthe.

I can't imagine what "Fraunt Hemelle" can be. Perhaps some reader can enlighten me. The recipe sounds as if the cook has gone mad, but I like its air of reckless abandon.

D.B.

WHAT EVERY COOK
SHOULD KNOW ABOUT

ROASTING THE TURKEY

First choose a medium-size bird, round about 10 to 11 lb. A turkey is easier to cook if not too big, is a better fit in the average oven and so has less chance of drying up during cooking. A hen turkey is supposed to have more delicate and tender flesh than a cock bird. Alternative methods of roasting:

ENGLISH FASHION:

For roasting use a good beef dripping, and if possible have a good proportion of bacon or ham fat mixed with it. This not only gives a good flavour, but a lovely brown and glistening finish to the bird. Heat the fat first in the roasting tin, which should be large enough to hold the turkey comfortably and leave room to baste easily. The fat should cover the bottom of the tin by about one inch. Set the bird, after stuffing, in the tin, baste, then cover with paper and put into a moderate oven, just under 400 deg. in temperature, or between Regulo 5 and 6. Roast, allowing approximately 15 minutes to the lb., and basting every 15 to 20 minutes. Take the paper off while doing so and replace it until about the last half hour, when it may be removed for the final browning. Turn the bird over fairly frequently during the roasting to ensure that the legs get a thorough cooking, and as much of the top heat of the oven as possible. So often the breast of a turkey, and particularly that of a large bird, gets stringy and overcooked, while the legs remain underdone. This can be avoided by cooking the bird for a greater part of the time on its side and turning it over as described. An indication of when the bird is cooked is when the meat tends to shrink away from the knuckle end of the drumstick. The flesh, however, should not crack or split, this means that the heat has been too great and the roasting too rapid. Remove paper and baste well for the final browning during the last half hour. Then dish.

FRENCH FASHION:

The advantage of this method of roasting is that the flesh of the turkey, always inclined to be on the dry side, will remain succulent and tender, and the gravy rich and full of flavour. It is a specially good method to use if the turkey is to be eaten cold. For roasting allow between 2 oz. and 4 oz. of butter according to the size of the turkey. Rub the butter well over the breast and legs of the bird, season well with freshly ground black pepper and a touch of salt, cover with paper and set in a roasting tin. Put the giblets in the tin with about a pint of hot water or stock, or alternatively use a well-flavoured stock previously made from the giblets. The liver is kept on one side for frying later, it is then sliced or diced and added to the gravy. Cook as for the first method in the same oven temperature, but allowing about 25 minutes to the lb. and removing the covering paper halfway during the cooking. It may be necessary to lower the heat a little at this stage. Care must be taken to see that the liquid in the tin does not reduce to less than half; more water or stock should be added to keep it to a good half pint. When the turkey is well browned and thoroughly cooked, dish and strain off the liquid from the tin into a saucepan. Skim off some of the butter, and mix a little of it with about a teaspoonful of flour. Work it to a creamy paste, then add to the gravy. Stir, boil up well, skim, adjust the seasoning; add the liver before serving.

STUFFINGS

CHESTNUT, *a classic stuffing for turkey, usually in the breast of the bird. One lb. chestnuts, weighed when peeled, 1-2 oz. onion, finely chopped, ½ oz. butter, 1 dessertspoonful mixed chopped herbs, salt and pepper. Cook in stock until tender. Strain and sieve. Add the onion to the purée with the butter, herbs and plenty of seasoning. Moisten if necessary with a little of the stock that the chestnuts were cooked in. Fill into the breast of the bird and sew up with a coarse thread.*

CELERY, FRENCH PLUM AND CHESTNUT *stuffing used for the breast of the bird and excellent with a veal forcemeat. One head of celery, chopped, 12 fine large prunes or French plums soaked overnight in ¼ pint red wine, or wine and water mixed, 1-2 oz. onion, finely chopped, ½ oz. butter, 1 dessertspoonful chopped mixed herbs, grated rind of half a lemon, ½ lb. chestnuts, weighed when peeled, and cooked until tender, salt and pepper, one small beaten egg. Simmer the plums in the wine in which they have been soaked, allowing it to well reduce, until they are barely soft. Stone and cut each into four. Melt the butter in a pan, add the celery and onion and allow to soften slightly. Then add the plums, herbs, lemon rind and chestnuts, broken into pieces. Stir lightly with a fork, seasoning well and adding the juice from the plums. When thoroughly cool, stir in the egg.*

SAUSAGE OR PORK FORCEMEAT, *also a classic and used for the carcase and goes well with any of the other stuffings. 1½ lb. of sausage meat or fresh minced pork or veal, if the latter is used add 3 oz. fresh white breadcrumbs. 1 dessertspoonful chopped mixed herbs, 1-2 oz. onion, finely chopped, 3 oz. minced fat bacon, 1 beaten egg. Mix all together, moistening with a little stock if necessary. These proportions as well as those of the following recipe may be altered according to the size of the turkey. They are enough for a 10-lb. bird.*

HERB AND ORANGE FORCEMEAT *may be used as an alternative to sausage or pork. One lb. fresh white breadcrumbs, 1 tablespoonful mixed chopped herbs, 2 tablespoonfuls chopped parsley, 1 tablespoonful finely chopped onion, 2 tablespoonfuls of chopped suet or 2 oz. butter or margarine. Grated rind and juice of two oranges, two small beaten eggs, salt and pepper and a little stock to bring the mixture to a moist paste, if necessary. Mix the ingredients in the above order and stuff into the bird.*

R.H.

————·•·————

The turkey is today the traditional Christmas roast and it is fairly obvious that the Christmas goose is really the true bird of tradition and that most Georgian squires thought little of any kind of poultry and stuck to their vast baron of peerless beef. The turkey if perfect is beyond all praise but many of the middle-sized birds can be most disappointingly dry. Often this is the fault of the cooking, for it requires rather careful basting and oven management to avoid overdoing the impressive but rather high breast while cooking the thighs and the chassis properly.

The goose has perhaps a less fashionable breast and is never dry as he "dresses in his own fat." In my opinion the goose is a great deal better bird than the *average* turkey and that the worst that can be said of him that many people consider him rather too rich. I also suspect that weight for weight there is more meat on a goose than on a turkey. Nevertheless turkey is better for the schoolroom with its heavy miscellaneous appetite and goose is perhaps best left to adults with more control.

In order to make the task of roasting an oversized bird more difficult we usually stuff the carcass with stuffing, sausage meat, and perhaps chestnuts. This mass of insulation means that the chassis and thighs take even longer to cook and are still almost raw when the breast is done to perfection.

Considered as a practical problem, the best thing to do is to partly cook the legs and heavy part of the chassis by boiling it in its deep baking pan not in the oven but on top of the stove. This, so to speak, gives the thick portion a start without affecting the breast, etc., which is above water level. The boiling water, which will be the basis of your gravy, is poured off after an hour's boiling and the bird conventionally roasted or rather baked in the oven in fat or, if possible, butter. "Fats" are today so variable that it is worth while saving any real pork or bacon fat in anticipation of the sacred bird. Remember that these vast baking dishes need a good depth of fat and that you will need more than you think.

As for time, the usual allowance of "fifteen minutes a pound" is as good as anything, but if you have parboiled it first for an hour the roasting time can be reduced by about half an hour or the heat reduced from your usual roasting oven value, say, "Six" to "Four" for part of the time.

Melt your fat in the oven tin and baste the bird all over, very carefully examining both sides for gaps – before it goes in the oven. You can, if your oven is "given to top heat," cover the breast with paper to prevent too great drying, but this is no substitute for basting and every ten minutes to a quarter of an hour the paper must come off and basting be repeated. If there is room in the pan to turn the turkey on its side do so, but all too often the bird is too big for tins. In any case the paper has to come off for the last three-quarters of an hour, and the best indication is the formation of enormous bubbles under the golden skin when the hot basting fat is poured over. If breast, legs and everything respond in beautiful bladders you can be fairly sure that things are all right. If they seem to diminish it is a warning that you are overcooking and the bird is drying out.

One word of advice. If you want to retain juice in any food do not put any salt on it till it is cooked.

For stuffing, the butcher's pork sausage meat is the basis but it needs flavouring with chopped onion and mixed herbs. Either this or chestnut stuffing fills the bow end of the bird. Chestnut stuffing has the advantage that it is put in cooked, while the sausage stuffing may be undercooked when the bird is just right.

Parboil a pound of chestnuts after having cut a cross with a sharp pointed knife on each of them. This opens as they boil and makes peeling a lot simpler. Finish cooking in stock and mash through a wire sieve, add about half an ounce of butter and a little ground pepper. Chopped onion and herbs can be added but I think it is better plain as you will probably fill the stern compartment with the usual herb, breadcrumbs, onion and chopped bacon stuffing. If it is goose in place of turkey you use sage and onion in place of the usual thyme or marjoram herbs and incidentally chestnut stuffing goes extremely well with goose!

The Americans always eat cranberry sauce with their turkey and it really is a very good combination. Technically it is not a "sauce" but simply stewed cranberries. A little very sharp apple sauce would be a possible substitute.

Essentially, turkey requires a good and preferably clear gravy. This should be made of the giblets, but I must say that the giblets often produce a rather dubious flavour more like a butcher's shop than delicate poultry. Faced by such a disaster simply substitute other stock if available, add a little of any of the meat extracts and about half a teaspoonful of dried marjoram, boil it for a couple of minutes or so and strain into a sauceboat and add a teaspoonful of strong sherry, an East India or any heavy type. You will then have a pure clear gravy which goes magnificently not only with turkey but with goose and indeed all game and poultry.

For the second appearance as a hot dish, a light re-warm of

turkey bits in a well-flavoured white sauce and accompanied by sweet corn fritters is something we can borrow from the Americans. Simply strain the corn as dry as possible and use an eggless batter of flour, water, salt and a dessertspoonful of olive oil. For the last appearance hot turkey drumsticks liberally devilled can be faced without that after-Christmas feeling!

H.B.C.P.

CONTRIBUTORS

A.A.	Anthony Armstrong, nom de plume of A.A. Willis, playwright, novelist, essayist
A.C.W.	Alwyne C. Wheeler, author of *Fishes of the World*
A.G.S.	A.G. Street, farmer, countryman, novelist, author of *Country Calendar, Farmer's Glory, Harvest of Shame*
A.M.	Arthur Moon
A.S-J.	Anne Scott-James, journalist and author of *The Cottage Garden, Down to Earth, Sissinghurst, the Making of a Garden* (see Introduction)
A.W.	Alan Walbank
B.M.N.	B. Melville Nicholas, author of *Teach Your Pet to Talk* and numerous books on birds
B.V.F.	Brian Vesey Fitzgerald, author of numerous books on wildflowers, dogs, trees and other country matters
C.M.	Cicely Mead, author of *A Concise Guide to Vegetable Gardening*
C.M.N.	Clare Marten
C.S.	Constance Spry, florist and teacher and author of numerous books on flower arranging and cookery. Designed flower arrangements for many state occasions, including the coronation of Queen Elizabeth II
C.T.	Cartwright Timms
C.W.	Colin Willock, author of *The Penguin Guide to Fishing, Rod, Pole or Perch, Anglers Encyclopedia*
D.B.	Daphne Bath, former Marchioness of Bath
D.F.	Daphne Fielding, author and socialite
E.B.	Effie Barker, expert on vegetables, cookery etc.
E.C.	Elizabeth Cross
E.G.	Evelyn Gibb
E.J.T.R.	E.J. Tonson Rye
E.P.D.	E. Philip Dobson, author of *The Garnett Story*
E.R.Y.	E.R. Yarham, author of *The Church of St Peter and St Paul, Cromer, Norfolk*
E.S.	Elizabeth Speed

F.C.P.	Charles Puddle, former President of the Royal Horticultural Society, holder of the Victoria Medal of Honour in Horticulture
F.E.	Frederick Evans
F.I.	Frank Illingworth, author of *Falcons and Falconry*
G.C.	Garth Christian, author of *While Some Trees Stand: Wild Fife in our Vanishing Countryside, Down the Long Wind: a Study of Bird Migration*
G.E.B.M.	G.E.B. de Maupas
G.R.W.	G.R. Winston
H.A.	Henry Avery
H.A.E.	Harold Evetts
H.B.C.P.	Hugh B.C. Pollard, author of *A History of Firearms, Game Birds and Game Bird Shooting, The Gun Room Guide, Shotguns: their History and Development*
H.D.	Humphrey Denham, author of *The Skeptical Gardener*
H.E.	Helen Evetts
H.M.	Henry Marshall
H.P.	Hubert Phillips, author of *The Pan Book of Card Games, How to Play Bridge*
J.E.	John Eastwood
J.F.	James Fisher, author, editor, naturalist and ornithologist. Joined Oxford Arctic Expedition of 1933 as ornithologist, editor of Collins New Naturalist series
J.F.	John Fleetwood
J.H.	John Hillaby, author of *Walking in Britain, Journey through Europe*
J.H-P.	Jack Hughes-Parry, author of *A Fishing Fantasy*
J.I.L.	J. Ivester Lloyd, author of *Come Hunting, Rabbiting and Ferreting, Beagling, Riders of the Heath*
J.K.H.	J. Kenneth Habgood
J.R.J.	James Robertson Justice, Scottish actor, Rector of Edinburgh University, devoted countryman
K.N.	Kathleen Naylor
L.G.A.	Leonard G. Appleby, author of *British Snakes*
L.H.M.	L. Harrison Matthews, author of *Life of Mammals, Senses of Animals* (with Maxwell Knight q.v.) *Living World of Animals, Beasts of the Field*
L.R.J.	L.R. James
M.B.	Maurice Burton, zoologist, author of *The Encyclopaedia of the Animal Kingdom*
M.B.R.	Marjorie Baron Russell, author of *Cooking for One*

M.H.   Macdonald Hastings, editor of *Country Fair* (see Introduction)

M.H.D. Margaret Holland

M.K.   Maxwell Knight (1900-1968), naturalist, writer, broadcaster, Head of MI5 and one of the models for Ian Fleming's M. Author of *Bird Gardening*

M.S.   Michael Shephard

N.A.B. Nell A. Broadhead

N.P.H. N.P. Harvey, author of *Fruit Growing for Amateurs* and *Encyclopedia of Modern Gardening*

P.H.C. P.H. Carne, author of *See the South by Car, Discovering Wessex*

P.M.   Patrick Murray

P.W.   Lady Patricia Ward

R.B.   Roy Beddington, author of *To Be a Fisherman*

R.F.   Richard Ford

R.G.   Roy Genders, author of *Pears Encyclopedia of Gardening, Book of Aromatics*

R.H.   Rosemary Hume, author of *The Penguin Dictionary of Cookery*

R.K.   Richard Kennaway

R.M.L. R.M. Lockley, Welsh naturalist. In 1927 Lockley took over the lease of the island of Skokholm, establishing the first British bird observatory there in 1933. The author of over fifty books, including *The Private Life of the Rabbit* (1965), which inspired Richard Adams's *Watership Down*

R.P.   Richard Perry, author of *Watching Sea Birds, Guide to Birds*

R.U.   Richard Usborne, editor of *Sunset at Blandings* (with P.G. Wodehouse), *Plum Sauce – a P.G. Wodehouse Companion, Vintage Wodehouse*

R.W.   Ralph Wightman, author of *Rural Rides, The Countryside Today*. Broadcaster and journalist on rural matters

R.W.H. Ruth W. How

S.M.   Sydney Moorhouse, author of *British Sheepdog, Companion into Northumberland, Walking Tours and Hostels in England*

S.M.T. S.M. Tritton, author of *Successful Wine and Beer Making, Amateur Wine Making*

S.R.   Sidney Rogerson, author of *Twelve days on the Somme: a Memoir of the Trenches*

T.F.   Thomas Firbank, author of *I Bought a Mountain*

V.M.	Victor MacClure, author of *Good Appetite, my Companion – a Gourmand at Large, Party Fare, The Crying Pig Murders, Mainly Fish – Meatless Menus*
V.T.	Vere Temple, author of *Butterflies and Moths in Britain*
W.E.M.	W.E. Matthews
W.H.	Willaton Hill
W.I.	Will Ingerswen, author of *Alpine Garden Plants, Alpines without a Rock Garden, The Dianthus: a Flower Monograph*
W.P.M.	W.P. Matthew, the first radio and TV handyman

INDEX